U·X·L
Protests, Riots, and Rebellions
Civil Unrest in the Modern World

U•X•L
Protests, Riots, and Rebellions
Civil Unrest in the Modern World

VOLUME 2

Tracey Vasil Biscontini, Editor
Kathleen J. Edgar, Project Editor

U·X·L
A part of Gale, a Cengage Company

Farmington Hills, Mich • San Francisco • New York • Waterville, Maine
Meriden, Conn • Mason, Ohio • Chicago

Protests, Riots, and Rebellions: Civil Unrest in the Modern World

Tracey Vasil Biscontini, Editor

Project Editor: Kathleen J. Edgar
Acquisition Editor: Christine Slovey
Editorial: Elizabeth Manar, Mark Mikula
Rights Acquisition and Management: Carissa Poweleit, Ashley M. Maynard
Imaging: John L. Watkins
Product Design: Kristine A. Julien
Composition: Evi Abou-El-Seoud
Manufacturing: Wendy Blurton

© 2018 Gale, a Cengage Company

ALL RIGHTS RESERVED. No part of this work covered by the copyright herein may be reproduced, transmitted, stored, or used in any form or by any means graphic, electronic, or mechanical, including but not limited to photocopying, recording, scanning, digitizing, taping, Web distribution, information networks, or information storage and retrieval systems, except as permitted under Section 107 or 108 of the 1976 United States Copyright Act, without the prior written permission of the publisher.

For product information and technology assistance, contact us at
Gale Customer Support, 1-800-877-4253.
For permission to use material from this text or product, submit all requests online at www.cengage.com/permissions.
Further permissions questions can be emailed to
permissionrequest@cengage.com

Cover art, front: Image of Umbrella Revolution, © Chris McGrath/Getty Images; Wounded Knee standoff, © Bettmann/Getty Images; Justice for All march against police violence, © Bill Clark/Getty Images; and child labor protest, courtesy of the Bain Collection/Library of Congress. Cover art, back: Image of sign held at immigration rally, © Jorge Salcedo/Shutterstock.com.

Inside art: Image of cheering crowd, © AlbertBuchatskyy/Shutterstock.com; document icon, © Colorlife/Shutterstock.com; and megaphone, © Gulnar Sarkhanl/Shutterstock.com.

While every effort has been made to ensure the reliability of the information presented in this publication, Gale, a Cengage Company, does not guarantee the accuracy of the data contained herein. Gale accepts no payment for listing; and inclusion in the publication of any organization, agency, institution, publication, service, or individual does not imply endorsement of the editors or publisher. Errors brought to the attention of the publisher and verified to the satisfaction of the publisher will be corrected in future editions.

Library of Congress Cataloging-in-Publication Data

Names: Biscontini, Tracey Vasil, editor. | Edgar, Kathleen J., editor.
Title: UXL protests, riots, and rebellions : civil unrest in the modern world / Tracey Vasil Biscontini, editor ; Kathleen J. Edgar, project editor.
Description: Farmington Hills, Mich. : UXL, a part of Gale, a Cengage Company, [2018] | Includes bibliographical references and index.
Identifiers: LCCN 2017045153 | ISBN 9781410339089 (set : alk. paper) | ISBN 9781410339102 (vol. 1 : alk. paper) | ISBN 9781410339119 (vol. 2 : alk. paper) | ISBN 9781410355874 (vol. 3 : alk. paper) | ISBN 9781410339096 (ebook : alk. paper)
Subjects: LCSH: Protest movements–History–Juvenile literature. | Civil rights movements–History–Juvenile literature. | Political participation–History–Juvenile literature.
Classification: LCC HM883 .U95 2018 | DDC 303.48/4–dc23
LC record available at https://lccn.loc.gov/2017045153

Gale
27500 Drake Rd.
Farmington Hills, MI 48331-3535

978-1-4103-3908-9 (set)   978-1-4103-3911-9 (vol. 2)
978-1-4103-3910-2 (vol. 1)   978-1-4103-5587-4 (vol. 3)

This title is also available as an e-book.
978-1-4103-3909-6
Contact your Gale sales representative for ordering information.

Printed in the United States of America
1 2 3 4 5 6 7   22 21 20 19 18

Table of Contents

Events by Topic of Protest (A Thematic Table of Contents) **ix**
Reader's Guide **xiii**
Chronology **xv**
Words to Know **xxxiii**

VOLUME 1

Chapter 1: Animal Rights **1**
    UCR Lab Raid to Protest Animal Testing **7**
    Bilbao Anti-bullfighting Protest **12**
    Global March for Elephants and Rhinos **18**
    Blackfish Documentary and SeaWorld Protests **25**

Chapter 2: Civil Rights, African American **35**
    Montgomery Bus Boycott **42**
    Little Rock Nine Crisis **47**
    Freedom Rides **54**
    Lunch Counter Protest, McCrory's **59**
    March on Washington for Jobs and Freedom **63**

Chapter 3: Civil Rights, Hispanic and Latino **71**
    East LA Blowouts **77**
    A Day without Immigrants **83**
    Mexican Indignados Movement **90**

Chapter 4: Economic Discontent **99**
    Secret Document of the Farmers of Xiaogang **105**

TABLE OF CONTENTS

Porkulus Protests, Tea Party **111**
15-M Movement **116**
Brexit **122**

Chapter 5: Environment **133**
Forward on Climate Rally **139**
Copenhagen Protests **144**
Global Frackdown **151**
Pacific Climate Warriors Blockade **157**
March for Science **163**

Chapter 6: Free Speech **171**
Harry Potter Book Burning **177**
Muslim Protests of Danish Cartoons **183**
"Je Suis Charlie" Protests **189**
Yale Student Protests on Free Speech **194**

Chapter 7: Globalization **203**
Battle in Seattle: World Trade Organization Protests **209**
Occupy Wall Street **216**
March against Monsanto **223**

VOLUME 2

Chapter 8: Gun Control/Gun Rights **233**
Black Panthers Carry Guns into California Legislative Building in Protest of Mulford Act **239**
March on Washington for Gun Control **246**
"I Will Not Comply" Rally **252**
Democratic Congressional Representatives Sit-in for Gun Control Legislation **256**

Chapter 9: Human Rights **263**
Attica Prison Riot **270**
Capitol Crawl **276**
March to Abolish the Death Penalty **284**
Dalit Protests in India **290**
Armenian Genocide Protests **297**

Chapter 10: Immigrant Rights **305**
1844 Nativist Riots **311**

TABLE OF CONTENTS

    Pro-Migrant Rallies in Europe and Australia **318**

    Protests against President Trump's Travel Ban **325**

Chapter 11: Independence Movements **335**

    Grito de Lares **342**

    Gandhi Leads Salt March **346**

    The Velvet Revolution **352**

Chapter 12: Indigenous Peoples' Rights **361**

    AIM Occupation of Wounded Knee **367**

    Aboriginal Land Rights Protest **375**

    Preservation of Amazon Rain Forest Awareness Campaign **379**

    Dakota Access Pipeline Protest **384**

Chapter 13: Labor Rights **393**

    Mother Jones's "Children's Crusade" **399**

    Flint Sit-Down Strike against General Motors **407**

    Delano Grape Strike and Boycott **414**

    Fast-Food Workers' Strike **422**

Chapter 14: LGBTQ Rights **429**

    Stonewall Riots **435**

    White Night Riots **441**

    Westboro Baptist Church Protests of Matthew Shepard **445**

    Shanghai Pride Festival **452**

    Protests of North Carolina House Bill 2 **458**

VOLUME 3

Chapter 15: Political/Government Uprisings **467**

    Tiananmen Square Protests **473**

    Fall of the Berlin Wall **478**

    Arab Spring and the Syrian Civil Uprising **486**

    Tahrir Square Protests (Egyptian Revolution) **493**

    Umbrella Revolution **498**

Chapter 16: Racial Conflict **509**

    Zoot Suit Riots **518**

    Detroit Riots **524**

    Soweto Uprising **530**

    Justice for All March **539**

TABLE OF CONTENTS

Chapter 17: Reproductive Rights **549**
- March for Women's Lives **556**
- Operation Rescue **562**
- One-Child Policy Riots **568**
- Planned Parenthood Protests **574**

Chapter 18: Resistance to Nazis **585**
- White Rose Movement **592**
- Holocaust Resistance in Denmark **597**
- Warsaw Ghetto Uprising **602**
- Treblinka Death Camp Revolt **607**

Chapter 19: Slavery **617**
- Louisiana Rebellion (German Coast) **623**
- Nat Turner's Rebellion/Anti-slavery Petitions **628**
- Christmas Rebellion/Baptist War **634**
- Harpers Ferry Raid **638**
- Fight to Stop Human Trafficking **643**

Chapter 20: War **651**
- International Congress of Women **657**
- Student Armband Protest of Vietnam War **663**
- Student Protest at Kent State **669**
- Candlelight Vigils against Invasion of Iraq **676**
- Chelsea Manning and WikiLeaks **684**

Chapter 21: Women's Rights **693**
- Hunger Strikes by Suffragettes in Prison **701**
- Women's Suffrage Protest at the White House **707**
- Baladi Campaign **714**
- Malala Yousafzai All-Girls School **718**
- Women's March on Washington **724**

Research and Activities Ideas **xlv**

Where to Learn More **li**

General Index **lxix**

Events by Topic of Protest (A Thematic Table of Contents)

The main entry events in *Protests, Riots, and Rebellions* are organized by theme and type in the list that follows. Entries may appear under more than one heading when numerous factors were involved. Boldface indicates volume numbers.

Animal Rights

Bilbao Anti-bullfighting Protest	**1:** 12
Blackfish Documentary and SeaWorld Protests	**1:** 25
Global March for Elephants and Rhinos	**1:** 18
UCR Lab Raid to Protest Animal Testing	**1:** 7

Children/Young Adult Issues

East LA Blowouts	**1:** 77
Harry Potter Book Burning	**1:** 177
Little Rock Nine Crisis	**1:** 47
Mother Jones's "Children's Crusade"	**2:** 399
Soweto Uprising	**3:** 530
Yale Student Protests on Free Speech	**1:** 194

Civil Rights

Baladi Campaign	**3:** 714
Day without Immigrants	**1:** 83
East LA Blowouts	**1:** 77
Freedom Rides	**1:** 54
Hunger Strikes by Suffragettes in Prison	**3:** 701
Little Rock Nine Crisis	**1:** 47
Lunch Counter Protest, McCrory's	**1:** 59
March on Washington for Jobs and Freedom	**1:** 63
Mexican Indignados Movement	**1:** 90
Montgomery Bus Boycott	**1:** 42
Women's Suffrage Protest at the White House	**3:** 707

Climate Change

Copenhagen Protests	**1:** 144
Forward on Climate Rally	**1:** 139
March for Science	**1:** 163
Pacific Climate Warriors Blockade	**1:** 157

Economic Issues

Battle in Seattle: World Trade Organization Protests	**1:** 209
Brexit	**1:** 122
Day without Immigrants	**1:** 83
Fast-Food Workers' Strike	**2:** 422
15-M Movement	**1:** 116
March on Washington for Jobs and Freedom	**1:** 63
Occupy Wall Street	**1:** 216
Porkulus Protests, Tea Party	**1:** 111
Secret Document of the Farmers of Xiaogang	**1:** 105

Education

East LA Blowouts	**1:** 77
Little Rock Nine Crisis	**1:** 47

ix

EVENTS BY TOPIC OF PROTEST (A THEMATIC TABLE OF CONTENTS)

Malala Yousafzai All-Girls School	**3:** 718
Soweto Uprising	**3:** 530
Yale Student Protests on Free Speech	**1:** 194

Energy, Power

Dakota Access Pipeline Protest	**2:** 384
Global Frackdown	**1:** 151
Pacific Climate Warriors Blockade	**1:** 157
Preservation of Amazon Rain Forest Awareness Campaign	**2:** 379

Environment

Battle in Seattle: World Trade Organization Protests	**1:** 209
Copenhagen Protests	**1:** 144
Dakota Access Pipeline Protest	**2:** 384
Forward on Climate Rally	**1:** 139
Global Frackdown	**1:** 151
March for Science	**1:** 163
Pacific Climate Warriors Blockade	**1:** 157
Preservation of Amazon Rain Forest Awareness Campaign	**2:** 379

Free Speech

Harry Potter Book Burning	**1:** 177
"Je Suis Charlie" Protests	**1:** 189
Muslim Protests of Danish Cartoons	**1:** 183
Yale Student Protests on Free Speech	**1:** 194

Globalization, Corporations

Battle in Seattle: World Trade Organization Protests	**1:** 209
March against Monsanto	**1:** 223
Occupy Wall Street	**1:** 216

Guns

Black Panthers Carry Guns into California Legislative Building in Protest of Mulford Act	**2:** 239
Democratic Congressional Representatives Sit-In for Gun Control Legislation	**2:** 256
"I Will Not Comply" Rally	**2:** 252
March on Washington for Gun Control	**2:** 246

Health Issues

Capitol Crawl	**2:** 276
March against Monsanto	**1:** 223
March for Women's Lives	**3:** 556
Planned Parenthood Protests	**3:** 574

Human Rights

Armenian Genocide Protests	**2:** 297
Attica Prison Riot	**2:** 270
Capitol Crawl	**2:** 276
Dalit Protests in India	**2:** 290
Gandhi Leads Salt March	**2:** 346
March to Abolish the Death Penalty	**2:** 284
Mexican Indignados Movement	**1:** 90

Immigration

Brexit	**1:** 122
Day without Immigrants	**1:** 83
1844 Nativist Riots	**2:** 311
Pro-Migrant Rallies in Europe and Australia	**2:** 318
Protests against President Trump's Travel Ban	**2:** 325

Income Inequality

Battle in Seattle: World Trade Organization Protests	**1:** 209
Delano Grape Strike and Boycott	**2:** 414
Fast-Food Workers' Strike	**2:** 422
Flint Sit-Down Strike against General Motors	**2:** 407
March on Washington for Jobs and Freedom	**1:** 63
Occupy Wall Street	**1:** 216

Independence Movements

Gandhi Leads Salt March	**2:** 346
Grito de Lares	**2:** 342
Velvet Revolution	**2:** 352

Indigenous Peoples' Rights

Aboriginal Land Rights Protest	**2:** 375
AIM Occupation of Wounded Knee	**2:** 367
Dakota Access Pipeline Protest	**2:** 384

Preservation of Amazon Rain Forest Awareness Campaign	**2:** 379

Labor

Battle in Seattle: World Trade Organization Protests	**1:** 209
Day without Immigrants	**1:** 83
Delano Grape Strike and Boycott	**2:** 414
Fast-Food Workers' Strike	**2:** 422
15-M Movement	**1:** 116
Flint Sit-Down Strike against General Motors	**2:** 407
March on Washington for Jobs and Freedom	**1:** 63
Mother Jones's "Children's Crusade"	**2:** 399
Secret Document of the Farmers of Xiaogang	**1:** 105

Land Rights

Aboriginal Land Rights Protest	**2:** 375
AIM Occupation of Wounded Knee	**2:** 367
Preservation of Amazon Rain Forest Awareness Campaign	**2:** 379

LGBTQ Issues

Protests of North Carolina House Bill 2	**2:** 458
Shanghai Pride Festival	**2:** 452
Stonewall Riots	**2:** 435
Westboro Baptist Church Protests of Matthew Shepard	**2:** 445
White Night Riots	**2:** 441

Police Brutality

Detroit Riots	**3:** 524
Justice for All March	**3:** 539
March on Washington for Jobs and Freedom	**1:** 63
Stonewall Riots	**2:** 435

Political Uprisings

Arab Spring and the Syrian Civil Uprising	**3:** 486
Fall of the Berlin Wall	**3:** 478
Tahrir Square Protests (Egyptian Revolution)	**3:** 493
Tiananmen Square Protests	**3:** 473
Umbrella Revolution	**3:** 498

Race Issues

Black Panthers Carry Guns into California Legislative Building in Protest of Mulford Act	**2:** 239
Detroit Riots	**3:** 524
East LA Blowouts	**1:** 77
Freedom Rides	**1:** 54
Justice for All March	**3:** 539
Little Rock Nine Crisis	**1:** 47
Lunch Counter Protest, McCrory's	**1:** 59
March on Washington for Jobs and Freedom	**1:** 63
Montgomery Bus Boycott	**1:** 42
Soweto Uprising	**3:** 530
Zoot Suit Riots	**3:** 518

Religion

"Je Suis Charlie" Protests	**1:** 189
Muslim Protests of Danish Cartoons	**1:** 183
Protests against President Trump's Travel Ban	**2:** 325

Reproductive Issues

March for Women's Lives	**3:** 556
One-Child Policy Riots	**3:** 568
Operation Rescue	**3:** 562
Planned Parenthood Protests	**3:** 574

Resistance to Nazis

Holocaust Resistance in Denmark	**3:** 597
Treblinka Death Camp Revolt	**3:** 607
Warsaw Ghetto Uprising (Poland)	**3:** 602
White Rose Movement	**3:** 592

Revolutions

Grito de Lares	**2:** 342
Tahrir Square Protests (Egyptian Revolution)	**3:** 493
Umbrella Revolution	**3:** 498
Velvet Revolution	**2:** 352

EVENTS BY TOPIC OF PROTEST (A THEMATIC TABLE OF CONTENTS)

Segregation/Desegregation

Freedom Rides	1: 54
Little Rock Nine Crisis	1: 47
Lunch Counter Protest, McCrory's	1: 59
March on Washington for Jobs and Freedom	1: 63
Montgomery Bus Boycott	1: 42

Slavery

Christmas Rebellion/Baptist War	3: 634
Fight to Stop Human Trafficking	3: 643
Harpers Ferry Raid	3: 638
Louisiana Rebellion (German Coast)	3: 623
Nat Turner's Rebellion/Anti-slavery Petitions	3: 628

Student Movements and Protests

East LA Blowouts	1: 77
15-M Movement	1: 116
Little Rock Nine Crisis	1: 47
Soweto Uprising	3: 530
Student Armband Protest of Vietnam War	3: 663
Student Protest at Kent State	3: 669
Tiananmen Square Protests	3: 473
Yale Student Protests on Free Speech	1: 194

Suffrage (Voting Rights)

Baladi Campaign	3: 714
Hunger Strikes by Suffragettes in Prison	3: 701
March on Washington for Jobs and Freedom	1: 63
Women's Suffrage Protest at the White House	3: 707

Violence

Bilbao Anti-bullfighting Protest	1: 12
Democratic Congressional Representatives Sit-In for Gun Control Legislation	2: 256
Global March for Elephants and Rhinos	1: 18
"Je Suis Charlie" Protests	1: 189
Justice for All March	3: 539
March on Washington for Gun Control	2: 246
March to Abolish the Death Penalty	2: 284
Mexican Indignados Movement	1: 90
White Night Riots	2: 441

War, Genocide, Ethnic Cleansing

Arab Spring and the Syrian Civil Uprising	3: 486
Armenian Genocide Protests	2: 297
Candlelight Vigils against Invasion of Iraq	3: 676
Chelsea Manning and WikiLeaks	3: 684
Holocaust Resistance in Denmark	3: 597
International Congress of Women	3: 657
Student Armband Protest of Vietnam War	3: 663
Student Protest at Kent State	3: 669
Treblinka Death Camp Revolt	3: 607
Warsaw Ghetto Uprising (Poland)	3: 602
White Rose Movement	3: 592

Women's Issues

Baladi Campaign	3: 714
Hunger Strikes by Suffragettes in Prison	3: 701
International Congress of Women	3: 657
Malala Yousafzai All-Girls School	3: 718
March for Women's Lives	3: 556
One-Child Policy Riots	3: 568
Operation Rescue	3: 562
Planned Parenthood Protests	3: 574
Women's March on Washington	3: 724
Women's Suffrage Protest at the White House	3: 707

Reader's Guide

The ancient Greek philosopher Heraclitus (535 BCE–475 BCE) once wrote that the only constant thing in life is change. Change is a natural part of human existence. It has driven everything from biological evolution to cultural advancement for thousands of years. Yet, despite the desire for change, accomplishing it can be difficult. Old ideas and prejudices are hard to overcome, and people often resist efforts to alter the current state of affairs.

For some, change involves the fight for human rights. Others seek to end war, to express ideas freely, or to live a lifestyle of their own choosing. Those who seek change use various forms of protest or civil unrest to make their voices heard. Although many protests are peaceful, some escalate into full-scale riots or rebellions. Nevertheless, the people involved in these movements strongly believe that their cause is worth fighting for.

U•X•L Protests, Riots, and Rebellions: Civil Unrest in the Modern World presents a detailed look at many of these efforts to enact change in the world. This 21-chapter work examines a wide range of diverse issues from the environment to free speech and racial conflict. Each chapter begins with a comprehensive overview designed to introduce readers to the topic. The text details 88 events as well as numerous sidebars that focus on various protests, conflicts, or social movements.

The entries are written in a style that makes complicated subjects easy for younger readers to understand. Each event is framed in the context of the historical period in which it occurred, examining not only the social forces that shaped the event but also the motivations of those who participated in it. Rather than solely focusing on what happened, each entry delves deeper into why it happened.

The chapters feature more than 200 photos and illustrations that help bring each event into sharper focus. In addition, each chapter includes a helpful

"Words to Know" box that defines key terms, and another box featuring questions designed to spark critical thinking. The set also includes 42 primary sources that provide additional information helpful in understanding the topic.

Additional Features

Protests, Riots, and Rebellions also contains a substantial and detailed chronology of events to help place each topic in its historical context. A "Where to Learn More" section lists books, periodicals, and websites to find additional information. The section "Research and Activity Ideas" provides students with ways to discuss and explore the topics further. Also included is a general glossary and a subject index.

Acknowledgments

The editors would like to acknowledge the following writers and editors at Northeast Editing, Inc. for their work on this volume: Tyler Biscontini, Eric Bullard, Cait Caffrey, Josephine Campbell, Mark Dziak, Angela Harmon, Jack Lasky, Elizabeth Mohn, Joanne Quaglia, Lindsay Rohland, Michael Ruth, Richard Sheposh, and Rebecca Zukauskas.

Special thanks to Susan Edgar, senior vocabulary editor at Cengage Learning, for sharing her expertise on historical events as we created the topic list. Additional thanks go to Justine Carson for her work on the index.

Suggestions Are Welcome

We welcome your comments on *U•X•L Protests, Riots, and Rebellions: Civil Unrest in the Modern World* and suggestions for other history topics to consider. Please write: Editors, *U•X•L Protests, Riots, and Rebellions* Gale, 27500 Drake Rd., Farmington Hills, MI 48331-3535; call toll free: 1-800-877-4253; fax to 248-699-8097; or send e-mail via http://www.gale.cengage.com.

Chronology

The chronology that follows contains a sampling of important events, protests, riots, and rebellions that occurred in the modern world.

c. 1760 to 1840	Period of transition beginning in Great Britain (and later spreading to Western Europe and North America) when manufacturing changed from hand to machine production. Some workers protested the loss of their jobs to machines during the Industrial Revolution.
1811	On January 8, several hundred slaves on Louisiana's German Coast near New Orleans stage an uprising that lasts for three days before military forces finally put it down.
1811	An anti-industrialization movement led by a group of angry textile workers and weavers called the Luddites begins in Great Britain.
1831–1832	A series of petitions sent to the Virginia General Assembly leads to a debate about the future of slavery in the state.
1835	On January 24, an uprising of Muslim slaves called the Malê revolt begins in Brazil.
1838	Author and poet Ralph Waldo Emerson (1803–1882) writes a letter to President Martin van Buren (1782–1862) in protest of the forced removal of the Cherokee in Georgia. The removal takes place and becomes known as the Trail of Tears.

McConnel & Company mills in England during the Industrial Revolution, c. 1820. PUBLIC DOMAIN

CHRONOLOGY

Ruins of the mission church destroyed during the Taos Revolt, 1847. © MATT RAGEN/SHUTTERSTOCK.COM

1844 — In May and July, anti-immigrant mobs attack Irish immigrants in a series of riots that rock the city of Philadelphia, Pennsylvania.

1847 — In January, a band of New Mexicans and Pueblo Indians revolt against the United States' occupation of northern New Mexico during the Mexican-American War (1846–1848). It becomes known as the Taos Revolt.

1848 — The first women's rights convention in US history takes place in Seneca Falls, New York.

1859 — Antislavery activist John Brown (1800–1859) leads an armed slave revolt at the US arsenal in Harpers Ferry, Virginia (now West Virginia).

1861 — The US Civil War begins.

1863 — In July, riots break out in New York City after Congress passes laws that allow the government to draft young men to serve in the US Civil War.

1865 — The US Civil War ends.

1868 — On September 23, Puerto Rican revolutionaries stage a brief uprising called the Grito de Lares in hopes of gaining their independence from Spain.

1880 — Growing resentment of incoming Chinese immigrants leads to rioting in Denver, Colorado.

1886 — On May 4, a labor rally near Haymarket Square in Chicago, Illinois, turns violent after someone throws a bomb at police.

1887 — Pioneering female journalist Nellie Bly (Elizabeth Cochran Seaman, 1864–1922) goes undercover as an inmate in a New York mental hospital to expose the many abuses occurring there. Her report is published in the *New York World* newspaper and later in the book *Ten Days in a Mad-House*. Bly's type of investigation is the first of its kind.

1890 — On December 29, tensions between the US Army and the Sioux on the Pine Ridge Reservation become intense. After

	a shot is fired, the army goes on to kill at least 150 Sioux men, women, and children in what becomes known as the Wounded Knee Massacre.
1898	The Spanish-American War begins in April after the USS *Maine* explodes in Havana Harbor, Cuba, in February. The war ends in August with the United States taking control of Guam, Puerto Rico, and the Philippines.
1903	In July, reformer Mary Harris "Mother" Jones (1837–1930) leads the Children's Crusade, also known as the March of the Mill Children, from Philadelphia, Pennsylvania, to Oyster Bay, New York, to bring attention to the problem of child labor.
1909	Women's rights activists imprisoned in Great Britain begin using hunger strikes to bring awareness to their cause.
1911	From September 14 to 22, El Primer Congreso Mexicanista, the first civil rights meeting for Mexican Americans, is held in Laredo, Texas.
1914	World War I begins in Europe.
1915	The International Congress of Women meets at The Hague in the Netherlands and creates several resolutions for peace.
1918	A group of National Women's Party members protest in front of the White House in Washington, DC, and call on the president to help women gain the right to vote.
1918	Between July and September, the anti-government Rice Riots break out in Japan in response to economic problems caused by low wages and high prices on goods such as rice.
1918	World War I ends.
1921	In August, thousands of frustrated West Virginian coal miners march on Blair Mountain and clash with coal company supporters and police for nearly a week in one of the largest labor uprisings in US history.

CHRONOLOGY

1929 — In November, women in Nigeria revolt against British colonial administrators in the Aba Women's War.

1930 — Indian independence movement leader Mohandas Gandhi (1869–1948) leads his famous Salt March in protest of the British Raj government's abuses of the Indian people.

1933 — On May 10, the Nazi Party holds a massive book burning in Germany, during which any books that do not support Nazi thinking or politics are destroyed.

1936 — General Motors employees in Flint, Michigan, go on a 44-day sit-down strike for better pay and improved working conditions.

1939 — World War II begins in Europe.

1942 — In February, President Franklin Roosevelt signs an executive order calling for people of Japanese ancestry on the West Coast to be relocated to internment camps. In March 1945 detainees at an internment camp near Santa Fe, New Mexico, rebel against guards in what becomes known as the Santa Fe Riot.

1942 — German medical student Hans Scholl (1918–1943) founds the White Rose movement, a resistance effort aimed at creating opposition to the Nazi Party.

People of Japanese descent are sent to internment camps, 1942. COURTESY OF LIBRARY OF CONGRESS.

1943 — People in Nazi-occupied Denmark begin resisting German rule and protecting Danish Jews from being sent to concentration camps.

1943 — On April 19, Jewish prisoners held in Poland's Warsaw Ghetto revolt against Nazi forces it what becomes known as the Warsaw Ghetto Uprising.

1943 — On June 3, chaos breaks out in Los Angeles, California, as angry American servicemen attack Mexican American and other minority youths in the Zoot Suit Riots.

1943 — In August, Jewish prisoners held by the Nazis at the Treblinka death camp in Poland revolt.

1945 — World War II ends.

CHRONOLOGY

1950   The Korean War begins.

1953   The Korean War ends.

1954   The Vietnam War begins.

1955   African Americans in Montgomery, Alabama, begin boycotting the public bus system after Rosa Parks (1913–2005) is arrested for refusing to give up her seat to a white passenger.

1957   In September, riots and other protests erupt in Little Rock, Arkansas, when nine African American students are admitted to the desegregated Little Rock Central High School.

1960   In April, a student uprising in South Korea known as the April Revolution leads to the overthrow of the First Republic of South Korea and the resignation of President Syngman Rhee (1875–1965).

1960   Chaos erupts in November when six-year-old Ruby Bridges (1954–) of Tylertown, Mississippi, becomes the first African American child to attend an all-white elementary school in the South.

Scene from the April Revolution in South Korea, 1960. © AP IMAGES.

1961   In January, nine African Americans stage a sit-in at a McCrory's lunch counter in Rock Hill, South Carolina, to protest the store's refusal to serve African American customers.

1961   Beginning In May, bus trips through the American South called the Freedom Rides are held in protest of Jim Crow laws and segregation at interstate bus stations.

1963   On August 28, about 250,000 people participate in the March on Washington for Jobs and Freedom in protest of racial segregation and other forms of discrimination. Civil rights icon the Rev. Dr. Martin Luther King Jr. (1929–1968) delivers his famous "I Have a Dream" speech.

1964   Between June and August, civil rights groups organize a voter registration drive called the Mississippi Summer Project in an effort to increase voter registration in that state.

CHRONOLOGY

Fannie Lou Hamer at Democratic National Convention. COURTESY OF LIBRARY OF CONGRESS.

1964 In August, voting rights and civil rights activist Fannie Lou Hamer shocks the nation during a speech at the Democratic National Convention in Atlantic City, New Jersey. She details the abuse she suffered at the hands of white citizens and police while trying to help register African American voters.

1964 The Free Speech Movement takes off at the University of California, Berkeley.

1965 On September 8, grape pickers in Delano, California, begin a labor strike with the help of the Agricultural Workers Organizing Committee and the United Farm Workers. The movement, which is led by César Chávez (1927–1993), continues until 1970.

1965 In December, students at several schools in Des Moines, Iowa, begin wearing black armbands to protest the Vietnam War.

1967 On May 2, members of the Black Panther Party stage a protest at the California State Capitol over a proposed gun control law that would prohibit them from conducting armed patrols of African American neighborhoods.

1967 On July 23, a race riot begins in Detroit, Michigan, after a police raid on an after-hours bar. The riot quickly becomes one of the worst of its kind in US history, resulting in 43 deaths, 7,200 arrests, and 2,000 damaged buildings.

1968 On March 1, Chicano students in Los Angeles, California, stage the first of a series of walkouts known as the East LA Blowouts in protest of unequal conditions at local high schools.

1968 On April 4, Martin Luther King Jr. is assassinated in Memphis, Tennessee.

May 1968 French student protest poster that reads "Be young and shut up." © ROGER VIOLLET/GETTY IMAGES.

1968 In May, civil unrest sweeps across France as student protests and widespread labor strikes temporarily disrupt the nation's government and economy.

CHRONOLOGY

1968 On September 7, several hundred feminists stage a protest against the Miss America Pageant on the Atlantic City boardwalk in New Jersey.

1968 In October, during the Olympic Games in Mexico City, Mexico, African American sprinters Tommie Smith (1944–) and John Carlos (1945–) raise their fists as they receive their medals in a gesture meant to promote human rights.

Protest of the Miss America Beauty Pageant, 1968. © BETTMANN/GETTY IMAGES.

1969 On June 28, a police raid on a New York City gay nightclub called the Stonewall Inn leads to a series of violent protests and riots.

1969 On November 20, a group of 89 Native Americans go to Alcatraz Island in San Francisco Bay and claim it as their own "by right of discovery." Their occupation of the island continues until June of 1971.

1970 On May 4, a protest against the Vietnam War at Kent State University turns deadly when members of the Ohio National Guard open fire on demonstrators and kill four students.

Bob Dylan and Joan Baez protested the Vietnam War through song. © TRINITY MIRROR/MIRRORPIX/ALAMY.

1971 Whistle-blower Daniel Ellsberg (1931–) reveals details from a secret US government report about US involvement in the Vietnam War to the *New York Times*. The report comes to be known as the Pentagon Papers.

1971 On September 9, prisoners demanding better living conditions and political rights at Attica Correctional Facility in upstate New York begin a violent four-day revolt. A total of 43 people are killed in the uprising.

1972 On January 30, British soldiers shoot and kill 28 unarmed people participating in a peaceful protest over the arrest of more than 300 people accused of working with the Irish Republican Army (IRA). This event soon becomes known as Bloody Sunday.

1973 On February 27, about 200 Native Americans led by members of the American Indian Movement (AIM) take control of Pine Ridge Reservation in South Dakota. Their occupation of the reservation continues until May 8.

The Pentagon Papers were released in 1971. © MPI/GETTY IMAGES.

U•X•L Protests, Riots, and Rebellions: Civil Unrest in the Modern World

CHRONOLOGY

1975 The Vietnam War ends.

1976 On June 16, hundreds are killed in Soweto, South Africa, when a student protest turns violent. The violence brings attention to the problem of racism in South Africa and plays an important role in eventually ending the apartheid system.

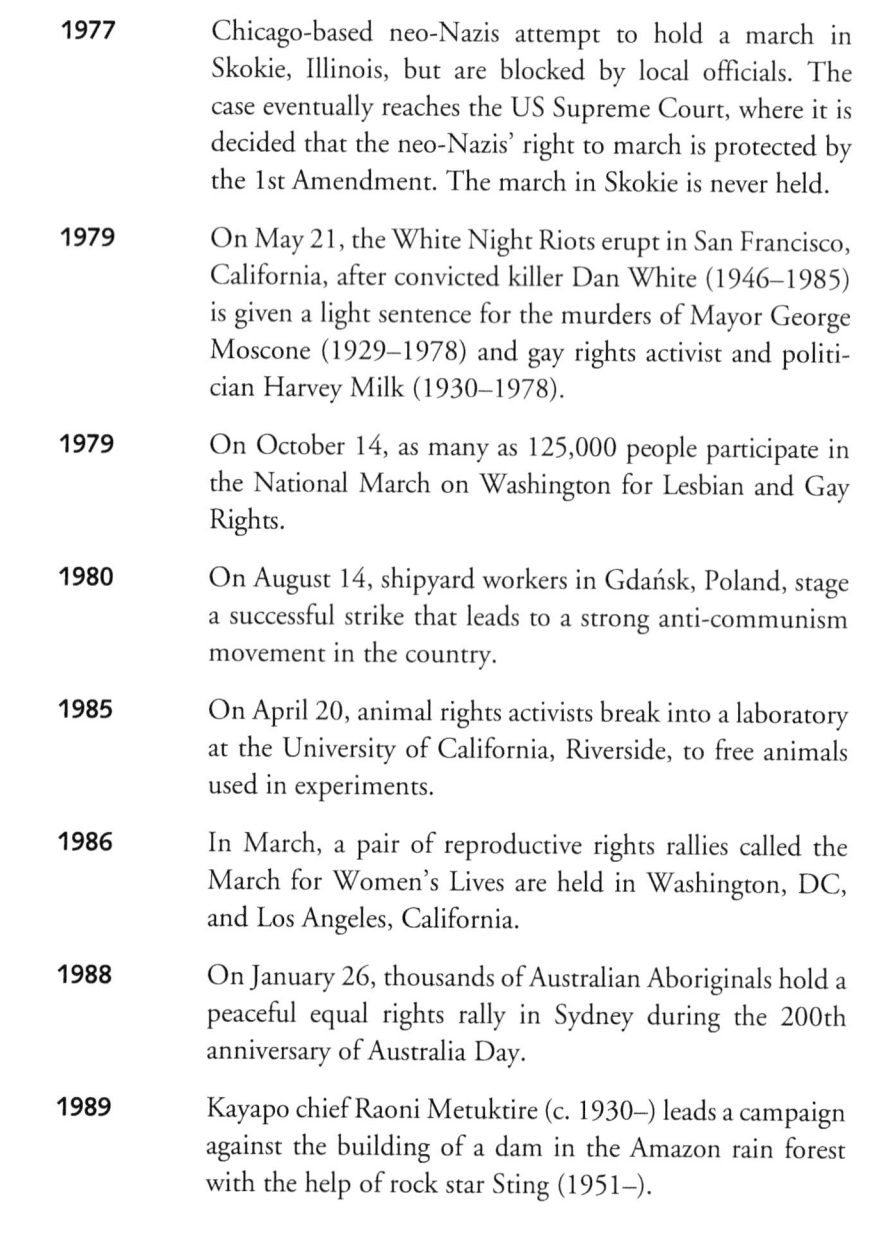

1977 Chicago-based neo-Nazis attempt to hold a march in Skokie, Illinois, but are blocked by local officials. The case eventually reaches the US Supreme Court, where it is decided that the neo-Nazis' right to march is protected by the 1st Amendment. The march in Skokie is never held.

1979 On May 21, the White Night Riots erupt in San Francisco, California, after convicted killer Dan White (1946–1985) is given a light sentence for the murders of Mayor George Moscone (1929–1978) and gay rights activist and politician Harvey Milk (1930–1978).

1979 On October 14, as many as 125,000 people participate in the National March on Washington for Lesbian and Gay Rights.

1980 On August 14, shipyard workers in Gdańsk, Poland, stage a successful strike that leads to a strong anti-communism movement in the country.

1985 On April 20, animal rights activists break into a laboratory at the University of California, Riverside, to free animals used in experiments.

1986 In March, a pair of reproductive rights rallies called the March for Women's Lives are held in Washington, DC, and Los Angeles, California.

1988 On January 26, thousands of Australian Aboriginals hold a peaceful equal rights rally in Sydney during the 200th anniversary of Australia Day.

1989 Kayapo chief Raoni Metuktire (c. 1930–) leads a campaign against the building of a dam in the Amazon rain forest with the help of rock star Sting (1951–).

CHRONOLOGY

1989   On November 9, the Berlin Wall falls.

1989   On November 17, a political movement called the Velvet Revolution begins in Czechoslovakia and ends just over a month later with the end of communism in that country.

1990   On March 12, disabled activists protest delays in passing the Americans with Disabilities Act (ADA) by crawling up the steps of the US Capitol in an event called the Capitol Crawl.

1990   In October, a Jewish group wants to lay a cornerstone for a temple at the site of the Al-Aqsa Mosque, a Muslim holy place in Jerusalem on a hill known as the Temple Mount. A group of Palestinians respond by throwing rocks and bottles at border police as well as at Jews, who are praying at the Western Wall just below the mosque on the hill. Israeli troops respond and kill 23 Palestinians; several hundred others are injured in the riots.

Temple Mount Riots, 1990. © MENAHEM KAHANA/AFP/GETTY IMAGES.

1991   In December, the collapse of the Soviet Union is complete.

1992   The pro-life organization Operation Rescue holds an anti-abortion protest called the Spring of Life.

1992   On April 29, riots break out in Los Angeles, California, after several city police officers are found not guilty in a criminal case concerning the beating of an African American man named Rodney King (1965–2012) during an arrest.

1992   In October, Irish singer Sinead O'Connor (1966–) appears on NBC's *Saturday Night Live* and sings Jamaican artist Bob Marley's (1945–1981) song "War." As she concludes her performance, she rips up a picture of Pope John Paul II (1920–2005), saying "fight the real enemy." She was protesting sexual abuse in the Catholic Church.

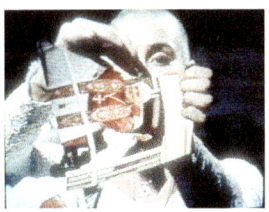

Sinead O'Connor causes a stir when she rips the pope's picture in 1992 on SNL. © YVONNE HEMSEY/HULTON ARCHIVE/GETTY IMAGES.

1994   Members of Greenpeace send two ships in an attempt to stop Norwegian ships from hunting whales.

1995   On October 16, Nation of Islam leader Louis Farrakhan (1933–) leads the Million Man March in Washington, DC, to raise awareness of the importance of American family values, unity, and civil rights.

Million Man March in Washington, DC, in 1995. © JAMES LEYNSE/GETTY IMAGES.

CHRONOLOGY

1998	On October 16, members of the Westboro Baptist Church protest at the funeral of Matthew Shepard (1976–1998), a young man who was murdered for being gay.
1999	On November 30, a series of protests known as the Battle for Seattle break out in Seattle, Washington, during the World Trade Organization (WTO) Ministerial Conference.
2000	On October 15, the first March to Abolish the Death Penalty is held in Austin, Texas. The inaugural event is called the March on the Mansion.
2001	On September 11, terrorists hijack airplanes that crash into the World Trade Center in New York City; the Pentagon in Washington, DC; and a field in western Pennsylvania. Almost 3,000 people are killed.
2001	In response to the September 11 attacks, the United States forms a coalition of nations and begins a war in Afghanistan on October 7.
2001	On December 30, Pastor Jack Brock of the Christ Community Church in Alamogordo, New Mexico, organizes a book burning at which copies of the Harry Potter series are destroyed.
2002	On November 30, various people in the United Kingdom protest the materialism rampant before the holidays by having a "Buy Nothing Day."
2002	Surfers against Sewage, a group in the United Kingdom, stages a protest to raise awareness about ocean pollutants, including plastics, and the need to keep the coasts clean.
2003	On March 16, thousands of candlelight vigils are held across the world in protest of the impending invasion of Iraq. The war begins on March 19.
2004	On August 29, a group called One Thousand Coffins participates in a march held in New York City to protest the Iraq War.

Organizer of Buy Nothing Day, Michael Smith, in 2002.
© ROGER BAMBER/ALAMY.

Participant in the Surfers against Sewage protest, 2002.
© SION TOUHIG/GETTY IMAGES.

CHRONOLOGY

2005	On September 30, the Danish newspaper *Jyllands-Posten* publishes several cartoons depicting the Muslim prophet Muhammad. Many Muslims voice concern over the portrayals and some protests turn violent.
2005	On December 3, the first Global Day of Action is held worldwide to protest climate change.
2006	On May 1, protests called a Day without Immigrants are held in cities across the United States. The event is also called the Great American Boycott.
2006	In late November and early December, damage to a statue of a Dalit hero triggers violent protests near Mumbai, India.
2007	In May, thousands of people riot in China against the government's controversial one-child policy.
2008	The women's rights group Soroptimist International of Great Britain and Ireland begins its Purple Teardrop campaign to combat human trafficking.
2008	In February, several Danish newspapers reprint the 2005 cartoon depicting the prophet Muhammad. At least 200 people are killed as protests flare in Denmark and several other nations.
2009	The conservative anti-tax Tea Party movement begins with protest rallies in cities across the United States.
2009	In June, the first Shanghai Pride Festival is held. The event is the first LGBTQ festival to take place on the Chinese mainland.
2009–2010	About 110 people are killed in ongoing protests in Iran over the election of President Mahmoud Ahmadinejad (1956–), which the protesters claim was fraudulent. The protests are known as the Iranian Green Movement.
2009	On October 11, thousands of members of the LGBTQ community and their supporters stage the National Equality March in Washington, DC.
2009	On December 16, about 1,700 people are arrested as thousands of protesters try to disrupt the United Nations Climate Change Conference in Copenhagen, Denmark.

Participants during the Global Day of Action, 2005, to fight climate change.
© PHOTOFUSION/GETTY IMAGES.

CHRONOLOGY

2010	Classified information stolen by US Army soldier Chelsea Manning (then Bradley Manning, 1987–) is first released on the website WikiLeaks.
2010	On August 21, protesters stage an anti-bullfighting rally in front of the Guggenheim Museum in Bilbao, Spain.
2010	In November in Nigeria, people march in conjunction with the Movement for the Survival of the Ogoni people. They are marking the 15th anniversary of the deaths of the Ogoni martyrs, who were executed by the government amid controversy.
2010	On December 17, a Tunisian street vendor named Mohamed Bouazizi (1984–2011) sets himself on fire in a protest against the government.
2011	In January, ongoing protests inspired by Mohamed Bouazizi's actions force Tunisia's president to resign. The protests spread to other nations in northern Africa and the Middle East, beginning a movement known as the Arab Spring.
2011	In January and February, massive anti-government demonstrations take place in Egypt's Tahrir Square.
2011	On March 11, a powerful earthquake strikes Japan, unleashing a massive tsunami. The earthquake and tsunami kill about 19,000 people and severely damage the Fukushima Daiichi Nuclear Power Station.
2011	In March, an uprising begins in Syria. It eventually turns into a brutal civil war that was still ongoing as of early 2018.
2011	The first "Slutwalk" is held after a police officer in Toronto, Canada, suggests women should stop dressing like "sluts" to avoid sexual assault. The protest took on rape culture, which includes blaming or shaming the victims of sexual assault.
2011	The March 28 killing of his son prompts Mexican poet Javier Sicilia (1956–) to organize several protest marches against drug violence in Mexico.
2011	On April 25, demonstrators hold several marches in France and Germany to protest the use of nuclear power.

March by the Movement for the Survival of the Ogoni People, 2010. © PIUS UTOMI EKPEI/ GETTY IMAGES.

Slutwalk, first held in 2011, is an annual event, shown here in 2014. © TYLER MCKAY/ SHUTTERSTOCK.COM.

CHRONOLOGY

2011 — On May 15, more than 80,000 people take part in a series of economic protests known as the 15-M movement in Spain.

2011 — On September 17, a global protest against economic inequality called Occupy Wall Street starts in New York City and spreads throughout the country and other parts of the world.

2011 — The Iraq War ends.

2011 — In December, residents of Wukan, China, protest illegal land grabs in their fishing village. Claiming that local officials sold communal land and provided no compensation to residents. the protesters become outraged when a local village leader is killed while in police custody.

Wukan, China, residents protest illegal communal land sales, 2011. © STR/GETTY IMAGES.

2012 — Starting in March, protesters in Fukushima, Japan, begin to meet in front of the prime minister's house to protest the use of nuclear power.

2012 — On November 29, fast-food workers at McDonald's and other restaurants begin going on strike to protest low wages.

2012 — Students in Montreal, Canada, take to the streets to protest a tuition hike and other rising fees at the country's universities.

2013 — On January 26, about 1,000 protesters take part in the March on Washington for Gun Control in honor of the 20 children and 6 staff members who were murdered in the Sandy Hook Elementary School shooting several weeks earlier.

Students protest tuition hikes in Montreal, 2012. © ROGERIO BARBOSA/AFP/ GETTYIMAGES.

2013 — On February 17, more than 40,000 environmentalists rally in front of the White House as part of the Forward on Climate rally in Washington, DC.

2013 — On May 25, people in 436 cities around the world protest against Monsanto, a multinational corporation that produces and promotes genetically modified foods.

2013 — In July, the Black Lives Matter movement forms.

2013 — On November 21, protests called the Euromaidan demonstrations begin to sweep across Ukraine and eventually lead to the 2014 Ukrainian revolution.

People participating in the Euromaiden protests in the Ukraine, 2013. © PROCESS/ SHUTTERSTOCK.COM

CHRONOLOGY

2014 — *Blackfish*, a documentary alleging the abuse of orca killer whales at SeaWorld, causes a significant number of animal rights activists to campaign against the parks.

2014 — In February, activists around the world protest against the Russian government's harsh policies on homosexuality days before the start of the Sochi Olympic Games.

2014 — On April 15, Islamist militants violently kidnap several hundred teenage girls from a boarding school in Nigeria. People around the world respond with the Bring Back Our Girls campaign.

2014 — In September, thousands of protesters in Hong Kong clash with police when China announces it will still not allow Hong Kongers to freely select their own leaders. This event is known as the Umbrella Revolution.

2014 — On October 3 and 4, animal rights activists around the world continue their annual protests against the poaching of elephants and rhinos in Africa.

2014 — On October 11, thousands of environmental activists march in protest of expanded fracking practices.

2014 — On October 17, Pacific Climate Warriors attempt to blockade Newcastle Harbor in Australia with kayaks, dinghies, and canoes to prevent coal ships from leaving the harbor.

2015 — Saudi Arabia allows women to vote and run in municipal elections for the first time in the country's history.

2015 — In January, tens of thousands of people attend rallies throughout France in response to a terrorist attack at the offices of the French magazine *Charlie Hebdo*.

2015 — On April 4, people protest the passage of the Religious Freedom Restoration Act in Indiana. They are concerned that the act will allow people to legally discriminate against people based on their sexual orientation or their gender identity.

Participants at the Religious Freedom Restoration Act protest in Indiana, 2015. © AP IMAGES/DOUG MCSCHOOLER.

CHRONOLOGY

2015 — On April 24, protesters around the world march to mark the 100th anniversary of the Armenian genocide. The protesters demand that Turkey acknowledge its role in the Armenian genocide.

2015 — Malala Yousafzai (1997–), who was shot by the Taliban for speaking out for girls' education, opens an all-girls school for Syrian refugees. A year earlier, she became one of the youngest people ever to win the Nobel Peace Prize.

2015 — On October 13, demonstrators in Turkey protest a double suicide bombing that occurred during a peace rally in Ankara several days earlier. The protesters hold signs of people killed by the blasts.

Anti-terrorism protest in Turkey, 2015. © ADEM ALTAN/GETTY IMAGES.

2015 — On November 21, following terror attacks in Paris, France, earlier that month, Muslims in Italy stage a rally to protest terrorism and violence. Many carry signs reading "Not in My Name."

2015 — In November, students at Yale University protest in response to racial issues at their school. The protests occur after the university issues advice on what types of Halloween costumes might be considered offensive to others.

Italian Muslims rally against terrorism, 2015. © EUGENIO MARONGIU/SHUTTERSTOCK.COM.

2016 — In January, armed anti-government militia members take over the Malheur National Wildlife Refuge near Burns, Oregon. They demand the federal government return the land to the people and release two local ranchers who were put in prison for committing arson on public land. Most of the protesters are not from Oregon but have traveled to the state from Arizona, Montana, and Idaho, among others.

Armed participants at the Malheur National Wildlife Refuge in Oregon, 2016. © ANADOLU AGENCY/GETTY IMAGES.

2016 — On January 24, activists in Greece hold a pro-migrant rally.

CHRONOLOGY

Participants protest lead in the water in Flint, Michigan, 2016. © BILL PUGLIANO/GETTY IMAGES.

Candelight vigil to protest deaths of Tibetans, 2016. © MANJUNATH KIRAN/AFP/GETTY IMAGES.

Counterprotesters urge people to reject hate at Stone Mountain protest, 2016. © AP IMAGES/BEN GRAY.

2016   On February 19, the Rev. Jesse Jackson (1941–) leads a national mile-long march in Flint, Michigan, to raise awareness and demand help to combat the water crisis in the city. A change in the city's water source had led to the corrosion of water pipes that began leaching harmful levels of lead into residents's tap water.

2016   In March, after the self-immolation of two Tibetans in Bangalore, India, a candlelight vigil is held. A schoolboy and a monk had set themselves on fire and died in protest of Chinese rule in the region of Tibet.

2016   Beginning in April, Native Americans and other protesters rally against the Dakota Access Pipeline in North Dakota.

2016   In April, dozens of pro-LGBTQ rights and anti-LGBTQ rights protesters demonstrate in Raleigh, North Carolina, after the passing of the state's Public Facilities Privacy and Security Act. The act pertains to which bathrooms transgender people can use.

2016   In April, white supremacists hold a protest at Stone Mountain, a monument to Confederate leaders, in Georgia. Their white power rally is interrupted by counterprotesters who urge people to reject hate and racism.

2016   On June 22, congressional Democrats stage a sit-in to protest the House of Representatives' refusal to vote on gun control.

2016   On June 23, the United Kingdom votes to leave the European Union. Thousands of people in London take to the streets to protest the decision.

2016   In the fall, San Francisco 49ers quarterback Colin Kaepernick (1987–) begins a protest against racial injustice and police brutality in the United States. He first sits and then later kneels when the national anthem is played at the team's games. Eventually, other athletes join his protest.

2016   In November, following the surprise victory of Republican candidate Donald Trump (1946–) in the US presidential election, protesters take to the streets in various cities to demonstrate against him. Many voice concerns about the negative remarks and promised policies that Trump made during the campaign that would impact women, Hispanics and Latinos, African Americans, Muslims, immigrants, gays, and others.

2017 On January 21, more than two million women march for women's rights and other issues in Washington, DC, on the first day of Donald Trump's (1946–) presidency.

2017 On January 28, protesters across the United States march against President Trump's immigration policy known as the travel ban.

2017 Protests erupt periodically at the University of California, Berkeley, in an attempt to stop controversial speakers from appearing at events on campus. Protests also erupt between pro-Trump supporters and counterprotesters.

2017 On February 11, antiabortion activists throughout the United States protest against Planned Parenthood. Counterprotests in support of Planned Parenthood funding are also held.

2017 On April 22, activists around the world gather in support of government funding for science. The event is known as the March for Science.

2017 On June 25, protesters march in Washington, DC, in support of traditional marriage.

2017 In August, white supremacist protesters and counterprotesters violently clash in Charlottesville, Virginia. The incident results in the death of counterprotester Heather Heyer (c. 1985–2017).

2017 In October, people use the hashtag #MeToo to raise awareness of sexual assault and harassment. Many people, especially women, document the various ways in which they have been victimized by sexual predators. The discussion prompts some of the accused people to resign from their jobs; others are fired.

CHRONOLOGY

2017 In December, protests erupt in the Middle East when President Donald Trump announces that the United States will recognize Jerusalem as the capital of Israel. The move stokes the Israeli-Palestinian conflict.

Words to Know

Ableism: Discrimination against disabled people.

Abolition: The act of ending or stopping something.

Abolitionist movement: A campaign held during the 19th century to end slavery in the United States.

Aboriginal: A member of the native people of region, such as Australia or Canada.

Accessibility: How easy or difficult it is for physically disabled individuals to navigate a building.

Activist: One who takes action to support or oppose an issue.

Advocate: One who defends a certain cause.

Allied powers: The group of nations that fought Nazi Germany and other Axis powers during World War II.

Amendment: A change in the wording of a law or bill.

Anarchist: A person who rebels against authority and believes governments should be overthrown.

Animal welfare: To assure the care and comfort of animals.

Apartheid: A series of laws in South Africa that legalized discrimination and ordered the separation of people by race.

Armory: A place where military weapons are made and stored.

Aryan: Adolf Hitler's idea of a master race of people who were tall and had blond hair and blue eyes.

Ashram: A religious retreat.

Assassination: The killing of someone for political reasons.

Asylum: Protection given to refugees that grants them the right to stay in a new country.

Austerity: Conditions of extreme spending cuts at a national level.

Autonomy: Self-government.

Background check: The process that allows authorities to examine the history of a person before he or she can purchase a gun.

Bill: A draft of a law that is presented to lawmakers for a vote.

Bloc: A group of nations that work together toward a common interest.

Boycott: A refusal to buy or use certain items, products, or services as a form of protest.

Bribery: Offering someone a gift in return for a favor.

Candlelight vigil: An assembly of people who hold candles to show support or opposition for a cause or event.

Capital punishment: A death sentence issued by a court to an individual found guilty of committing a serious crime; also known as the death penalty.

Capitalism: An economic system in which land and wealth are mostly owned by private individuals.

Captivity: The state of being held under the control of someone and not allowed to leave.

Cartridge: A tube that contains a bullet that the user puts into a gun.

Caste system: A system that groups people into different social classes based on wealth, occupation, or other factors.

Censorship: The act of removing any content considered harmful or offensive from books, newspapers, or other media.

Census: Provides a count of a population for specific information about the people living in a country.

Chemical weapons: Weapons that use chemicals to kill or seriously injure people.

Chicano: A term used to describe a Mexican American individual.

Christianity: A religion based on the teachings of Jesus Christ.

Civil disobedience: A public refusal to follow certain laws as a peaceful form of protest.

Civil rights: Guarantees of equal political, social, and economic freedoms to all citizens of a country.

Civilian: A person who is not active in the military or a member of law enforcement.

Climate change: Long-term, significant, measured change in the climate as seen in temperature, wind patterns, precipitation, and other factors. The term is often used today to describe any changes to global weather patterns that result from human practices.

Climate refugee: Any person who has been forced to leave his or her home as a direct result of changes to the environment.

Colonialism: An economic system in which Western European nations controlled various underdeveloped countries located around the world.

Colony: A country or other area that is controlled by a more powerful country.

Communism: A political system in which private ownership of property is eliminated and government directs all economic production. The goods produced and accumulated wealth are, in theory, shared relatively equally by all.

Conception: The moment when a male's sperm fertilizes a female's ovum.

Conservative: A view that favors traditional beliefs concerning social issues and wants limited government spending.

Constitution: A country's document of laws.

Consumerism: An economic concept based on buying and using goods.

Contraceptive: A method or device used to prevent pregnancy.

Corporatism: Occurs when big businesses become powerful enough to take control of the state.

Crusade: An important mission, usually involving moral beliefs and often requiring a long journey.

WORDS TO KNOW

D

Dalit: A member of the lowest social class in India's caste system. They were previous known as Untouchables, a term that is considered derogatory.

Death camp: Prison camps where Nazis killed hundreds of thousands of Jews and other prisoners from across Europe during World War II.

Deforestation: The clear-cutting of forests for such human purposes as homes, businesses, and farms.

Delegate: A person at a meeting who represents others.

Democracy: A form of government in which people choose leaders by voting.

Deport: To remove immigrants from a nation and send them back to their home country.

Depression: A period in which economic activity is limited and joblessness is widespread.

Desegregate: To end the practice of keeping different groups of people separated by joining them together as one.

Desertification: A process in which land becomes increasingly dry and unusable due to climate change.

Developing countries: Poor nations that are looking to advance economically and socially.

Dictator: Ruler who has total power over a country.

Disability: A physical, developmental, or mental condition that limits a person's activities in certain areas of life.

Discrimination: Unfair treatment based on one's race, ethnicity, or other distinction.

Draft: A process by which young men are required to serve in the armed forces. Some countries also draft women.

Drug cartel: A group that produces and sells illegal drugs.

E

Economic inequality: A large difference in income between the poor and the wealthy.

Economy: The combined wealth and other resources of a country.

Electoral votes: Votes cast by a select group of people from each state to elect the president of the United States.

Embassy: The office in one country where a representative of another country lives and works.

Endangered: A plant or animal that is in danger of becoming extinct.

Environmentalism: The idea that people must actively take part in political and social movements to bring about positive changes that improve the health of the planet.

Ethnicity: A division of human beings by culture, language, or home country.

Etiquette: A social custom or skill that guides the way people behave in the presence of others.

Execution: The killing of a person who has been sentenced to die.

Extinct: A term to describe a species that has completely died out.

F

Factory farm: A farm where many animals are raised, often indoors, for food.

Fetus: An unborn, developing human.

Final Solution: A plan for killing all Jews in Nazi-controlled areas.

Fiscal responsibility: When the government taxes just enough to pay for necessary expenses.

Force-feed: To make a person eat by forcefully putting food down his or her throat.

Fossil fuels: Energy sources such as gas, oil, and coal that result from ancient natural processes, such as the decay of ancient plants and animals.

Fracking: A method of getting natural gas and oil from rock by injecting water at high pressure into the ground.

Free trade: The buying and selling of goods and services between nations without any special taxes or rules to limit trade.

G

Gender expression: Individuals' external presentation of gender, including how they dress, style their hair, and refer to themselves.

WORDS TO KNOW

Gender identity: Individuals' personal inner experience of their gender, which may not match the sex they were assigned at birth.

Genocide: The killing of many members of the same race, religion, ethnicity, or culture.

Ghetto: Poor area of a city where certain groups of people live.

Global warming: Rising temperature of Earth's atmosphere caused by an increase of greenhouse gases.

Globalization: Occurs when countries do business on an international level.

Greenhouse gases: Gases that collect in the upper atmosphere of Earth and are believed to be responsible for changes to the planet's climate and weather patterns.

Gun control: Any attempt to create policies that offer more protections from gun violence.

Gun rights: A term used to describe attempts to protect the ability of Americans to own and use guns.

H

Handgun: A firearm that can be held and fired with one hand.

Hate crime: A crime committed against a person because of his or her race, religion, national origin, gender, sexual orientation, or disability.

Hate group: A group that supports hatred, anger, or violence toward members of a certain race, religion, national origin, gender, or sexual orientation.

Hispanic: A person who is from or who has ancestors from a Spanish-speaking country.

Hitler Youth: Nazi Germany's children's organization that taught Nazi ideas to youths so they would grow up supporting the Nazi Party.

Holocaust: Nazi Germany's mass killing of European Jews and others during World War II.

Hostage: A person who is captured and held against his or her will until certain demands are met.

Housing bubble: An increase in housing prices caused by high demand that eventually decreases, causing values of properties to decline sharply.

Human trafficking: The practice of forcing people to perform labor or participate in sex work.

Humane: Acting in a caring or considerate manner.

Hunger strike: The act of refusing to eat to bring about a desired change.

Hydroelectric energy: Energy that is generated from the force of moving water.

I

Idol worship: The worship of a false god.

Immigrant: A person who enters a new country after leaving his or her home country.

Impoverished: Extremely poor.

Indentured servant: A person who works for another person in exchange for travel, food, and housing for a specified amount of time.

Indigenous: Originating in or living naturally in a certain region.

Industry: The production of goods from raw materials in factories.

Integration: The practice of combining different groups in society to make them equal.

Islamization: A shift in a society's culture toward the religion of Islam.

Ivory: The hard, white substance that makes up the tusks and some teeth of certain animals.

J

Jim Crow laws: Laws created mostly in the American South in the late 19th and early 20th centuries that kept black citizens from enjoying the same rights as white Americans.

L

Labor union: An organization of workers that is formed to protect their rights and interests.

Latin America: A region south of the United States that includes Mexico, Central America, South America, and islands in the Caribbean.

Latino: A person who is from or who has ancestors from a Latin American country.

Legislature: A group of people responsible for making laws.

Liberal: A view that favors new ideas.

M

Market economy: An economic system of free competition in which prices are determined by supply and demand.

Maroons: Freed Spanish slaves who lived in the mountains of Jamaica.

Migrant: A person who moves from one place to another in search of work.

Militant: Using violent or aggressive means in support of a cause.

Militia: A group of citizens with military training who are called to service only in the event of emergencies.

Minimum wage: The lowest hourly rate that an employer can pay a worker.

Monopoly: When a single company or person is the sole provider of a product or service.

Mortgage: Payments made on a loan from a bank to help pay for the purchase of a home.

Multinational company: A company that does business in many countries around the world.

Muslim: A follower of Islam, a religion founded by the prophet Muhammad.

N

National Guard: A branch of the armed forces that usually deals with problems within the United States.

Nativism: A policy that protects the rights of a country's native people over immigrants' rights.

Natural resources: Water, soil, minerals, and other materials that are found in nature and are important to humans.

Nazi Party: A political party that controlled Germany from 1933 to 1945 under the leadership of Adolf Hitler.

Negotiate: To discuss something in hopes of making a deal.

North Atlantic Treaty Organization (NATO): A military partnership of the United States, Canada, and various European countries.

O

Occult: Matters that deal with the supernatural or magic.

Ovum: A female reproductive cell, sometimes called an egg.

P

Pacifist: Someone who is strongly opposed to war and fighting.

Parliament: A lawmaking body.

Partisans: Members of armed organizations that fight against forces that are controlling their country.

Pepper spray: A spray made from cayenne pepper that can cause a burning feeling in a person's eyes and throat when applied.

Petition: A written request made to an official person or organized body.

Picket: A protest that involves a group of people marching at a site with signs on posts or pointed sticks.

Pipeline: A system of connected pipes that are used to transport liquids and gases over a long distance.

Plantation: A large area of land that is usually worked by manual labor.

Poaching: The illegal hunting or killing of an animal.

Police brutality: The use of more force than necessary by police.

Political correctness: The act of avoiding certain language or activities that could offend a particular person or group.

Pork barrel spending: Funds attached to legislation for projects that benefit a lawmaker's home district.

Pro-choice: A term used to describe people who support a woman's right to choose whether or not to have an abortion.

Pro-life: A term used to describe people who are against abortion.

Prophet: A messenger of God.

R

Racial diversity: To include people from various racial backgrounds.

Racial insensitivity: A lack of understanding of the experiences of people of other races.

Racism: The belief that one human being is better than another because of his or her race.

Radical: Someone who favors extreme measures to make a point or bring about change.

Recession: A period when trade and economic production slow.

Reformer: A person who tries to bring changes to society.

Refugee: A person who leaves his or her home country because of war or mistreatment based on race, religion, or political opinion.

Renewable energy: Sources of energy that can be naturally replaced by the environment and include solar, wind, and water sources.

Repeal: To cancel or withdraw something, especially a law.

Reservation: An area of land set aside for use by certain people.

Reservoir: A human-made lake created to store water for use by a community.

Resistance: The effort to fight against a powerful force.

Revolution: The overthrow of one type of government in favor of another.

S

Sanction: An official punishment usually imposed on a country by another nation or group of nations.

Sanctuary: A refuge for animals where they are protected from harm and able to roam freely.

Segregation: The separation of groups of people.

Semiautomatic weapon: A type of gun that allows the user to fire bullets quickly due to an automatic reloading process.

Sexual orientation: A person's sexual identity, which relates to whom a person is attracted. Sexual orientation includes gay, lesbian, bisexual, straight, and asexual.

Sexual reproduction: Occurs when two individuals have sex and produce an offspring.

Sharia: Islamic law based on the teachings of the Koran.

Sit-down strike: A protest in which a group of workers sit down on the job and refuse to complete any work.

Sit-in: A peaceful protest in which people occupy a place for long periods, often in a seated position, to call attention to a certain social issue.

Slave driver: A slave who is responsible for organizing and punishing other slaves.

Socialism: A political system in which the central government provides goods and services to all members of a society equally.

Sperm: A male reproductive cell.

Stimulus: An action that causes another action to take place.

Strike: An organized work stoppage to force employers to meet certain demands.

Suffocate: To die from not being able to breathe.

Suffrage: The right to vote.

Suffragist: A person who works to gain voting rights for people who are not allowed to vote.

Sustainable: A method of using natural resources without depleting them or damaging them permanently.

Sweatshop: A small factory where people work long hours for low pay.

T

Tactic: Something used to effect change.

Tariff: A tax or fee added to foreign products to make them more expensive.

Terrorism: The use of fear and violence to achieve political goals or social change and to create fear.

Terrorist: Someone who uses fear and violence to influence others.

Trafficking: The act of buying or selling an illegal product or service.

Traitor: Someone who has betrayed his or her country.

Transgender: A term used to describe a person whose gender identity differs from the sex he or she was assigned at birth.

Tribunal: A decision-making body that has authority in a specific area.

Trimester: A period of pregnancy lasting about three months, during which the fetus develops.

U

Unconstitutional: Going against the US Constitution.

Undocumented or unauthorized immigrants: Immigrants who enter a country without permission or who stay longer than they are allowed.

Union: An organized group that protects workers' rights.

Universal Declaration of Human Rights: A document that defines the rights that the United Nations believes should belong to every person in the world.

US Supreme Court: The highest court of the federal government.

V

Visa: A government document that allows a person from another country to stay in the United States.

Voluntary manslaughter: A sentence for a crime in which a person has no previous intent or plans to kill another person, which usually happens in the moment.

W

Weapons of mass destruction (WMD): Powerful weapons that can destroy entire cities or regions.

Whistle-blower: A person who publicly reports the illegal or unethical activities of an organization or a government.

White supremacist: A person who believes the white race is superior to other races.

Z

Zoot suit: A flashy oversized suit that was popular in the 1940s.

8

Gun Control/Gun Rights

Black Panthers Carry Guns into Capitol **239**

March on Washington for Gun Control **246**

"I Will Not Comply" Rally **252**

Democratic Congressional Representatives Sit-In **256**

The effect of guns on society has been a source of continuing debate. People on both sides of the issue often feel very strongly about gun laws. They argue about how much control the government should have over gun ownership. Gun control supporters want more limits on the use of guns. Gun rights advocates hope to have as few rules as possible controlling the purchase, use, and ownership of guns.

About 33,000 Americans die each year from gunshot wounds, according to the Centers for Disease Control and Prevention. Gun control supporters and opponents have different views about what is the best way to lower this number. Gun control supporters argue that stronger laws would limit the number of guns available to people. They believe fewer guns would mean fewer deaths. Gun rights supporters say that the only way to lower the number of gun-related deaths is to make sure everyone has the same ability to own these weapons.

History of gun ownership and gun laws in the United States

The United States has a strong history of gun ownership. The first colonists of America relied on guns to hunt and protect themselves. During the American Revolutionary War (1775–1783), the American forces relied on a type of gun called a musket to defend themselves. Guns were so important to the success of the American revolutionaries that the founding fathers guaranteed citizens the right "to bear arms" in the 2nd Amendment to the US Constitution.

The first national limits on guns were created in 1934. During this period of American history, the country was coming out of a period called Prohibition (1920–1933). During Prohibition the sale of alcoholic beverages was against the law. Many criminal organizations had stepped in to sell

233

Gun Control/Gun Rights

WORDS TO KNOW

Background check: Allows authorities to examine the history of a person before he or she can purchase a gun.

Bill: A draft of a law that is presented to lawmakers for a vote.

Cartridge: A tube that contains a bullet that the user puts into a gun.

Civil disobedience: A nonviolent method of protesting.

Civilian: A person who is not active in the military or a member of law enforcement.

Gun control: Any attempt to create policies that offer more protections from gun violence.

Gun rights: A term used to describe attempts to protect the ability of Americans to own and use guns.

Handgun: A firearm that can be held and fired with one hand.

Semiautomatic weapon: A type of gun that allows the user to fire bullets more quickly due to an automatic reloading process.

Sit-in: A peaceful protest in which people occupy a place for long periods, often in a seated position, to call attention to a certain social issue.

alcohol illegally, creating a culture of violence. To help reduce the amount of violent crimes, the US government passed the National Firearms Act. Firearms are portable guns that use gunpowder to shoot bullets. This law established a national list of all guns that were legally owned in the United States. It also placed a tax on companies that made certain types of guns.

Congress passed the Gun Control Act in 1968. A troubling event that took place in the early 1960s led to the creation of this law. In 1963 Lee Harvey Oswald (1939–1963) killed President John F. Kennedy (1917–1963) using a rifle. Authorities later discovered that Oswald had purchased this gun through the mail. The Gun Control Act limited the ability of people to buy guns and move them between various states. This law allowed only licensed dealers and the makers of guns to transport firearms. In 1976 Washington, DC, banned the ownership of guns, a rule that remained in place until the US Supreme Court overturned the law in 2007. In 1985 and 1986, two more gun laws were passed, the Law Enforcement Officers Protection Act and the Firearms Owners' Protection Act.

In 1994 the Federal Assault Weapons Ban stopped the making of assault weapons for use by private citizens. An assault weapon is a high-powered firearm such as an AK-47 that can shoot many bullets very quickly. These types of guns have occasionally been linked to mass shootings that killed many people. Many gun rights groups opposed the ban of assault weapons, so the law was limited to a 10-year period. In 2004 the ban expired. Since then, assault weapons have been legal in the United States.

The percentage of Americans owning guns in the United States is higher than in any other country. This is partly because of the rights of the 2nd Amendment. According to the Pew Research Center, as of 2017, 30 percent of Americans said they owned a gun, while 42 percent lived in a home in which at least one person owned a gun. In addition, 55 percent of Americans have fired a gun at some point in their lives.

Gun control and gun rights debate

Compared to most other countries, the United States has loose federal gun laws. Individual states often have their own gun laws that differ from one another. For instance, as of July 2017, 45 of 50 US states allowed gun owners to carry handguns openly in public, known as open carry, according to the Law Center to Prevent Gun Violence.

A handgun is a firearm that can be held and fired with one hand. This type of gun includes revolvers and pistols but not rifles. The only states that banned open carry of handguns were California, Florida, Illinois, New York, and South Carolina, as well as the District of Columbia. In the other 45 states, the laws for open carry of handguns varied. In some states, the owners of handguns had to have a license to carry their weapons openly. Other states required gun owners to keep their handguns in a holster in public places. A holster is a case a person wears to carry guns when the weapons are not in use.

Gun control arguments Gun control supporters argue that stronger gun control laws would mean fewer deaths from gun-related incidents. They believe the large number of guns available in US society leads to more gun violence. They note that according to 2016 statistics, when there is a gun in a household, people are more than three times as likely to be the

Gun Ownership by Adults in the United States, 2017

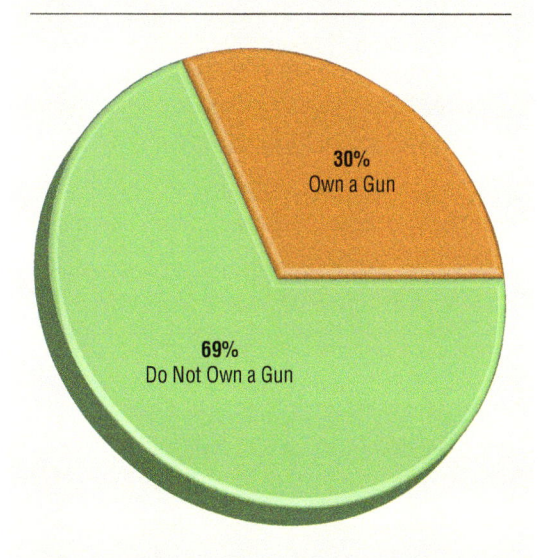

- 30% Own a Gun
- 69% Do Not Own a Gun

Note: The percentages do not total 100 due to rounding.

SOURCE: Parker, Kim, Juliana Menasce Horowitz, Ruth Igielnik, Baxter Oliphant, and Anna Brown. "The Demographics of Gun Ownership." *America's Complex Relationship with Guns*. Pew Research Center, June 22, 2017. http://www.pewsocialtrends.org/2017/06/22/the-demographics-of-gun-ownership/.

More than two-thirds of adults in the United States do not own guns. © 2018 CENGAGE®.

CRITICAL THINKING QUESTIONS

1. What are some ways to reduce gun violence in the United States? Do you think more gun control laws or increased gun rights is a better way to reduce gun violence?

2. Why is gun ownership debated much more in the United States than in other countries?

3. Do you think the activities of the Black Panthers during the 1960s were effective? Why or why not?

4. Do you think the Mulford Act was designed specifically to limit the actions of the Black Panthers? Why or why not?

5. Would the March on Washington for Gun Control have had as much support if it had taken place a year later? Explain.

6. Do you think background checks are an effective way to prevent dangerous people from buying guns? Why or why not?

7. Should someone who has signs of mental illness be able to own a gun? Why or why not? Should someone who has been violent toward others be able to own a gun? Why or why not?

8. Should someone who is on the Federal Bureau of Investigation's terrorism watch list be able to own a gun? Why or why not?

9. What do you think about the actions of Democrats during the sit-in at the House of Representatives? Were their actions effective?

victims of gun violence. Up to 1.7 million American children lived in a home that contained a loaded and unlocked weapon. Gun control supporters note that while violent crime has decreased by about 0.7 percent from 2011 to 2016, guns were used in almost three-quarters of the murders committed in 2015, according to an article by Alan Neuhauser in *U.S. News & World Report*.

Gun control backers also favor background checks. A background check allows authorities to examine the history of a person before he or she can purchase a gun. A federal law passed in 1993 made background checks required for the purchases of all guns bought from a federally licensed dealer. If a background check reveals that a person is a convicted criminal or has a history of violent behavior, he or she might not be allowed to purchase a gun. Gun control advocates believe that background checks keep guns out of the hands of violent people.

One of the leading gun control organizations is the Brady Campaign to Prevent Gun Violence. This group is named after James Brady (1940–2014), the former press secretary to President Ronald Reagan (1911–2004). Brady was badly injured when John Hinckley Jr. (1955–) tried to assassinate Reagan in 1981. Reagan was wounded but several of the

Gun Control/Gun Rights

bullets hit Brady and left him severely injured. The Brady Campaign believes that stronger gun control laws can save lives. Other well-known organizations that fight for more gun control measures include the Coalition to Stop Gun Violence, Everytown for Gun Safety, Stop Handgun Violence, and the Violence Policy Center.

Gun rights arguments Gun rights supporters place great value on the 2nd Amendment, which protects the right of citizens to own guns under the US Constitution. The 2nd Amendment is part of the Bill of Rights. The Bill of Rights also grants freedom of speech, freedom of religion, and the right to a fair trial. To limit gun ownership, gun rights supporters say, is not what the creators of the US Constitution intended. Instead, more laws only serve to limit people's ability to defend themselves.

They also argue that gun control laws do not actually reduce crime. Instead, gun rights backers believe that gun owners are better at limiting crime. They point out that only law-abiding citizens follow the rules to buy guns. Criminals will continue to buy guns illegally regardless of what laws are passed. They argue that even if there were fewer guns in the United States, criminals would use other weapons such as knives to commit crimes. They suggest that criminals are responsible for gun violence; the guns are not to blame for crimes. Rather than pass more laws, gun rights supporters want to see existing laws defended more

People gather in front of the Idaho capitol for a pro-gun rights rally. © TXKING/SHUTTERSTOCK.COM.

Gun Control/Gun Rights

strongly. Many gun rights supporters view background checks as interfering with privacy and the right to own guns.

The National Rifle Association (NRA), which is an organization that strongly supports gun rights, was founded in 1871. Two veterans of the Union Army created the NRA after the US Civil War (1861–1865). When the NRA was first established, its leadership wanted to help Americans prepare for a possible war by improving their shooting skills. The group established several gun ranges to train people to shoot better. Since then, the NRA has become one of the most powerful defenders of gun rights. Other groups committed to protecting gun rights include Gun Owners of America, the National Association for Gun Rights, the National Shooting Sports Foundation, and the Second Amendment Foundation.

Gun protests in the United States

Many experts suggest that guns became a topic of great debate in the 1970s. This began with the NRA's changed position on guns. The group had previously focused on issues such as hunting, sports, and safety. However, many members were upset about the growing bans on some types of guns that they enjoyed using. The NRA leadership became more

Georgia State Senator Elena Parent, a Democrat, speaks at a Moms Demand Action anti-gun, anti-NRA rally in Woodruff Park in April 2017 in Atlanta, Georgia.
© BLULZ60/ SHUTTERSTOCK.COM.

active in gun politics. As the NRA grew more political, it pushed to limit gun laws. Its membership grew once the organization became more politically active. This allowed the NRA to become more powerful.

The NRA clashed with groups that supported gun laws. A number of high-profile mass shootings stirred the debate even further. After mass shootings, the issue of gun control often becomes the focus of great media attention. People ask what changes can be made to prevent such events from happening again. This often leads to fierce debate between gun rights and gun control supporters. Both groups stage protests. Often, members from both sides of the issue appear at the same event. The goal of both groups is to try to influence people to support their side of the debate. Protesters hope that by staging demonstrations and making their points on the subject heard, they will push lawmakers to support changes to gun policies.

Black Panthers Carry Guns into California Legislative Building in Protest of Mulford Act

LOCATION: State Capitol, Sacramento, California

DATE: May 2, 1967

In 1966 a group called the Black Panther Party formed in Oakland, California. This organization was made up of African American activists. At the time, the civil rights movement was going strong. This movement wanted to gain full civil rights for black citizens. The Black Panthers were upset with the slow progress of gaining equal civil rights in the United States. They took a different approach than the peaceful protests used by the broader civil rights movement. The Black Panthers used militant, or radical, means to achieve civil rights. For example, they began to patrol African American neighborhoods of Oakland armed with guns.

Members of the group carrying guns in public, even though it was legal, made some politicians and residents uncomfortable. Lawmakers wanted to limit the ability of civilians to carry firearms openly in public.

Civilians are people who are not active in the military or members of law enforcement. California politicians proposed passing a law that made it illegal for civilians to carry loaded guns on the streets. The Black Panthers believed this law was directed at them. They responded by having armed members of the group enter the state capitol in Sacramento, California, while this law was being debated. This protest placed the Black Panther Party in the national spotlight.

The Black Panthers

College students Huey P. Newton (1942–1989) and Bobby Seale (1936–) formed the Black Panther Party for Self-Defense (later shortened to the Black Panther Party or Black Panthers) on October 15, 1966. The two men had followed news of violent conflicts between African American demonstrators and the police in cities around the nation. Locations such as Detroit, Michigan; Chicago, Illinois; Harlem in New York City; and the Watts neighborhood of Los Angeles were all in the news for riots between police and local black residents. While the Black Panthers admired civil rights leaders such as the Rev. Dr. Martin Luther King Jr. (1929–1968), they disagreed with the peaceful methods these figures used.

Instead, Newton and Seale believed that each community should make decisions for itself. They pictured a community in which its members were fully independent of outsiders. They would not need or want help from people who were not members of the group. They hoped this type of community would bring greater power and independence to African Americans. They issued what they called the Ten-Point Program. This document included demands for freedom, jobs, housing, education, land, food, clothing, legal justice, and peace for African American citizens.

Part of the Black Panthers' strategy involved self-defense. They fearlessly carried loaded firearms in black neighborhoods. They were sometimes forceful in their dealings with the police. All of this was intended to show police that they were not afraid of them. They would defend African Americans from what they saw as police hostility toward their community. They believed these actions would allow them to gain control of their neighborhoods.

The Black Panthers wore matching black uniforms that had a military design. This included a type of military hat called a beret, sunglasses, and black leather jackets. However, their use of guns was most upsetting to lawmakers and police. The Black Panthers primarily carried shotguns.

Part of the Black Panthers' strategy involved self-defense. They fearlessly carried loaded firearms in black neighborhoods. They were sometimes forceful in their dealings with the police. All of this was intended to show police that they were not afraid of them.

While this show of force was fully legal, many people found the Black Panthers and their display of weaponry in public to be threatening and frightening.

Background to the protest in Sacramento

On the morning of April 1, 1967, police responded to reports of a break-in at a liquor store in the small town of North Richmond, California. This community was located just east of the city of Oakland and had a mostly African American population. When officers from the nearby Martinez, California, sheriff's department arrived at the liquor store, they saw two suspects. One suspect fled, while police shot the other. The police reported that the suspect who was killed, 22-year-old Denzil Dowell (1944–1967), had failed to respond to warnings to stop running.

Police reported finding burglary tools at the site. They further discovered a hole in the wall that police thought Dowell and his partner used to enter the building. The officers told inspectors they fired two shots after Dowell tried to escape. However, the medical investigator found that Dowell had been shot six times. He believed that Dowell likely had his hands up at the time of his death. This was a sign that Dowell intended to surrender. A mostly white jury later decided that the police acted responsibly when they shot Dowell. This angered many African Americans in the Oakland community.

After Dowell's death, the Black Panther Party became involved. They investigated the details of the crime on their own. They offered protection to the Dowell family. They held rallies asking for greater justice for African American victims such as Dowell. They also began carrying large weapons in public. They approached people being arrested with law books in hand. While police were taking suspects away, members of the Black Panthers would shout their legal rights at them.

The Black Panthers were careful to follow the law. They made sure to leave 10 feet (3 meters) between themselves and the arresting officers as the law required. They did not want to appear as if they were interfering with arrests. On April 25, 1967, the Black Panthers held a rally in Oakland that attracted media attention. This rally drew hundreds of people. Many of the people in attendance signed up to join the Black Panthers. Dozens of people came to the event carrying guns.

Gun Control/Gun Rights

Bobby Seale on the Mulford Act

In this primary source excerpt from Black Panthers founder Bobby Seale, he discusses the passing of the Mulford Act in an interview with Amber Slater of the McDaniel Free Press *at McDaniel College. The interview was published on October 17, 2013.*

By the end of May 3 or 4, weeks later they made law of the Mulford Act. And the Mulford Act said no one could carry loaded weapons inside city limits. That's very important: inside city limits. Why did they do that? That meant you could carry a loaded weapon still outside of city limits. What happens is if they had said no one could carry a loaded weapon anywhere in the state of California that meant hunters could not carry a loaded weapon. So that meant the law was specifically structured for who? For the Black Panther Party who did have legal weapons when they patrolled the police. They observed the police. And the action was very legal because we had researched the law. Huey P. Newton was two years in law school by this time and we had found the law in a California State Supreme Court ruling that all citizens had the right to stand and observe a police officer carrying out their duties as long as they stood a reasonable distance away.

So with our guns we stood a reasonable distance away. But they didn't want that so they made a law that you couldn't carry a loaded weapon in city limits and they further went to say and you couldn't carry that weapon in city limits within 150 feet of public property. Now, you're thinking about public buildings, right? But the Mulford Act went further to say that public property included all roadways and byways. In other words if you're on the street and if you have a sidewalk, that's public property. And you have to be 150 away from that public property before you can do what? Load your weapon. Ah, interesting, right, the way they did that. They concocted a law so that we could not carry loaded weapons while we stood a reasonable distance away and observed the police.

SOURCE: Slater, Amber. "An Exclusive Interview with Bobby Seale." *McDaniel Free Press* (October 17, 2013). Available online at http://www.mcdanielfreepress.com/2013/10/17/an-exclusive-interview-with-bobby-seale/ (accessed October 13, 2017). Courtesy of the *McDaniel Free Press*.

The Mulford Act

Politicians began to worry about the tactics of the Black Panthers. In particular, Republican California assemblyman Donald Mulford (1915–2000) was upset about the group's use of guns. In 1967 Mulford proposed a law that would ban citizens from carrying loaded weapons in public. Both Democratic and Republican lawmakers in California supported this bill. A bill is a draft of a law that is presented to lawmakers for a vote. If the bill was approved, it would become a law.

This proposed bill upset members of the Black Panthers. They recognized that while the law would affect everyone, including members

Gun Control/Gun Rights

of all races, it was especially drafted to end their armed patrols. If California passed this bill, it would force the Black Panthers to use other methods. This was disturbing to the leaders of the Black Panthers. They saw this as another attempt to limit the ability of African Americans to protect themselves. Passage of the Mulford Act would prevent the Black Panthers from having armed members patrol neighborhoods under their watch. They decided to show their opposition to the creation of the Mulford Act.

The protest at the California State Capitol

While the bill was being debated at the California legislature on May 2, Newton asked 30 Black Panthers, including 24 men and 6 women, to go to Sacramento. Sacramento is the capital city of California and houses the main buildings of the state government. These Black Panthers, many of whom carried loaded weapons, entered the capitol building where the lawmakers meet. The Black Panthers' protest of the Mulford Act was peaceful; they broke no laws. Nonetheless, the sight of so many armed black people in matching military outfits entering a state building drew much attention from the news media. Images of armed Black Panthers standing in the capitol were shown in news stories across the United States.

Two members of the Black Panthers are met on the steps of the state capitol in Sacramento, California, by police on May 2, 1967. The police officer informs the men that they will be allowed to keep their guns as long as they do not cause any trouble or disturb the peace.
© BETTMANN/GETTY IMAGES.

Huey P. Newton Gun Club Demonstrations

The Huey P. Newton Gun Club is an organization of African American activists who openly carry guns to patrol areas of Dallas, Texas. Group members consider themselves to be like the Black Panthers. The name of the group honors Huey P. Newton, a cofounder of the Black Panther Party. The organization addresses concerns about police violence against African Americans. The founders of the club worried that crimes against African Americans were not being investigated properly by police.

On August 20, 2014, the Huey P. Newton Gun Club held a demonstration in a south Dallas neighborhood. About 24 members of the club were armed with guns as they marched down Martin Luther King Jr. Boulevard. Police monitored the demonstration. The protesters wanted to encourage African American self-defense and community policing. They also wanted to demonstrate their right to carry guns in public without being stopped by police. In Texas, people who are licensed to own firearms are also allowed to openly carry their weapons in public. The peaceful demonstration lasted about 90 minutes.

The club drew support from national African American groups such as Black Lives Matter. This movement campaigns against violence and unfair treatment toward African Americans. The Huey P. Newton Gun Club called for African Americans to arm themselves nationwide. The organization believed that an armed African American citizenry could reduce possible conflicts between black residents and police. However, the club leadership also said that gun owners should legally follow the gun laws in individual communities.

The Black Panthers were careful not to upset or frighten anyone at the capitol building. They kept their guns pointed only up or down, and not facing anyone. They tried to seem nonthreatening. They wished to appear like any other California resident who was concerned about the debate over a bill. As the bill related to their use of guns, the Black Panthers reasoned it was fair to bring the guns in question. Many members of the news media circled around the Black Panthers as they entered the wing of the building that contained the chambers. The second floor viewing room of the California legislative chambers were open to the public, but the floor where the representatives debated bills was not.

Several members of the media pushed out onto the floor of the chambers. Seale and other Black Panthers followed them. The Black Panthers and the media were quickly asked to leave. As the Black Panthers debated among themselves where to go, the state police surrounded them. Several police officers tried to take their guns away. The Black Panthers attempted to resist, but they were escorted into an elevator. These events attracted even more attention, so Seale read a prepared statement about the Mulford Act in front of the media several times. He called the Mulford Act a racist attack on black communities. He called on African Americans to arm themselves. Upon finishing reading the statement for the last time, the Black Panthers headed back to their cars to leave.

Members of the police and the news media followed the Black Panthers as they drove away. When the Black Panthers stopped at a gas station, police arrested them. They charged them with breaking a little-known law of California's Department of Fish and Game that banned people from driving with loaded weapons in their cars. Police arrested the members of the Black Panthers in front of news media.

Effects of the protest

The Black Panthers who went to the state capitol building knew their demonstration probably would not convince the lawmakers debating the Mulford Act to change their minds. Instead, they hoped that their efforts would bring increased attention to their cause. In this way, at least, they were successful. Video of Seale reading his statement and photographs of the armed Black Panthers walking through the capitol were broadcast to the nation. The *San Francisco Chronicle*, a California newspaper, printed 12 stories about the demonstration. For many African Americans who were disappointed by the slow pace of civil rights progress, this new form of activism expressed by the Black Panthers appealed to them. Within months, thousands of people were attending Black Panther rallies and hundreds were joining their movement.

The Black Panthers' rally at the capitol building did not convince lawmakers to allow civilians to carry loaded guns in public. In fact, it probably had the opposite effect. California legislators were concerned that an armed group of people could legally enter the state capitol. The California governor at the time, Ronald Reagan, signed the Mulford Act into law on July 26, 1967. Members of both the Democratic and Republican political parties supported the law. The National Rifle Association (NRA), which is an organization that seeks to defend the rights of gun owners, also supported the Mulford Act. The NRA would later become a strong backer of Reagan when he ran for president in 1980.

Over the next decade, the Black Panther Party became a well-known group. Some members were involved in a shootout in April 1968 with Oakland police that left 17-year-old Black Panther Bobby Hutton (1950–1968) dead and two officers wounded. The Black Panthers claimed that during this period, many of its leaders were unfairly arrested. Despite these issues, the Black Panthers had chapters in cities across the United States by the end of the 1960s. High-profile actions such as the protest in Sacramento helped the Black Panther Party grow in popularity and numbers. Between 1966 and 1982, the Black Panthers played a large role in civil rights activities. The group broke up in the early 1980s.

March on Washington for Gun Control

LOCATION: Washington, DC

DATE: January 26, 2013

On January 26, 2013, thousands of people gathered to participate in the March on Washington for Gun Control. Organizers held the march to honor victims of a mass shooting at an elementary school a month earlier. The protesters hoped to bring attention to their desire for stronger gun control laws. They believed such laws would help save lives in the future. Several groups supported the event, including One Million Moms for Gun Control, Foundry United Methodist Church, Trinity United Church of Christ, and the Washington National Cathedral.

The march ended at the Washington Monument, where the participants listened to speakers including lawmakers, survivors of gun violence, celebrities, and organizers of the event. The marchers included people from a variety of backgrounds who gathered on a cold winter day. They listened to people voice their concerns about what they saw as a growing problem with gun violence in the United States. Cities across the country held other related events. Demonstrators hoped the march would begin a national discussion about creating stricter gun laws.

Background to the march

On December 14, 2012, a 20-year-old man named Adam Lanza (1992–2012) entered Sandy Hook Elementary School in Newtown, Connecticut. Using a high-powered rifle, he killed 20 children and 6 staff members. He had already shot and killed his mother earlier in the day. He ultimately killed himself. The event was very upsetting for people across the United States.

The reason for Lanza's actions are unknown. He left no notes and destroyed the hard drive on his computer. Without being able to identify a reason for his actions, many people instead focused on other aspects of the crime. People questioned such things as Lanza's mental health and his easy access to guns.

Gun Control/Gun Rights

Lanza's surviving family described him as hard to reach and often alone. He enjoyed violent video games and researched other mass shootings. Lanza's mother had difficulty relating to her son and worried about his inability to relate to the people around him. She learned that her son shared her love of guns. She thought it would be a good way for her to bond with her son. She bought several weapons that she allowed him to use. All of her guns were purchased legally, and she regularly took her son to gun ranges to teach him to shoot properly. However, under Connecticut law, at 20 years of age, Lanza was too young to own or carry any type of gun by himself.

After the sad event at Sandy Hook, people wondered if stricter gun laws might have prevented the shooting, or at least limited the number of deaths. Lanza brought four different guns with him to the school that day. These included a semiautomatic shotgun, a semiautomatic rifle, and two semiautomatic handguns. Semiautomatic weapons reload bullets automatically and do not require the gun's user to reload after each shot. The user only has to pull the trigger to shoot each bullet as long as there are bullets available. A clip or magazine can hold many bullets and can be attached to an automatic weapon. This allows a gun or rifle to be fired repeatedly, until all the bullets in the magazine are gone.

Lanza primarily used the semiautomatic rifle during the shooting. The rifle used a magazine that held 30 bullets at one time. This limited the number of times Lanza had to reload the gun. This weapon allowed Lanza to fire 154 shots within five minutes. Many people who buy semiautomatic weapons say the guns can be used safely for sport hunting, target shooting, and self-defense. Supporters of gun control argue that the sale of such powerful weapons enabled Lanza to kill many people before the police arrived.

Organization of the march

The events in Newtown renewed the debate over firearms between gun control and gun rights supporters. While the two sides disagreed over how to react to the shooting at Sandy Hook, both agreed that it was an awful event. Molly Smith, a director of a theater in Washington, DC, and Native American activist Suzanne Blue Star Boy decided to take action. The pair used their Washington connections to

After the sad event at Sandy Hook, people wondered if stricter gun laws might have prevented the shooting, or at least limited the number of deaths. Lanza brought four different guns with him to the school that day.

Gun Control/Gun Rights

2016 Vocal Majority Tour

In the fall of 2016, Gabrielle Giffords (1970–) and her husband, Mark Kelly (1964–), organized a bus tour to promote increased gun control laws. Giffords had been the victim of a mass shooting in Tucson, Arizona, on January 8, 2011. At the time, she was a member of the US Congress. She had been meeting with voters in her congressional district when Jared Lee Loughner (1988–) opened fire with a pistol, hitting 19 people. Six people died, including a nine-year-old girl and a federal judge. Although Giffords was shot in the head, she survived.

After the shooting, Giffords was in a coma, or a deep sleep, to let her brain heal. Once she awoke, she faced a long period of recovery. She had to relearn how to walk, talk, and eat due to the seriousness of her injuries. Even after she mastered these skills, she suffered permanent disabilities from the shooting. She lost some vision in both eyes, was not able to move her right hand, and struggled to form sentences. She was able to return to Congress in August 2011 but decided to leave in 2012 to focus on her health and promote gun control.

Together with her husband, astronaut Mark Kelly, Giffords created Americans for Responsible Solutions (ARS). They founded the organization with the hope of establishing new protections against gun violence. ARS is dedicated to electing politicians who support limitations on guns. In particular, ARS supports a rule that requires all gun owners to undergo background checks.

As part of their efforts, Giffords, Kelly, and ARS created the Vocal Majority Tour, which led a number of rallies across the United States. They

Gabrielle Giffords and Mark Kelly started the Americans for Responsible Solutions organization to address gun violence. © DEBBY WONG/SHUTTERSTOCK.COM.

held events in 43 cities in 14 states over 40 days during the 2016 election season. They promoted political candidates who agreed with their ideas about gun control. The Vocal Majority Tour began in the city of Orlando, Florida, on September 27, 2016. Orlando was chosen for the start of the tour because it had recently been the site of one of the deadliest mass shootings in American history. ARS organized meetings in each city to discuss ways to limit gun violence and to push their supporters to vote in the 2016 election.

stage a protest march in favor of increased gun control. They gained the backing of the One Million Moms for Gun Control, an organization that supported Smith's gun control goals.

The biggest goal of the march was to influence members of Congress to renew a ban on semiautomatic weapons like those used by Lanza. In 1994 legislators had passed a ban on the making of military-style semi-automatic weapons to be used by civilians. When the bill originally passed, it had a 10-year limit. As a result, the ban ended in 2004 when it was not renewed. The demonstrators had other gun control goals as well. They wanted to end the sale of magazines that hold large numbers of bullets. Finally, they wanted background checks on all purchases of guns. A background check examines whether someone attempting to purchase a gun has a criminal or violent history that might affect the ability to own a gun responsibly. Smith used Facebook and Twitter to publicize the event.

The March on Washington for Gun Control

Participants gathered at the Capitol Reflecting Pool in Washington, DC. They marched down Constitution Avenue to a site near the Washington Monument. There, participants listened to speakers from a variety of backgrounds. These speakers included US Secretary of Education Arne Duncan (1964–). He cited figures from his time as the head of Chicago's public schools. He noted that, on average, one Chicago student had died every two weeks from gun violence. Another speaker was Colin Goddard, a survivor of a mass shooting. Goddard was wounded in a shooting spree at Virginia Tech in 2007 that killed 32 people. After college,

Two teenagers from Newtown, Connecticut, march for stricter gun control laws in January 2013 in Washington, DC. Demonstrators joining the march included survivors of the shootings at Virginia Tech and Newtown. © BRENDAN HOFFMAN/GETTY IMAGES.

Goddard joined the Brady Campaign to Prevent Gun Violence. At the march, he was able to provide a personal account of the effects of a mass shooting. Other speakers included several members of Congress and Vincent Gray (1942–), mayor of Washington, DC.

The families of many people who died in the Sandy Hook shooting attended the march. Organizers noted their participation, and several speakers called out to them to express sorrow for their loss. Many marchers carried posters of victims of gun violence. Speakers like Duncan said the event was not a protest against the 2nd Amendment. Rather, it was meant to show the concerns of Americans who wanted laws that favor increased gun responsibility.

Smith, the organizer of the event, had deep roots in the city's theater community. Upon completion of the march, she arranged for several plays about gun control to be performed around the city. Actors from different participating theaters performed new works by various writers. Other marches were held in such cities as Austin, Texas, and San Francisco, California.

Aftermath

Protesters at the march hoped to influence the debate about gun control. They wore pictures of shooting victims on their clothes, carried candles, and waved signs in support of both the victims' families and stronger gun laws. The march was organized to start a discussion about gun control. Also happening in Washington around the same time was an official White House meeting on guns.

In response to the Sandy Hook shooting, Vice President Joe Biden (1942–) headed a task force to study gun violence. Biden and his team met with leaders of the National Rifle Association (NRA) in January 2013. The NRA is an organization dedicated to strengthening the rights of gun owners. The NRA recognized the tragedy of the Sandy Hook shooting but noted that guns are merely the tools of the people who use them. The organization argued that guns are not the problem. It said the people who use guns to hurt others on purpose should be the central issue in the gun control debate. Instead of more gun laws, the NRA sought to enforce existing laws. The organization also wanted to create new laws that would allow guns to be carried in schools. The NRA argued that if staff members at Sandy Hook had been armed, they could have prevented the loss of so many lives.

President Obama on Gun Violence

In this primary source excerpt from October 2015, US President Barack Obama speaks about gun violence in the United States following a mass shooting at Umpqua Community College in Roseburg, Oregon. The transcript of the president's speech appeared in Time *magazine.*

Earlier this year, I answered a question in an interview by saying, "The United States of America is the one advanced nation on Earth in which we do not have sufficient common-sense gun-safety laws—even in the face of repeated mass killings." And later that day, there was a mass shooting at a movie theater in Lafayette, Louisiana. That day! Somehow this has become routine. The reporting is routine. My response here at this podium ends up being routine. The conversation in the aftermath of it. We've become numb to this.

We talked about this after Columbine and Blacksburg, after Tucson, after Newtown, after Aurora, after Charleston. It cannot be this easy for somebody who wants to inflict harm on other people to get his or her hands on a gun.

And what's become routine, of course, is the response of those who oppose any kind of common-sense gun legislation. Right now, I can imagine the press releases being cranked out: We need more guns, they'll argue. Fewer gun safety laws.

Does anybody really believe that? There are scores of responsible gun owners in this country—they know that's not true. We know because of the polling that says the majority of Americans understand we should be changing these laws—including the majority of responsible, law-abiding gun owners.

There is a gun for roughly every man, woman, and child in America. So how can you, with a straight face, make the argument that more guns will make us safer?...

We spend over a trillion dollars, and pass countless laws, and devote entire agencies to preventing terrorist attacks on our soil, and rightfully so. And yet, we have a Congress that explicitly blocks us from even collecting data on how we could potentially reduce gun deaths. How can that be?...

When Americans are killed in mine disasters, we work to make mines safer. When Americans are killed in floods and hurricanes, we make communities safer. When roads are unsafe, we fix them to reduce auto fatalities. We have seatbelt laws because we know it saves lives. So the notion that gun violence is somehow different, that our freedom and our Constitution prohibits any modest regulation of how we use a deadly weapon, when there are law-abiding gun owners all across the country who could hunt and protect their families and do everything they do under such regulations doesn't make sense.

So, tonight, as those of us who are lucky enough to hug our kids a little closer are thinking about the families who aren't so fortunate, I'd ask the American people to think about how they can get our government to change these laws, and to save lives, and to let young people grow up.

SOURCE: Obama, Barack. "President Obama's Statement on the Shootings in Oregon." *Time* (October 1, 2015). Available online at http://time.com/4058961/oregon-shooting-president-obama-transcript-speech/ (accessed October 13, 2017). Courtesy of Time Inc.

Gun Control/Gun Rights

Supporters of gun control have continued to gather on a regular basis to protest outside of the NRA building in Fairfax, Virginia. The NRA has a strong influence on gun laws in the United States. Protesters hoped to influence the NRA on supporting stricter gun control measures. On July 14, 2017, hundreds of people gathered for a Women's March to protest outside the NRA headquarters. The group then marched 17 miles to the Justice Department's headquarters to hold a rally there. Gun control supporters have credited events like the March on Washington for Gun Control with helping to push tougher gun laws in states such as Connecticut, Maryland, and New York.

"I Will Not Comply" Rally

LOCATION: Olympia, Washington

DATE: December 13, 2014

In the November 2014 election, residents in Washington State voted to pass a law increasing background checks on individuals buying guns. Background checks allow authorities to examine the history of a person before he or she can buy a gun. The findings in a background check can sometimes prevent a person from buying a gun. This idea of expanding background checks upset some gun owners in Washington. They did not like limits on gun ownership. Others were concerned about authorities being able to look into their past. They saw such searches as an attack on their privacy. On December 13, 2014, opponents of background checks held a protest in Olympia, the capital city of Washington. They called the demonstration the "I Will Not Comply" rally.

Many protesters worried that such laws might eventually lead to stronger laws on gun ownership. They viewed such controls as overstepping their 2nd Amendment rights. The 2nd Amendment to the US Constitution promises that Americans have the right to bear arms, or own guns. The demonstrators used their rights as guaranteed in the US Constitution to make their voices heard. They hoped to bring more attention to their views on gun rights.

Background to the protest

Performing background checks on people buying guns from licensed dealers became a federal law in 1993. Licensed dealers generally include all people who sell guns in a store. Bill Clinton (1946–), the president of the United States at the time, signed the Brady Handgun Violence Prevention Act, also known as the Brady Bill, into law on November 30, 1993. The Brady Bill was meant to keep dangerous people from purchasing guns. Because of the law, the Federal Bureau of Investigation (FBI) created the National Instant Criminal Background Check System. This system allows authorities to run a check on a person before he or she is allowed to buy a gun. If the background check shows, for example, that a person has a criminal history, he or she will not be allowed to purchase a gun from a licensed dealer. The federal law, however, does not require background checks on private gun sales. These include purchases that take place over the Internet or at gun shows. It is up to each state to pass laws that would expand background checks to include private sales.

In November 2014 Washington State put the Universal Background Checks for Gun Purchases, Initiative 594 (I-594), up for a vote. Voters would decide on a new law to expand background checks on all gun purchases, both commercial and private. If passed, I-594 would change gun control laws in the state. The new law would require background checks not only at licensed dealers but also for guns purchased privately, for example, between friends. Background checks would also be required for purchases over the Internet and at gun shows.

Before Washington's 2014 election, there had been a number of deadly shootings in the United States. These shootings made some states want to increase their gun control measures. On December 14, 2012, Adam Lanza killed 26 people at Sandy Hook Elementary School in Newtown, Connecticut. Twenty of the victims were six or seven years old. On September 16, 2013, Aaron Alexis (1979–2013) gunned down 12 people at the Navy Yard in Washington, DC. Most recently before the vote, on October 24, 2014, 15-year-old freshman Jaylen Fryberg (c. 1999–2014) killed 4 of his classmates at Marysville Pilchuck High School before turning the gun on himself. Since this high school was located in Marysville, Washington, it was particularly troubling for residents of the state. While the language of I-594 had been written before the Marysville shooting, the incident was on the minds of many Washington residents when they went to vote in November. I-594

The new law would require background checks not only at licensed dealers but also for guns purchased privately, for example, between friends. Background checks would also be required for purchases over the Internet and at gun shows.

Gun Control/Gun Rights

passed with 59 percent of voters in favor and 41 percent opposed. The new law went into effect on December 4, 2014.

The "I Will Not Comply" protest

The passage of I-594 angered many gun owners in Washington State. They believed the government was unfairly targeting them for the actions of criminals. Gun rights supporter Gavin Seim (1985–), a Republican, decided to hold a rally to protest the new law. Seim believed that the government should have less involvement in people's lives. He suggested that people gather at the state capitol building on December 13, 2014, to protest the law.

Seim requested that protesters practice civil disobedience at the rally. Civil disobedience is a public refusal to follow certain laws as a peaceful form of protest. As part of Seim's beliefs about a limited government, he refused to get the required permits to protest. This initially created a problem, since another gun rights group was already scheduled to protest at the state capitol building on December 13. Seim told the local media that he was opposed to government interference in people's lives. He said he did not recognize the government's ability to decide whether he could hold a rally.

Gun rights activists hold signs during the "I Will Not Comply" event at the state capitol in Olympia, Washington, in December 2014. © STEPHEN BRASHEAR/GETTY IMAGES.

Between 1,000 and 1,500 people gathered in Olympia, the capital city of Washington for the rally. The protesters assembled outside the capitol building and traded guns with one another. They believed that trading guns in this way was against the new law. By breaking the law, they hoped to bring attention to their cause. However, the police noted that the law allowed gun sellers to take several weeks to fill out the required paperwork. As such, they said that they could not prove that the protesters' trading of guns was illegal and did not arrest anyone.

The rally featured many speakers who warned against too many government controls on guns. They argued that the new law went against the spirit of the 2nd Amendment. Congresswoman Elizabeth Scott, a state politician and a Republican, suggested she would try to pass a law allowing guns in school to prevent further shootings like the one in Marysville. Seim told the crowd that he believed residents had the right to own any weapons that the police possessed. This included guns, tanks, and other high-powered weapons. He further suggested that the government does not have the power to limit gun rights. He said the 2nd Amendment banned creating laws that limit gun ownership. Many protesters wore military uniforms and openly carried guns, which is legal in Washington. They chanted gun rights and anti-government slogans. Many attendees expressed disappointment with the law and vowed to vote for political candidates who would support greater gun rights.

Effects of the protest

After the protest ended, several gun rights groups challenged the law in the courts. When the courts ruled in favor of keeping I-594, these groups pushed their elected officials to make legal changes to the rule. Among the changes were to allow former members of the military and security guards to buy or trade guns without a background check. Gun control organizations, on the other hand, such as Moms Demand Action for Gun Sense in America and Everytown for Gun Safety, opposed these changes. Instead, they wanted to make gun laws stronger. They asked for changes to Washington's gun laws that would protect people who might be in danger from a gun owner. In such cases, guns could be taken away from a dangerous person such as a domestic abuser for up to 14 days. People who might be protected under this included abused women and children. Such people would be able to ask the court to have a relative's gun taken away for a short time until the person was determined to not be a threat.

In October 2016 the first arrest was made for someone breaking I-594. Mark Mercado (c. 1991–) was arrested for not getting a background check when selling a gun to a man named David Nunez (c. 1997–). The gun Nunez purchased from Mercado was later used in the murder of a 17-year-old male. Nunez and Mercado were not involved in the shooting. Gun control groups noted in the first 14 months after I-594 had passed, background checks had blocked 50 gun sales. They said I-594 had prevented possibly dangerous people from owning guns. They suggested that stopping these gun sales may have saved lives.

Gun rights supporters argued that the Mercado-Nunez sale would have been illegal even without I-594. At the time of the purchase, Nunez was only 19, which is too young to buy a handgun legally under federal law. Only people 21 years of age and over are allowed to legally buy handguns from a licensed dealer under federal law. They also pointed out that before Mercado was arrested, there had not been any arrests related to I-594 since it became law in 2014. They suggested that this meant that the law was unnecessary.

According to the Law Center to Prevent Gun Violence, 19 states and the District of Columbia have expanded background checks to include at least some private sales. In addition to Washington, 8 states, California, Colorado, Connecticut, Delaware, Nevada, New York, Oregon, and Rhode Island, along with the District of Columbia, require background checks on all gun sales.

Democratic Congressional Representatives Sit-In for Gun Control Legislation

LOCATION: Washington, DC

DATE: June 22, 2016

On June 22, 2016, some members of the Democratic Party refused to leave the floor of the US House of Representatives. They wanted House members to vote on a set of new laws to strengthen gun control. June 22 was the last day of voting before the members of Congress ended business for several weeks. The Republican Party leadership wanted to finish voting on its list of scheduled bills without including the Democrats' gun control measures. The Republicans had more elected members of Congress. This allowed them to control which bills would be voted on by the full House of Representatives. The Democrats were upset. They felt that their concerns were being ignored. They tried to think of ways to force Republicans to consider their gun control bills.

The House was scheduled to finish its business on June 22 for the month. After that, the representatives had a break until after the 4th of July holiday. When the Democrats realized that the gun control bills would not be considered, they staged a sit-in on the House floor. A sit-in is a type of demonstration in which individuals sit down at a protest site and refuse to move. The demonstration lasted for almost 24 hours. During this time, Republicans voted on a spending bill without the support of Democrats. After taking a vote on this budget issue, Republicans ended the session and left for the pre-scheduled break. Although the House Democrats received widespread media attention for their sit-in, they were unable to get a vote on their gun control legislation.

Background of the protest

A gun tragedy partly inspired the Democrats' sit-in. On June 12, 2016, a gunman killed 49 people at the Pulse nightclub in Orlando, Florida. It was one of the deadliest mass shootings in American history. The shooter was a man named Omar Mateen (1986–2016). During the shooting, Mateen announced his support for a terrorist group called the Islamic State (ISIS). Before the 2016 shooting, Mateen's name had been on a terrorist watch list two different times. The Federal Bureau of Investigation (FBI) creates this watch list. It includes people who may be members of terrorist groups. Mateen's name was briefly placed on the watch list in both 2013 and 2014. The FBI investigated Mateen and later removed his name from the list because there was not enough evidence to arrest him.

Democrats wanted laws that made it harder for people like Mateen to obtain guns. To avoid another tragedy like the Pulse nightclub shooting, they tried to gain support for bills that had failed to pass the previous year. In 2015 Democrats had tried to stop people whose names were on the FBI's terrorist watch list from being able to buy guns. They also wanted to increase background checks at gun shows. Background checks allow authorities to examine the history of a person before he or she can buy a gun. The National Rifle Association (NRA) opposed these measures. The NRA believed that these rules would place unfair limits on gun ownership. With the support of NRA members, Republicans in Congress killed the bill. However, Democrats thought that the Pulse tragedy might cause Americans to support these gun control bills. They tried to force a vote to make Congress take a stand on gun control.

In late June, Democrats asked for consideration of their bills. Since Republicans held a majority in the House of Representatives, they could determine whether the gun control bills were heard. Democrats tried to use a number of allowed congressional means to bring their bills to the floor for a vote. They were blocked at every turn. Democrats made

A gun tragedy partly inspired the Democrats' sit-in. On June 12, 2016, a gunman killed 49 people at the Pulse nightclub in Orlando, Florida. It was one of the deadliest mass shootings in American history.

speeches about gun control on the House floor, and they gave interviews to the news media. However, they realized that these efforts were not going to convince Republicans to vote on their bills. They tried to think of other ways to bring attention to their cause. They wanted to make sure that even if the Democratic bills failed, Republican members would be forced to explain in the coming 2016 elections why they had voted against gun control.

Democrats in the Senate were having similar problems. Senator Christopher Murphy (1973–) of Connecticut gave a 15-hour speech to block other bills from coming to the floor until Republicans voted on the Democrats' gun control measures. Murphy's speech worked, and the Senate agreed to consider gun control legislation. During the week of June 20, 2016, the Senate voted on four bills regarding gun control. Democrats authored two of the bills, while Republicans wrote two others. All four failed. There was little agreement between members of the two political parties regarding gun control legislation.

The Democratic sit-in at the House of Representatives

On the night of June 21, some Democrats gathered to come up with a plan that might get their bills to a vote. They decided to try to use a form of civil disobedience. This small group of Democrats decided they would sit on the House floor until their demands were heard. This was similar to a practice that Republicans had used in 2008 while Democrats were in control of the House. At that time, Republicans wanted to bring attention to an energy bill. However, the Republican sit-in had occurred during a break called a recess. During a congressional recess, there are no scheduled votes on bills. So the Republicans' actions did not interrupt congressional business. The Democrats decided to stage their sit-in so that it would occur while Congress was still in session. This would prevent Republicans from voting on other bills.

On June 22, Representative John Lewis (1940–) of Georgia led about two dozen Democrats onto the House floor. Lewis had great respect among Democrats. He had been a key figure during the civil rights movement of the 1950s and 1960s. During this period, Lewis had worked to gain rights for African Americans alongside the Rev. Dr. Martin Luther King Jr. Sit-ins had been among the actions that civil rights leaders had most commonly used. Together, the Democrats sat down at the front of the room and

Gun Control/Gun Rights

refused to move until the Republican membership considered their bills. They hoped the publicity of the sit-in would pressure Republicans to take action on gun control.

The sit-in caught Republicans off guard. Republicans tried to close business for the day, but the Democrats remained. C-SPAN, which is a television network that broadcasts many events of the federal government, was not allowed to televise the sit-in. The party with the majority decides whether C-SPAN is allowed to broadcast the official video from the House of Representatives. Republicans insisted that the Democrats' sit-in should not be shown live.

The Democrats remained on the floor of the House chambers overnight. They made speeches about the importance of gun control. Democrats used social media sites including Facebook and Periscope to show their efforts during the night. C-SPAN soon started to broadcast the video being recorded by Democrats at the sit-in. Eventually, more than 170 lawmakers from the Democratic Party joined the sit-in at various points during the night. Live broadcasts of the sit-in drew more than 1 million hits on the Periscope live-streaming video app. The sit-in became news on other social media sites such as Twitter. President Barack Obama (1961–) and former President Bill Clinton both tweeted their support of the sit-in.

US Rep. John Lewis (seated, lower right) leads a group of Democrats from the House and Senate to stage a sit-in on the floor of the US House of Representatives. They are staging a protest to demand a vote on gun control legislation in June 2016. © PLANETPIX/ALAMY LIVE NEWS.

U•X•L Protests, Riots, and Rebellions: Civil Unrest in the Modern World

Gun Control/Gun Rights

Finally, at 3 a.m., Republican Speaker of the House Paul Ryan (1970–) called for a vote on an unrelated budget bill. His goal was to end the Democratic sit-in. He called for a vote without any debate. It was an unusual step, as debate over bills is a major part of congressional practices. After the vote, Republicans quickly left. Democrats chanted after them, "No bill! No break!" This was a reference to their desire to have a vote on gun control before Congress broke for the 4th of July holiday recess.

Effects of the protest

Democrats believed that the sit-in had achieved its purpose. They noted their efforts to voters in their home districts and promised to keep trying to get Republicans to vote on gun control measures. Democrats believed stricter gun laws were what most Americans wanted. Democrats pointed to a poll taken during the week of the sit-in that showed 90 percent of Americans supported stronger background checks for gun purchases.

Once they returned from the 4th of July break, Republicans moved onto new business. Speaker Ryan spoke against the Democratic sit-in. He suggested that it was the wrong way to try to pass laws. He further mentioned his personal opposition to the Democrats' gun control bills. He suggested that banning people whose names appear on terror watch lists from buying guns takes away their rights as Americans.

Susan Collins (1952–), a Republican senator from Maine, blamed the House sit-in for her difficulties in trying to pass gun control legislation in the Senate. She noted that her bill had support from members of both the Republican and Democratic Parties. Her bill failed, and she wondered whether the sit-in had stopped some senators from backing it.

In January 2017 the House of Representatives passed rules that made it more difficult for members of either party to have sit-ins in the future. Republicans established a series of fines that were to be given to any member of Congress trying to protest on the House floor. As of fall 2017, the Democrats' bill to prevent people whose names appear on terror watch lists from buying guns had still not reached a vote. A new call for stricter gun laws was being pursued by Democrats in early October 2017. It followed the largest mass shooting in modern US history. Nearly 60 people were killed and more than 500 others injured when a 64-year-old American named Stephen Paddock fired into the crowd at a country music festival in Las Vegas, Nevada.

Democrats believed stricter gun laws were what most Americans wanted. Democrats pointed to a poll taken during the week of the sit-in that showed 90 percent of Americans supported stronger background checks for gun purchases.

For More Information

BOOKS

Cross, Nathaniel, and Michael A. Sommers. *Understanding Your Right to Bear Arms.* New York: Rosen, 2012.

Cunningham, Anne. *Critical Perspectives on Gun Control.* Berkeley Heights, NJ: Enslow, 2017.

Doeden, Matt. *Gun Control: Preventing Violence or Crushing Constitutional Rights?* Minneapolis: Lerner, 2012.

Hampton, Henry, and Steve Fayer. "Birth of the Black Panthers, 1966–1967." In *Voices of Freedom: An Oral History of the Civil Rights Movement from the 1950s through the 1980s.* New York: Bantam Books, 1991, 349–372.

Henderson, Harry. *Gun Control.* 2nd ed. New York: Facts on File, 2005.

PERIODICALS

Collins, Eliza. "Thousands Rally in Washington for Gun Control." *USA Today* (January 26, 2013). Available online at https://www.usatoday.com/story/news/nation/2013/01/26/gun-control-march-newtown/1866295/ (accessed August 8, 2017).

Goldstein, Jessica. "Arena's Molly Smith, Others in Theater Community Join Gun-Control March." *Washington Post* (January 22, 2013). Available online at https://www.washingtonpost.com/lifestyle/style/arenas-molly-smith-others-in-theater-community-join-gun-control-march/2013/01/22/1780d0f0-64c7-11e2-85f5-a8a9228e55e7_story.html?utm_term=.ccaa7fcff2d0 (accessed August 8, 2017).

Havard, Kate, and Lori Aratani. "Nearly 1,000 March in D.C. for Gun Control." *Washington Post* (January 26, 2013). Available online at https://www.washingtonpost.com/local/trafficandcommuting/newtown-residents-among-those-at-dc-march-for-gun-control/2013/01/26/1813a3f6-67cb-11e2-85f5-a8a9228e55e7_story.html?utm_term=.c1c727450d42 (accessed August 8, 2017).

Herszenhorn, David M., and Emmarie Huetteman. "House Democrats' Gun-Control Sit-In Turns into Chaotic Showdown with Republicans." *New York Times* (June 23, 2016). Available online at https://www.nytimes.com/2016/06/23/us/politics/house-democrats-stage-sit-in-to-push-for-action-on-gun-control.html (accessed August 8, 2017).

Neuhauser, Alan. "U.S. Crime Rate Rises Slightly, Remains Near 20-Year Low." *U.S. News & World Report* (September 26, 2016). Available online at https://www.usnews.com/news/articles/2016-09-26/us-crime-rate-rises-slightly-remains-near-20-year-low (accessed October 5, 2017).

O'Sullivan, Joseph. "'I Will Not Comply' Rally Draws Gun-Rights Supporters to Olympia." *Seattle Times* (December 13, 2014). Available online at http://www.seattletimes.com/seattle-news/lsquoi-will-not-complyrsquo-rally-draws-gun-rights-supporters-to-olympia/ (accessed August 8, 2017).

Rajwani, Naheed. "Armed Demonstrators March through South Dallas to Protest Police Shootings." *Dallas Morning News* (August 20, 2014). Available online at https://www.dallasnews.com/news/news/2014/08/20/armed-demonstrators-march-through-south-dallas-to-protest-police-shootings (accessed August 8, 2017).

Richmond, Emily. "Civics Lessons from the House Democrats' Sit-in." *Atlantic* (June 28, 2016). Available online at https://www.theatlantic.com/education/archive/2016/06/civics-lessons-from-the-house-democrats-sit-in/489167/ (accessed August 8, 2017).

WEBSITES

Americans for Responsible Solutions. http://americansforresponsiblesolutions.org/?nosplash=true (accessed October 5, 2017).

Bade, Rachael, and Heather Caygle. "How Democrats Mounted Their Guns Sit-In." Politico, June 22, 2016. http://www.politico.com/story/2016/06/democrats-sitin-gun-control-224687 (accessed August 8, 2017).

"Gun Violence." Brady Campaign to Prevent Gun Violence. http://www.bradycampaign.org/gun-violence (accessed August 8, 2017).

"Huey P. Newton Story: State Capitol March." Public Broadcasting Service, 2002. http://www.pbs.org/hueypnewton/actions/actions_capitolmarch.html (accessed August 8, 2017).

Igielnik, Ruth, and Anna Brown. "Key Takeaways on Americans' Views of Guns and Gun Ownership." Pew Research Center, June 22, 2017. http://www.pewresearch.org/fact-tank/2017/06/22/key-takeaways-on-americans-views-of-guns-and-gun-ownership/ (accessed August 8, 2017).

National Rifle Association (NRA). https://home.nra.org/ (accessed August 8, 2017).

Neiwart, David. "New Washington Gun-Control Law Spurs 'We Will Not Comply' Rally Led by Youthful 'Patriot.'" Southern Poverty Law Center, November 29, 2014. https://www.splcenter.org/hatewatch/2014/11/29/new-washington-gun-control-law-spurs-%E2%80%98we-will-not-comply%E2%80%99-rally-led-youthful-%E2%80%98patriot%E2%80%99 (accessed August 8, 2017).

Simpson, Ian. "Thousands March against Gun Violence in Washington." Reuters, January 26, 2013. http://www.reuters.com/article/us-usa-guns-march-idUSBRE90P0DE20130127 (accessed August 8, 2017).

Smith, Aaron Lake. "Huey P. Newton Gun Club in Dallas Are Responding to Police Brutality with Armed Community Patrols." Vice, January 5, 2015. https://www.vice.com/en_us/article/5gk85a/huey-does-dallas-0000552-v22n1 (accessed August 8, 2017).

"U.S. Gun Laws: A History." National Public Radio, June 26, 2008. http://www.npr.org/templates/story/story.php?storyId=91942478 (accessed August 8, 2017).

Walsh, Deirdre, et al. "Democrats End House Sit-In Protest over Gun Control." CNN, June 24, 2016. http://www.cnn.com/2016/06/22/politics/john-lewis-sit-in-gun-violence/ (accessed August 8, 2017).

9

Human Rights

Attica Prison Riot **270**

Capitol Crawl **276**

March to Abolish the Death Penalty **284**

Dalit Protests in India **290**

Armenian Genocide Protests **297**

Human rights are rights that belong to all human beings by nature. Rights are guarantees that people and governments will treat individuals in certain ways. Human rights are based on principles such as equality, fairness, and respect for all. Examples of human rights include the right to live, the right to liberty, the right to express opinions openly, the right to education, and the right to work. In an ideal world, human rights would apply equally to all people, regardless of race, nationality, sex, religion, culture, or other status. Human rights are accepted almost everywhere in the world in the 21st century.

Human rights have several qualities that separate them from other legal protections. One quality of human rights is that they are supposed to be universal, or shared by all people. To many, this means that the governments of every country in the world should protect the human rights of their citizens. Human rights should be protected no matter what kind of political system or culture exists in a country. Another quality of human rights is that they are supposed to be absolute. This means that the rights should not be able to be taken away unfairly. In some cases, people may give up some of their rights, such as if they commit crimes and go to prison.

Human rights are supposed to be indivisible, which means that they exist as wholes. Governments are not supposed to be able to partially take away human rights. Human rights depend on one another to exist. If a government takes away one right from its citizens, other rights may suffer, too. For instance, if a government limits people's right to speak freely, it may indirectly limit people's right to practice their religion. Finally, human rights are supposed to apply equally to everyone in the world. No one should be able to enjoy more or fewer rights than anyone else. People of different cultures, sexes, races, or skin colors should all have the same human rights. All people should be able to be born free and equal and remain so for their entire lives.

WORDS TO KNOW

Ableism: Discrimination against disabled people.

Accessibility: How easy or difficult it is for physically disabled individuals to navigate a building.

Capital punishment: A death sentence issued by a court to an individual found guilty of committing a serious crime; also known as the death penalty.

Caste system: A system that groups people into different social classes based on wealth, occupation, or other factors.

Dalit: A member of the lowest social class in India's caste system.

Disability: A physical, developmental, or mental condition that limits a person's activities in certain areas of life.

Execution: The killing of a person who has been sentenced to die.

Genocide: The killing of many members of the same race, religion, ethnicity, or culture.

Hostage: A person who is captured and held against his or her will until certain demands are met.

Imperialism: A policy of expanding the rule of one nation over foreign countries.

Militarism: A state of being in high military preparedness.

Nationalism: A strong loyalty to one's own nation and the quest to be independent from other nations.

Negotiate: To discuss something in hopes of making a deal.

Reservation: A system in India that requires reserving a certain number of seats in jobs or schools for people from lower castes.

Universal Declaration of Human Rights: A document that defines the rights that the United Nations believes should belong to every person in the world.

Human rights have not always been part of human societies. Few governments in ancient times and during the Middle Ages guaranteed human rights to their people. The Middle Ages was a period in European history that lasted from the 5th century to the 15th century. People in Western Europe truly started to develop the idea of human rights during the Enlightenment in the 17th and 18th centuries. During the Enlightenment, many Europeans studied science, philosophy, and politics. They came to believe that all people deserve to enjoy human rights.

The idea continued to develop over the next few centuries. Numerous countries around the world started including human rights protections in their laws. An international organization called the United Nations (UN) formed in 1945 to make sure governments around the world protected their citizens' human rights. In modern times, people in many countries protest their governments for abusing human rights.

Development of human rights

Human rights did not truly begin to develop as an idea until the Enlightenment and the centuries that followed. However, some individual examples of human rights appeared in history earlier than the 17th century. In 539 BCE King Cyrus the Great (c. 580–529 BCE) of Persia created one of the first documents of human rights in history. Cyrus took over the great city of Babylon (pronounced BA-buh-len) that year.

Unlike previous rulers of the city, Cyrus allowed the people of the city to be free. He told the people they could choose any religion they wanted and live anywhere in the city. Cyrus allowed them to work any job they chose as long as they did not abuse other people's rights. Many ancient historians praised Cyrus for his kindness. In the 21st century, the British Museum in London owns the clay Cyrus Cylinder on which Cyrus wrote these laws.

Cyrus's ideas about human rights did not spread. The concept of human rights remained absent from most societies for many centuries. Another early example of human rights was a law King Henry II (1133–1189) of England created in 1166. The law ended the part of England's legal system that required suspected criminals to fight others or touch fire to prove their innocence. Instead, Henry's law created juries of 12 people to judge the guilt or innocence of suspects.

Another Middle Ages law that protected human rights was the Magna Carta of 1215. This English document allowed people to receive a fair trial before being imprisoned. Before the Magna Carta was written, English kings and queens had the power to jail anyone at any time. The Magna Carta created a fairer system of laws in England. These examples of early human rights protections were individual events, though. They were not part of a larger movement to protect human rights.

The 17th century

Western European philosophers and other thinkers started to form the idea of human rights in the late 17th century. The Enlightenment began during this time, and new advances in science, math, and philosophy were introduced. One major idea of the Enlightenment was the belief that God had given basic rights to all people. These rights included the rights to liberty, religion, and political power. Enlightenment thinkers believed that people should be able to express their opinions openly or follow any religion they wanted without fear of punishment.

Human Rights

CRITICAL THINKING QUESTIONS

1. Do you agree with the United Nations that all people should enjoy human rights, no matter who they are? Are universal human rights a good idea? Explain your answer.

2. Do you agree with opponents of the death penalty that the United States should ban capital punishment? Why, or why not?

3. Do you think that protests like the March to Abolish the Death Penalty can influence people's opinions on the death penalty in the United States? Explain your answer.

4. Why do you think it is important to Armenians for Turkey to label the 1915–1923 killings as a genocide? Explain your answer.

5. Why do you think that direct actions, like those taken by ADAPT, have been particularly effective in the fight for disability rights? Explain your reasoning.

6. Could anything have been done to prevent the Attica riot? Explain.

7. Do you think the prisoners at Attica were right to do what they did? Why or why not?

8. In what ways does caste discrimination in India affect Dalits' human rights? Explain your answer.

9. India's government has considered creating a reservation system for private-sector jobs for more than a decade. Do you think reservation in the private sector would help or hurt Dalits in India? Why?

10. Why do you think Dalits became so angry after someone vandalized the statue of Bhimrao Ramji Ambedkar?

Thinkers such as English philosopher John Locke (1632–1704) claimed that people had the right to choose individuals to represent them in their governments. This belief opposed the style of government that existed in most European countries at that time. Most countries were monarchies in which kings and queens ruled over their people. Locke believed politicians could hold power in government only if the citizens of a country gave them permission to do so.

One important English document created during the Enlightenment was the English Bill of Rights of 1689. The document was written in response to the actions of King James II (1633–1701), who ruled England from 1685 to 1688. James canceled laws the English government had passed and collected taxes the government had not actually created. A revolution removed James from power in 1688. The English Bill of Rights stated that the English people had the right to request government changes from their monarch. The bill made it illegal for monarchs to punish people for complaining in this way. The bill also stated that monarchs had to obey the laws that the government passed. Suspected criminals had to receive trials. Monarchs were not to sentence guilty criminals to especially violent punishments. The English Bill of Rights shifted England from a complete monarchy to a fairer government system.

The 18th century

Another important European document that resulted from the Enlightenment was France's Declaration of the Rights of Man and of the Citizen in 1789. The document was a product of the French Revolution. The French Revolution occurred in the late 1780s and 1790s. The French people overthrew the French monarchy and tried to establish a free, fair government called a democracy. A democracy is a type of government in which the citizens elect representatives to create laws for them.

The Declaration of the Rights of Man and of the Citizen drew many of its ideas from the Enlightenment. The declaration stated that people were free from birth and had rights that could not be taken away. People had a right to be free, own property, and feel safe and secure in society. Individuals had a right to resist harsh treatment from their governments. According to the declaration, the power to govern a nation comes directly from the people of that nation. The French Revolution caused great violence throughout France, but the country eventually became a democracy.

In 1791 the newly created nation of the United States passed its own Bill of Rights into law to protect the human rights of its citizens. The Bill of Rights was a list of 10 amendments, or changes, to the US Constitution, the United States' document of laws. The amendments described the basic rights of American citizens. Americans had the right to speak freely and the right to assemble peacefully. They were allowed to form free presses, or newspapers, and had the right to practice any religion they chose. The Bill of Rights guaranteed suspected criminals the right to a fair trial. The US government could not take away any of these rights.

Several countries around the world passed more human rights laws in later centuries. For example, the United Kingdom and the United States ended the practice of slavery in the 19th century. British citizens had protested the African slave trade in the late 18th century. It took until the early 19th century for the antislavery movement to become truly influential. Slavery opponents wanted to end the suffering of African slaves. In 1807 the United Kingdom outlawed the African slave trade. This was only one victory in the antislavery fight. Opponents now wanted to end slavery altogether. Many British citizens, especially slave owners, still supported slavery. After years of debate among politicians, the United Kingdom outlawed slavery with the Slavery Abolition Act of 1833.

The path to the abolition of slavery in the United States took more time. The United States banned the African slave trade in 1807, the same year as the United Kingdom. However, many Americans still supported continuing the existing system of slavery within the country. Others opposed slavery, calling it an evil practice. The issue divided the United States into the 1860s, when southern states broke away from the Union and formed the Confederate States of America. The North and South fought the US Civil War (1861–1865) mostly over whether slavery would continue in the United States. The North won the war in 1865. At the end of that year, the 13th Amendment to the US Constitution was ratified, or approved. This ended slavery throughout the United States. The abolition of slavery in the United Kingdom and the United States is seen as an important advancement of human rights.

United Nations

The mid-20th century became an important period for human rights worldwide. The United States, the United Kingdom, the Soviet Union, China, and numerous other countries formed the UN in 1945. The UN is an international partnership of countries. It was created as a result of World War II (1939–1945). The war had been extremely violent in Europe and Asia; millions of people were killed worldwide. Some 6 million Jews were killed by the Nazis during the war; some were shot and others were gassed. Other people were victims of abuse, which included forced labor and sexual abuse. The UN was formed to prevent another world war from happening. Since then, the UN has worked to protect human rights in every country around the world.

The UN's founding charter, or document, describes the protection of human rights as one of the organization's purposes. In 1948 the United Nations created the Universal Declaration of Human Rights (UDHR). The document defines the human rights that the UN believes should belong to every person in the world. The declaration is not an actual set of laws. However, the UN encourages countries to adopt the declaration and work toward protecting the rights of their citizens.

Human Rights

The United Nations works to protect human rights for people around the world. Some of the people they have tried to help are the Korean "Comfort Women." These women were forced to serve as sex slaves to Japanese soldiers during World War II. Here, protesters sit next to a statue of a South Korean teenage girl in a traditional costume, which is part of a comfort women monument. Demonstrators protest at the Japanese Embassy in Seoul weekly demanding justice for the women. © JUNG YEON-JE/AFP/GETTY IMAGES.

The UDHR states that people of all races, sexes, nationalities, religions, and political groups have human rights. Everyone is born free and has the rights to life, freedom, and safety. People may practice any religion they choose. Everyone has the right to be a citizen of a country. No one may be arrested unfairly or sentenced to cruel punishments. Laws protect everyone equally. The UN keeps track of countries that abuse these rights and works to stop the abuses.

Human rights protests

Although the idea of human rights has existed for centuries, many governments around the world continued to abuse citizens' human rights in the 21st century. People in countries where human rights abuses occur sometimes protest their governments for change. Nations with powerful leaders that do not want to lose power often fight back against protesters.

For example, thousands of people in Venezuela protested their government in 2017. They claimed that the government was abusing human rights in many ways. The people wanted the government to hold new elections, release prisoners, and allow the Venezuelan National Assembly to make laws again. Government forces fought with protesters in the streets. The government tried to stop journalists from reporting the event.

Police in Belarus also opposed protesters and human rights supporters in 2017. People in that country were protesting the government's tax on unemployed people and its failure to help people living in poverty. Human rights groups said the Belarusian government jailed protesters and journalists. Belarus still tried to keep good relations with Western Europe despite these problems.

Human rights have greatly expanded and improved for people around the world since ancient times. Most governments in the 21st century recognize the UN's definitions of human rights, but some still abuse these rights. In countries where human rights abuses occur, people often protest for change. They believe they should have the same human rights as everyone else in the world.

Attica Prison Riot

LOCATION: Attica, New York

DATE: September 9–13, 1971

The criminal justice system is the source of some of American society's most difficult challenges. Dealing with criminals and making sure that justice is served can be a very complicated matter. While it is important to see that people who commit crimes receive an appropriate punishment, it is also necessary to protect prisoners' human rights while they are paying their debt to society. This usually means providing them with food and water, medical care, and healthy living conditions. In reality, these standards are not always met. Many prisoners are forced to live in harsh environments where abuse and mistreatment are all too common. When this happens, prisoners sometimes find themselves pushed to the brink and end up acting out in violence.

Poor conditions have led to prisoner uprisings many times in history. One of the most notable incidents of an uprising in the United States was the Attica prison riot in 1971. At the time, New York's Attica Correctional Facility was one of America's roughest prisons. Prisoners there endured terrible conditions and poor treatment from prison staff. The situation at Attica was so bad that anger and mistrust between prisoners and guards eventually led to a major riot that lasted for several days. More than 40 people were killed before the riot was finally brought to an end.

Strangeways Prison Riot

The Strangeways prison riot was a 1990 prisoner uprising in Manchester, England. Prisoners at Strangeways were frustrated with the poor conditions they were forced to endure. At Strangeways and other overcrowded British prisons, prisoners were locked in their cells for as long as 22 hours a day. They were mistreated in many other ways as well.

After several earlier protests, a riot broke out in the Strangeways chapel on April 1, 1990. About 300 prisoners were in the chapel when the rioting started. They easily took control of the prison and began calling for change. Some rioters climbed onto the roof and protested in front of the massive number of media outlets that soon surrounded the prison. Many of the prisoners surrendered as the riot continued day after day. Others refused to give up. As word of the riot spread, similar incidents began to happen at other prisons across the United Kingdom. In total, the Strangeways prison riot lasted 25 days. Although only one person was killed, nearly 200 people were injured before the last rioters finally surrendered on April 25.

The Strangeways riot forced the British government to take a serious look at how it could improve the prison system. The resulting trials and investigations led to a number of important reforms. Special officials were appointed to address prisoner complaints. In addition, telephones were installed on prison landings to make it easier for prisoners to stay connected with their families and the outside world. These changes, made possible by the Strangeways riot, made life better for prisoners throughout the United Kingdom.

To make matters worse, many of the prisoners involved in the riots were subjected to brutal abuse as authorities worked to regain control. When the public learned what happened during the incident, the Attica prison riot came to be seen as one of the worst human rights abuses ever committed in the American criminal justice system.

The Attica prison riot sent a powerful message about the importance of human rights. It demonstrated that people would go to great lengths to achieve fair treatment even in the worst situations. Even though the Attica riot did not do much to change prison conditions in the end, it brought attention to the American criminal justice system's many problems and shed light on the mistreatment faced by prisoners across the country.

Troubles mount at Attica

The Attica Correctional Facility located near Buffalo, New York, was a maximum security prison. This meant that it housed some of the most dangerous prisoners in the United States. It also meant that it was a place where prisoners were forced to live under the most difficult circumstances. Prisoners at Attica were housed in cells that were only 6 feet (1.8 meters) wide, 9 feet (2.7 meters) long, and 7 feet (2.1 meters) high. Prisoners were locked in their cells for up to 14 hours a day. With more than 2,000 prisoners housed at Attica in 1971, the prison was also very overcrowded. On top of that, prisoners were underfed, allowed to shower only once a week, and provided just one roll of toilet paper per month.

In addition to poor living conditions, prisoners at Attica also had to endure a great deal of racism. Racism is the unfair treatment of people because of their race. Most of the prisoners at Attica were African Americans and Latinos from urban areas. At the same time, because the prison was located in rural upstate New York, the guards and other staff members were white. This created an uneasy environment in which prisoners did not trust guards and guards did not understand prisoners' feelings. Racism was a constant problem that only worsened the already terrible conditions that prisoners had to endure at Attica.

The Attica prison itself was also part of the problem. Built in the 1930s, Attica was old and outdated by 1971. It had only a very basic communication system that made it difficult to get information from one part of the prison to another. It also lacked a proper riot control plan. Overstuffed with prisoners, the aging Attica prison was simply unable to keep up with the needs of either its residents or its staff.

The road to violence The situation at Attica began to spiral out of control as the summer of 1971 began. Around that time, a group of prisoners calling themselves the Attica Liberation Faction sent a letter to New York's commissioner of prisons. The prisoners explained that they felt the staff at Attica no longer treated them as human beings. They demanded improved prison conditions and better medical care. When the staff at Attica heard about the letter, they quickly punished any and all prisoners who had a copy of it.

The situation only got worse in the weeks that followed. Guards began to notice that the normal racial and religious divides between the prisoners were beginning to break down. The prisoners were coming together as one to oppose the harsh treatment they were receiving. A movement was building. Guards began to worry that the ongoing prisoner movement was going to get out of control, and prisoners worried that guards would start using force against them for taking a stand. Confusion and uncertainty had everyone concerned.

Attica Prison Rioters' Manifesto of Demands

This primary source excerpt lists some of the demands made by the prisoners in Attica to Russell Oswald, the commissioner of corrections, and Nelson Rockefeller, governor of New York, on July 2, 1971.

MANIFESTO OF DEMANDS

We Demand a change in medical staff and medical policy and procedure. The Attica Prison hospital is totally inadequate, understaffed, and prejudiced in the treatment of inmates. There are numerous "mistakes" made many times; improper and erroneous medication is given by untrained personnel. We also demand periodical check-ups on all prisoners and sufficient licensed practitioners 24 hours a day instead of inmates' help that is used now. . . .

We Demand an end to the segregation of prisoners from the mainline population because of their political beliefs. Some of the men in segregation units are confined there solely for political reasons and their segregation from other inmates is indefinite.

We Demand an end to political persecution, racial persecution, and the denial of prisoner's rights to subscribe to political papers, books, or any other educational and current media chronicles that are forwarded through the U.S. Mail. . . .

We Demand that inmates be granted the right to join or form labor unions.

We Demand that inmates be granted the right to support their own families; at present, thousands of welfare recipients have to divide their checks to support their imprisoned relatives, who without outside support, cannot even buy toilet articles or food. Men working on scale wages could support themselves and families while in prison. . . .

We Demand an immediate end to the agitation of race relations by the prison administration of this State. . . .

We Demand an end to the discrimination in the judgment and quota of parole for Black and Brown people. . . .

We Demand that better food be served to the inmates. The food is a gastronomical disaster. We also demand that drinking water be put on each table and that each inmate be allowed to take as much food as he wants and as much bread as he wants, instead of the severely limited portions and limited (4) slices of bread. Inmates wishing a pork-free diet should have one, since 85% of our diet is pork meat or pork-saturated food.

We Demand an end to the unsanitary conditions that exist in the mess hall: i.e., dirty trays, dirty utensils, stained drinking cups and an end to the practice of putting food on the table's hours before eating time without any protective covering over it.

SOURCE: Kaba, Mariame. "Attica Prison Rioters Manifesto of Demands." *Attica Prison Uprising 101: A Short Primer.* Project NIA, 1971. Available online at https://niastories.files.word press.com/2011/08/attica_primerfinal.pdf (accessed October 13, 2017). Courtesy of Project NIA.

The worsening atmosphere of fear and misunderstanding at Attica reached a new height when a small outbreak of violence occurred on September 8, 1971. After the incident, several guards were seen carrying a

Human Rights

limp prisoner back to his cell. Many of the other prisoners incorrectly thought the guards had killed the man and were angered by what they saw. With emotions running high, the stage was set for chaos.

The riot

The situation at Attica finally exploded on September 9. That morning, the prison went on alert when a prisoner in lockdown was released after another prisoner flipped a switch to open his cell. Guards immediately took action in response to this emergency. One group of prisoners, who were on their way back from breakfast, was suddenly locked in a passage called Tunnel A as a security measure. The confused prisoners did not know what was going on and thought that they were about to be attacked by guards. When one of the prisoners attacked a guard moments later, a riot began.

The rioting prisoners quickly broke out of Tunnel A and moved into a central part of the prison known as Times Square. Once they took control of Times Square, the prisoners were able to access all of the cellblocks. This allowed most of Attica's other prisoners to join the riot. At that point, rioters began storming through the whole prison. They attacked guards and set fire to the prison chapel. One guard named William Quinn was beaten and thrown out of a second-story window. He died two days later.

Inmates at Attica prison give a black power salute while leaders of the takeover meet with prison officials.
© BETTMANN/GETTY IMAGES.

The New York State Police quickly set to work trying to end the riot. They used tear gas and other weapons to take back control of three of Attica's four cellblocks by 10:30 a.m. Tear gas is a substance that hurts people's eyes but does not cause permanent injury or death. Unable to stay inside any longer, the prisoners moved into an outside exercise field called D Yard. They also took hostages, which meant that the prisoners held people against their will in hopes of getting authorities to give in to their demands. Thirty-nine guards and other prison employees were taken hostage, blindfolded, and held in a circle surrounded by armed prisoners. The prisoners then produced a list of demands. At the same time, New York Governor Nelson A. Rockefeller (1908–1979) called in the National Guard to help with the riot. The National Guard is a branch of the armed forces that often helps with emergencies within the country.

The authorities tried to negotiate, or come to an agreement, with the prisoners at first. It looked like an agreement was actually going to be reached for a while, but the negotiation process broke down when the prisoners demanded to be released and provided with safe passage to other countries. Many people thought the problem could be solved peacefully if Rockefeller went to the prison himself, but he refused to do so. This only made matters worse.

The riot and hostage situation finally came to an end on September 13. That morning, the prisoners were ordered to surrender. In response, the prisoners threatened to kill the hostages. At about 9:45 a.m., helicopters flew over D Yard and dropped tear gas. Police officers and guards entered the yard moments later. They fired blindly into the clouds of tear gas and killed 29 inmates. They also accidentally killed 10 hostages. About 89 others were injured. In the hours that followed, police officers and guards brutally attacked and abused the prisoners. At least one injured prisoner was forced to crawl naked through blood and broken glass. Others were shot or beaten with batons. Most prisoners were denied medical care, and many did not receive treatment for days or even weeks.

Results

After the riot, a special commission investigated what happened and why. The commission found the riot was the result of prison officials' failure to follow through on promises to improve conditions for the prisoners. The commission also found that certain reforms were needed. Only a few of these suggested reforms were actually made, however. For a time, at least, many state criminal justice systems tried to give more thought to prisoners' rights and to improve prison conditions. Such reforms helped to ensure that prisoners were treated like human beings.

Lawyers working on behalf of the 1,281 prisoners involved in the riot filed a $2.8 billion lawsuit against the prison and state officials in 1974. The suit did not go to trial for 18 years, but the prisoners eventually received an $8 million settlement for the pain and suffering they endured.

The Attica prison riot happened in large part because prisoners there began to recognize that they were entitled to basic human rights. When prison officials were reluctant to recognize those rights, prisoners responded the only way they could. Although the Attica riot did not lead to major changes, it did help bring attention to the mistreatment of prisoners and the many problems facing the American prison system.

Capitol Crawl

LOCATION: Washington, DC
DATE: March 12, 1990

In 2010 the US Census Bureau reported that nearly 57 million Americans had a disability. This means one in five people in the country is disabled. Disabled people have a physical, developmental, or mental condition that limits their activities in certain areas of life. Even though disabled citizens represent a large part of the population, their rights have often been overlooked in the fight for human and civil rights.

Disabled people have had to fight for their own rights in many instances by challenging society's ableism. Ableism refers to the negative and harmful ideas that nondisabled people often have about disabled people. Examples of ableism include making assumptions about disabled individuals' intelligence, treating disabled people as if they are children, or using language to suggest that they are suffering in some way. Such ideas lower the importance of the lives of disabled people.

Because ableism is so widespread, disabled people are often mistreated. Not too long ago, many disabled people ended up in institutions or nursing homes for much of their lives. Many disabled children could not attend public schools because of discrimination and a lack of accessible buildings. Discrimination occurs when people are treated unfairly due to their race, sex, religion, or disability. Accessibility refers to how easy or difficult it is for a person with a physical disability to navigate a building. Accessible buildings often have ramps and elevators to make them manageable for people who use wheelchairs, canes, crutches, or other assistive devices.

Because society often did not consider the needs or rights of disabled people, they have, at times, had to take direct action to bring about change. One example of this was seen on the steps of the US Capitol in 1990. During an event that became known as the Capitol Crawl, disabled activists, many of whom used wheelchairs, crawled up the steps of the Capitol to protest the delay in passing the Americans with Disabilities Act (ADA). This federal legislation prevents discrimination against disabled people in all areas of public life, including in the workplace, at school, and in communities.

History of disability rights movement

Disabled people have been fighting for their rights for hundreds of years. In the United States, the disability rights movement started making progress in the 20th century. Following World War I (1914–1918), activists worked to help disabled veterans return to the workforce. Several universities also established programs specifically for disabled veterans. Some colleges even worked to make their campuses accessible to wheelchair users.

Although many people assumed that disabled people could not take on important roles, Franklin D. Roosevelt (1882–1945) proved the opposite was true. Roosevelt had contracted polio, a disease that left him unable to walk, when he was nearly 40. Despite needing the use of a wheelchair, Roosevelt became president of the United States and was reelected three times. Many people did not know that Roosevelt used a wheelchair because he rarely was photographed in it.

Later in the century, parents of disabled children began fighting to get their children access to public education. At the time, many disabled children were not able to attend private or public schools. Disabled children who did attend school were often put in separate classes, where they received little real education. Parents brought lawsuits against their states. The lawsuits claimed that preventing disabled children from

Despite needing the use of a wheelchair, Franklin Roosevelt became president of the United States and was reelected three times. Many people did not know that Roosevelt used a wheelchair because he rarely was photographed in it.

Human Rights

Nellie Bly and the Need for Reform

Elizabeth Cochrane Seaman (1867–1922), more commonly known by the name Nellie Bly, was a reporter in the late 19th century. Many of her stories were published in the newspaper the *New York World*, which was known for printing sensational stories.

However, not all of Bly's work was aimed at attracting readers through dramatic tales. One of her earliest assignments involved going undercover at a mental institution. In 1887 mental institutions, sometimes called insane asylums, housed people with mental health problems in terrible conditions. Bly was determined to expose the horrific treatment that patients suffered at these institutions. To do this, she pretended to be insane. Police officers took her to the Municipal Mental Hospital on Blackwell's Island in the East River near Manhattan. What Bly discovered during her 10 days there shocked many people.

Bly wrote an article, "Behind Asylum Bars," and a book, *Ten Days in a Mad-House*, about her experience. In both, she claimed that doctors and hospital staff members were abusive to patients. She reported that patients were given terrible food and they received clothing that was not warm enough. Instead of receiving needed care, patients were often left alone all day with nothing to do. Bly said that such treatment would likely only make patients with mental health issues worse, not better.

Thanks to Bly's work, people pushed for reform at mental institutions. After her story was published,

Nellie Bly was the pen name of Elizabeth Cochrane Seaman. Her undercover assignment in a mental facility exposed the harsh treatment that the inmates were receiving there. COURTESY OF THE LIBRARY OF CONGRESS.

a grand jury investigation was called in New York. Eventually, the city agreed to provide more money in its budget for mental institutions and for patient care.

Bly continued to make and report news. In 1889 she made a trip around the world in 72 days and wrote about her experiences.

---

attending public school denied them their rights under the Constitution. In 1975 this effort helped to pass the Education for All Handicapped Children Act, which was later renamed the Individuals with Disabilities Education Act (IDEA).

Also in 1975, the US Supreme Court ruled in the case of *O'Connor v. Donaldson*. The Supreme Court is the highest court in the United States. *O'Connor v. Donaldson* involved the rights of a man named Kenneth Donaldson whose father had committed him to a state hospital in the late 1950s. Donaldson, who had been diagnosed with schizophrenia, spent 18 years in the hospital. Schizophrenia is a mental disorder that makes it difficult for patients to tell fantasy from reality. Donaldson was not a danger to himself or others, so he sued. He believed that the hospital was denying him his right to liberty because of his mental disorder. The court ruled in his favor, saying that the state could not imprison someone against his or her will forever. This led to the release of many patients with mental disabilities from state hospitals.

By this time, there was a federal law that was meant to protect disabled people from discrimination. The Rehabilitation Act of 1973 included Section 504, which stated that disabled individuals could not be denied participation in society based solely on their disability. It also said such individuals could not be discriminated against by any program that received federal money. However, the law would provide little protection if there was no way to enforce it.

Disability rights groups take action

By the end of the 1970s, several groups were taking direct action to effect change. They tried to get lawmakers to either enforce or change laws regarding disability rights. One such group was the American Coalition of Citizens with Disabilities (ACCD). This group lodged protests in several major cities in 1977 in an effort to force the government to pass regulations that would enforce the protections provided by Section 504 of the Rehabilitation Act. The ACCD's protests were successful, and the regulations were issued.

Another group taking direct action to force society to confront disability issues was American Disabled for Accessible Public Transit (ADAPT). ADAPT had formed in Denver, Colorado, in 1978, when a group of disabled activists surrounded two public buses for a full day and night, refusing to move out of the buses' way. The group was protesting the city's refusal to provide public transportation that was accessible to wheelchair users and other disabled citizens.

ADAPT members said they would not move until the city promised to add wheelchair lifts to the buses. The protest worked, and the city

Human Rights

Americans with Disabilities Act (ADA)

This primary source excerpt contains information from the Americans with Disabilities Act of 1990 (ADA) and the ADA Amendments Act of 2008. It describes how people with disabilities have often been discriminated against and addresses the need for equal opportunity for disabled people.

TITLE 42—THE PUBLIC HEALTH AND WELFARE

CHAPTER 126—EQUAL OPPORTUNITY FOR INDIVIDUALS WITH DISABILITIES

Sec. 12101. Findings and purpose

(a) Findings

The Congress finds that

1. physical or mental disabilities in no way diminish a person's right to fully participate in all aspects of society, yet many people with physical or mental disabilities have been precluded from doing so because of discrimination; others who have a record of a disability or are regarded as having a disability also have been subjected to discrimination;
2. historically, society has tended to isolate and segregate individuals with disabilities, and, despite some improvements, such forms of discrimination against individuals with disabilities continue to be a serious and pervasive social problem;
3. discrimination against individuals with disabilities persists in such critical areas as employment, housing, public accommodations, education, transportation, communication, recreation, institutionalization, health services, voting, and access to public services;
4. unlike individuals who have experienced discrimination on the basis of race, color, sex, national origin, religion, or age, individuals who have experienced discrimination on the basis of disability have often had no legal recourse to redress such discrimination;
5. individuals with disabilities continually encounter various forms of discrimination, including outright intentional exclusion, the discriminatory effects of architectural, transportation, and communication

agreed to meet their demands. ADAPT soon became a leading disability rights group. People now understood that disabled citizens were willing to put themselves at risk to gain their civil rights.

Battle over the ADA

Following changes made to the Rehabilitation Act in 1974, the White House held a Conference on Handicapped Individuals in May 1977. At the time, Jimmy Carter (1924–) was president, and his administration seemed willing to work with disabled activists on amending the 1964 Civil Rights Act, which provided protections against discrimination to barriers, overprotective rules and policies, failure to make modifications to existing facilities and practices, exclusionary qualification standards and criteria, segregation, and relegation to lesser services, programs, activities, benefits, jobs, or other opportunities;

6. census data, national polls, and other studies have documented that people with disabilities, as a group, occupy an inferior status in our society, and are severely disadvantaged socially, vocationally, economically, and educationally;

7. the Nation's proper goals regarding individuals with disabilities are to assure equality of opportunity, full participation, independent living, and economic self-sufficiency for such individuals; and

8. the continuing existence of unfair and unnecessary discrimination and prejudice denies people with disabilities the opportunity to compete on an equal basis and to pursue those opportunities for which our free society is justifiably famous, and costs the United States billions of dollars in unnecessary expenses resulting from dependency and nonproductivity.

(b) Purpose

It is the purpose of this chapter

1. to provide a clear and comprehensive national mandate for the elimination of discrimination against individuals with disabilities;
2. to provide clear, strong, consistent, enforceable standards addressing discrimination against individuals with disabilities;
3. to ensure that the Federal Government plays a central role in enforcing the standards established in this chapter on behalf of individuals with disabilities; and
4. to invoke the sweep of congressional authority, including the power to enforce the fourteenth amendment and to regulate commerce, in order to address the major areas of discrimination faced day-to-day by people with disabilities.

SOURCE: "Americans with Disabilities Act of 1990, as Amended." US Department of Justice. Available online at https://www.ada.gov/pubs/adastatute08.htm (accessed October 14, 2017). Courtesy of US Department of Justice.

African Americans and others. The amendment would include disabled people in this important federal civil rights legislation.

However, the Carter administration did little to move this effort forward. By late 1980, Carter had lost reelection. Disability rights activists worried that the new president, Ronald Reagan (1911–2004), would not support an amendment to the Civil Rights Act. Their concerns were confirmed when the administration tried to remove the protections provided by the Rehabilitation Act. Vice President George H. W. Bush (1924–) ended these efforts after thousands of activists called and wrote letters to the White House protesting the administration's plans.

Human Rights

Led by 8-year-old Jennifer Keelan, a group of disabled people crawl up the steps of the US Capitol in Washington, DC, in March 1990, to gain support for a bill that would improve the civil rights of people with disabilities. The protest brought to light the difficulties people in wheelchairs had when trying to enter public buildings with stairs and no accessible ramps.
© AP PHOTO/JEFF MARKOWITZ.

Still, disability rights activists knew that they needed to come up with a plan to get comprehensive, or complete, federal disability rights legislation passed. In the early 1980s, Justin Dart Jr. (1930–2002) was appointed to the National Council on the Handicapped (NCH), now known as the National Council on Disability. Dart, who had been disabled since age 18, was a businessperson who worked in Mexico and Japan. Dart became the vice chair of the NCH in 1982.

Dart worked with Robert L. Burgdorf Jr., a lawyer, on the NCH. They worked on putting together a proposal that would become the basis for the Americans with Disabilities Act (ADA). The first draft of the legislation was introduced to Congress in 1988. Although the new president, Bush, had said he would support disability rights, efforts to pass the ADA had stalled in Congress by the spring of 1990.

The Capitol Crawl

The Senate passed the ADA in September 1989. However, the bill stalled in several committees in the House of Representatives. Some House members had concerns over certain parts of the act. By the spring of 1990, the bill was still in committee. Many disability rights activists were disappointed by the delays, and they said they would not wait any longer for their civil rights.

In 1990 leaders from ADAPT helped organize the Wheels of Justice march in Washington, DC. About 1,000 disabled protesters from across the country came to the capital on March 12, 1990, to call for passage of the ADA. At one point during the protest, nearly 100 demonstrators abandoned their wheelchairs, crutches, and other assistive devices and started crawling up the steps of the US Capitol building, where lawmakers do their work. The crawl was partly symbolic, as the ADA would require only new buildings that serve the public, but not old ones, like the Capitol, to be accessible to disabled individuals. One of these protesters was eight-year-old Jennifer Keelan, who used a wheelchair due to a medical condition. She used her hands and elbows to pull herself up the steps of the Capitol. According to ShareAmerica, Keelan was quoted by media at the time as saying, "I'll take all night if I have to."

Protesters also occupied part of the Capitol building. Some protesters even chained their wheelchairs together. Because protesting is not allowed in the building, the police started arresting demonstrators. Officers had to use chain cutters to separate the wheelchairs before wheeling protesters out. The process, which took about two hours, ended in the arrest of about 104 people.

The Capitol Crawl and the protests inside the building were effective. The Senate and the House passed the ADA in early July 1990. On July 26, 1990, President Bush signed the ADA into law in front of more than 2,000 disability rights advocates. The ADA contained five titles that provided disabled people with protection against discrimination in employment, state and local government, public accommodations, transportation, and telecommunications.

Continued fight for disability rights

While the ADA did provide disabled people with many civil rights protections, disability activists continued the fight for their rights into the 21st century. Ableism and discrimination continued to be major issues for disabled activists. In the 2010s, ADAPT remained one of the main organizations using direct action to fight for disability rights.

In 2017 efforts by lawmakers to cut Medicaid spurred ADAPT and many other disability organizations into action in Washington, DC. Medicaid is a joint federal and state insurance program that covers health care for many disabled Americans. In June 2017, members of ADAPT occupied the Capitol building to urge Republican senators to vote against a bill that would cut Medicaid funding. Some protesters were connected to devices to help them breathe as they held signs or chanted slogans. Some ADAPT members managed to drop to the floor from their wheelchairs to lie in the hallways in protest About 43 protesters were arrested during the demonstration. Many of the protesters refused to move and had to be picked up and carried out by police.

Every protest needs a good slogan. Here are some shouted out by ADAPT members.
© 2018 CENGAGE®.

ADAPT Slogans

ADAPT is a disability rights activist group that drew attention in 2017 when Republican lawmakers tried to make large cuts to Medicaid. Many ADAPT members rely on Medicaid, government-provided health insurance for people needing financial help. ADAPT members protested the cuts, often from their wheelchairs, and many were arrested.

Here are some of the slogan they used during the protests:
- "No Cuts to Medicaid, Save Our Liberty"
- "We'd rather go to jail than die without Medicaid"
- "Hey! Hey! Ho! Ho! These Medicaid cuts have got to go!"
- "No Medicaid! No Life! No Medicaid! No Liberty!"
- "Don't put your wealth before our health!"
- "Save our Medicaid, don't give us death!"
- "Medicaid is Liberty for people with disability!"

SOURCE: "Toolkit to ADAPTandRESIST to SaveMedicaid." ADAPT. http://adapt.org/toolkit-to-adaptandresist-to-savemedicaid/.

The protesters argued that cutting Medicaid would reduce access to health care and community-based services. Many activists feared that such cuts would force disabled individuals back into institutions, reversing the progress made since the passage of the ADA. Others worried that some disabled people would die without access to services provided by Medicaid. The fight against cuts to Medicaid continued into the fall of 2017.

March to Abolish the Death Penalty

LOCATION: Texas

DATE: Beginning in 2000

One of the most widely accepted human rights in the world is the right to life. All other human rights build upon this basic right. Capital punishment, or the death penalty, is a punishment that a court issues to an individual who has been convicted, or found guilty, of committing a serious crime. A person who receives the death penalty may be killed for his or her crimes. For this reason, opponents believe that the death penalty denies people their human rights.

As of late 2017, a majority of the world's nations had abolished the death penalty. Several more had not banned it but had stopped using it. In the United States, laws allowed the death penalty to continue in 31 states, though it was abolished in the 19 others. Courts still handed down death sentences, and some states still carried out executions. Other states with the death penalty did not. An execution is the killing of a person who has been sentenced to die. People in prison who are awaiting execution are said to be on "death row."

According to a 2016 Pew Research Center survey, the number of Americans opposed to the death penalty is rising. Evidence of the increasing opposition to the death penalty is the annual March to Abolish the Death Penalty. This march has been held every year since 2000 in either Austin or Houston, Texas. Texas has one of the highest execution rates in the United States. The state was responsible for more than one-third of all executions in the United States between 1976 and 2013, according to the Cornell Center on the Death Penalty Worldwide.

Several anti–death penalty groups organize the march in Texas. People who received death sentences and were later found to be innocent and families with loved ones who were or are on death row have participated in the marches.

History of the death penalty

The death penalty has existed since ancient times. Babylonian king Hammurabi (died 1750 BCE) developed a written code of laws in the 18th century BCE. The Code of Hammurabi included the death penalty as punishment for several crimes. Later both the ancient Greeks in the 7th century BCE and the ancient Romans in the 5th century BCE permitted death sentences for various crimes. Methods of execution could be quite harsh. They included drowning, beating, and burning someone alive.

By the 10th century CE, England mainly used hanging to carry out death sentences. During the 16th century, however, King Henry VIII (1491–1547) began to use other methods, such as boiling, burning at the stake, and beheading. Over the next 200 years, the number of crimes punishable by death in England and Great Britain (formed in 1707) greatly increased. Even crimes such as theft could be punished by death. During the 19th century, Britain began to change its laws to lower the number of capital crimes (crimes punishable by death).

The first colonists who came to North America from England in the early 17th century brought capital punishment with them. In some colonies, capital crimes included relatively harmless acts such as stealing fruit or trading with Native Americans. Efforts to abolish the death penalty in the early days of the United States began in the late 18th century and continued into the 19th century.

During the early 20th century, a few states abolished the death penalty for a short time but then brought it back. Some states continued to use capital punishment but looked for less painful ways to execute people. During the 1930s, use of the death penalty reached an all-time high. That decade averaged about 167 executions per year, according to CNN. During the 1960s, some death penalty opponents argued that capital punishment was "cruel and unusual punishment," which is outlawed in the 8th Amendment to the US Constitution. These arguments led to changes in death penalty laws in the later decades.

During the 1960s, some death penalty opponents argued that capital punishment was "cruel and unusual punishment," which is outlawed in the 8th Amendment to the US Constitution. These arguments led to changes in death penalty laws in the later decades.

Background on modern death penalty laws

In 1972 the US Supreme Court decided the case *Furman v. Georgia*. The court's decision basically stated that the methods that juries used to sentence people to death were unconstitutional, or were against the laws of the Constitution. As a result, several states' death penalty laws became illegal. These laws had to be rewritten. The court's decision suspended the death penalty for a time. States were not allowed to use it until they rewrote their laws.

In 1976 the Supreme Court reviewed new death penalty laws from Florida, Georgia, and Texas. The court determined that the new laws were constitutional. They allowed use of the death penalty to continue in those states. Other states soon wrote similar laws and began to use the death penalty again. Between 1976 and August 2017, there were 1,459 people executed in the United States.

The Supreme Court continued to narrow death penalty rules. In *Ford v. Wainwright* (1986), the court banned the death penalty for insane people. In 2002 the court ruled in *Atkins v. Virginia* that intellectually disabled people could not be sentenced to death. Three years later, the court ruled in *Roper v. Simmons* (2005) that the death penalty could not be applied to people who were under the age of 18 when they committed their crimes. These decisions suggest that the Supreme Court will continue to redefine how the death penalty is applied to people convicted of crimes.

Most people who receive a death sentence have been convicted of committing crimes that killed one or more people. Examples of these crimes include murder and terrorism. Terrorism is the use of violence for political gain or social change. Other crimes punishable by death are treason and espionage. Treason is trying to overthrow the government of one's own nation. Espionage (pronounced EH-spee-uh-naj) is the act of spying on one's own nation to learn secret information and then sharing that information with an enemy nation.

Support and opposition to the death penalty

The death penalty has divided Americans for decades. Death penalty supporters offer several reasons why capital punishment is necessary. They argue that the death penalty gives justice to the families of victims of violence and helps them deal with their grief. Supporters also say that the threat of the death penalty is enough to prevent some people from committing similar crimes. Supporters believe that executing prisoners helps keep prisons from becoming overcrowded. In addition, they argue that the death penalty makes it impossible for violent criminals to commit future crimes.

Opponents argue that the death penalty is more expensive to states than keeping a person in prison for life. It is not the execution itself that is costly. The costs come from the trial and all the appeals leading up to an execution. An appeal is when a court case moves from a lower court to a higher court for review. Studies from Kansas, California, Florida, Texas, and other states have shown that the cost of using the death penalty is much higher than the cost of life imprisonment.

Aside from cost, opponents question whether killing the people who killed others sends the right message. Some opponents believe that life in prison is a harsher sentence than death. It forces convicted criminals to live with their crimes forever. In addition, the majority of the world's nations have banned or stopped using the death penalty. Opponents believe that banning the death penalty would improve the United States' image to the rest of the world. Perhaps most importantly, opponents believe that ending the death penalty would prevent the killing of innocent people. Between 1973 and 2017, 160 people who received death sentences were later found to be innocent, according to the Death Penalty Information Center.

Religious leaders and activists rally against the death penalty in Texas in July 2014. Texas is one of the states that puts the most prisoners to death.
© J. G. DOMKE/ALAMY.

The annual March to Abolish the Death Penalty

Many opponents of capital punishment have started protests to support ending the death penalty. One such event is the annual March to Abolish the Death Penalty in Texas. Since 2000 groups such as the Texas Moratorium Network, Texas Death Penalty Abolition Movement, and Texas Students against the Death Penalty have worked together and with national groups to organize the anti–death penalty march.

The March to Abolish the Death Penalty is usually held in Austin, Texas, the state's capital, in October. A few times it has been held in Houston, the state's largest city. Although the march is held in Texas, anti–death penalty

Human Rights

supporters from around the country participate in it. They carry signs with messages such as "Stop Executions," "Texas Executes Innocent People," and "Abolish the Death Penalty." A popular chant during the marches is "Death row? Hell no!"

The march has changed names several times in its history. The first march in 2000 was known as the March on the Mansion. During the march, death penalty opponents marched up to the gates of the Texas governor's mansion. In 2001 and 2002, the event was called the March for a Moratorium (pronounced more-uh-TOR-ee-um). A moratorium is the stopping of a certain activity. From 2003 to 2009, the name changed to the March to Stop Executions. The named changed to the March to Abolish the Death Penalty in 2010. The 18th annual march, which still bears this name, was held October 28, 2017, in Austin.

Notable marches

A few of the anti–death penalty marches in Texas have been notable. During the first March on the Mansion in 2000, George W. Bush (1946–) was the governor of Texas. He was elected president later that year. Rick Perry (1950–) took over as governor when Bush left office to serve as president. Perry served as governor until 2015. During this period, 14 anti–death penalty marches took place.

The family of Cameron Todd Willingham (1968–2004) traveled from Oklahoma to participate in the 7th annual march in 2006. In 1991 a fire killed Willingham's three daughters. Willingham was convicted of starting the fire that killed his three girls and was executed in 2004. He maintained that he was innocent until the moment he died. Experts who later reviewed Willingham's case believed that the original investigation was flawed. Although Willingham was executed, his family has continued to fight to prove his innocence. During the 2006 march, Willingham's family slipped a letter to Governor Perry through the gates of the governor's mansion. In the letter, the Willinghams accused the state of Texas of putting an innocent man to death.

In 2011 a group of 26 people who had been on death row led the march. These people had been convicted of crimes they did not commit. All had been sentenced to die. They spent years in prison awaiting their executions. When evidence finally proved that they were innocent, they were released from prison. Stories like theirs encourage opponents of the death penalty to continue marching each year.

The death penalty in decline

Since the start of the 21st century, both support for the death penalty and executions in the United States have been declining. According to the Death Penalty Information Center, since 1976 executions reached a high of 98 in 1999. In 2000 that number dropped to 85. In 2016 only 20 executions were performed. As of October 5, 2017, 18 people had been executed in the United States that year.

By the start of the 21st century, 12 states and Washington, DC, already had banned the death penalty. Between 2007 and 2016, seven more states banned capital punishment. Governors in a few other states placed a moratorium on the death penalty or refused to allow executions during their time in office. As of 2017, many of the states that still allowed the death penalty had not executed anyone in years.

According to a Pew Research Center survey from 2016, support for the death penalty decreased and opposition increased between 2000 and 2016. Support for the death penalty reached a high of about 80 percent in the late 1990s. By 2016 just 49 percent of Americans still supported the death penalty. In the same period, opposition to the death penalty increased from about 16 percent in the late 1990s to 42 percent in 2016.

Another reason for the decline in executions is a shortage of the drugs used for executions. The most common method of execution is called lethal injection. Lethal injection is designed to end the person's life as quickly and painlessly as possible. It involves using a needle to push a deadly mixture of drugs into a person's veins. However, some of these drugs are not made in the United States. They must be purchased from other countries. Because most countries around the world have banned the death penalty, they refuse to sell these drugs to prisons in the United States.

As a result of the shortage of lethal injection drugs, some states have tried using combinations of other drugs with mixed results. In some instances, prisoners have suffered for minutes or even hours before dying. Some states have considered returning to older methods of execution—such as hanging, firing squad, or the electric chair—if lethal injection drugs become unavailable. Opponents of capital punishment will likely continue to organize events like the March to Abolish the Death Penalty until the United States ends all methods of execution.

As a result of the shortage of lethal injection drugs, some states have tried using combinations of other drugs with mixed results. In some instances, prisoners have suffered for minutes or even hours before dying.

Human Rights

Dalit Protests in India

LOCATION: Maharashtra, India; New Delhi, India

DATE: November 30, 2006; December 5, 2006

The Universal Declaration of Human Rights (UDHR) was adopted by the United Nations (UN) in 1948. It states that all humans are "equal in dignity and rights." The UDHR also states that neither social origin nor birth can be used to deny people their basic human rights. Yet, for centuries members of the lowest social class in India, called Dalits (pronounced DAH-lits), have been denied these rights simply for being born into a low social class. Dalits have faced discrimination. Discrimination is unfair treatment of a person or group of people. Members of upper social classes have called Dalits mean names. Upper-class business owners have refused to hire Dalits. Schools have refused to accept Dalit students. Worst of all, Dalits have been victims of class-based violence.

In early 2006, Dalits in India had hopes that a new law added to India's constitution would create new opportunities for education and jobs. By late 2006, however, several events, including the murder of a Dalit family and damage to a statue of a Dalit hero, showed that Dalits' human rights were still being trampled.

Background on Hinduism

The class structure in India dates back thousands of years. It has its roots in Hinduism (pronounced HIN-due-is-zum). Hinduism is the most widespread religion in the South Asian nation of India. Followers of Hinduism are called Hindus (pronounced HIN-dues). According to the BBC, about 80 percent of India's people consider themselves Hindus. Hinduism is often called "the oldest religion in the world." It began in the Indus River valley (now in the nation of Pakistan) between 500 and 300 BCE.

The Vedas (pronounced VAY-duhz) are the sacred writings of Hinduism. The Vedas provide Hindus with guidelines for living their lives. One of the four Vedas is the Rig Veda, written about 3,000 years ago. The Rig Veda identifies four separate castes, or classes, of humans. These castes are the Brahmans, or priests; the Kshatriyas (pronounced ksha-TREE-uhz), or warriors and rulers; the Vaishyas (pronounced VI-shaz), or merchants and traders; and the Sudras, or servants. This caste system is known as *varna*. A caste system groups people into different social classes based on wealth, occupation, or other factors.

The varna system includes a fifth caste not named in the Rig Veda. This caste falls below the Sudras. Historically, members of this caste have been considered impure. For this reason, they were excluded from, or left out of, the rest of Hindu society. The varna system has some similarities to and some differences from the modern caste system in India.

Caste system in India

The modern caste system in India is called *jati* (pronounced JAH-tee). It differs from the varna system, although some jati castes fit within varna castes. Unlike the varna system, which has four castes, the jati system has more than 3,000 castes. The castes vary somewhat from one region of India to another. The thousands of castes are based mostly on people's jobs and are determined at birth. Castes often were formed to get people to work together for a particular reason, such as education or politics.

Upper castes are considered purer than lower castes. The traditional jobs of the lowest caste, such as working with animal skins or cleaning up human waste, are considered unclean. For this reason, members of the lowest caste became known as "untouchables."

In the 21st century, referring to members of the lowest caste as untouchable is offensive. Members of this caste call themselves Dalits. *Dalit* means "oppressed." Due to their low status in Indian society, many Dalits live or have lived in poverty. Discrimination against Dalits in India continues. Some Dalits are called names. Others have been victims of violence.

Dalits in India's history

Dalits have been fighting to improve their lives since the 1890s. In the 20th century, one outspoken supporter of equal rights for Dalits was politician Bhimrao Ramji Ambedkar (1891–1956; pronounced BEEM-rou RAHM-jee ahm-BED-kahr). Although Ambedkar was born into a Dalit caste, he became a powerful force in India's government. He participated in activities that led to India's independence from the United Kingdom in 1947. Later, he became one of the main forces behind the Constitution of India, which went into effect in 1950.

In the 21st century, referring to members of the lowest caste as untouchable is offensive. Members of this caste call themselves Dalits. Dalit means "oppressed."

Human Rights

Bhimrao Ramji Ambedkar

Bhimrao Ramji Ambedkar was born into a poor family in the state of Madhya Pradesh (pronounced mah-DYAH pruh-DESH) in central India. He was the youngest of 14 children. His family belonged to a Dalit caste, a social group considered "untouchable" in the Hindu caste system. Dalits often worked in jobs that upper-caste Hindus thought of as unclean. These jobs included patrolling the village, sweeping streets, and picking up dead animals from the road.

Ambedkar and his family had a slightly better life than other members of his caste because his father was a soldier. However, they were still treated unfairly by many people. One day, a young Ambedkar went with his brother and sister to visit their father. They found a cart driver willing to take them to the village where their father worked. When the driver stopped to eat at an inn along the way, the children were forced to wait outside. They had to drink water from a muddy stream. Ambedkar never forgot how that experience made him feel.

Because their father was a soldier, Ambedkar and his brothers and sisters were able to go to school. They were not allowed to sit inside with the other children. Ambedkar was a very smart child. He graduated from high school and enrolled in college. He received a scholarship to study in the United States. He also earned a doctoral degree from the London School of Economics in England.

Ambedkar returned to India to work as a lawyer. Even though he had accomplished much, he still had a hard time attracting customers because of his caste. He already had spoken out against the caste system, but he decided to devote his life to helping improve conditions for the Dalits. He gave speeches, wrote newsletters, and organized groups to fight for Dalit rights.

In 1926 Ambedkar became a member of the government in the Indian city of Bombay (now known as Mumbai). His new role allowed him to become more active in helping end the caste system. He tried to get Hindu leaders to let Dalits enter religious temples and drink from the same wells as other people. He also tried to convince the Indian government to give Dalits a stronger voice in forming the country's laws.

Ambedkar continued to work for Dalit rights for many years. In 1947 India declared its independence from the United Kingdom. The country's new leader named Ambedkar its first minister of law. He also was one of the main people who worked on India's new constitution. Under Ambedkar's leadership, the new constitution gave people of all backgrounds more rights.

Ambedkar had worked very hard to end the caste system. However, he was upset with Hindu religious leaders for constantly trying to stop him. In 1956 he decided to change his religion from Hinduism to Buddhism, which does not have a caste system. Many thousands of his supporters also switched to Buddhism. Just months after he became a Buddhist, Ambedkar died on December 6, 1956.

The Constitution of India abolished, or ended, the practice of "untouchability." It made discrimination against Dalits punishable by law. It established strict consequences for violence against members of lower castes. The constitution also created a reservation system. The system requires reserving a certain number of public-sector jobs (jobs controlled by the government) and seats in public schools for members of lower castes. The idea behind reservation is to help members of lower castes receive more education and obtain better jobs to improve their lives.

Ambedkar fought for equal rights for Dalits until the end of his life. In 1956, a few months before he died, Ambedkar converted from Hinduism to Buddhism. To convert is to switch from one belief system to another. Followers of Buddhism believe that a person's standing in life should be determined by actions rather than by birth. Ambedkar encouraged other Dalits to protest the caste system by converting from Hinduism to Buddhism. Many Dalits followed, and continue to follow, his lead.

Dalits in 21st-century India

By the early 21st century, the laws in India's constitution had provided some help to Dalits. Reservation made it easier for Dalits to receive more education and get public-sector jobs. However, public-sector jobs were limited in number. Although Dalits occupied more seats in government at the federal, state, and local levels, the private sector remained out of reach.

Businesses owned and operated by individuals, rather than governments, make up the private sector. Most of India's businesses are in the private sector. Many private businesses and private schools still discriminated against Dalits. To begin to change this, India's government passed a new amendment to its constitution in early 2006. An amendment is a change in the law. The amendment required private schools to reserve 25 percent of their seats for members of lower castes.

The new amendment stirred debate. Many believed that reservation in private schools was just the first step toward reservation of jobs in privately owned businesses. After the amendment passed, government leaders tried to encourage private businesses to hire more Dalits without a new law requiring them to do so. Many private business owners and members of India's upper castes did not approve of the amendment. They did not think that the government should start meddling in the private sector. Dalits supported the amendment. They believed it would open new educational opportunities. They hoped it would lead to better jobs in the future.

Dalit murder in Khairlanji

At the same time people were debating reservation in the private sector, the murder of a Dalit family occurred. The Bhotmange family lived in

Khairlanji (pronounced care-LON-jee), a village in India's Maharashtra (pronounced mah-huh-ROSH-truh) state. The family included husband Bhaiyyalal, wife Surekha, 21-year-old son Roshan, 19-year-old son Sudhir, and 17-year-old daughter Priyanka. The Bhotmanges were Dalits who lived in a small home built from loose bricks. The family owned some land but were in a land battle with members of an upper caste in their village.

In early September 2006, a mob attacked a police officer in the village. The officer later filed a report accusing 15 men of attacking him. Surekha and Priyanka gave statements to the police that supported the officer's report. Twelve of the 15 men who had been arrested for the attack were released from jail on September 29. That evening, an angry upper-caste mob, which according to witnesses included those 12 men, showed up at the Bhotmanges' door. Bhaiyyalal was not home at the time, but the rest of the family was there.

The mob dragged the Bhotmanges from their home. Mob members brutally beat the Bhotmanges with bicycle chains and sticks. They murdered Roshan and Sudhir. They removed Surekha and Priyanka's clothes and sexually assaulted them. The mob then paraded the women through the village streets before killing them. Mob members dumped the women's bodies in a nearby canal. Bhaiyyalal was the only member of the Bhotmange family to escape the violence.

News of the attack spread quickly throughout the Dalit community, although little was reported in the national news. Many believed the killings were a caste-based hate crime and an act of revenge. As police investigated, Dalits became more upset. Reports were changed to protect members of the upper castes. The reports did not mention caste hatred or the sexual violence involved in the attack. Investigators denied that Surekha and Priyanka had been sexually assaulted.

Lead-up to the Dalit protests

Two weeks after the murders in Khairlanji, Dalits found some reason to celebrate. October 14, 2006, marked the 50th anniversary of Ambedkar's conversion to Buddhism. Across India, many Dalits followed Ambedkar's lead and converted to Buddhism to escape the caste system. Despite the celebration, the violence in Khairlanji was not forgotten.

Also in October, India's government formed a committee to discuss creating a reservation system for private businesses. The system would be

Human Rights

Indian Dalits attend an anti-government rally put on by the National Conference of Dalit Organisations in New Delhi in December 2006. Thousands of protesters gathered to accuse the government of not honoring its promise to help the Dalits become more empowered in the private sector. © RAVEENDRAN/AFP/GETTY IMAGES.

designed to help Dalits find better jobs. Although the system would benefit Dalits, the formation of the committee was another reminder of the discrimination Dalits still faced.

Later in October, a few protests began in Maharashtra in response to the Khairlanji murders. The protesters believed that the state government had moved too slowly in investigating the crime. They also believed that the crime had not received the attention it deserved. Police used brutal force to stop the protests.

Then, on November 29, 2006, a statue of Ambedkar in Kanpur (pronounced KAHN-pour), in the state of Uttar Pradesh (pronounced oot-er pruh-DESH), was vandalized, or damaged on purpose. Dalits already were upset about the murders in Khairlanji and the discrimination they faced. The damage to the Ambedkar statue caused even more outrage.

Dalit protests erupt

The Dalits' growing anger finally caused a massive protest in the state of Maharashtra. On November 30, 2006, a crowd of about 2,000 Dalits gathered in Mumbai, India's largest city, and surrounding areas.

The protesters first targeted public transport systems. They threw rocks at city buses, damaging at least 100 of them. They set fire to 5 cars on a train called the Deccan Queen. Protesters torched 15 vehicles. They damaged public property. Amid the violence and unrest, at least 2 people were killed. Another 60 were injured. Police arrested about 1,500 protesters. At the time, police reported that at least 400 of them had been involved in acts of violence.

On December 5, about a week after the protests in Mumbai, Dalit activists gathered in New Delhi, India's capital city, for a rally. The rally was organized by the National Conference of Dalit Organisations. Thousands of Dalits attended. They came to accuse the government of doing too little to improve Dalits' lives. The activists expressed their dismay that the government had made little progress toward creating a reservation system for private-sector jobs.

Aftermath of the Dalit protests

Following the protests, little changed for Dalits in India. In late December 2006, Indian prime minister Manmohan Singh (1932–) recognized that caste discrimination was a very real problem. He became the first prime minister to note the similarities between caste discrimination and racism. Racism is the unfair treatment of a person because of his or her race. Singh's statement pleased Dalits, who had made a similar argument at the UN human rights conference years earlier.

In Khairlanji, police eventually arrested 46 people in connection with the murder of the Bhotmange family. However, 35 of those people were released. Eight of the 11 people charged with the murders were found guilty in 2008. They were sentenced to death. The other three were found not guilty and were released. In 2010 a higher court changed the death sentences of the guilty people to sentences of life in prison. Bhaiyyalal Bhotmange, whose family was murdered during the massacre, passed away in January 2017.

Ten years after the caste-based murders in Khairlanji, the *Times of India* reported that life for Dalits in the state of Maharashtra seemed to have worsened. The National Crime Record Bureau (NCRB) showed an

The protesters first targeted public transport systems. They threw rocks at city buses, damaging at least 100 of them. They set fire to 5 cars on a train called the Deccan Queen. Protesters torched 15 vehicles. They damaged public property.

86-percent increase in violence against Dalits in Maharashtra. The NCRB reported a 105-percent increase in major violent acts, such as murder and sexual assault.

As of 2017, India's government still had not passed a law requiring reservation in the private sector. Caste discrimination against Dalits had lessened somewhat in cities but remained common in rural areas. Dalit activists continued to work to protect the human rights of India's lowest caste.

Armenian Genocide Protests

LOCATION: Worldwide

DATE: April 24, 2015

Armenian (pronounced are-MEE-nee-an) people and others around the world protested against the country of Turkey on April 24, 2015. This date marked the 100th anniversary of the Armenian genocide, which was carried out by the Ottoman Empire from 1915 to about 1923. Genocide is the killing of many members of the same race, religion, ethnicity, or culture. The word is most often associated with the Holocaust of the 1940s, when the Nazis killed millions of Jews and people from other minority groups.

Armenians protested against Turkey in 2015 and in many other years because Turkish officials still would not identify the killings as genocide. About 1.5 million Armenians died during the genocide. This mass violence resulted from centuries of political tensions between the Ottomans and Armenians.

Background

The Ottoman Empire was a vast territory that included parts of northern Africa, western Asia, and southeastern Europe. It existed for more than 600 years but reached its peak of power during the 15th and 16th centuries. The Ottoman Empire was centered in Turkey.

Armenia was an ancient Christian kingdom. The Ottoman Empire took over Armenia in the 15th century. The majority of the Ottoman people were Muslims, followers of the religion of Islam. The Ottoman Empire treated the Armenian people unfairly. As Christians, the

Armenians had to pay higher taxes than Muslims did. They also had fewer human and political rights than Muslims.

By the late 19th century, the Ottoman Empire was failing. Ottoman leaders became suspicious of the Armenians over time. They thought the Armenians would join with Russia on the empire's unstable eastern border and overthrow the government. By this time, Armenians had already started calling on the government to give them basic human rights. Ottoman leaders wanted to silence the protesting Armenians because they believed it would prevent the collapse of the empire.

Between 1894 and 1896, the Ottomans began killing hundreds of thousands of Armenians. In 1908 a new political party called the Young Turks came to power in the Ottoman Empire. The party wanted to make the empire more modern. Armenians thought the Young Turks would finally provide them and other Christians with basic rights. However, the Young Turks only wanted to build up the Turkish identity of the Ottoman Empire. They saw Christians and other non-Turks as enemies of the empire. The Armenian genocide was the Ottoman Empire's solution to what the government saw as the Armenian threat.

Armenian genocide

The origins of the Armenian genocide lie partly in the Ottoman Empire's entrance into World War I (1914–1918) in 1914. World War I was a global war fought mostly in Europe. It resulted from militarism, nationalism, and imperialism. Over time, European nations and empires had built up their armies (militarism). They believed themselves to be better and stronger than other countries (nationalism) and frequently tried to expand their territories (imperialism). This eventually led to a worldwide conflict.

The Ottoman Empire joined Germany and Austria-Hungary in the war. After entering the war, the Ottoman leaders became even more distrustful of the Armenians living in their territory. They thought the Armenians would betray the empire by helping Russia, one of the Ottomans' enemies in the war. Armenians did exactly this. They organized army units to help Russia fight the Ottomans in the eastern part of the empire and in western Russia. Ottoman leaders responded to the Armenians' activities by approving a plan to execute a mass killing against them. To the Ottoman leaders, this was the only solution they saw to the Armenian threat.

About 2 million Armenians lived in the Ottoman Empire in early 1915. On April 24, 1915, the Ottoman government arrested about 250

Armenian Genocide Survivors

This is an excerpt from a letter written by an American humanitarian named Stanley Kerr about Armenian genocide survivors that he observed in Turkey. The letter, written to Kerr's father, is part of the Stanley Kerr Archives at the Zoryan Institute.

I've never seen a sadder sight than the poor Armenians who came in the next few hours prepared to leave Marash with the troops. Old women, children, men, all loaded with what belongings they could carry came crowding into the college compound to wait for the departure. Not one wanted to stay. You will remember Pastor Solakian whose wife and children were killed by the Turks a week ago. He said to me, "If I knew I would freeze to death an hour after leaving here, I would rather go than be here when the Turks come. And you, too, will get no mercy from them."

It had turned cold. The ground was covered with snow and with a bitter wind the night was the most terrible one this winter. Not a man would go with me to the French barracks [to bring] the flour they offered for those who must stay behind. I went [through] the trenches myself to locate the supply room and before I returned [I] decided not to ask men to carry it that cold night. At the barracks men were destroying everything of military value, buryin[g] what they could not break. It was on my return and after supper that each of us wrote our farewell letters. It was decided that the American women must go with the French. Mrs. Wilson refused to go without Dr. Wilson, all missionaries decided to stay and so did Miss Trostle. The Armenian men were asked to leave so that when [the] Turks should come we who were staying behind might ask protection for women and children. The men didn't need any coaxing, but the parting scenes were pitiful. All our orphanages were abandoned, the children coming to the college and the adjoining orphanage belonging to the mission. The older orphans were to go with the French. "Beit—schallum" orphanage, on the far side of the city, was out of our reach. We had already been told that Miss Buckley, the American in charge, had been butchered by the Turks at the Rescue Home, and that the Turks had slain all the girls there except one who escaped. It turned out later that the girl must have escaped before the killing began. Miss Buckley and most of the girls are safe. But [our] information was that she had been slain, so the [rest] of us expected the same fate.

SOURCE: Kerr, Stanley. Letter from Stanley Kerr, Humanitarian, to His Father Regarding Genocide Survivors in Turkey (January 21, 1920). Available from Zoryan Institute; submit request online at http://zoryaninstitute.org/wp-content/uploads/2017/02/Stanley-Kerr-Archives-Catalogue-.pdf (accessed October 13, 2017). Courtesy of Zoryan Institute.

prominent Armenians in the Ottoman capital of Constantinople (pronounced kahn-stan-teh-NO-puhl), now called Istanbul. Government forces executed most of these people.

Following this, the Ottoman government arrested and executed Armenians by the thousands. This happened not only in the Ottoman Empire but also in the historical lands of Armenia. Ottoman forces killed

Armenians in many ways. Sometimes they sent Armenians to the deserts. There the Ottomans forced the Armenians to walk under the hot sun with no food or water until they died. In other cases, the Ottomans used "killing squads" to murder Armenians in various cruel ways. Many Armenians were deported to other countries as well. Government forces also kidnapped Armenian women and children and forced them to become Muslims.

The killings ended around 1923. By this point, the Ottoman Empire had been defeated. The Republic of Turkey was established as the country underwent many reforms. By the early 1920s, only about 388,000 Armenians lived in Turkey. Almost 2 million Armenians had lived there in early 1915. About 1.5 million Armenians died in the genocide. Many others had left the country to search for a new place to live.

Disagreement over killings

The government of Turkey refused to call the mass killing of the Armenians a genocide. The word *genocide* was invented in the early 1940s, but Turkey denied the killings had even been a crime. In later years, the Turkish government claimed the killing of Armenians was an unfortunate result of World War I. Government officials said the Armenians were a wartime enemy who had joined with Russia to fight the Ottoman Empire. Therefore, the Ottomans had to defend the empire against the Armenians.

Whether the killings should be called a genocide remained a serious political issue for Turkey in the early 21st century. The country banned mentions of the Ottoman government's killing of Armenians. Turkish leaders also became angry whenever a foreign country officially labeled the killings as a genocide. In the 21st century, Armenia, France, Germany, and Russia were among the countries that used *genocide* to describe the killings. Presidents of the United States refused to use the word because they did not want to anger Turkish leaders. Turkey is an important American ally in the Middle East.

Western Asian protests against Turkey

The Armenian genocide affected the populations of numerous countries. Armenians claimed Turkey's denial of the genocide insulted their national identity. They wanted Turkey to admit its history as a sign of respect to the Armenian people. Some Turkish leaders claimed the country would never call the killings genocide because the Armenian people might then demand reparations. Reparations are payments made to crime victims or their relatives as apologies for past wrongs.

The 100th anniversary of the start of the Armenian genocide on April 24, 2015, brought new international attention to the historic event. Armenians around the world protested on that day for Turkey to recognize the 1915 killings as a genocide. The Armenian government held a ceremony marking the event in the capital of Yerevan (pronounced yer-eh-VAHN). Armenians placed flowers around a monument that featured an eternal flame. The flame was meant to honor the 1.5 million Armenians killed by the Ottomans.

People of Armenian descent from many other countries also attended the Yerevan event. Many traveled there from Iran, Russia, and the United States. The Armenians said they wanted to show their respect to their ancestors who had died during the genocide. Some people there criticized Turkey for continuing to deny what had happened. They claimed Turkey and Armenia would never become friendly again unless the Turkish government apologized for the killings.

Also on the 100th anniversary, Armenians from numerous countries gathered in the Turkish city of Istanbul to honor victims of the killings. Some Armenians there claimed they wanted Turkey to admit to the genocide simply so the world could know the full history of the

Members of the Armenian community march on the 100th anniversary of the Armenian genocide in Los Angeles in 2015. Similar marches were planned throughout the world to mark the anniversary.
© HAYK_SHALUNTS/ SHUTTERSTOCK.COM.

Armenian people. The Turkish government held to its traditional position on this issue, though.

American protests against Turkey

The protests on April 24, 2015, were not limited to Armenia and Turkey. That day, thousands of Armenian Americans publicly marched in cities across the United States. They demanded that Turkey identify the 1915 killings as a genocide.

An especially large protest took place in Los Angeles, California. The Los Angeles area was home to about 200,000 people of Armenian descent in the mid-2010s. About 100,000 people marched in the city. They carried Armenian flags and held signs calling for Turkey to admit to the genocide.

The marchers eventually reached the Turkish consulate (pronounced KAHN-seh-let) in the city. A consulate is a government building in which officials from foreign countries assist people from their homeland. The Turkish official in the Los Angeles consulate restated that the Ottoman Empire's 1915 killings of Armenians had simply been part of the disorder of World War I.

About 1,000 Armenian Americans and others in Chicago, Illinois, also marched to protest Turkey on April 24, 2015. Some of the protesters' relatives had managed to survive the Ottoman Empire. The protesters said their families had been struggling for many years to convince Turkey to admit to the genocide. Armenians continued protesting Turkey on the anniversaries of the Armenian genocide after 2015.

For More Information

BOOKS

Freedman, Jeri. *The Armenian Genocide*. New York: Rosen, 2009.

Jaffrelot, Christophe. *Dr. Ambedkar and Untouchability: Fighting the Indian Caste System*. New York: Columbia University Press, 2005.

McNeese, Tim. *Disability Rights Movement*. North Mankato, MN: Abdo, 2014.

Thompson, Heather Ann. *Blood in the Water: The Attica Prison Uprising of 1971 and Its Legacy*. New York: Vintage Books, 2016.

PERIODICALS

"Dalit Anger Singes West India." *Times of India* (December 1, 2006). Available online at https://www.pressreader.com/india/the-times-of-india-new-delhi-edition/20061201/281552286366605 (accessed September 21, 2017).

Eaton, William J. "Disabled Persons Rally, Crawl Up Capitol Steps: Congress: Scores Protest Delays in Passage of Rights Legislation. The Logjam in the House Is Expected to Break Soon." *Los Angeles Times* (March 13, 1990). Available online at http://articles.latimes.com/1990-03-13/news/mn-211_1_capitol-steps (accessed September 21, 2017).

Etehad, Melissa. "Marchers Gather to Commemorate 102nd Anniversary of Armenian Genocide." *Los Angeles Times* (April 24, 2017). Available online at http://www.latimes.com/local/lanow/la-me-ln-armenian-genocide-march-20170423-htmlstory.html (accessed September 8, 2017).

Gopalakrishnan, Amulya, and Vaibhav Ganjapure. "10 Years Later, Khairlanji Shows How Caste Crimes Fester." *Times of India* (September 28, 2016). Available online at http://timesofindia.indiatimes.com/city/nagpur/10-years-later-Khairlanji-shows-how-caste-crimes-fester/articleshow/54568908.cms (accessed September 19, 2017).

Holmes, Steven A. "Disabled Protest and Are Arrested." *New York Times* (March 14, 1990). Available online at http://www.nytimes.com/1990/03/14/us/disabled-protest-and-are-arrested.html (accessed September 21, 2017).

Huggler, Justin. "India's Untouchables Turn to Buddhism in Protest at Discrimination by Hindus." *Independent* (October 12, 2006). Available online at http://www.independent.co.uk/news/world/asia/indias-untouchables-turn-to-buddhism-in-protest-at-discrimination-by-hindus-419870.html (accessed September 21, 2017).

Iracheta, Michelle. "Houston Group Protests Texas' Death Penalty." *Houston Chronicle* (October 26, 2014). Available online at http://www.chron.com/news/houston-texas/houston/article/Houston-group-protests-Texas-death-penalty-5848226.php (accessed September 7, 2017).

Mejia, Brittny, et al. "Armenian Genocide: Massive March Ends at Turkish Consulate in L.A." *Los Angeles Times* (April 24, 2015). Available online at http://www.latimes.com/local/lanow/la-me-ln-armenian-genocide-march-los-angeles-20150424-story.html (accessed September 8, 2017).

Stein, Perry. "Disability Advocates Arrested during Health Care Protest at McConnell's Office." *Washington Post* (June 22, 2017). Available online at https://www.washingtonpost.com/local/public-safety/disability-advocates-arrested-during-health-care-protest-at-mcconnells-office/2017/06/22/f5dd9992-576f-11e7-ba90-f5875b7d1876_story.html?utm_term=.5a04b8487c3d (accessed September 21, 2017).

WEBSITES

"About." 18th Annual March to Abolish the Death Penalty—Oct 28, 2017. http://marchforabolition.org/about-2/ (accessed September 7, 2017).

"Bill of Rights of the United States of America (1791)." Bill of Rights Institute. https://www.billofrightsinstitute.org/founding-documents/bill-of-rights/ (accessed September 19, 2017).

"Death Penalty 2015: Facts and Figures." Amnesty International, April 6, 2016. https://www.amnesty.org/en/latest/news/2016/04/death-penalty-2015-facts-and-figures/ (accessed September 7, 2017).

"Death Penalty Fast Facts." CNN, September 3, 2017. http://www.cnn.com/2013/07/19/us/death-penalty-fast-facts/index.html (accessed September 7, 2017).

"The Death Penalty in United States of America." Cornell Center on the Death Penalty Worldwide, March 10, 2014. http://www.deathpenaltyworldwide.org/country-search-post.cfm?country=united+states+of+america (accessed September 7, 2017).

"Death Sentences Dropped for Mob Murder of Dalit Family." BBC News, July 14, 2010. http://www.bbc.com/news/10627073 (accessed September 21, 2017).

"Facts about the Death Penalty." Death Penalty Information Center, October 13, 2017. https://deathpenaltyinfo.org/documents/FactSheet.pdf (accessed October 13, 2017).

"Hinduism: At a Glance." BBC, September 29, 2009. http://www.bbc.co.uk/religion/religions/hinduism/ataglance/glance.shtml (accessed September 21, 2017).

Kauffman, Stephen. "They Abandoned Their Wheelchairs and Crawled Up the Capitol Steps." ShareAmerica, March 12, 2015. https://share.america.gov/crawling-up-steps-demand-their-rights/ (accessed September 21, 2017).

"Nearly 1 in 5 People Have a Disability in the U.S., Census Bureau Reports." US Census Bureau, July 25, 2012. https://www.census.gov/newsroom/releases/archives/miscellaneous/cb12-134.html (accessed September 21, 2017).

Office of the United Nations High Commissioner for Human Rights. http://ohchr.org/EN/Pages/Home.aspx (accessed October 7, 2017).

Robertson, Albert. "Declaration of the Rights of Man and of the Citizen." Digital Public Library of America. https://dp.la/primary-source-sets/sets/declaration-of-the-rights-of-man-and-of-the-citizen/ (accessed September 19, 2017).

"States with and without the Death Penalty." Death Penalty Information Center, November 9, 2016. https://deathpenaltyinfo.org/states-and-without-death-penalty (accessed September 7, 2017).

Thompson, Heather Ann. "Editorial: Lessons from the Attica Prison Uprising, 45 Years Later." NBC News, September 9, 2016. https://www.nbcnews.com/news/nbcblk/lessons-attica-prison-uprising-45-years-later-n645276 (accessed September 27, 2017).

"Universal Declaration of Human Rights." United Nations. http://www.un.org/en/universal-declaration-human-rights/index.html (accessed September 19, 2017).

"What Are Human Rights?" Office of the United Nations High Commissioner for Human Rights. http://www.ohchr.org/EN/Issues/Pages/WhatareHumanRights.aspx (accessed September 19, 2017).

10

Immigrant Rights

1844 Nativist Riots **311**

Pro-Migrant Rallies in Europe and Australia **318**

Protests against President Trump's Travel Ban **325**

Migration, or the movement of people from one place to another, has been a part of human history for thousands of years. About 60,000 to 70,000 years ago, ancestors of modern humans left their homes in Africa and began to move into Asia. Scientists do not know exactly why these early humans moved, but they guess that Earth's climate may have changed and forced them to leave. Eventually humans moved into Europe and the islands of the Pacific Ocean. By about 15,000 years ago, they had migrated into North and South America.

Humans began to live in cities and formed their first civilizations about 5,000 years ago. In time they established nations and empires. They created borders, or boundaries, around their territories to separate them from other regions. The people who lived within these boundaries began to think of themselves as citizens of their nations. In times of food shortages, war, or disease, however, people often had to leave their homes. They would search for food or safety in lands belonging to other nations.

A person who moves from his or her home in search of a new place to live is called a migrant. When a migrant enters a new nation, he or she is called an immigrant. Throughout history, many immigrants have lived peacefully with the native citizens of their new homes. Other immigrants were treated harshly and unfairly. Examples of both can be found in the history of the Roman Empire (27 BCE–476 CE).

The Roman Empire was a powerful civilization that ruled much of the ancient world for hundreds of years. Early in its history the empire often welcomed immigrants. Romans sometimes gave newcomers land and accepted them into Roman culture. In return, the Romans asked the newcomers to become soldiers in the army. In the final years of the empire, the Romans allowed a group of immigrants called the Goths to

Immigrant Rights

> ## WORDS TO KNOW
>
> **Asylum:** Protection given to refugees that grants them the right to stay in a new country.
>
> **Christianity:** A religion based on the teachings of Jesus Christ.
>
> **Immigrant:** A person who enters a new country after leaving his or her home country.
>
> **Islamization:** A shift in a society's culture toward the religion of Islam.
>
> **Nativism:** A policy that protects the rights of a country's citizens over immigrants' rights.
>
> **Migrant:** A person who moves from his or her home area to another region.
>
> **Muslim:** A follower of Islam, a religion founded by the prophet Muhammad.
>
> **Refugee:** A person who leaves his or her home country because of war or mistreatment based on race, religion, or political opinion.
>
> **Terrorist:** A person who uses violence and murder as a way to force political or social change.

settle in their territory. The Romans, however, mistreated the Goths. In the early 5th century, the Goths rebelled against the empire and destroyed the city of Rome.

Early history of US immigration

Viking explorers from Iceland landed in North America around the year 1000, but they did not stay. Italian explorer Christopher Columbus (c. 1451–1506) was the first European to land in the Caribbean islands, in 1492. His journey was the first of many as explorers and settlers from Europe began arriving in North and South America around the year 1500. By the early 1600s, England, France, and the Netherlands had built several colonies in the eastern sections of the continent. Spain had built settlements in South America and the southern areas of North America. All four nations contributed to the culture of the new territories.

England later defeated France, Spain, and the Netherlands in separate wars to win control over much of the eastern regions of North America. During the American Revolution (1775–1783), the 13 American colonies under British control rebelled against England. The colonists declared their independence in 1776 and formed a new nation called the United States of America. The people of the new United States may have come from many cultures, but they saw themselves as Americans. The United States is a nation built by immigrants.

The United States continued to grow in the early 1800s. At the same time, war, poverty, and unfair treatment affected people in several European countries. Many Europeans began arriving in the United States to start new lives. Most immigrants during this time came from Ireland and Germany. Some did not speak English and had religious beliefs that differed from most Americans.

Rising tensions

Millions of Irish and German immigrants arrived in the United States in the 19th century. Many Irish immigrants settled in larger cities on the East Coast. Many Germans moved to states in the Midwest. By the middle of the century, Chinese immigrants began arriving on the West Coast. By 1890 more than 100,000 Chinese immigrants lived in the United States.

Many Americans did not welcome the newcomers. Irish immigrants often were very poor and were treated unfairly because of their Catholic religion. Some people feared that the Irish would work for lower wages and take jobs away from Americans. Business owners looking for workers often posted signs in their windows reading "No Irish Need Apply." In some cities, people even rallied against the Irish. In 1844 anti-Irish protests in Philadelphia, Pennsylvania, turned into deadly riots that killed several people.

Chinese immigrants who settled in the western United States also received unfair treatment and were victims of violence. In 1880 a riot in Denver, Colorado, killed one man and left the city's Chinese section in ruins. Anti-Chinese attitudes were so strong that in 1882 the United States passed the Chinese Exclusion Act. The law made it illegal for Chinese workers to enter the United States. The law remained in effect until 1943.

An immigration boom

Despite the treatment some immigrants received, many Europeans viewed the United States as a land of opportunity. To them it was far better than the poverty and mistreatment they experienced in their homelands. From about 1890 to 1920, a new wave of immigrants came to the United States. More than 20 million people arrived during that

HELP WANTED
NO IRISH NEED APPLY

The Irish in the United States faced much discrimination. Signs such as this one told the Irish they were not welcome to work at that business. © 2018 CENGAGE®.

time. Many came from countries in eastern and southern Europe, such as Italy, Austria-Hungary, Russa, Poland, Greece, and Slovakia. Like the immigrants who arrived before them, many newcomers received poor treatment. They worked long hours for low wages in places such as factories and coal mines.

The immigration boom ended with the start of World War I (1914–1918). This war was fought in Europe between the Central Powers (Germany, Austria-Hungary, and the Ottoman Empire) and the Allies (France, the United Kingdom, Russia, the United States, and others). When the war ended, the US government worried that millions of immigrants would leave their damaged homelands and move to the United States. In 1924 the United States placed limits on the number of immigrants who could enter the country. These limits stayed in place until 1965.

Changing face of immigration

Immigration limits were based on the immigrants' homeland and slowed the number of arrivals from Europe and Asia. The government did not put any limits on immigrants from Mexico and Latin America. Latin America refers to countries south of the United States where people speak Spanish, Portuguese, and/or French. These languages came from Latin, the main language of the Roman Empire. A person from a Latin American nation is called a Latino (pronounced luh-TEE-no).

In the first 30 years of the 20th century, more than 600,000 Mexican immigrants came to the United States. By the late 20th century, millions of Mexican and Latino immigrants were living in the country. Many arrived looking for work and were willing to accept low wages. Low wages in the United States were still higher than what they could earn in their homelands.

Some Americans were especially concerned with the number of Mexican and Latin American immigrants entering the United States without proper approval. Immigrants need certain documents to be allowed to stay in the country. People who enter the United States without such documents are called undocumented or unauthorized immigrants. Some Americans worried that undocumented immigrants would take jobs and benefits away from Americans and legal immigrants.

According to the Pew Research Center, about 44.7 million immigrants were living in the United States in 2015. Nearly 12 million came

Immigrant Rights

CRITICAL THINKING QUESTIONS

1. What are some fears people have about immigrants' influence on their new countries?

2. What were some reasons why people in Europe did not want to allow migrants or refugees into their countries?

3. Why were some Eastern European nations angry when Germany agreed to allow Syrian refugees to apply for asylum?

4. Why were the people of Philadelphia worried about the growing number of Irish Catholic immigrants in the 1840s?

5. Why were people so concerned about the large influx of Chinese immigrants to the United States beginning in the 1850s?

6. Why did opponents of Donald Trump's executive order argue that it was a ban on Muslims? How did Trump respond to this argument?

7. Based on the US Constitution, does Trump's travel ban violate freedom of religion?

---

from Mexico, but large numbers also arrived from China, India, and the Philippines. The number of immigrants from Asia is rising at such a rate that by 2055, Asians are expected to become the largest immigrant group in the United States.

Situation in Europe

In the nations of the European Union (EU), immigration between countries is common. The EU is a group of 28 nations that work together on political and economic matters. The citizens of the EU can cross over national borders into other EU countries freely. A person who lives in Germany, for example, can work in Denmark without having to get a visa or fill out paperwork. Migrants from outside the EU who want to enter a country must follow a common set of rules that most EU nations use. Each country also has its own immigration rules.

EU countries faced a difficult test starting in 2015 when more than a million people from the Middle East, Africa, and Asia tried to find new homes in Europe. This became known as the migrant or refugee crisis in Europe. Many of these migrants had fled war and poverty in their homelands. The journey to Europe was long and dangerous. People had to travel more than 1,000 miles (1,600 kilometers) just to reach the borders of the EU nations. Many migrants faced danger as they traveled across the Mediterranean Sea in unsafe, overcrowded boats and rafts. More than 5,000 died trying to cross the Mediterranean in 2016. Among those who made it to Europe, many were stopped at these borders as the EU tried to find a way to help such a large number of people.

The migrant crisis that started in 2015 was the largest human migration in Europe since World War II (1939–1945). World War II was the deadliest war in history. Many of the world's nations were involved in the conflict, and millions of people died. Because much of the fighting took place in Europe, about 60 million Europeans were forced from their homes. More than five years after the war ended, about 1 million people still had not found a new place to live.

The flow of migrants into Europe beginning in 2015 divided the EU nations and their citizens. Some leaders decided to help the migrants. They offered to accept thousands of people into their countries. Other nations worried about the expense of caring for the new arrivals. As EU nations debated how to respond, thousands of European citizens across the continent rallied in support of the migrants. At the same time, other groups called on their countries to keep the newcomers out.

A different fear

Fear of change is a common reason why people have been against immigration throughout history. Immigrants from a new land bring new customs. They are new workers often willing to take jobs for lower wages. People who already live in a country sometimes fear that immigrants will replace them. These native-born citizens believe they will lose their traditions, religious beliefs, or jobs to immigrants. In the early 21st century, some countries began to fear that immigrants could cause harm to their nations.

As EU nations debated how to respond to the migrant crisis, thousands of European citizens across the continent rallied in support of the migrants. At the same time, other groups called on their countries to keep the newcomers out.

Many people worried about terrorism. Terrorism is the use of violence and murder to try to force political or social change. Several terrorist attacks occurred around the world in the first decades of the century. As a result, fears arose that terrorists pretending to be immigrants could gain entry into the United States, EU nations, or other regions of the world.

In 2017 the fear of terrorism led the new president of the United States, Donald Trump (1946–), to try to stop people from several Middle Eastern and African nations from entering the country. The official religion in all these nations is Islam. Many people believed Trump's order was unfair because it targeted immigrants based on their religious faith. Thousands of protesters rallied against the law. Protests were held in the United States and in some cities in Europe.

1844 Nativist Riots

LOCATION: Philadelphia, Pennsylvania
DATE: May 6–8 and July 6–7, 1844

Most people who lived in the British colonies in North America in the early 1700s considered themselves English citizens. When the colonists rebelled against England in 1776, they formed a new nation called the United States of America. By the 1840s the United States had been an independent country for more than 60 years. People who lived in the United States at that time thought of themselves as "Americans." When immigrants from Europe began arriving in the United States in the early 1800s, many Americans were against it. They saw these new arrivals as outsiders with different customs and religious beliefs.

In 1844 a dispute over the Bible began between Irish immigrants and native-born citizens. The Bible is the holy book of Christianity, a religion founded in the 1st century CE. The argument led to protests and riots in the city of Philadelphia, Pennsylvania. Two separate riots occurred in May and July 1844. A local military force came in to stop the riots but not before dozens of people were killed.

A new world

In the late 1400s and early 1500s, European explorers searched for a faster way to reach the rich trade markets of Asia. As they sailed west, they found the continents of North and South America blocking their path. They called these lands the New World and began building towns and settlements there.

To Europeans the New World represented hope and freedom. Some saw it as a place that offered a chance for a better life and more economic opportunities. To others it was a place where people were free to practice their religious beliefs. In the early 1600s several groups arrived in the British colonies of North America after fleeing religious persecution in England. Religious persecution is unfair treatment against those with different religious beliefs.

The Molly Maguires

Many Irish immigrants who came to the United States in the mid-1800s left their homeland because of a food shortage called the Great Potato Famine. Potatoes were an important source of food in Ireland. When a disease killed much of the country's potato crop, many people in Ireland starved. More than 1 million Irish citizens left the country to seek a new life in the United States. Others immigrated to Canada.

When the Irish arrived in the United States, many settled on the East Coast. This region was a large coal-producing area and the site of numerous coal mines. Many Irish immigrants started working in the mines. The job was very hard. Miners worked long hours under dangerous conditions for very little pay. They often had to live in houses the mining companies owned. They had to buy food and other goods from company stores. Sometimes miners worked just to get enough money to pay the company what they owed.

Many miners tried to join labor unions, groups that wanted to improve working conditions and wages. The mine owners tried to stop the unions and prevent miners from joining. In the early 1860s a group of Irish mine workers in northeastern Pennsylvania began to revolt against the unfair working conditions. They called themselves the Molly Maguires, a name that may have been taken from a secret organization in Ireland. Instead of protests and marches, they used violence to make their point.

In the 1860s and 1870s the Molly Maguires were accused of killing about 24 mining bosses and officials. They threatened people who spoke out against their group. They attacked police officers who took the mine owners' side. The Molly Maguires organized riots, blew up train cars filled with coal, and destroyed mining property.

In 1873 the owner of a Pennsylvania railroad company hired a detective to go undercover and spy on the group. The detective gathered information on the group and reported what

Religious divide

Most settlers arriving in the New World from England were Protestant. A Protestant is a follower of Christianity. Christianity is based on the teachings of Jesus Christ (c. 4 BCE–29 CE), whom Christians believe is the son of God. For centuries the Catholic Church was the largest and most powerful Christian church. For most of its existence, the Catholic Church has been based in Vatican City, which is located in Rome, Italy. The leader of the Catholic Church is called the pope.

In 1517 a German priest named Martin Luther (1483–1546) questioned the authority of the Catholic Church and the pope. He began a religious movement called the Protestant Reformation. During the

Immigrant Rights

he found to authorities. In 1876 dozens of Molly Maguires were arrested. Among those arrested were some of the group's leaders. After several trials, 20 Molly Maguires were found guilty of murder and sentenced to death.

The Molly Maguires were a secret organization of Irish immigrants who worked in the coal region of Pennsylvania.
© EVERETT HISTORICAL/SHUTTERSTOCK.COM.

Protestant Reformation, several groups split from the Catholic Church. These groups formed new branches of Christianity that became the Protestant churches. The divide caused conflict and anger among Protestants and Catholics in Europe for many years.

When settlers founded the first British colonies in North America in the early 1600s, Catholics were not allowed. Later the colonies permitted Catholic settlers but often stopped them from voting or running for office. By the 1700s each of the 13 British colonies had its own laws. Some colonies accepted Catholics while others limited their rights. When the United States formed after the American Revolution (1775–1783; the American colonists' fight for independence from England), some states kept their anti-Catholic laws for several years.

Immigrant Rights

Nativist Riots in Philadelphia

This primary source excerpt is from John B. Perry's 1844 book A Full and Complete Account of the Late Awful Riots in Philadelphia. *In it, the author describes the early stages of the riot.*

[During the Nativist Party meeting on May 7, 1844], Mr. Levin took the stand, but had not proceeded far before a storm of wind and rain came on.

Many persons ran from the meeting, to seek shelter elsewhere, but the majority adjourned over to the market, on Washington street, above Master. During the time they were running in this direction, to avoid the rain, a great deal of hallooing and shouting was kept up, and every one in the street seemed to be excited, but apparently with no angry feelings.

A few minutes after the meeting was re-organised under the market house, a commotion occurred from some cause or other, and some twelve or fifteen persons ran out of the market, on the west side, pursued by about an equal number. A scuffle ensued; two desperate fellows clinched each other, one armed with a brick, and the other with a club, and exchanged a dozen blows, any one of which seemed severe enough to kill an ordinary man. Some stones and bricks were now thrown on both sides, and several pistol shots were fired by persons on both sides. At the report of the fire-arms, the majority of the meeting dispersed precipitately, while a number took position at the south end of the market, where they displayed the American flag.

Several stones were thrown against the Hibernia Hose House, situate[d] in Cadwalader street, west

Growing conflict

Among the first European immigrants who arrived in North America before the American Revolution were the Irish and Germans. Another large wave of immigrants began arriving in the early 1800s. Again, a large number of the immigrants during this period were Irish. Many were very poor. They settled on the East Coast in large cities such as New York, Boston, and Philadelphia. Most Irish immigrants were Catholic.

From 1830 to 1850 the number of Catholics in Philadelphia increased from about 35,000 to 170,000. The city's native residents were mostly Protestant. Many of these native residents were unhappy with the growing number of Catholic immigrants. They worried that the newcomers would gain a strong voice in the city's politics and force changes to their way of life. They supported a policy called nativism. Nativism is the belief that the rights of a country's native citizens are more important than immigrants' rights.

In the early 1840s Irish Catholic bishop Francis Patrick Kenrick (1796–1863) began to worry about Catholic students in Philadelphia's of the market, and some persons were pursued up Master street. A frame house in the … [area] was stormed, and the windows and doors demolished.… Two or three muskets were discharged at this time by the retreating party, and a rally attempted. The persons who had been in the meeting still kept their ground, and volleys of bricks and stones were continually kept up by both sides. A number of persons, evidently Irishmen, then rallied at Germantown Road and Master street, and came down at a brisk pace upon the others with stones and two or three guns. The Native Americans retreated, but maintained a fire with stones, and one or two pistols. Several persons were severely wounded at this point of time, and the rioters became furious. The Native Americans again rallied, and recovered a temporary advantage, but finally retreated, under a sharp fire of every kind of missiles, and two or three discharges of a musket carried by a gray-headed Irishman who wore a seal-skin cap.

During the firing a young man, named George Shifler, between eighteen and nineteen years of age, … was shot.…

While the contest raged with its greatest fury, the main body of the belligerent parties were posted east and west of the market house, in Master street, each rallying and retreating in turns, while others were engaged in skirmishes in every direction, for some distance round. Houses were attacked, and the inmates driven out with the utmost consternation and alarm.

SOURCE: Perry, John B. *A Full and Complete Account of the Late Awful Riots in Philadelphia*. New York: Nafis & Cornish, 1844. Available online at https://digital.library.villanova.edu/Item/vudl:94648#?c=0&m=0&s=0&cv=12&z=-0.5073%2C0.4846%2C1.2006%2C0.468 (accessed October 15, 2017). Courtesy of Villanova University Digital Press.

schools. Catholic students were learning Protestant hymns, or religious songs. They were reading from Protestant versions of the Bible. Kenrick asked the city school board to allow Catholic children to read a Catholic version of the Bible. The school board agreed.

The decision angered many Protestant leaders. They used Kenrick's complaints about the Bible to inspire and gather followers. They began to hand out papers containing anti-Catholic messages. In 1842 several Protestant religious leaders formed the American Protestant Association. A year later a newspaper editor formed an anti-Catholic political party called the American Republican Association. Both groups wanted to defend the United States against what they viewed as a Catholic threat.

Riots begin

In February 1844 a Catholic school director from Kensington, an Irish section of Philadelphia, realized that reading two versions of the Bible was causing confusion at a girls' school. He suggested stopping Bible readings until both Catholics and Protestants could agree on a solution. Rumors began to spread in the Protestant community that the director had demanded Bible readings to stop completely. Many believed this was an example of Catholic interference in their Protestant beliefs.

On May 3, 1844, thousands of members of the American Protestant Association staged a protest in Kensington. The rally angered many Irish Catholics from the neighborhood. Catholic residents yelled at the rally's Protestant speakers and threw objects at them. Eventually the protesters were forced to leave. Three days later the protesters returned in larger numbers. Fights began between Catholics and Protestants. Shots were fired, and several protesters were killed.

The deaths angered the crowd. Many began to attack Irish Catholics, destroying several homes and a religious school. A local police force tried but failed to stop the violence. By the end of the first day, four nativist protesters were killed, and dozens of people were injured.

On May 7 rioters burned down a fire station and about 30 homes. Both sides fired guns at each other. In an effort to stop the violence, Bishop Kenrick asked Catholics to avoid fighting. People in the Kensington neighborhood hung signs from their windows that read "Native American" in hopes that rioters would leave them alone. A military force arrived to help the local police and temporarily chased the crowds away.

More riots began in Kensington on May 8, and they started to spread to central Philadelphia. Dozens more homes were attacked, and several Catholic churches were burned. A crowd in central Philadelphia cheered as a pointed steeple on top of a burning church fell to the ground. The mayor of Philadelphia requested help from the US Army and Navy, police from surrounding communities, and private citizens. The additional forces helped end the riots. In three days about 14 people were killed, and the city suffered $150,000 in damage.

More violence

For several weeks after the riots Philadelphia was calm, but anger among Catholics and Protestants remained high. The mayor ordered people to be in their homes and off the streets by a certain time each night. He put military forces near Catholic churches to guard them. An investigation into the cause of the riots put the blame on Irish Catholics.

As July approached, nativists and their supporters planned a large protest for July 4, the day the United States celebrates its independence. A Catholic priest at the Church of St. Philip de Neri in the Southwark section of

The Nativist Riots pitted Protestants against Catholics in Philadelphia in 1844. The "June 7th" date at the bottom of the illustration was a misprint. It should have read July 7th. COURTESY OF THE LIBRARY OF CONGRESS.

Philadelphia heard about the march. He worried that protesters would attack his church. He began to collect and store guns in the church basement.

The day after the march, thousands of nativists surrounded the church. They demanded that the priest surrender the guns. On July 6 the crowd gathered again, and a small military force was called in to defend the church. Some fighting occurred, and several nativists were taken prisoner inside the church.

On July 7 the crowd of nativists returned armed with a cannon. They pointed it at the church and forced the men guarding the church to surrender. Later that evening a larger military force arrived and tried to move the crowd from the area around the church. More violence occurred as the crowd began attacking the military with bricks, knives, and broken bottles. The military fired back, killing several people. The fighting continued for hours. By the next morning about 15 people had been killed, and more than 50 had been injured.

Aftermath

An official from the Southwark section arranged for the military to leave the area without further violence. The city called in thousands of additional troops to patrol the city and keep the peace. Irish Catholics' situation in Philadelphia changed little after the riots. Another investigation again blamed Irish Catholics for starting the violence. In elections held later in 1844, nativist politicians won several key positions.

The riots did help Philadelphia officials realize that they needed a stronger police force. In 1845 the city passed a law requiring one police officer for every 150 tax-paying citizens. Five years later it created a unified police department that covered the entire city.

Pro-Migrant Rallies in Europe and Australia

LOCATION: Europe and Australia

DATE: 2015–2016

In the early years of the 2010s, millions of people in the Middle East, Africa, and central Asia fled their homes because of war, poverty, or unfair treatment by their governments. With nowhere to go, many tried to find new homes in Europe. Some people died trying to reach Europe. Others had to live in camps while they waited for permission to enter a country and find new homes.

With hundreds of thousands of people trying to enter Europe at once, many countries struggled to help the new arrivals. Some nations welcomed them, but others tried to keep them out. Many European citizens wanted their governments to do more to help the situation. In 2015 tens of thousands of people marched through the capitals of Europe to show their support for migrants and refugees.

Fleeing war and poverty

In late 2010 and early 2011 a series of large protests in the northern African nation of Tunisia (pronounced too-NEE-zhuh) helped remove the country's president from power. The uprising inspired similar protests in other nations in northern Africa and the Middle East. The movement became known as the Arab Spring.

In March 2011 the unrest spread to Syria, a nation on the eastern coast of the Mediterranean Sea. Syrian President Bashar al-Assad (pronounced buh-SHAR al-AW-sawd; 1965–) ordered the nation's army to fire on protesters. The attack further angered the Syrian people, who began to organize larger demonstrations. Hundreds of thousands of protesters marched in Syria and called for Assad to leave. The president responded to the protests with even more force. By 2012 Syria was involved in a civil war, a conflict between citizens of the same country.

Many people in Syria died in the fighting. The United Nations (UN), an organization of countries from around the world, said about 90,000 people had been killed by June 2013. Just two years later that number had risen to 250,000. Millions more people were displaced, or forced to leave their homes because of the war. Many left Syria to find a new place to live in other countries. According to the UN, more than 5 million people fled Syria between 2011 and 2017.

The conflict in Syria may have been the most destructive, but it was not the only country in chaos. In the central Asian country of Afghanistan, a war started by the United States and some allies in 2001 caused millions of people to flee their homes. The UN said about 2.6 million people left in 2014 alone. Poverty and war forced people to flee the nations of Somalia, Iraq, Kosovo, Albania, Pakistan, Eritrea (pronounced air-uh-TREE-uh), Iran, Nigeria, and Ukraine in large numbers, too.

Turning toward Europe

Most displaced people first traveled to the nations of Turkey, Jordan, or Lebanon. These three nations share a border with Syria; Jordan and Turkey also border Iraq. By 2014 more than 3 million people had arrived in these nations from Syria alone. The number of people crossing their borders strained the countries' ability to feed and house the new arrivals. Many displaced people lived in tents in large camps while they waited to find new homes. The living conditions in some of these camps were very poor.

As people continued to arrive, the camps became more crowded and the conditions worsened. In some cases, people died while trying to reach Europe directly. Many drowned attempting to cross the Mediterranean Sea in unsafe, overcrowded boats. Others were beaten or robbed by smugglers who had promised to take them to Europe.

A person who moves from his or her home often for a better job or more opportunity is called a migrant. A person who flees his or her homeland because of a natural disaster, war, or mistreatment based on race, religion, or political reasons is a refugee. Under laws created by the UN, nations must protect refugees and cannot force them to return to their home country. Refugees who want to live in their new country can ask the government for permission to stay there. This is called seeking asylum (pronounced uh-SIGH-lum).

The migrants' and refugees' situations began to attract the European Union's (EU) attention. The EU is a group of 28 countries that work together on political and economic matters. In response to the growing crisis, some EU nations began taking in migrants and refugees. According to the British Broadcasting Corporation (BBC), 280,000 migrants entered EU nations in 2014.

Number of migrants increases

In 2015 the flow of migrants and refugees into Europe increased. Many wanted to reach countries in Western Europe, such as Germany, Sweden, Denmark, France, and the United Kingdom. The easiest path to the region was through Eastern European countries such as Greece, Bulgaria, Serbia, Hungary, and Austria. Some nations allowed migrants to pass through freely on their way to other locations.

Other nations did not want large numbers of people crossing their borders. Bulgaria and Hungary began building large fences to keep out migrants. Thousands of migrants fled into Hungary before the fence was completed. Others traveled to Greece and Italy. Because these people were migrants fleeing poor economic conditions, the UN's refugee laws did not protect them. Many migrants became stuck in camps in Italy, Hungary, and Greece as officials tried to figure out who was a refugee and who was not.

As more people tried to reach Europe, the situation in the camps worsened. Some Europeans began asking their governments to do more to help the migrants and refugees. They wanted their leaders to allow more migrants to enter their nations. Others did not want to let any new arrivals into their countries. They believed that the cost of paying for food and housing for the migrants was too high. Some worried that the newcomers would bring higher rates of crime with them.

In August 2015 the chancellor, or leader, of Germany, Angela Merkel (pronounced ahn-GA-luh MAIR-kuhl; 1954–), announced that her nation would accept any refugees fleeing the war in Syria. She said that if they could make it to Germany, they could apply for asylum. From January to July 2015, about 200,000 people asked for asylum in Germany. By the end of the year, about 1 million refugees had arrived in the country.

Merkel's decision put pressure on other European leaders to accept more Syrian refugees. It angered some Eastern European nations that already struggled with the amount of people in their countries. Many worried that they could not handle an increased number of people passing through on their way to Germany and Western Europe.

Pro-migrant demonstrations

Rallies and protests both for and against migrants and refugees had been common across Europe since the crisis began. In January 2015 a group of about 25,000 anti-migrant protesters staged a rally in the German city of Dresden. About 35,000 migrant supporters met them. Large pro-migrant rallies also were held in the German cities of Leipzig and Munich.

In August 2015, shortly after Merkel announced her refugee policy, an anti-migrant rally in Dresden turned violent. About 250 protesters attacked police and threw objects at buses carrying people seeking asylum. On August 29 about 5,000 people demonstrated in Dresden against the attacks. Many held signs saying "Refugees Welcome. Racists Not." The slogan often was used at pro-migrant rallies across Germany.

As leaders in other EU nations considered their response to the crisis, protesters in several European capitals and Australia gathered on September 12 to make their voices heard. Tens of thousands of people carried signs reading "Open the Borders" and "Refugees In" as they marched in London. The protesters called for David Cameron (1966–), the prime minister of the United Kingdom, to agree to take in more refugees. Earlier Cameron had announced that the United Kingdom would accept 20,000 refugees. Protests were held in several other cities in the United Kingdom, too.

In August 2015, shortly after German Chancellor Angela Merkel announced her refugee policy, an anti-migrant rally in Dresden turned violent. About 250 protesters attacked police and threw objects at buses carrying people seeking asylum.

Immigrant Rights

Anti-Islam Movement

Some people and countries were against accepting migrants and refugees for many reasons. Some worried that their nation could not afford to feed, house, and provide health care to such a large number of people. Others worried that the newcomers would cause crime to rise. Some groups of people feared that the religious beliefs of many of the migrants and refugees would destroy the culture of their homelands.

Most of the refugees from Syria, Iraq, and other Middle Eastern and African nations were Muslims, or followers of Islam. Islam is a very popular religion in the Middle East, northern Africa, and central Asia. The prophet Muhammad (c. 570–632) founded Islam about the year 610.

Some Europeans feared that Muslim migrants and refugees would try to spread their religious beliefs once they arrived in their new countries. These Europeans believed the goal of Islam was to replace the religions and cultures of Europe. This idea is known as Islamization. In 2014 the group PEGIDA (also written as Pegida) formed in Germany to try to stop Muslims from entering the country. In English, the letters PEGIDA stand for Patriotic Europeans against the Islamisation of the West.

PEGIDA organized a series of large anti-migrant protests across Germany on January 11, 2015. The largest rallies were in the German cities of Dresden, Leipzig, Munich, and Hannover. Many protesters said they did not want to feel like outsiders in their own country. In each city, larger crowds of pro-migrant supporters met the protesters.

In August 2015 German Chancellor Angela Merkel said her country would accept any Syrian refugees who could make it to Germany. This policy angered anti-Muslim protesters. They staged more than 200 demonstrations in Germany in the last three months of 2015.

In January 2016 about 8,000 PEGIDA supporters marched in the city of Cologne, Germany. They were angry about several

About 30,000 pro-migrant supporters rallied in Copenhagen, the capital of Denmark. Some 1,000 people demonstrated in support of migrants and refugees in Stockholm, Sweden. Pro-migrant rallies were held in France, Germany, the Netherlands, and Australia. Australia is not part of Europe, but protesters there marched in support of migrants. They also called on their government to do more to help refugees.

On September 12 people in several Eastern European nations demonstrated against accepting more migrants or refugees. These nations are not as wealthy as the countries in Western Europe. Many are having trouble dealing with the new arrivals they already had. About

attacks that had occurred during New Year's Eve celebrations in the city. Many of those arrested in the attacks were refugees seeking asylum. In 2016 and 2017 PEGIDA rallies continued in Germany and also were held in other European nations.

Supporters of the PEGIDA movement in Dresden, Germany, march with their country's flags during one of their weekly protests in 2015. A PEGIDA leader spoke out against any form of violence against refugees but called for a major change in Europe's policy of accepting so many refugees and migrants. Many PEDIGA supporters believe that Muslim immigration is a threat to Germany. © SEAN GALLUP/GETTY IMAGES.

5,000 people attended an anti-migrant rally in Warsaw, Poland. In Prague, the capital of the Czech Republic, marchers carried signs reading "Get out of EU is the solution." Another rally was held in Slovakia's capital city of Bratislava.

Deadly journey

According to the BBC, about 1.3 million migrants and refugees arrived in Europe in 2015. Slightly more than 1 million made the trip by boat. About 35,000 traveled by land. The World Economic Forum, an international group that works to improve business and economic matters

Immigrant Rights

Demonstrators shout slogans during a pro-migrant rally in Orestiada, Greece, in January 2016. They were protesting against a security fence, which was intended to stop the flow of migrants across the Turkey-Greece border. Protesters demanded the opening of safe passages for migrants two days after at least 45 refugees drowned at sea. © SAKIS MITROLIDIS/AFP/GETTY IMAGES.

around the world, reported that about 370,000 migrants came to Europe in 2016. About 173,000 arrived in Greece, and 167,000 arrived in Italy. About 3,777 died while trying to make the sea crossing from northern Africa in 2015. In 2016 about 5,000 people died on the journey across the Mediterranean.

On January 24, 2016, hundreds of protesters gathered on the border of Turkey and Greece to call for the removal of a security fence. The fence was set up in 2012 to stop people from crossing into Greece from Turkey. The protesters wanted Greece to open its land borders after an accident caused 45 people to drown two days earlier while trying to make the journey to Greece by sea. Many protesters wore life jackets to remember those who died.

Trying to find a solution

On September 22, 2015, EU officials met to vote on a plan to help with the migrant crisis. They approved a system through which most EU countries were expected to accept at least a certain number of refugees. For example, Germany was supposed to take in at least 40,000 refugees, France about 30,700, Spain about 19,200, and Poland about 12,000. The United Kingdom, Ireland, and Denmark could choose whether to participate in the system. EU officials had hoped to find homes for about 160,000 refugees by September 2017.

At first, Romania, the Czech Republic, Slovakia, and Hungary voted against the plan and refused to accept any refugees. Slovakia and Hungary went to court in May 2017 to try to fight the plan. At that time, Poland, Hungary, and Austria had yet to take in any refugees. Other EU nations followed the EU order and began accepting people in 2015. By summer 2017, however, the process was moving more slowly than expected. As a result, EU officials lowered the number of people each nation was supposed to accept.

Protests against President Trump's Travel Ban

LOCATION: Across the United States and several cities worldwide

DATE: January 28–29, 2017

The topic of immigration played a key role in the 2016 presidential election in the United States. As a candidate, Donald Trump (1946–) said he would build a wall on the US-Mexican border to keep out unauthorized immigrants. Unauthorized, or undocumented, immigrants enter another country without proper approval from that country's government. Some people who visit from other countries remain in the country illegally after overstaying their visas. During the campaign, Trump also said he would ask for a ban on Muslims entering the United States. Trump later changed his position to call for a ban on Muslims from nations he said were home to terrorists. A terrorist is a person who uses violence and murder to try to force political or social change.

Trump was elected in November 2016 and officially became president on January 20, 2017. Seven days after taking office, he signed an order to ban immigration from seven Middle Eastern and African nations whose people mainly practiced the Islam religion. The president's actions made many people angry. Opponents of the ban said it unfairly targeted Muslims because all seven nations on the list named Islam as their official religion. Others believed the ban went against the laws of the United States. They took legal measures to try to stop the ban.

Immigrant Rights

Countries Included in Trump's First Travel Ban, January 27, 2017

© 2018 CENGAGE®.

On January 28 thousands of people demonstrated against the ban in cities across the United States. Many staged protests at airports where some travelers from the banned nations had been held by authorities or forced to return home. The protests continued through the next day. In some places, they lasted for several days. Protests also were held in the United Kingdom and other cities around the world.

A US court eventually blocked Trump's travel ban. Trump tried to pass a different version of the ban in March 2017, but the courts stopped that ban, too. In June the US Supreme Court, the highest court in the United States, allowed some parts of the ban to take effect. It also agreed to listen to arguments on whether Trump's plan was legal in October 2017. However, Trump adjusted his travel ban again in late September 2017, so the Supreme Court canceled its hearing on the previous ban.

Incidents of terrorism

Terrorism was a major concern for many people in the United States both before and after the 2016 election. The country had been the site of several terrorist attacks in the 21st century. The largest occurred on September 11, 2001, when 19 terrorists took control of four airplanes. The terrorists crashed two of the planes into the two towers of the World Trade Center in New York City, killing 2,753 people. They crashed another plane into the Pentagon, the headquarters of the US Department of Defense in Washington, DC, killing 184 people. Another 40 people died when a fourth hijacked airplane crashed in a field in Pennsylvania. The attacks shocked the United States and made many Americans angry and fearful of future terrorism.

The terrorists who hijacked, or used force to take control of, the airplanes were all Muslims from Islamic countries in the Middle East (Egypt, Lebanon, Saudi Arabia, and the United Arab Emirates). They all entered the United States legally, claiming to be either students or tourists. The hijackers were not typical of Muslims or the Islamic religion. Most Muslims in the United States and around the world are peaceful

Immigrant Rights

California State Senate Resolution No. 16

This primary source excerpt is from the California Legislature in response to the travel ban issued by US President Donald Trump in January 2017. The excerpt comes from "Senate Resolution No. 16," and it contains some of the reasons given for the Senate's condemnation of the executive order.

WHEREAS, The United States was founded as a refuge for those escaping religious and political persecution; and

WHEREAS, Wave after wave of immigrants seeking a better life have enriched our nation's culture, increased our productivity and innovation, and bolstered our economy; and

WHEREAS, President Donald J. Trump signed an executive order on January 27, 2017, that desecrates our American values and panders to fears and nativist instincts that have resulted in some of our nation's most shameful acts; and

WHEREAS, The executive order bans individuals from the predominately Muslim countries of Sudan, Syria, Yemen, Iran, Iraq, Libya, and Somalia from entering the United States for 90 days, prevents all refugees from entering the United States for 120 days, and indefinitely suspends the entry of refugees from Syria; and

WHEREAS, The executive order titled "Protecting the Nation From Foreign Terrorist Entry Into the United States" ignores the fact that those being denied entry are themselves victims of terrorism and are fleeing the savagery, death, and destruction of the Syrian civil war; and

WHEREAS, The executive order is an affront to religious freedom—a principle so cherished by our nation's founding fathers that it was included in the First Amendment to the United States Constitution; and....

WHEREAS, The executive order is against our national interests as it exacerbates the United States' anti-Muslim reputation, providing a recruitment tool for terrorist organizations while alienating the more than 3.3 million Muslims living in the United States; and

WHEREAS, While President Trump has falsely stated there is no refugee-vetting system in place, refugees are subjected to the most stringent vetting system of any traveler seeking entry into the United States—a system that can take up to two years or longer to complete; and

WHEREAS, While the executive order references the September 11, 2001, terrorist attacks as why his executive order is necessary, the 19 terrorists who carried out the attacks were from countries not listed in the ban— Saudi Arabia, Egypt, Lebanon, and the United Arab Emirates....

SOURCE: California State Senate. "Senate Resolution No. 16. Senate, California Legislature— 2017–18 Regular session." Available online at http://leginfo.legislature.ca.gov/faces/billTextClient.xhtml?bill_id=201720180SR16 (accessed October 15, 2017). Courtesy of California State Senate.

people. They were angered and upset by the attacks. Many Muslims spoke out against the attacks. The hijackers were religious extremists, or people who believe in using extreme methods such as violence to achieve their goals.

Immigrant Rights

Anti-Chinese Riots in Denver, 1880

Anti-immigration feelings were also popular in the past. In the 1850s thousands of Chinese immigrants began arriving in the United States. Many Chinese immigrants had fled from poverty and political unrest at home. Some came to seek their fortunes in the California gold rush. Because the immigrants arrived in the western United States, many took jobs in the farming and railroad industries in addition to the mines. These businesses were common in the West during the mid- to late 19th century.

Chinese immigrants often accepted lower wages than American workers. They gained a reputation for working hard; many took dangerous railroad jobs. For these reasons, many Americans and other immigrants feared that the Chinese would replace them in the workforce. In California in the 1850s, Chinese immigrants were forced to pay a tax just to work in the mines. They also faced violence and unfair treatment in the community. Many Chinese immigrants left California and moved east to the states of the Great Plains.

By 1880 Chinese immigration had become a national concern. Politicians called for a ban on all Chinese immigration to the United States. The city of Denver, Colorado, had a Chinese population of about 238 in 1880. One of the city's newspapers was very critical of the Chinese. The paper printed stories calling them "pests" and stating that white citizens could starve if any more Chinese immigrants moved to the city.

On October 31, 1880, several men began insulting two Chinese immigrants at a Denver saloon. The immigrants tried to leave but were attacked when they stepped outside. A large crowd had gathered to watch. Denver's police

Incidents of terrorism in the United States and the world increased from 2009 to 2016. Muslims did not carry out all the attacks. Militant Islamists, however, were responsible for some of the deadlier attacks. In November 2015 a group of attackers killed 130 people in Paris, France. In December 2015 two Muslims—one a US citizen and the other his wife, a permanent resident—killed 14 people in San Bernardino, California. An attack in Brussels, Belgium, killed more than 30 people in March 2016.

Trump's executive order

Several days after the attacks in San Bernardino, Trump said that if he were elected president, he would ban all Muslims from entering the United States. He said he would lift the ban once the United States found a better way to check whether the new arrivals posed a threat. However, one of the San Bernardino shooters was an American, born in force could not control the crowd. The city's mayor ordered the fire department to spray the crowd with water hoses. The angry mob moved to the Chinese section of town and began attacking people and destroying businesses and homes. One Chinese man was killed.

The police placed Chinese immigrants in the city jail to protect them from the crowd. Several Denver citizens took immigrants into their homes and business to protect them. By the end of the day, police had restored order. Most of Denver's Chinatown section, however, had been destroyed. A representative from China's government asked US officials to pay for the damage, but the request was denied. None of the rioters was punished for his role in the violence.

In 1882 the US Congress passed the Chinese Exclusion Act, which banned Chinese workers from entering the country. The law remained in effect until 1943.

This sketch by N. B. Wilkins, which appeared in Frank Leslie's Illustrated Newspaper *in 1880, depicts the anti-Chinese riot that occurred in Denver in October of that year.* COURTESY OF THE LIBRARY OF CONGRESS.

Chicago. The other was his wife, a legal permanent resident. Later in the campaign, Trump said his ban would apply only to countries with a history of terrorism against the United States and Europe.

After Trump became president, one of his first acts was to create his immigration ban. Trump issued an executive order to put the ban in place on Friday, January 27, 2017. An executive order is the power of the president to create new policy without having to get approval from the two houses of Congress. The order blocked refugees from any part of the world from entering the United States for 120 days. It blocked refugees from Syria indefinitely. It banned citizens from Iraq, Syria, Iran, Libya, Somalia, Sudan, and Yemen from entering the country for 90 days.

Trump said those seven nations had been labeled as "countries of concern" for supporting terrorism against the United States. He argued that the ban would help protect against an attack similar to the September

Immigrant Rights

11, 2001, attack. Opponents said the order was an unfair ban on Muslims. They noted that none of the hijackers from September 11 was a citizen of the seven banned countries. They pointed out that most of the suspects involved in terrorist attacks in the United States since 2001 were US citizens or people who had lived in the United States for a long time.

Protests begin

Trump's order caused confusion at airports across the country. Airport security officials did not receive proper instructions on how to follow the order. Some travelers from the blocked nations were sent home. Others who were legally allowed to be in the United States were kept at airports and denied entry. Some people were held by authorities.

In New York's John F. Kennedy (JFK) International Airport, protesters began demonstrating on Saturday, January 28, 2017, after two men from Iraq were held by authorities. Officials at JFK Airport shut down several security checkpoints to make room for the protesters. About 2,000 people gathered in New York. Many carried signs criticizing the ban and shouted "Let them in!" Similar protests formed at other airports across the United States. Many protests were organized through social media.

People against President Trump's travel ban come together to protest at Los Angeles International Airport in California on January 29, 2017. It was the second day of protests at that airport. © AYDIN PALABIYIKOGLU/ANADOLU AGENCY/GETTY IMAGES.

Thousands of people demonstrated at O'Hare International Airport in Chicago, Illinois. Hundreds of protesters at Los Angeles International Airport in California shouted anti-Trump slogans. Military veterans and members of Congress joined a rally at Dulles International Airport in Washington, DC. At Philadelphia International Airport in Pennsylvania, people sang protest songs and carried signs that read "Welcome Muslims."

Demonstrations were held at airports in large cities such as San Francisco, California; Dallas, Texas; Seattle, Washington; and Atlanta, Georgia. People even staged rallies at smaller airports such as those in Boise, Idaho, and Albuquerque, New Mexico. On Saturday night a judge in New York City issued an order that temporarily blocked parts of the travel ban.

Tens of thousands of protesters arrived at the nation's airports on Sunday, January 29, to continue the rally against Trump's ban. Lawyers who handle immigration cases volunteered their services in many airports to help stranded travelers. More than 10,000 people rallied Sunday in Battery Park in New York City near the Statue of Liberty. The statue has been a symbol of immigration in the United States since it was built in the 1870s–1880s.

Protests spread worldwide

Later on Sunday a crowd of about 30,000 people marched in downtown Manhattan in New York City. Other large demonstrations were held at the White House in Washington, DC, and in Boston, Massachusetts. Police in Columbus, Ohio, used pepper spray on a crowd of protesters who refused to leave the area in front of the main state government building. Pepper spray is a substance made from cayenne pepper that can cause a burning feeling in a person's eyes, nose, and throat.

Many world leaders spoke out against the travel ban. German Chancellor Angela Merkel told Trump that his order broke UN rules that required countries to help refugees. The protests also spread to several cities in Europe. Thousands of marchers in London, United Kingdom, held signs and chanted, "Hey, hey! Ho, ho! Donald Trump has got to go!" Smaller demonstrations were held in other cities throughout the United Kingdom; in Paris, France; and in Berlin, Germany.

By Sunday night every person who had been held by authorities or stalled by Trump's order was either released or sent back to his or her home nation. Some protests in the United States continued on Monday, January 30. On February 4 thousands of people in London rallied against British leader Theresa May (1956–). Protesters were unhappy with what they saw as her support of Trump. May was one of the first foreign leaders to visit Trump after he became president. She did speak out against the travel ban when it was first issued.

A new ban

In the days after Trump signed his executive order, several states filed lawsuits in federal court to try to overturn the ban. A lawsuit is a legal dispute that is decided by a judge. A federal court hears cases regarding the laws and policies of the United States. On February 3, 2017, a federal court judge blocked the travel ban nationwide. Trump asked another court to reverse that decision, but he was denied. On February 16 Trump said he would change the travel ban to make it more acceptable to the court.

Immigrant Rights

On March 6 Trump signed another executive order. This second travel ban included some of the same rules as the first ban. Under the new order, Syrian refugees would be blocked for only 120 days. The order removed Iraq from the list of banned nations. It allowed citizens of banned nations to enter the country if they were also citizens of the United States or had a proper visa. A visa is a government document that allows a person from another country to stay in the United States.

The new travel ban led to several more protests across the United States. The protests in March were not as large as the ones held in January. Hundreds of people rallied outside the White House and in airports in cities such as San Francisco and San Diego, California. Several states again filed lawsuits against the ban. On March 15 a federal judge in Hawaii blocked it.

The US Supreme Court announced in June that it would decide whether Trump's executive order was legal under the laws of the United States. The court said it would begin hearing arguments in the case in October 2017. In the meantime, the court allowed part of the ban to take effect. It did rule that travelers from the six banned nations must be allowed into the United States if they have close relatives already living there. In late September Trump issued yet another version of his travel ban, which caused the Supreme Court to cancel its hearing on the earlier ban. The new order indefinitely banned people from Chad, Iran, Libya, North Korea, Somalia, Syria, Yemen, and various groups from Venezuela. In December 2017, the US Supreme Court allowed implementation of Trump's third ban pending the completion of challenges to the ban in lower courts. In late December, the US Court of Appeals for the 9th Circuit ruled Trump's ban was unlawful. In mid-January 2018 the US Supreme Court agreed to hear the case. A decision was expected around June 2018.

For More Information

BOOKS

Biddle, Wendy. *Immigrants' Rights after 9/11*. New York: Chelsea House, 2008.

Townsend, Riley M. *The European Migrant Crisis*. Morrisville, NC: Lulu, 2015.

PERIODICALS

"Anti-Islam Movement Stages Anti-Immigration Protests across Europe." *Christian Science Monitor* (February 6, 2016). Available online at https://www.csmonitor.com/World/2016/0206/Anti-Islam-movement-stages-anti-immigration-protests-across-Europe (accessed July 31, 2017).

Bacon, John, and Alan Gomez. "Protests against Trump's Immigration Plan Rolling in More than 30 Cities." *USA Today* (January 29, 2017). Available online at https://www.usatoday.com/story/news/nation/2017/01/29/homeland-security-judges-stay-has-little-impact-travel-ban/97211720/ (accessed August 3, 2017).

Barnes, Robert. "Supreme Court Allows Trump Refugee Ban but Backs Broader Exemptions for Relatives." *Washington Post* (July 19, 2017). Available online at https://www.washingtonpost.com/politics/courts_law/supreme-court-allows-trump-travel-ban-enforcement-but-says-it-must-allow-broader-exemptions-for-relatives/2017/07/19/6945e01e-6bf8-11e7-96ab-5f38140b38cc_story.html?utm_term=.2090312877f9 (accessed August 3, 2017).

Davis, Kenneth C. "America's True History of Religious Tolerance." *Smithsonian* (October 2010). Available online at http://www.smithsonianmag.com/history/americas-true-history-of-religious-tolerance-61312684/ (accessed August 1, 2017).

Dearden, Lizzie. "Poland's Prime Minister Says Country Will Accept No Refugees as EU Threatens Legal Action over Quotas." *Independent* (May 17, 2017). Available online at http://www.independent.co.uk/news/world/europe/poland-no-refugees-eu-legal-action-infringement-quotas-resettlement-beata-szydlo-commission-a7741236.html (accessed July 31, 2017).

Eddy, Melissa. "Big Anti-Immigration Rally in Germany Prompts Counterdemonstrations." *New York Times* (January 12, 2015). Available online at https://www.nytimes.com/2015/01/13/world/europe/big-anti-immigration-rally-in-germany-prompts-counterdemonstrations.html (accessed July 27, 2017).

Gambino, Lauren, Sabrina Siddiqui, Paul Owen, and Edward Helmore. "Thousands Protest against Trump Travel Ban in Cities and Airports Nationwide." *Guardian* (January 29, 2017). Available online at https://www.theguardian.com/us-news/2017/jan/29/protest-trump-travel-ban-muslims-airports (accessed August 3, 2017).

Hingston, Sandy. "Bullets and Bigots: Remembering Philadelphia's 1844 Anti-Catholic Riots." *Philadelphia Magazine* (December 17, 2015). Available online at http://www.phillymag.com/news/2015/12/17/philadelphia-anti-catholic-riots-1844/ (accessed August 1, 2017).

Horn, Heather. "The Staggering Scale of Germany's Refugee Project." *Atlantic* (September 12, 2015). Available online at https://www.theatlantic.com/international/archive/2015/09/germany-merkel-refugee-asylum/405058/ (accessed July 31, 2017).

WEBSITES

Batha, Emma. "Europe's Refugee and Migrant Crisis in 2016. In Numbers." World Economic Forum, December 5, 2016. https://www.weforum.org/agenda/2016/12/europes-refugee-and-migrant-crisis-in-2016-in-numbers (accessed July 27, 2017).

"Early American Immigration Policies." US Citizenship and Immigration Services, September 4, 2015. https://www.uscis.gov/history-and-genealogy/

our-history/agency-history/early-american-immigration-policies (accessed August 7, 2017).

Ellis, Mark R. "Denver's Anti-Chinese Riot." Encyclopedia of the Great Plains. http://plainshumanities.unl.edu/encyclopedia/doc/egp.asam.011 (accessed August 7, 2017).

"Europe Migrant Crisis: Protests at Greece-Turkey Border Fence Follow Latest Deadly Water Crossings." Australian Broadcasting Corporation, January 24, 2016. http://www.abc.net.au/news/2016-01-25/greece-turkey-fence-protest-follows-deadly-water-crossings/7110956 (accessed July 27, 2017).

Grinberg, Emanuella, and Eliott C. McLaughlin. "Travel Ban Protests Stretch into Third Day from US to UK." CNN, January 31, 2017. http://www.cnn.com/2017/01/30/politics/travel-ban-protests-immigration/ (accessed August 3, 2017).

López, Gustavo, and Kristen Bialik. "Key Findings about U.S. Immigrants." Pew Research Center, May 3, 2016. http://www.pewresearch.org/fact-tank/2017/05/03/key-findings-about-u-s-immigrants/ (accessed August 7, 2017).

"Migrant Crisis: Migration to Europe Explained in Seven Charts." BBC News, March 4, 2016. http://www.bbc.com/news/world-europe-34131911 (accessed July 27, 2017).

"Pro-Migrant Rallies in Europe and Australia Draw Thousands." BBC News, September 12, 2015. http://www.bbc.com/news/world-europe-34233725 (accessed July 27, 2017).

Schrag, Zachary M. "Nativist Riots of 1844." Encyclopedia of Greater Philadelphia. http://philadelphiaencyclopedia.org/archive/nativist-riots-of-1844/ (accessed August 1, 2017).

Zong, Jie, and Jeanne Batalova. "Chinese Immigrants in the United States." *Migration Information Source*, September 29, 2017. http://www.migrationpolicy.org/article/chinese-immigrants-united-states (accessed November 7, 2017).

11

Independence Movements

Grito de Lares **342**

Gandhi Leads Salt March **346**

The Velvet Revolution **352**

People have fought for their independence throughout history. Powerful nations and empires have stretched out and taken control of distant lands to increase their wealth and power for many centuries. They usually did this through colonization, colonialization, or occupation. Colonization refers to creating a colony in a foreign land and sending people to live there. Colonialization involves taking control of an area by establishing governmental power over the people who live there. Occupation occurs when another country takes control of a populated place by force. Often times, the people who have colonized or those who lived in conquered lands believed they had a better understanding of how they should be governed. Growing tired of foreign rule, they decided to rise up and take control of their countries. These independence movements have taken many different forms and played out in very different ways.

Independence movements have helped to shape the world's political makeup. Many countries that are part of the modern world started out as colonies. A colony is an area where a group of people have settled or live that is away from their homeland. Usually, the colony is governed by the country of origin of its members. Some of the countries that were once colonies include Australia, Mexico, and the United States. There are many others as well. Modern independence movements, such as those related to Morocco's occupation of Western Sahara and Greenland's struggle to gain full independence from Denmark, continue to shape the world and the lives of everyone in it.

Independence movements in history

One of the most famous independence movements in modern history was the American Revolution (1775–1783), also known as the American War

Independence Movements

WORDS TO KNOW

Activist: One who takes action to support or oppose an issue.

Ashram: A religious retreat.

Autonomy: Self-government.

Bloc: A group of nations that work together toward a common interest.

Civil disobedience: A public refusal to follow certain laws as a peaceful form of protest.

Colonialism: An economic system in which Western European nations controlled various underdeveloped countries located around the world.

Colonies: Territories that are settled by emigrants from a distant land and remain subject to or closely connected with the parent country.

Communism: A political system in which private ownership of property is eliminated and government directs all economic production. The goods produced and accumulated wealth are, in theory, shared relatively equally by all.

Labor union: An organization of workers that is formed to protect their rights and interests.

Resistance: The effort to fight against a powerful force.

Revolution: An attempt to end the rule of one government and begin another one.

Strike: The temporary stoppage of work by employees as a form of protest.

of Independence. By the start of the 16th century, European countries including Spain, Great Britain, and France had already established colonies in the New World.

Problems between Great Britain and its colonies in North America slowly grew over time. Because Great Britain wanted to make as much money from its colonies as possible, the British government forced colonists to pay many different taxes. There were taxes on everything from stamps to tea, sugar, and paper. Eventually the colonists became upset about how much money they were being forced to pay in taxes. They also grew angry because they felt their voices were not being heard in Parliament. Parliament was Great Britain's main lawmaking body. By the middle of the 18th century, the colonists were ready to think seriously about seeking independence.

As things got worse in the colonies, one especially important protest took place. On December 16, 1773, a group of unhappy colonists in Massachusetts held a protest against the Tea Act. British Parliament passed the Tea Act in May 1773. It placed no new taxes on the colonies, but the colonists viewed the act as another policy created without their

Independence Movements

THE DESTRUCTION OF TEA AT BOSTON HARBOR.

An illustration depicting the Boston Tea Party. COURTESY OF THE LIBRARY OF CONGRESS.

consent. In the middle of the night, colonists climbed aboard three British ships docked in Boston Harbor. Once on board, they dumped the tea the ships were carrying into the water. This famous act of protest became known as the Boston Tea Party. The Boston Tea Party helped turn the colonists' anger into a full revolution.

The American colonists' struggle for freedom turned violent just two years after the Boston Tea Party. The American Revolution broke out in 1775. A colonial lawmaking body called the Continental Congress wrote the Declaration of Independence the next year. The Declaration of Independence laid out all of the colonists' complaints against Great Britain. It also announced the colonists' desire to become their own nation. The fight for independence continued until colonists defeated the British Army and a peace agreement was reached in 1783. With that, the United States of America was born.

Independence Movements

Independence across the Americas Many other European colonies in the Americas also began seeking independence after the United States won its freedom. Many of these other independence movements took place in the colonies that Spain and France established outside of the United States and Canada. Most began in the 19th century. By the beginning of the 20th century, almost all of the Spanish and French colonies in the Americas were independent.

Among the first and most important of these independence movements was the Haitian Revolution (1791–1804). France governed Haiti for many years, bringing in thousands of slaves from Africa to work on sugar plantations. In 1791 the African slaves began to rebel against French control. By 1804 the slaves were victorious. Their defeat over the French inspired many others in the Caribbean and Central and South America to fight for freedom themselves.

Just a few years after the Haitian Revolution, Mexico started its own independence movement. Mexico had been a Spanish colony for hundreds of years. In 1810 Catholic priest Miguel Hidalgo (pronounced e-thal-go; 1753–1811) began calling for independence. Mexico's fight for freedom lasted until rebel forces finally overcame Spanish forces in 1821.

Several South American colonies also began seeking independence from Spain around the same time as Mexico. These movements were headed by military and political leader Simón Bolívar (pronounced bo-lee-var; 1783–1830). Bolívar's success eventually resulted in the creation of Venezuela, Bolivia, Colombia, Ecuador, Peru, and Panama as independent nations.

Simón Bolívar. COURTESY OF THE LIBRARY OF CONGRESS.

The last Spanish colony in the Americas to become independent was Cuba. The people of Cuba began pushing back against Spanish rule in the late 19th century. Spain tried to control the island by force, but Cuba had a powerful friend in the United States. The United States traded goods with Cuba and did business with its people. There were also many Americans who lived on the island. When an American naval ship exploded in Havana Harbor, Cuba, in February 1898, the United States blamed Spain and declared war. After the three-month Spanish-American War (1898), Spain surrendered Cuba, Puerto Rico, the Philippines, and Guam to the United States. The latter three initially became US territories, but the Philippines eventually gained independence in 1946. Cuba was granted its independence in 1902.

Peaceful independence Not all independence movements involve war. Some colonies win their independence in more peaceful ways. One country that gained its independence peacefully was Jamaica. The island of Jamaica was claimed by Spain in the early 16th century. After almost 150 years of Spanish rule, it was taken over by the British. Jamaica remained a British colony for several hundred years.

During that time, many Jamaicans were unhappy being ruled by Great Britain. While some rebel groups used violence to fight back, most Jamaicans did not. The Jamaican independence movement was mainly carried out through political action and labor protests. This approach allowed Jamaica and Great Britain to work together in establishing Jamaica as an independent nation in 1962.

Independence in the East Many Asian countries that were controlled by European powers also won their freedom through independence movements. Vietnam was one of these. France took control of Vietnam in the late 19th century. When this happened, Vietnam became part of a larger French-controlled region called French Indochina. This region also included Cambodia and Laos.

Many Vietnamese people wanted to break away from France. Vietnamese rebels fought against the French for many years. Their best chance for success came during World War II (1939–1945). Japan entered Vietnam during the war and pushed the French out of power. After Japan was defeated in the war, the Vietnamese declared their independence. France was not ready to give up its claim to the region, however.

Early talks between the French and Vietnamese did not go well and war soon began. Fighting continued until the Vietnamese won a key battle at Dien Bien Phu in 1954. The French had no choice but to give in after this defeat. The resulting peace talks led to Vietnam being divided in half. While a government controlled by the Communist Party took over in the north, a non-Communist government came to power in the south. The two sides then struggled for power in what became known as the Vietnam War (1954–1975), with North Vietnam supported by the Soviet Union and China and South Vietnam supported by the United States When the war

Independence Movements

During the Vietnam War, the country was divided into North and South Vietnam. © 2018 CENGAGE®.

finally ended, the north's Communist government took complete control of independent Vietnam.

Protest and independence

Most independence movements involve some type of protest. These protests may be violent or peaceful. Whatever form they take, protests can go a long way toward helping an independence movement succeed. Some of the most successful independence movements are those that are fueled by strong acts of protest. The effect that the Boston Tea Party had on the American Revolution is a prime example of this. The Boston Tea Party inspired colonists and helped them overcome the British. In short, protest and revolution go hand in hand.

Grito de Lares Puerto Rico was one of the Spanish colonies that started to move toward independence in the 19th century. Many Puerto Ricans were tired of Spanish rule and wanted to control their own country. Others wished to have more of a say in their government but still wanted to be part of Spain. These disagreements made independence a difficult goal to achieve. It would take a big shift for all Puerto Ricans to get behind the idea of independence.

The event that put Puerto Rico on the path to independence was the Grito de Lares uprising. Although short-lived, the uprising pitted Puerto Rican revolutionaries against Spanish rule. The rebels took over the town of Lares and tried to set up an independent Puerto Rican government. The uprising lasted only one day before it was put down by Spanish forces. Even though it failed, the Grito de Lares uprising helped bring the people of Puerto Rico together and created more interest in independence. This interest eventually led to Puerto Rico becoming a territory of the United States when Spain finally gave up its claim on the island after the Spanish-American War in 1898.

Gandhi's Salt March One of the biggest independence movements in history was India's 20th-century struggle for freedom from British control. The British ruled over India for hundreds of years and often mistreated the

CRITICAL THINKING QUESTIONS

1. Why was the Grito de Lares an important part of Puerto Rican history, even though it failed to achieve its goal?

2. Can independence movements be considered a success even when they do not lead to independence? Why or why not?

3. Do you think peaceful protests are an effective way to achieve change? Why or why not?

4. How do peaceful protests help to drive independence movements?

5. What do you think was the importance of Gandhi choosing the Salt Acts to protest?

6. Do you think Gandhi's arrest and imprisonment helped advance India's independence movement? Why or why not?

7. What do you think was the biggest success of the Velvet Revolution?

8. Why do you think the Soviet Union banned patriotic music and other cultural activities in Estonia and other areas it occupied?

9. How did Solidarity, the first independent trade union in Communist Poland, help bring an end to Communism in Poland?

Indian people. Many Indians wanted to be free of British rule, but all efforts failed. By the middle of the 20th century, they were ready to try again but needed someone to kick-start the independence movement. That person was lawyer and activist Mohandas Gandhi (pronounced gahn-DEE; 1869–1948). An activist is a person who fights for political or other types of change. Gandhi was often called Mahatma, which refers to a person who is admired for his or her wisdom and thoughtfulness of others.

Gandhi was a strong supporter of Indian independence. He also believed in using nonviolent means of resistance. Resistance is the effort to fight against a powerful force. Gandhi wanted to use nonviolent protest as a way of advancing the Indian independence movement. His idea was to focus on a set of unfair British laws called the Salt Acts. The Salt Acts prevented Indians from collecting or selling salt, which was a vital mineral in their diet. In 1930 Gandhi led a march to the seaside where salt deposits were found. He and his followers extracted salt from the sea in protest of the law. Gandhi's Salt March played an important part in starting the Indian independence movement once again and eventually bringing an end to British rule in India.

The Velvet Revolution Some independence movements are nonviolent. Such was the case with the Velvet Revolution in Czechoslovakia (pronounced

Independence Movements

check-o-slo-VAH-kee-a). The nation was one of the Communist countries in central Europe that were beginning to turn against the Soviet Union in the late 1980s. The Communist government enforced strict rules on the people of Czechoslovakia, and the Czechs were ready for change. The Velvet Revolution was the key to their success.

The Velvet Revolution was a nonviolent movement in which the people of Czechoslovakia called for the Communist government to give up its power and allow democracy to take root. It included a series of protests and other activities that brought people together and put a great deal of pressure on the government. In the end, it led to the fall of the Communist Party in Czechoslovakia and the establishment of a new democratic government. It also helped lead to Czechoslovakia's split into the separate countries of Slovakia and the Czech Republic in 1993.

Grito de Lares

LOCATION: Puerto Rico

DATE: September 23, 1868

The Grito de Lares (the Cry of Lares), or the Lares Uprising, was a short-lived revolution of the 19th century. It occurred when the people of Puerto Rico tried to win their independence from Spain. Puerto Rico is an island located between the Caribbean Sea and the Atlantic Ocean. At the time, Puerto Rico was a colony of Spain. A colony is an area of land where a group of people have settled or live that is away from their homeland. Usually, the colony is governed by the country of origin of its members. This armed uprising began on September 23, 1868. It lasted only one day and ended when Spanish forces defeated the rebel fighters. Although it did not lead to independence, the Grito de Lares was one of the most successful revolutions in Puerto Rican history, as it marked the beginning of the end of Spanish control.

At the time of the revolution, Puerto Rico had been under Spanish colonial rule for several hundred years. Puerto Rican citizens had endured centuries of abuse at the hands of their Spanish rulers. By the late 1860s, angry Puerto Ricans were ready to revolt.

The rebels fighting in the Grito de Lares were no match for Spanish forces. After their defeat, the rebels knew they could not win Puerto Rican independence by force. More people from different parts of Puerto Rican society then came together in the independence movement. This set in motion the events that led to Spain's exit from Puerto Rico at the end of the 19th century.

Colonial Puerto Rico

Puerto Rico became a colony of Spain in the late 15th century. Christopher Columbus arrived on the island on November 19, 1493. He claimed the island for Spain. At the time, about 30,000 to 60,000 native people called Taino (pronounced ti-NO) lived on the island. When Columbus arrived, he called the island San Juan Bautista. He named it after the biblical figure St. John the Baptist (c. 4 BCE–c. 31 CE). The first permanent European settlement in Puerto Rico was Caparra. It was founded in 1508.

The Spanish colonized Puerto Rico by sending groups of people to live there. Spain set up a colonial government, which authorized the colonists to enslave the Taino people, forcing them to work the land. The Taino staged an unsuccessful revolt in 1511. After this, King Ferdinand II (1452–1516) of Spain let the colonists recruit the native people, but they were still forced into labor. This outlawed punishment of the Taino and improved their working conditions. Over the next few decades, however, most of the Taino were wiped out by disease and violence. The Spanish then brought in African slaves to help with planting and harvesting crops.

The Spanish colonization of Puerto Rico continued throughout the 16th century. The Caribs, a local raiding tribe, often threatened early Spanish settlements, but Spain never lost control of the island to them. The Spanish also successfully defended the island from several attempted French, English, and Dutch invasions over the next few centuries.

Colonial life Puerto Rico became a major agricultural center. By the mid-19th century, the colony was producing large quantities of sugar, coffee, tobacco, and other goods. It eventually grew into one of the world's largest exporters of these goods. The money Puerto Rico made on trade was good for Spain's economy. The Puerto Ricans worked hard to produce these goods to benefit Spain.

The rebels fighting in the Grito de Lares were no match for Spanish forces. After their defeat, the rebels knew they could not win Puerto Rican independence by force.

Life was difficult for the people of Puerto Rico. Most people lived in poverty and few had access to a proper education. The agriculture industry was strong, but many farmers lacked the tools necessary to do their jobs efficiently. A poor system of roads also made transporting goods difficult. On top of all that, Spain created many taxes that hurt poor Puerto Ricans. Many Puerto Ricans were unhappy under Spanish control.

Puerto Ricans rebelled against Spain many times but failed. Between 1702 and 1711, for example, a group of rebels from several Puerto Rican towns overthrew Spanish authorities and created their own town councils. Spain eventually regained control in these areas, though. Another organized attempt to achieve independence unfolded in the town of San Germán in the early 19th century. The Spanish military quickly ended the uprising. Similar small-scale revolts also took place in 1823 and 1838.

Part of the reason so many rebellions failed was because Puerto Ricans were not fighting for full independence. Most citizens wanted more say in what went on in their local governments while remaining under Spanish control. As time went on, a growing movement for full independence began to take shape. Puerto Ricans realized that a complete split from Spain was the only way to solve the island's problems. It was the rise of this movement that eventually led to the Grito de Lares.

Grito de Lares

The Puerto Rican independence movement began to heat up in 1866. Starting that year, pro-independence activists took the first steps toward revolution. They began to speak openly against Spanish tyranny in public places. Tyranny is a harsh form of government control. They also called on the Spanish government to give them greater control of their own country. Spain ignored these requests and instead created more taxes for Puerto Ricans to pay. Puerto Rico's Spanish governor also ordered the arrest of anyone calling for reform.

Spain's refusal to address Puerto Ricans' complaints fueled the independence movement. It set the wheels of revolution in motion. Two revolutionaries who headed the independence movement were Ramón Emeterio Betances (pronounced bay-TAN-ces; 1827–1898) and Segundo Ruiz Belvis (pronounced BELL-vis; 1829–1867). The two were previously forced out of Puerto Rico by Spanish authorities for their political activities. In 1867 Betances and Ruiz Belvis founded the Revolutionary Committee of Puerto Rico. They hoped to build a forceful resistance to Spanish rule. Betances wrote a series of statements that criticized the Spanish government and called on Puerto Ricans to revolt. These statements were passed around the entire colony. These writings helped to convince people that it was time to take a stand against Spain.

Between 1867 and 1868 the Revolutionary Committee secretly worked to build a resistance force. People from all levels of Puerto Rican society, from wealthy landowners to merchants, workers, and even slaves, wanted to fight against Spain. Once this force was gathered, plans were made for an armed uprising. Organizers originally planned for the revolt to take place on September 29, 1868. The date was moved up to September 23 when news of the plan reached Spanish authorities.

On the day of the uprising, several hundred rebels met at a hacienda (pronounced HA-cee-en-da), or estate, in a small town outside Lares. After making their final preparations, the rebels marched into Lares around midnight and began their assault. They started by robbing stores owned by Spanish businesspeople. Eventually they moved to city hall and took control of the city. Once they claimed authority, the rebels declared Puerto Rico's independence. They introduced a new constitution, established a new government, and began arresting Spanish merchants and officials.

A statue of Ramón Emeterio Betances was placed in the Plaza de la Revolución in Lares, Puerto Rico. © EDDTORO/SHUTTERSTOCK.COM.

The rebels named Francisco Ramírez Medina president of the newly independent Puerto Rico. Afterward they moved to the nearby city of San Sebastián del Pepino to continue the uprising. When they arrived, however, Spanish forces were ready and waiting. Unable to overcome the Spanish defenses, the rebels were defeated and the survivors were arrested. With that, the Grito de Lares uprising came to an end.

Results

Even though it was considered a failure, the Grito de Lares was an important moment in Puerto Rican history. It marked the beginning of the island's move away from Spanish control.

After the revolt, the Spanish government was finally convinced to recognize Puerto Ricans' demands for greater autonomy, or self-government. Spain also began allowing Puerto Ricans to have their own political parties. They were also granted freedom of the press and freedom of assembly. These changes also cleared the way for the end of slavery of Africans in Puerto Rico.

Puerto Rico continued to be a Spanish colony until the late 19th century. In 1897 Spain approved the Charter of Autonomy. This made the island an independent nation. Although a Spanish-appointed governor led it, Puerto Rico finally had a local lawmaking body made up mostly of elected officials. The new government did not remain in place for long. At the time, Spain began fighting the Spanish-American War (1898). This war was fought between Spain and the United States for control of Cuba. Puerto Rican revolutionaries who still wanted full independence tried to get the United States to include Puerto Rico in its struggle against Spain. This led to a fight between American and Spanish forces in Puerto Rico that lasted from May to August 1898. In a peace treaty signed that December, Spain agreed to leave Puerto Rico. It turned control of the island over to the United States. Puerto Rico has remained a US territory since that time.

The Grito de Lares continues to be seen as a symbol of Puerto Rico's struggle for independence. The site of the uprising was designated a National Historic Site in 1969, honoring the Puerto Rican desire for self-rule.

Gandhi Leads Salt March

LOCATION: India

DATE: 1930

The Salt March was an important nonviolent protest against British rule in India. It was also called the Dandi March. Indian civil rights leader Mohandas Gandhi led the protest in 1930. Gandhi's Salt March was an act of civil disobedience. Civil disobedience is a public refusal to follow certain laws as a form of peaceful protest. The protest targeted the Salt Acts, which banned Indians from gathering or selling salt. The Salt March was a chance for Indians to take a stand against the British government. It marked the start of a serious campaign for Indian independence from Britain.

India was controlled by Britain in one way or another for nearly 350 years. During that time, the British government exercised strict control over the Indian people. The British denied Indians a political voice in their own country. Indians were forced to follow British law without having a role in their own government. As a result, there was a great deal of tension between the Indian people and the British government. Even though activists worked hard to win a limited role in government for Indians by the early 20th century, the possibility of India's full independence from Britain still seemed unlikely.

The 1920s marked the beginning of a new era in Indian history. Activists such as Gandhi strongly supported Indian independence. Gandhi thought independence should be gained through peaceful protests and acts of civil disobedience. He believed that these were the best ways to challenge authority and achieve meaningful change. Gandhi's biggest success when it came to peaceful protest was the Salt March. This protest united the Indian population against the British. The Salt March sparked the Indian independence movement and eventually led to the end of British rule in India.

Rise of the British Raj

The British government first took an interest in India in the early 17th century. At the time, the Dutch controlled a nearby chain of islands called the Spice Islands. Seeking to establish a British presence in the region, Elizabeth I (1533–1603), queen of England, signed a royal charter creating the British East India Company (EIC). The EIC oversaw British trade in India.

To do its job in organizing Indian trade, the EIC had to establish its authority over the region. This was difficult because India was divided into separate territories ruled by different leaders. Over time, the EIC made agreements with each of these leaders. The EIC then slowly united most of the separate Indian territories. This eventually made the EIC a powerful organization with a great deal of political influence.

As the EIC rose to power, a growing number of Indians began to rebel against British involvement in their country. While the EIC had little trouble dealing with such rebellions in the 18th century, the situation

Activists such as Gandhi strongly supported Indian independence. Gandhi thought independence should be gained through peaceful protests and acts of civil disobedience. He believed that these were the best ways to challenge authority and achieve meaningful change.

Independence Movements

The Singing Revolution, Estonia, 1988

In the 1980s Estonia and a number of other republics or states along the Baltic Sea in northern Europe worked to win their independence from the Soviet Union. Unlike other republics, Estonia's most powerful weapon in the fight for freedom was its culture. One of Estonia's oldest and strongest cultural traditions was the creation and performance of choral music. As the Estonian people began to push for independence in the mid-1980s, they used their rich tradition of choral music to stir national pride and drive opposition to Soviet rule.

For several years, determined Estonians regularly gathered in large crowds to sing traditional songs and inspire a sense of patriotism. Many of these events also included the performance of songs that were banned by Soviet leadership. Also banned were the display of symbols that reflected Estonian culture. This simple act of nonviolent protest became known as the Singing Revolution. It was remarkably successful in bringing Estonians together and putting pressure on Soviet leadership to accept that change was coming.

The Singing Revolution reached its high point in 1988. In the summer and fall of that year, around 860,000 Estonians signed a petition, which is a formal written request. The petition declared the end of Soviet rule and the formation of the Republic of Estonia. Estonia then began the process of becoming an independent nation. By the early 1990s, Estonia had its own government institutions and held its first democratic elections. Since that time, Estonia has remained a free and independent country. It continues to celebrate its long-standing cultural traditions and the music that freed it from Soviet control.

began to spiral out of control in the 19th century. The EIC's breaking point came in 1857 with the Indian Mutiny (1857–1858). Although the British managed to overcome the rebellion in the end, it was clear that the EIC no longer had the ability to control India. At that point, the British government did away with the EIC and took direct government control of India. The system of government that was created became known as the British Raj.

Life under the Raj The British Raj enforced strict rules over India. Almost from the beginning, the Indian people were forced to pay heavy taxes. This left many in poverty and struggling to survive. Many Indians also faced starvation because of widespread famine, or lack of food. There was little the Indian people could do to improve their situation. They were not permitted to hold any important political positions in the early Raj government. Life during the Raj was a challenge.

By the late 19th century, Indians began pushing to have more control over their country. Their first major success came with the creation of the Indian National Congress (INC) in 1885. The INC was an organization that worked to promote increased Indian involvement in the Raj government. At first, this was as much as the organization hoped to accomplish. After India played an important role in helping Britain achieve victory in World War I (1914–1918), however, the INC began calling for full independence.

When the independence movement began, Gandhi was becoming one of the INC's most prominent members. After leaving India as a young man to study law in Britain, Gandhi went to work as a lawyer in South Africa. He first became a civil rights activist there. When he returned to India in 1915, Gandhi joined the INC. Within just a few

Gandhi before the Salt March

This primary source excerpt is from a speech that Mahatma Gandhi gave on March 11, 1930. It occurred on the night before Gandhi's historic Salt March.

In all probability this will be my last speech to you. Even if the Government allow me to march tomorrow morning, this will be my last speech on the sacred banks of the Sabarmati. Possibly these may be the last words of my life here.

I have already told you yesterday what I had to say. Today I shall confine myself to what you should do after my companions and I are arrested. The programme of the march to Jalalpur must be fulfilled as originally settled. The enlistment of the volunteers for this purpose should be confined to Gujarat only. From what I have been and heard during the last fortnight, I am inclined to believe that the stream of civil resisters will flow unbroken.

But let there be not a semblance of breach of peace even after all of us have been arrested. We have resolved to utilize all our resources in the pursuit of an exclusively nonviolent struggle. Let no one commit a wrong in anger. This is my hope and prayer. I wish these words of mine reached every nook and corner of the land. My task shall be done if I perish and so do my comrades. It will then be for the Working Committee of the Congress to show you the way and it will be up to you to follow its lead. So long as I have reached Jalalpur, let nothing be done in contravention to the authority vested in me by the Congress. But once I am arrested, the whole responsibility shifts to the Congress. No one who believes in non-violence, as a creed, need, therefore, sit still. My compact with the Congress ends as soon as I am arrested. In that case volunteers. Wherever possible, civil disobedience of salt should be started. These laws can be violated in three ways. It is an offence to manufacture salt wherever there are facilities for doing so. The possession and sale of contraband salt, which includes natural salt or salt earth, is also an offence. The purchasers of such salt will be equally guilty. To carry away the natural salt deposits on the seashore is likewise violation of law. So is the hawking of such salt. In short, you may choose any one or all of these devices to break the salt monopoly.

SOURCE: Gandhi, Mahatma. "On the Eve of the Historic Dandi March." Bombay Sarvodaya Mandal & Gandhi Research Foundation. Available online at http://www.mkgandhi.org/speeches/dandi_march.htm (accessed October 15, 2017). Courtesy of Bombay Sarvodaya Mandal / Gandhi Book Centre.

years, he became one of the organization's most important leaders. Once the INC started its push for full independence, Gandhi, who was always opposed to violence, argued that the best way to pursue that goal was through peaceful protest and civil disobedience. Gandhi wanted to get the Raj government's attention and show British leaders that Indians were serious about independence. He knew he needed to stage a demonstration that could not be ignored.

The Salt March

Gandhi's protest focused on the Salt Acts. The British Salt Acts were a series of laws that caused Indians much suffering. Under these laws, Indians were forbidden from collecting or selling salt. This meant that they had to purchase their salt from British merchants at high prices. Because Indians generally ate little meat and depended on added salt for their diet, the Salt Acts were extremely harsh. Gandhi decided that protesting the Salt Acts would be a good way to unite the people of India against the British Raj.

Once he set his sights on targeting the Salt Acts, Gandhi began planning his protest. He initiated a demonstration centered around a symbolic act of civil disobedience. Gandhi planned to lead a march from his ashram (pronounced ASH-rum), which is a religious retreat. He would march from his ashram near the city of Ahmedabad in the western state of Gujarat to the coastal town of Dandi. Once there he and his followers would intentionally break the law by collecting salt at the shoreline.

Gandhi's march began on March 12, 1930. That morning, he and 78 followers left the ashram and began their 240-mile (386-kilometer) journey to the sea. They traveled about 10 to 15 miles (16 to 24 kilometers) per day. Along the way, Gandhi stopped and spoke to large crowds of people who came to hear his message of achieving independence. As Gandhi moved from town to town, more people joined the march. By the time Gandhi reached Dandi on April 5, he was accompanied by thousands of fellow protesters.

Protest at Dandi Once he arrived at Dandi, Gandhi began the main part of his protest. He walked to the seaside to work the salt flats there. Police tried to prevent him from succeeding by stamping the salt deposits into the muddy ground. Gandhi persisted and plucked a clump of salt from the earth. With this act, Gandhi welcomed the thousands gathered with him to begin collecting salt in protest.

In the weeks that followed, similar peaceful acts of civil disobedience took place across India. Many people began making and selling their own salt. As many as 60,000 people were arrested. One of them was Gandhi himself. He was arrested on May 5, 1930, after announcing that he would lead a peaceful march on the Dharasana salt works. While the march went on without him, Gandhi remained behind bars until early 1931.

Independence Movements

Indian spiritual leader Mahatma Gandhi and politician Mrs. Sarojini Naidu (center, front) are shown during the Salt March as they protest the government's rules on who can produce salt. © KEYSTONE/GETTY IMAGES.

Results

When Gandhi was released from prison, he was considered a national hero. He was also granted a meeting with Lord Irwin (1881–1959), the British viceroy of India. A viceroy is a governor of a colony who represents the king or queen of the ruling country. At their meeting, Gandhi agreed to end the ongoing salt protests if Lord Irwin allowed Indians an equal role at an important upcoming conference. The conference would be held in London to discuss India's future. Although that conference did not go as well as Gandhi hoped, it was a major step forward for India.

The real success of the Salt March was the influence it had on the broader independence movement. The Salt March drew a great deal of attention to the suffering Indians faced under British rule. This put pressure on the British government to reconsider its position. It also helped to unite the Indian people in their opposition to the Raj. With Gandhi's leadership, the independence movement continued into the late 1940s. Britain finally agreed to surrender control of India in 1947. With that, India finally won its independence.

The Velvet Revolution

LOCATION: Czechoslovakia
DATE: 1989

The 1989 Velvet Revolution, or Gentle Revolution, was a nonviolent movement that led to the fall of Communism in Czechoslovakia. Communism is a political system in which one ruling party controls all businesses and means of production in a country. Property is owned collectively and people are paid according to what they need. The revolution also marked the end of Czechoslovakia's association with the Soviet Union and its exit from the Eastern Bloc. The Eastern Bloc was a group of European nations that were associated with the Soviet Union. The Velvet Revolution helped pave the way for the Velvet Divorce. This was the 1993 division of Czechoslovakia into the Czech Republic and Slovakia.

The people of Czechoslovakia struggled to maintain their rights since 1948. In that year, the Communist Party first came to power in the country. The party gained complete control in 1968 and ruled over Czechoslovakia with absolute authority. Communist leaders restricted everything from economic activity to education to free speech. Criticism of the government was not allowed, and many of those who dared to speak out were often arrested and imprisoned.

By the late 1980s, things began to change in Czechoslovakia. Chaos erupted during a peaceful student protest in November 1989. After this, a movement of nonviolent resistance arose and shook the Communist government in Czechoslovakia. The Soviet Union was already struggling to survive because of the collapse of Communism there. The Czechoslovakian Communists had little choice but to surrender control of the country and allow democracy to take hold.

Independence Movements

The rise of Communism

Czechoslovakia is located in central Europe. It was first founded in 1918 as an independent nation after World War I (1914–1918). The nation was formed by joining the Czech Republic and Slovakia together. Prior to that, the two countries were part of the Austro-Hungarian Empire. During World War II Germany took partial control of Czechoslovakia. As a result, the nation was divided until the war's end. It later reunited and became part of the Soviet Union in 1948. It joined several other European countries in forming the Eastern Bloc.

The Communist Party rose to power in Czechoslovakia after the country joined the Soviet Union. The Communists exerted strong control over the people. Early on, the party's authority was not widely challenged. Over time, however, a movement to loosen the party's hold on Czechoslovakia began to form. For a brief time in the late 1960s, this movement seemed likely to succeed.

Prague Spring The political reform movement in Czechoslovakia reached its height in 1968. Early that year, reform leader Alexander Dubček (1921–1992) was elected first secretary of the Communist Party of Czechoslovakia. This marked the beginning of a brief period during which the government scaled back its unfair tactics. It even encouraged liberties such as human rights and freedom of the press. This period came to be known as the Prague Spring.

The reforms of the Prague Spring were helpful for the people of Czechoslovakia. The changes did not sit well with the leaders of the Soviet Union, though. In August 1968 the Soviets sent troops to Czechoslovakia to gain control of the government. Determined Czechs responded with various types of nonviolent civil resistance. These acts delayed the Soviet takeover for about eight months. A hard-line Communist government was then put in place and Dubček was removed from power.

Communist control After the Prague Spring, the Communists in Czechoslovakia quickly became one of the harshest governments in the Eastern Bloc. All of the rights that the Czechoslovakian people had just been granted during the Prague Spring were taken away. Freedom of speech was severely restricted. Opportunities for education and economic gain became very limited. Any opposition to the Communist government was banned. Those who did speak out against the government were dealt with harshly. Between 1948 and 1989, about 250,000 Czechs were

Freedom of speech was severely restricted. Opportunities for education and economic gain became very limited. Any opposition to the Communist government was banned.

Independence Movements

The Red Army along with troops from Hungary, Poland, Bulgaria, and East Germany invaded Czechoslovakia on August 20, 1968. The action put an end to the popular demonstrations known as the Prague Spring. © KEYSTONE-FRANCE/GAMMA-KEYSTONE VIA GETTY IMAGES.

imprisoned for political reasons. Almost 250 were executed. Thousands more were placed in forced labor camps.

Many Czechs were unhappy with the Communist government and its brutal tactics. The government's unwillingness to accept opposition left little room for open resistance. Most resistance instead played out in secretive groups. Educated people got together secretly to discuss the political situation and make plans for achieving change in Czechoslovakia. Much opposition was also expressed culturally through songs and plays. A fully open resistance movement finally arose more than 20 years after the Prague Spring.

The Velvet Revolution

On November 17, 1989, a large crowd of students gathered in the Czech capital of Prague. They were there to mark the 50th anniversary of the death of demonstrator Jan Opletal (1915–1939). Opletal was killed during a protest against the German takeover of his country in the early stages of World War II. The anniversary demonstration began peacefully. However, it soon turned into an anti-Communist protest. When the students began moving toward Wenceslas Square, which is the center of business and culture in Prague, police surrounded and attacked them. About 167 protesters were injured.

The Prague incident immediately sparked a strong anti-Communist movement in Czechoslovakia. Additional protests were held across the country. Workers' unions also organized labor strikes to put pressure on the Communist government. A strike is a temporary stoppage of work by employees as a form of protest. As a result, the demand for democracy grew quickly.

The most important part of the rising anti-Communist movement was led by author, poet, and activist Václav Havel (pronounced hav-EL; 1936–2011). Havel was part of the Prague Spring and was deeply committed to the ideals of democracy. In response to the violence in Prague, Havel formed a political group known as the Civic Forum. The Civic Forum called for the end of the Communist government. It also demanded the release of political prisoners and an investigation into the Prague attack on the student protesters.

The Civic Forum began a series of peaceful activities designed to draw attention to its cause and to force the Communist government to back down. These activities became known as the Velvet Revolution and included numerous marches and other protests. During these demonstrations, protesters rattled their keys as a symbol of unlocking the doors so that the Communist government could leave. To show their national pride, the public sang songs that the Communist government had banned. There were also many public gatherings. At these events, concerned people spoke openly about the problems with the Communist government and the need for change. Additional labor strikes also helped to demonstrate the movement's ability to impact society.

The Communist government tried to resist the Civic Forum's calls for change. However, a growing movement made it impossible for the government to withstand the mounting public pressure for long. By early December, the party's hold on power was quickly slipping away. Unable to maintain control, the entire Communist decision-making body, called the politburo (pronounced pa-LET-byur-o), resigned later in the month.

Independence Movements

Gdansk Shipyard Strike, Poland, 1980

Poland was one of the countries that fell to Communism and joined the Eastern Bloc after World War II. Like Czechoslovakia, it became a democratic nation after Communism's collapse in the late 1980s. Poland's shift to democracy started with the spread of a nationwide labor movement.

Poland was faced with serious economic problems in 1980. In response, the Polish government raised food prices while lowering wages. This made life difficult for Polish workers who suddenly could not afford to feed their families. Before long, workers across the country began to go on strike.

In the middle of Poland's economic crisis, a forklift operator named Anna Walentynowicz (pronounced vah-len-teen-OH-vitch; 1929–2010) was fired from her job at the Lenin Shipyard in the city of Gdansk. She participated in labor union activities and was believed to be fired because of this. A labor union is an organization of workers that is formed to protect their rights and interests. Walentynowicz was a popular employee at the shipyard, and her firing upset many people. Her coworkers started a sit-down strike to get her job back. The protesters numbered 17,000 and they demanded that Walentynowicz be rehired.

The Polish government tried to stop news of the strike from spreading, but word got out. This led to many more strikes across the country. After days of tense debate, the government came to an agreement with the workers. Walentynowicz got her job back, and the strike ended. A short time later, Polish workers under the leadership of Lech Wałesa (1943–) formed a national trade union called Solidarity, the first union not controlled by the Communist Party. Over time, Solidarity grew into a widespread social movement that gained Western support. It eventually helped bring an end to Communism in Poland and other Eastern European nations in the late 1980s and early 1990s. Wałesa was later elected president of Poland.

On December 29, 1989, a new democratic government with Havel as president was formed.

Results

The success of the Velvet Revolution had an immediate effect. Czechoslovakia quickly began to change over to a democratic nation. Many of the old Communist limits on free speech and other liberties were lifted. The new government also started rebuilding the economy and creating a free society.

The new government's work was not easy. This was partly because the Communist government left behind a complicated political structure. There were many different political parties and ruling bodies in the government. This made it almost impossible to achieve a majority decision on any significant issue. In addition, Slovaks in the nation began to call for

Independence Movements

Friends and relatives of striking workers listen to labor leader Lech Wałesa outside the gates of the Lenin Shipyard in Gdansk, Poland, in August 1980. The new trade union that formed at that time, called Solidarity, eventually included 10 million members. Wałesa went on to become president of Poland. © AFP/GETTY IMAGES.

Slovakia to become an independent country again. The country had been joined with the Czech Republic after World War I.

Before long, it started to look like Czechoslovakia was not going to survive as a unified nation. Czechs and Slovaks had different ideas about how the country should be run. The two groups simply could not agree on how to move forward. For example, one such issue that raised debate was the question of what the new nation's name should be. While most Slovaks wanted to call the country Czecho-Slovakia, the Czechs mostly favored Czechoslovakia. This illustrated the differing political views of Czechs and Slovaks. For a time after World War I, the country was called Czecho-Slovakia. During the Communist era, it became known as Czechoslovakia. Afterward, Slovaks who wished to move as far away from their Communist history as possible wanted to restore the hyphen. More conservative Czechs, on the other hand, wanted to keep the Communist era spelling. Both spellings were used informally.

By 1992 a separation between the two sides seemed unavoidable. After elections were held in June of that year, it became clear that Czechoslovakia was divided beyond repair. As a result, the country officially broke into the Czech Republic and Slovakia on January 1, 1993. This division was known as the Velvet Divorce.

In the years after their split, the Czech Republic and Slovakia both grew as independent democratic nations. Both also came to earn high marks from the international community for their commitment to human rights. The end result may have been a little different than what was expected, but the Velvet Revolution was successful at achieving major political change through nonviolent means.

For More Information

BOOKS

Duany, Jorge. *Puerto Rico: What Everyone Needs to Know*. New York: Oxford University Press, 2017.

Duberstein, John. *A Velvet Revolution: Vaclav Havel and the Fall of Communism*. Greensboro, NC: Morgan Reynolds, 2006.

Henderson, Timothy J. *The Mexican Wars for Independence*. New York: Hill and Wang, 2009.

Jimenez de Wagenheim, Olga. *Puerto Rico's Revolt for Independence: El Grito de Lares*. Princeton, NJ: Markus Wiener, 1993.

Kuhn, Betsy. *The Force Born of Truth: Mohandas Gandhi and the Salt March, India, 1930*. Minneapolis, MN: Twenty-First Century Books, 2010.

Pierce Flores, Lisa. *The History of Puerto Rico*. Santa Barbara, CA: Greenwood Press, 2010.

Weber, Thomas. *On the Salt March: The Historiography of Mahatma Gandhi's March to Dandi*. New Delhi, India: Rupa, 2009.

Wheaton, Bernard, and Zdeněk Kavan. *The Velvet Revolution: Czechoslovakia, 1988–1991*. Boulder, CO: Westview Press, 1992.

PERIODICALS

"Caribbean Independence: Past, Present and Future: A Reckoning (Pt I)." *Gleaner* (Jamaica; September 7, 2012). Available online at http://jamaica-gleaner.com/gleaner/20120907/news/news1.html (accessed August 8, 2017).

Engler, Mark, and Paul Engler. "How Did Gandhi Win? Lessons from the Salt March." *Dissent* (October 10, 2014). Available online at https://www.dissentmagazine.org/blog/gandhi-win-lessons-salt-march-social-movements (accessed August 2, 2017).

Schwab, Katharine. "A Country Created through Music." *Atlantic* (November 12, 2015). Available online at https://www.theatlantic.com/international/archive/2015/11/estonia-music-singing-revolution/415464/ (accessed August 2, 2017).

WEBSITES

"Czech Republic Slovakia: Velvet Revolution at 25." BBC News, November 17, 2014. http://www.bbc.com/news/world-europe-30059011 (accessed August 4, 2017).

"The Grito de Lares: The Rebellion of 1868." Library of Congress. https://www.loc.gov/collections/puerto-rico-books-and-pamphlets/articles-and-essays/nineteenth-century-puerto-rico/rebellion-of-1868 (accessed July 31, 2017).

Kurtz, Lester. "Czechoslovakia's Velvet Revolution (1989)." International Center on Nonviolent Conflict, March 2008. https://www.nonviolent-conflict.org/czechoslovakias-velvet-revolution-1989 (accessed August 4, 2017).

Moscoso, Francisco. "The Grito de Lares, 1868." Encyclopedia of Puerto Rico. https://enciclopediapr.org/en/encyclopedia/the-grito-de-lares-1868/#1463492689874-dd12c211-136e (accessed July 31, 2017).

"Spanish-American War for Cuba's Independence." Exploring Florida: A Social Studies Resource for Students and Teachers. https://fcit.usf.edu/florida/lessons/s-a_war/s-a_war1.htm (accessed August 8, 2017).

"The Velvet Revolution, November 1989." Association for Diplomatic Studies and Training. http://adst.org/2015/10/the-velvet-revolution-november-1989 (accessed August 4, 2017).

12

Indigenous Peoples' Rights

AIM Occupation of Wounded Knee 367

Aboriginal Land Rights Protest 375

Preservation of Amazon Rain Forest Campaign 379

Dakota Access Pipeline Protest 384

Indigenous (pronounced in-DI-juh-nus) people are the original inhabitants of a region. They are natives who lived in an area before colonists or other people arrived there from the outside world. According to the organization Amnesty International, there were about 5,000 different indigenous groups living in more than 70 countries around the world in 2017.

Many indigenous people have been absorbed into larger countries and cultures over time. When this happens, indigenous people are often denied the same rights as others in society and are treated like second-class citizens. They are often expected to leave their traditional practices and beliefs behind and accept the customs of the larger culture they are joining. These challenges make life difficult for indigenous people and put their traditional cultures at risk of disappearing forever.

Indigenous people also risk losing control of their lands when colonists move into their homelands. Many indigenous people throughout history have been forced off their lands by colonists and others looking to expand their own territories. This can be a major challenge because most indigenous people have a very close relationship with the land on which they live. Leaving that land by choice or force is often quite troubling for indigeous people.

Most indigenous people view the lands on which they live as sacred and an essential part of what defines them as a group. This means that indigenous people are often very protective of their lands. When other people arrive and try to take over these lands, indigeous peoples end up in a very difficult situation. They have to defend their lands to preserve their culture. This is why land rights are such an important issue for indigenous people. Without the land, there is little chance that their culture will survive.

WORDS TO KNOW

Aboriginal: A member of the indigenous people of a region, such as Australia or Canada.

Census: Provides a count of a population for specific information about the people living in a country.

Hydroelectric energy: Energy that is generated from the force of moving water.

Indigenous: Originating in or living naturally in a certain region.

Natural resources: Water, soil, minerals, and other materials that are found in nature and are important to humans.

Pepper spray: A spray made from cayenne pepper that can cause a burning feeling in a person's eyes and throat when applied.

Pipeline: A system of connected pipes that is used to transport liquids and gases over a long distance.

Reservation: An area of land set aside for use by certain people.

Reservoir: A human-made lake created to store water for use by a community.

Second-class citizen: A person who belongs to a social or political group with fewer rights and opportunities than the dominant members of the group.

Tribunal: A decision-making body that has authority in a specific area.

Indigenous rights in history

Indigenous people in North America struggled to maintain control over their lands when Europeans arrived in the 15th century. It is believed that there were millions of indigenous people living in North America when the first European explorers reached the New World. The later arrival of permanent European settlers soon caused problems for these people.

From the beginning, European settlers in North America established communities on lands that previously belonged to indigenous people. As more settlers arrived over time, their colonies grew. This meant that the indigenous people in what is now Canada, Mexico, Central America, and the United States had to give up more of their lands, sometimes pushed off their lands by force. This often resulted in violence and death. At the same time, European settlers brought diseases to North America that were especially harmful to indigenous people. Between the effects of disease and fighting over control of the land, the number of indigenous people quickly declined.

In the United States, the problems Native Americans faced got worse after the colonies gained their independence from Great Britain. When the young United States expanded west during the 19th century, Native Americans were pushed off their lands again. In many cases, this happened by force. Losing their lands continued to make it difficult for Native

CRITICAL THINKING QUESTIONS

1. Why do you think the AIM protesters chose to occupy Wounded Knee in 1973?

2. Do you think the Lakota Sioux leaders at Pine Ridge did the right thing by calling for an end to the standoff? Why or why not?

3. Why do you think Aboriginals chose to hold their march in connection with Australia Day? Why was this important?

4. Which of the different names for Australia Day do you think is most accurate? Why?

5. Do you think the benefits of a dam outweigh the risks to indigenous communities? Why or why not?

6. Why was it important that Chief Raoni Metuktire worked with Sting during his campaign to stop the dam project? How did this help Raoni to be successful?

7. What were the main concerns the Standing Rock Sioux had against the Dakota Access Pipeline?

8. Do you think the Army Corps of Engineers did an adequate study of the Standing Rock site before the pipeline was started? Why or why not?

Americans to maintain their traditional culture and way of life. This led their numbers to drop even lower. By the early 20th century, there were only about 250,000 Native American people left in the country.

Many of the Native Americans who survived were forced to live on reservations. These reservations were special areas of land set aside just for Native Americans. Life on reservations was not easy. Native Americans living on reservations had little chance to improve their lives because they did not have the same rights and freedoms as other Americans. Many people thought the best solution to this problem was to help Native Americans become more like the European American members of society. This meant that Native Americans would have to give up their own way of life. In some cases, this too happened by force.

The challenges surrounding Native American land rights continued even into the 21st century. Many Native Americans still live on reservations and struggle to maintain their culture. As they continue to lose control of their lands, their connection to their traditions grows weaker. This means that the Native American way of life is still in danger of one day being lost forever. Even hundreds of years after the first European settlers arrived, Native Americans still face great dangers because of the loss of their traditional lands.

The Māori Indigenous land rights issues are not unique to the United States. Indigenous people around the world struggle to protect their lands from governments and others who want to use them to their advantage. The Māori are one such group of people. The Māori are an indigenous people from New Zealand who spent much of the 20th century trying to maintain control of their traditional lands.

European settlers first arrived in New Zealand in the 19th century. The indigenous Māori tried to work with their new neighbors at first. They agreed to the Treaty of Waitangi in 1840, New Zealand's founding document. The Māori thought that the terms of the agreement protected their land rights, but they were wrong. Over time, the New Zealand government passed special laws that allowed it to take control of many Māori lands. Within only 100 years, the Māori lost most of their territory.

Eventually the Māori began to fight back against the New Zealand government. Their biggest success in this fight came in 1975. In that year, the Māori held a large protest march to Wellington, which is New Zealand's capital city. Once there, the protesters met with government leaders and called for an end to the theft of Māori land. This peaceful protest raised a great deal of awareness and led the New Zealand government to create a body called the Waitangi Tribunal. A tribunal is a decision-making body that has authority in a specific area. The Waitangi Tribunal reviewed and settled many of the Māori's land claims. Much of the land taken from the Māori in the 19th century was eventually returned. Although the Māori's struggle for control of their lands still continues, they have made much progress in their fight.

Land rights protests

Like the Māori, many other indigenous people have used peaceful protests to fight for their land rights. These sorts of protests can do much to change the way people view the importance of indigenous land rights. Although not all indigenous protests are successful, those that are can go a long way toward helping others in their efforts to preserve their culture and homelands.

American Indian Movement (AIM) occupation of Wounded Knee Native Americans have long been mistreated by the US government. Many have been forced off their lands and made to live on special reservations removed from society where their rights and needs are often ignored. Some Native Americans decided the best way to overcome this abuse was to bring attention to the poor treatment they received from the US government. This led to the American Indian Movement (AIM) of the 1960s and 1970s. The

Various groups of native people have protested the loss of their lands and the destruction of that land and the environment. A group of Aboriginal peoples in Canada called Idle No More formed in 2012 to voice their concerns about social injustice, inequality, destruction of the environment, and other issues. Here, the group is shown protesting in Vancouver, British Columbia, Canada, in 2013. They were demonstrating against the government's treatment of Aboriginal peoples. © SERGEI BACHLAKOV/SHUTTERSTOCK.COM.

point of AIM was to force the US government to start treating Native Americans with the respect and dignity they deserved.

The most well-known AIM protest was held at Wounded Knee in 1973. Wounded Knee is a site in South Dakota where American soldiers killed several hundred Native Americans in 1890. On February 27, 1973, about 200 AIM protesters gathered at Wounded Knee to demonstrate against the government's disregard for Native Americans' civil rights. The demonstration quickly turned violent as armed protesters and government agents occasionally fired shots at one another for weeks. Tensions continued until the protest finally ended on May 8. The protesters did not achieve their goal of convincing the US government to live up to its previous treaties and other promises. However, they did manage to draw attention to the poor treatment Native Americans received from the government and created more public pressure for change.

Aboriginal land rights protest Like Native Americans, the indigenous people of Australia suffered after the arrival of European settlers in their lands. Indigenous Australians are known as Aboriginals (pronounced aa-bah-RIJ-eh-nulz). Aboriginals were forced from their lands and treated like second-class citizens after the arrival of Europeans on the continent in 1788. The day British ships first arrived in Australia is celebrated each year as Australia Day on January 26. Although other Australians remember this as the day their country began, many Aboriginals remember it as the day their way of life became threatened.

Australia Day has long been a day of sorrow for Aboriginals. They often mark the day with protests and marches meant to call attention to their suffering. The biggest march of this kind ever held took place during the 200th anniversary of Australia Day in January 1988. More than 40,000 Aboriginals and other marchers took to the streets of Sydney to bring their concerns to the world about how they were being mistreated. By protesting, the Aboriginals drew attention to their cause and helped to improve their standing in Australian society.

Preservation of Amazon rain forest awareness campaign The Amazon rain forest in South America is home to many indigenous people who are struggling to keep control of their traditional lands. The Kayapo (pronounced ky-AH-poh) are one of these peoples. They live in a region found along the banks of the Xingu (pronounced SHEEN-goo) River. Their lands were threatened in the 1980s when the Brazilian government decided to build a dam on the river. The Kayapo leader Chief Raoni Metuktire (pronounced REE-oh-nee may-TUK-tire; c. 1930–) led a movement against the dam project in 1989 that was a major victory for indigenous rights.

Raoni used his position as chief to raise awareness about the risks the dam posed to his people. He worked with rock musician Sting (full name Gordon Sumner; 1951–) to bring the Kayapo struggle to the world's attention. Raoni was eventually able to put enough pressure on the government that the dam project was put on hold for many years. Although the dam was later built, Raoni's campaign in the 1980s was one of the most successful indigenous rights movements in history at that time.

Dakota Access Pipeline protest Indigenous people are sometimes forced to fight not only to maintain control of their lands but also to protect those lands from damage by dangerous activities. Such a challenge brought about the 2016 Dakota Access Pipeline protest in North Dakota. The issue began when an energy company announced that it wanted to build an oil pipeline that would pass near the Standing Rock reservation, which stretches across both North Dakota and South Dakota. A pipeline is a system of connected pipes used to transport liquids and gases over a long distance. Many people were against this pipeline because they worried that the oil being transported might spill and cause the water in the area to be unusable.

Native Americans ride their horses through the protesters camp on the edge of the Standing Rock Reservation in December 2016. The group was attempting to halt the construction of the Dakota Access Pipeline. © HELEN H. RICHARDSON/THE DENVER POST VIA GETTY IMAGES.

Efforts to build the pipeline eventually led to a protest in 2016. Protesters gathered and began a demonstration at a site called the Sacred Stone Camp. Protesters stayed at the camp for months to call attention to their fight against the pipeline and persuade the government to take action. They remained there until police finally forced them to leave in February 2017. By that time, President Donald Trump (1946–) had already signed an order allowing the project to move forward. Although the Standing Rock protest was not a success, the fact that it gained widespread support across the United States and even inspired the November 15 National Day of Action against the pipeline demonstrated the power indigenous people have to sway public opinion when they stand up for their rights.

AIM Occupation of Wounded Knee

LOCATION: Wounded Knee, South Dakota

DATE: February 27–May 8, 1973

Throughout US history, the government has clashed with Native Americans many times over land rights, governing issues, and respect for the indigenous people's way of life. In 1973 an armed group of Native Americans, who were angry with the treatment of their people, took control of some land in South Dakota. The place they chose was the site of a deadly conflict between the US Army and Native Americans in 1890. The group held several people captive. Police and federal agents responded to the incident, and the two sides faced off for 71 days. By the time the incident was over, two Native Americans had been killed and a federal agent was badly hurt.

Treatment of Native Americans

Experts are not sure how many indigenous people lived in North America (including Canada, Mexico, Central America, and the United States) before the Europeans arrived. Based on historical evidence, they estimate the number could have been between 2 million and 12 million. By the 1800s, the Native American population in the United States had fallen considerably. The 1860 census recorded about 339,000 Native Americans living in the United States. A census provides a count of a population for specific information about the people living in a country. In 1890 that number was down to roughly 307,000.

As the United States continued to grow, the government needed to find more land for its expanding population. It looked to lands in the south and southeastern part of the country—lands settled by Native Americans. Many were moved onto "reserved lands," or reservations, west of the Mississippi River. The government signed treaties, or agreements, with the Native Americans. Some of these treaties purchased the land, requiring the indigenous people to relocate. Some of these treaties promised native people the right to own the land where the Native Americans made their new homes.

In some cases, the treaties promised Native Americans the right to govern their own reservation in return for their land. If the indigenous people resisted, the government would often use military force to make them move. At times, Native Americans were pushed into signing treaties they did not fully understand. Even with an agreement in place, Native Americans were sometimes forced to move from the land promised to them. After 1871 the US government stopped signing treaties with Native Americans.

Once indigenous people were settled on reservations, many Americans believed the native people would fit into society better if they gave up their traditional practices. The native people were encouraged to adopt an

"American" way of life and religious beliefs. Many native children were removed from their homes and sent to special schools where they were made to learn English. They were not allowed to speak their indigenous languages or practice their traditions.

Wounded Knee Massacre of 1890

By 1890 almost all Native Americans were living on reservations. A belief had begun to spread among many tribes that if they performed a special dance, called the Ghost Dance, the white settlers who took their land would be defeated. They believed that by performing the dance, their dead ancestors would come back to life, increasing their numbers in order to push back the settlers. They also believed that the special shirts they made for the dance would protect them from bullets. US military leaders were worried that the Ghost Dance would inspire Native Americans to stage an uprising.

The Ghost Dance was especially popular among the Lakota Sioux (pronounced lah-KOH-tah SOO). Many members of the tribe were living on reservations in southern South Dakota. In December 1890 police came to the Standing Rock Reservation to arrest Chief Sitting Bull (c. 1834–1890), the leader of the Lakota Sioux. Authorities believed he was a leader in the Ghost Dance movement. During the arrest, a fight broke out and Sitting Bull was killed.

This illustration of the Sioux performing the Ghost Dance appeared in the Illustrated London News *on January 3, 1891.* COURTESY OF THE LIBRARY OF CONGRESS.

Indigenous Peoples' Rights

Occupation of Alcatraz

Alcatraz Island is located in San Francisco Bay in California. A fortress was built on the island in 1850 and was used to hold military prisoners. In the early 20th century, the fortress was turned into a highly secure prison. In 1934 Alcatraz became a federal prison. Some of the most dangerous criminals in the United States were sent to Alcatraz. The prison, nicknamed "The Rock," closed in 1963.

After the prison closed, Native Americans wanted to build a cultural center and school on the island. On November 9, 1969, a small group of Native Americans led by Richard Oakes (1942–1972) landed on Alcatraz Island. The group called themselves Indians of All Tribes and claimed the island in the name of all Native Americans.

The group was removed from the island by authorities on November 10. Oakes returned with about 100 Native Americans and reclaimed Alcatraz on November 20. The group ignored warnings to leave and began moving into the houses built for the former prison guards. On top of a large water tower, they spray-painted the slogan, "Home of the Free Indian Land."

Rather than use force to remove the protesters, the government at first allowed them to stay as long as they were peaceful. Officials tried to work out a deal with the occupiers, but the Native Americans insisted they be granted full ownership of the island.

As the occupation moved into 1970, some protesters left the island. Oakes himself left in January 1970 after his stepdaughter fell down a stairway and was killed. As time went on, living conditions got worse. More people left Alcatraz until only 15 people remained by June 1971, when federal agents arrived and forced them to leave. The occupation may not have achieved its goal, but it did inspire similar Native American protests at historical sites across the United States. In the end, the occupation of Alcatraz was instrumental in the establishment of the

---

Other Native Americans in the region were afraid they would be the victims of violence as well. A group of several hundred Lakota Sioux fled Standing Rock and headed for the larger Pine Ridge Reservation, where they believed they would be safer. Along the way, they were surrounded by US Army soldiers at Wounded Knee Creek.

As the army searched the camp for weapons, someone fired a gun. No one knows for sure who fired first, but the soldiers thought they were under attack and began shooting. The soldiers outnumbered the Native Americans and had better weapons. Some Native Americans tried to run away but were killed by the soldiers. Historians believe as many as 300 Lakota Sioux were killed. Many of those killed were women and children. The Wounded Knee Massacre, as it came to be called, angered Native Americans.

Indigenous Peoples' Rights

self-governance policy set in place by US President Richard M. Nixon (1913–1994). This policy gave back the rights of Native Americans to make decisions about their own welfare.

A man stands outside a tepee set up on Alcatraz during the Indians of All Tribes' takeover of the abandoned federal penitentiary. The Golden Gate Bridge in San Francisco Bay is behind him. © BETTMANN/GETTY IMAGES.

American Indian Movement

Wounded Knee was the last major battle between Native Americans and the US military. In the 20th century, the US government tried to change many of the ways it handled Native American issues. It no longer forced native people to give up their culture. It also stopped making native children attend special schools. Living conditions for many Native Americans, however, continued to be harsh. Many could not find jobs and faced unfair treatment in the white community. Native reservations were also some of the poorest areas in the United States.

In 1968 a group of Native Americans gathered in Minnesota to discuss the problems facing their community. They were angry about the years of mistreatment their people had endured. They blamed the US government for breaking its promises to Native Americans. They also felt many federal programs that were supposed to help them were not working. To help address the problems they were facing, the group formed the American Indian Movement (AIM).

AIM staged several protests in the late 1960s and early 1970s. In 1969 the group Indians of All Tribes (IAT) was involved in the takeover of Alcatraz Island in California's San Francisco Bay. In 1972 AIM members marched on Washington, DC, to protest the 371 Native American treaties they said the government broke. During the march, AIM members also occupied the offices of the Bureau of Indian Affairs (BIA). The BIA is the government agency that manages reservation land.

The occupation begins

In early 1973, the Lakota Sioux at the Pine Ridge Reservation in South Dakota wanted their tribal chief removed from office. They thought he was dishonest and his decisions were hurting the reservation. When an attempt to replace him failed, reservation leaders asked AIM to help. The chief went to the offices of the BIA police for protection.

About 200 AIM members in trucks and cars drove into Pine Ridge on the night of February 27, 1973. They were led by Russell Means (1939–2012) and Dennis Banks (1937–2017), two of the cofounders of AIM. The group decided to take over the small town of Wounded Knee, the site of the 1890 massacre. They chose the site because they felt it was a symbol of the US government's mistreatment of Native Americans.

The AIM members carried guns and took 11 residents of the town captive. Police and federal agents were called in and surrounded the protesters. On February 28 the members of the opposing sides began firing shots at one another. AIM gunmen also shot at any car or small airplane that came too close. Protest leaders made several demands in return for the release of the people being held captive. They wanted the US government to investigate the BIA and the leaders of the Lakota Sioux reservations in South Dakota. They also wanted the government to address the broken Native American treaties.

Occupation turns deadly

As the occupation at Wounded Knee lasted several weeks, members of AIM and federal agents continued to fire shots at one another. About a month after the standoff began, a federal agent was shot. His injuries left

Indigenous Peoples' Rights

Witnesses at Wounded Knee, 1890

This primary source excerpt from the Annual Report of the Commissioner of Indian Affairs *in 1891 contains eyewitness accounts of what transpired at Wounded Knee Creek, South Dakota, on December 29, 1890. Specifically, this excerpt includes the "Account Given by Indians of the Fight."*

TURNING HAWK, Pine Ridge. [We heard people were coming toward our agency.] These people were coming towards Pine Ridge Agency, and when they were almost on the agency they were met by the soldiers and surrounded and finally taken to the Wounded Knee Creek, and there at a given time their guns were demanded. When they had delivered them up the men were separated from their families, from their tepees, and taken to a certain spot. When the guns were thus taken and the men thus separated there was a crazy man, a young man of very bad influence and in fact a nobody, among that bunch of Indians fired his gun, and of course the firing of a gun must have been the breaking of a military rule of some sort, because immediately the soldiers returned fire and indiscriminate killing followed....

AMERICAN HORSE. The men were separated as has already been said from the women, and they were surrounded by the soldiers. Then came next the village of the Indians and that was entirely surrounded by the soldiers also. When the firing began, of course the people who were standing immediately around the young man who fired the first shot were killed right together, and then they turned their guns ... upon the women who were in the lodges standing there under a flag of truce, and of course as soon as they were fired upon they fled, the men fleeing in one direction and the women running in two different directions. So that there were three general directions in which they took flight.

There was a woman with an infant in her arms who was killed as she almost touched the flag of truce, and the women and children of course were strewn all along the circular village until they were dispatched.... The women as they were fleeing with their babes on their backs were killed together, shot right through, and the women who were very heavy with child were also killed. All the Indians fled in these three directions, and after most of them had been killed a cry was made that all those who were not killed or wounded should come forth and they would be safe. Little boys who were not wounded came out of their places of refuge, and as soon as they came in sight a number of soldiers surrounded them and butchered them there.

SOURCE: "Account Given by Indians of the Fight at Wounded Knee Creek, South Dakota, December 29, 1890." *Annual Report of the Commissioner of Indian Affairs, for the Year 1891.* Available online at http://images.library.wisc.edu/History/EFacs/CommRep/AnnRep91p1/reference/history.annrep91p1.i0004.pdf (accessed October 15, 2017). Courtesy of University of Wisconsin.

him unable to walk. In an effort to force the protesters to surrender, the agents turned off the electricity and water to the town. They also tried to cut off food supplies to the protesters. Some people who supported AIM flew planes over the town and dropped shipments of food.

Indigenous Peoples' Rights

Oscar Bear Runner, a member of the American Indian Movement (AIM), stands with a rifle at Wounded Knee, South Dakota, on the Pine Ridge Reservation. AIM was negotiating with US government officials in an effort to settle the situation in the town in 1973. © BETTMANN/GETTY IMAGES.

On the 50th day of the occupation, several AIM members ran out to get one of the food shipments. The federal agents began firing and a protester was killed. On April 26 another Native American was killed. AIM leaders wanted to keep holding out at Wounded Knee. The second death, however, made the Lakota Sioux leaders call for an end to the occupation.

Protest ends

The two sides began to talk about ways to end the standoff. The government promised it would investigate some of AIM's complaints. On May 8, 1973, the Native American protesters put down their guns and surrendered. Some AIM members managed to escape, but Means, Banks, and most of the group were arrested. In September 1973, criminal charges against all AIM members were dropped. A judge ruled the federal authorities had mishandled witnesses and key evidence.

In the years after the occupation, AIM members and federal authorities fought several battles at Pine Ridge. In 1975 two federal agents were killed in a shootout. An AIM member was arrested and convicted of the crime. However, many claim he is innocent. By 1978 many of the group's members were in jail, and the leadership disbanded. However, AIM is still active today.

The occupation of Wounded Knee did not accomplish most of the goals AIM wanted. It did raise awareness about Native American rights. Many people watched the standoff on television news, and the protesters received a great deal of public support. The occupation even inspired a protest by famed movie actor Marlon Brando (1924–2004). On March 27, 1973, Brando sent a Native American woman to the Academy Awards to decline his award for best actor. In a speech on national television, the woman mentioned Wounded Knee and called for an end to the mistreatment of Native Americans.

Aboriginal Land Rights Protest

LOCATION: Sydney, Australia

DATE: January 26, 1988

European nations including Great Britain, Spain, and France worked for centuries to increase their wealth and power by founding colonies around the world. When colonists arrived in a new land, trouble often followed for the native people who were already living there. In many places, settlers forced native people from their lands. Sometimes this even involved violence and killing. Native people were often mistreated in other ways as well. Often, they were denied equal rights by new governments. In other cases, colonists disliked indigenous people just for being different. Simply put, the arrival of colonists frequently led to suffering for native people.

Australia was one of the many places where indigenous people underwent great change when colonists arrived. Australia's indigenous people, known as Aboriginals, have endured much suffering since British colonists first arrived in 1788. At the start, the native people were pushed out of their lands by force. Many were killed while trying to defend their homelands. Later, the Aboriginals were often denied equal rights and prevented from having a voice in Australian government.

No matter what challenges they have faced, Australia's many indigenous people have always been willing to stand up for their rights. The Aboriginal community has staged many marches, protests, and other demonstrations over the years in its fight for equal rights. One of the most famous of these protests took place during the 200th anniversary of Australia Day in 1988. On that day, thousands of Aboriginals and others marched into the middle of a celebration marking the day that British colonists first arrived in Australia. The peaceful march brought a great deal of attention to the Aboriginal cause. It helped to remind the world that the Aboriginal community is as much a part of Australia as the rest of its people.

A painful history

The suffering of Australia's Aboriginal population dates back to 1787, when Great Britain first set its sights on the continent. That year, King George III (1738–1820) of Britain officially made Australia part of the British Empire. Australia was not going to be an ordinary colony, however. Instead, it was going to be used to help solve a pressing problem. Britain's prisons were dangerously overcrowded at the time, so government officials decided to start a prison colony in Australia. Even though the British knew that there were native people living in Australia, they laid claim to the land using a principle called terra nullius. This meant that the British believed they were free to take control of Australia because it did not belong to anyone else as far as they were concerned.

The first group of British ships to set sail for Australia was called the First Fleet. The First Fleet landed in what is now called Sydney Harbour on January 26, 1788. The new colonists quickly encountered Aboriginals who were living in the area. There was little conflict at first. When the colonists began to move farther inland, however, the Aboriginals felt threatened. Many violent battles for control of the land took place in the years that followed, and many Aboriginals were killed.

The Aboriginals' suffering continued, even as Australia went from being a British colony to an independent country. As Australian communities grew, more Aboriginals were forced off their lands. Thousands also died because of the diseases the British brought with them to Australia. Most indigenous people who survived were badly mistreated as Australians worked to do away with Aboriginal practices. One 20th-century law even allowed for Aboriginal children to be taken away from their parents and placed with white families. Life for Aboriginals was very difficult.

Australia Day The day of the First Fleet's arrival in Sydney Harbour has long been celebrated as one of the most important days in Australian history. The anniversary of the fleet's arrival was often marked by special dinners in the colonial era. At different times, it was known as First Landing Day or Foundation Day. It later became known as Australia Day and made a national holiday.

Australia Day has always been a difficult day for the country's Aboriginal population. To many Aboriginals, Australia Day marked the day their traditional way of life ended. Aboriginals tend to think of it as the day of invasion or the day they had to start doing whatever it took to survive. That is why most Aboriginals call it Invasion Day or Survival Day instead of Australia Day. Many Aboriginals also find Australia Day hurtful because they are often left out of traditional celebrations.

While most Australians celebrate Australia Day with parades and parties, Aboriginal groups often use it as a day to hold protests and marches. One of the first of these marches took place on Australia Day in 1938. That year's celebration marked the 150th anniversary of the First Fleet's landing. About 100 people took part in a march through Sydney called the Day of Mourning and Protest. The marchers protested the treatment of Aboriginals. They called on the Australian government to start making up for all the wrongs done to Aboriginals over the years. While the Day of Mourning and Protest was the first major protest movement of its kind, it was not the last or the most effective.

The march

Australia Day 1988 marked the 200th anniversary of the First Fleet's arrival. The Australian government planned an especially big celebration in honor of this historic anniversary. It was highlighted by a re-creation of the First Fleet's arrival in Sydney. This celebration was designed to bring all Australians together as one nation, but it did little to include Aboriginals or address their concerns. Even so, determined Aboriginals still made their voices heard.

While the Australian government spent millions of dollars putting together their grand celebration, a group of Aboriginals planned a protest. The group arranged to hold a march during which they would protest the Australia Day celebration and call on the government to restore their land rights. The resulting protest ended up being one of the largest of its kind in Australian history.

January 26, 1988, marked the day of the elaborate Australia Day celebration. In protest, more than 40,000 Aboriginal and non-Aboriginal demonstrators marched through the city to Hyde Park near Sydney Harbour. As they paraded through the streets of Sydney, the protesters chanted in support of Aboriginal rights and called for change. When the marchers arrived in Hyde Park, several Aboriginal leaders and activists

In protest, more than 40,000 Aboriginal and non-Aboriginal demonstrators marched through the city to Hyde Park near Sydney Harbour. As they paraded through the streets of Sydney, the protesters chanted in support of Aboriginal rights and called for change.

Indigenous Peoples' Rights

The Aboriginal land rights protest occurred on the 200th anniversary of Australia Day in Sydney, Australia, in 1988. © TIM GRAHAM/GETTY IMAGES.

spoke to the crowd. They praised people of different cultural backgrounds for coming together for an important cause and taking a stand against unfairness. They also called on government leaders to accept that Australia was a better country when people of all races and beliefs were treated as equals.

The 1988 Australia Day march was successful for Aboriginals in many ways. It demonstrated that while setting policies, the Australian government failed to include the Aboriginal point of view. It also showed that Aboriginals were tired of being treated like second-class citizens in their own country and would no longer be silent. The march also brought attention to the poor living conditions and other challenges that Aboriginals faced. It reminded people that Aboriginal suffering started on the same day that other Australians were celebrating.

Results

The Australia Day march did much to help Aboriginals reach their goal of improving their situation. The march increased public awareness of the challenges Aboriginals faced and persuaded many people that something had to be done to help. This put pressure on the government to take action and led to some real change.

Just months after the march took place, Prime Minister Bob Hawke (1929–) announced that the government would make a new treaty, or agreement, with the Aboriginal community. Although this never actually happened, it did lead to a real victory for the indigenous people when the Aboriginal and Torres Strait Islander Commission (ATSIC) was formed in 1990. The ATSIC was a new organization through which Aboriginal people could play a role in the Australian government. Another important step forward came when former Labor Party leader Kevin Rudd (1957–) issued a public apology to Australia's aboriginal people in his first act as prime minister in 2008. In a speech delivered before Parliament, Rudd apologized to Aboriginals for the pain, suffering, and mistreatment they endured at the hands of the Australian government.

The Australia Day march gave Aboriginals a more important place in Australian society. It also put them in a position to start healing old wounds caused by the centuries of mistreatment their people endured. The march allowed Aboriginals to begin working with the government to reclaim some of their rights as the first people of Australia.

Preservation of Amazon Rain Forest Awareness Campaign

LOCATION: Brazil

DATE: 1989

Indigenous people often have to fight to save the lands on which they live. Many people in the modern world want to take advantage of the natural resources these lands offer. Natural resources include water, soil, minerals, and other materials that are found in nature and are important to humans. Indigenous people are frequently forced from their traditional lands so that others can benefit from the area's natural resources. This can be very harmful for indigenous people because it puts their way of life at risk of being lost forever. When this happens, native people who want to preserve their lands have no choice but to fight back.

Some indigenous people of Brazil had to fight to save their homelands from being taken over in 1989. The government of Brazil wanted to build a dam on the Xingu River as a way to create electricity. The Xingu runs through the heart of the Amazon rain forest. A rain forest is a tropical

Indigenous Peoples' Rights

woodland that receives a high amount of rain and contains tall trees and much plant life. The river also runs through the homeland of a native people called the Kayapo. The Kayapo worried that they would be forced from their land if the dam was built. To stop this from happening, they started a movement against the dam project.

Chief Raoni Metuktire (pronounced REE-oh-nee may-TUK-tire; c. 1930–), leader of the Kayapo, took charge of the movement against the dam project and brought his people's concerns to the world. He also teamed up with famous rock-and-roll musician Sting to bring more attention to the protest. Raoni's efforts eventually helped to put the dam project on hold for many years. His success demonstrates the power that indigenous people can have when they take a stand to save their homelands and preserve their way of life.

The Kayapo and the Xingu

The Xingu is a river that runs for more than 1,000 miles (1,609 kilometers) through parts of central and northern Brazil. It flows northward from a state called Mato Grosso until it meets with the Amazon River. About 25,000 people from different indigenous groups live along the Xingu River's banks. Among these are the Kayapo. More than 300 miles (428 kilometers) of the Xingu are in Kayapo territory. This source of water is vital to the Kayapo's ability to survive.

The Kayapo are one of Brazil's many indigenous peoples. Like many of their neighbors, the Kayapo live away from modern society. In fact, they did not make contact with the outside world at all until the mid-20th century. Because they are cut off from the modern world, the Kayapo depend on the land to survive. They rely on the plants and animals found in their territory for food and medicine. Without the Xingu, these resources would not exist. As a result, the Xingu is a central part of the Kayapo way of life. The importance of the river to the Kayapo is even demonstrated in their name. *Kayapo* means "the men from the water place."

Raoni Metuktire is one of the most important Kayapo leaders. He was born in a small village sometime around 1930. He had no contact with the outside world until he met three brothers, Orlando (1914–2002), Claudio (1916–1998), and Leonardo Villas Boas (1918–1961), in 1954. The brothers were activists against the destruction of the indigenous way of life along the Xingu River. They worked with Raoni, teaching him to speak Portuguese, the official language of Brazil. They introduced him to the

The Kayapo are one of Brazil's many indigenous peoples. Like many of their neighbors, the Kayapo live away from modern society. In fact, they did not make contact with the outside world at all until the mid-20th century.

modern world by showing him how others lived in Brazilian society. The brothers also helped him to understand the importance of preserving the Kayapo way of life. This became Raoni's greatest goal as leader of his people—preserving the Kayapo way of life.

The dam The Brazilian government has long wanted to build dams on the Xingu River. Dams are often used to create a kind of energy called hydroelectric power. Hydroelectric power is electric energy that is created by the movement of water. Building dams is one way to harness this power and provide it to modern cities and towns. Brazilian officials first thought about building a series of dams on the Xingu in the 1970s. The Kayapo and other indigenous peoples who lived along the river were against this idea, however. As a result of indigenous resistance, these dams were not built at that time.

For a while it looked like there would be no dams built on the Xingu. This changed when the Brazilian government announced a new plan in the late 1980s. Instead of a series of dams, the government now wanted to build one dam near the town of Altamira. It was to be called the Belo Monte Dam. The Kayapo were against this dam project because it would change their way of life.

The government wanted to build the Belo Monte Dam at a site that was south of where the Kayapo lived. Since the river flows north, this meant that the part of the Xingu that flowed through Kayapo lands would dry up if the dam was built. If the river dried up, the Kayapo would no longer be able to continue their traditional way of life and would have to leave their lands. This left the Kayapo with no choice but to take a stand against the Belo Monte Dam.

The movement

Stopping the Belo Monte Dam was a difficult task for the Kayapo. The Brazilian government planned to build the dam with the support of the World Bank. The World Bank is an international banking organization that gives loans to different countries for development projects. If the Kayapo were going to succeed in preventing the Belo Monte Dam from being built, they would have to convince the World Bank to pull out of the project. For a remote indigenous people living deep in the Amazon rain forest, this seemed to be all but impossible.

Chief Raoni stepped up to lead the fight against the Belo Monte Dam. Unlike most other Kayapo, he already had some experience with the outside world. He met French filmmaker Jean-Pierre Dutilleux (pronounced

Indigenous Peoples' Rights

Cree First Nations Battle Hydro-Québec

In the early 1970s, the government of the Canadian province of Québec announced plans to begin a large hydroelectric project on James Bay on the southern end of Hudson Bay. Hydroelectric energy is generated from the force of moving water. The project included a large dam and several stations where electricity would be produced. The project was to be built in two phases and managed by a government-run company called Hydro-Québec.

In Canada, the indigenous inhabitants are also known as Aboriginals, which include the First Nations, Métis, and Inuit. The Cree are First Nations people who live in the region around James Bay. They realized that the proposed dam would flood some of their communities. It would also destroy much of their traditional hunting and fishing areas.

In 1973 the Cree went to court and asked a judge to stop the project. Although the judge at first did stop the project, a ruling by another court allowed it to continue. The Cree tried to keep up their fight, but they were not able to stop Hydro-Québec from constructing the first part of the project.

In 1975 the Canadian government agreed to give the Cree $255 million and granted them the right to continue to hunt and fish in the area. The government also paid to relocate several Cree villages and promised money to help with education and health care.

When the dam was completed in 1981, it had a harmful effect on the environment. Many caribou were killed by the flooding. Caribou are a source of food and clothing for the Cree. The flooding also created pollution that harmed the area's fish. The Cree were angry at the environmental damage. They also said that the government did not keep many of the promises it had made.

The second phase of the Hydro-Québec project began in 1989. The leaders of the Cree met and began an effort to stop construction. Because some of the electricity produced by the dam would be sold to the United States, the Cree decided to take their case to the American people.

They began speaking at American colleges to raise awareness about the Cree way of life. They made movies, posters, and T-shirts supporting their cause. They even built a large, traditional Cree kayak and paddled it to New York City. The Cree also spoke to lawmakers in several US states and asked them not to support the project. In 1992 New York Governor Mario Cuomo (1932–2015) canceled the state's deal with Hydro-Québec. Other states soon did the same.

Because of the effort of the Cree and environmental groups, the government of Quebéc canceled the second part of the project in 1994. The government and the Cree continued to discuss the issue for several years. In 2002 the two sides agreed to allow the next phase of the project to continue. This time, the Cree were more involved in the process. They insisted that they keep control over their traditional lands. The government also agreed to share some of the money earned by the sale of natural resources with the Cree.

DOO-tee-yeh; 1949–) in the 1970s. In 1977 Dutilleux made a film called *Raoni*. Dutilleux's film helped make Raoni a recognized figure around the world. Because Raoni was already well known, he was the perfect person to be the public face of the Kayapo struggle to save their homeland.

Indigenous Peoples' Rights

Raoni did several things to build up opposition to the Belo Monte Dam. First, he brought the Kayapo together with the other indigenous peoples whose homes were threatened by the dam project. This united a large number of people whose concerns the Brazilian government could not simply ignore. Raoni also reached out to others for help in bringing the Kayapo struggle to the world stage. His biggest supporter in this effort was rock musician Sting. The two men first met when Sting visited the region in 1987.

When Raoni fought against the Belo Monte Dam, Sting stood by his side and carried his message to the rest of the world. Sting and Raoni also went on a world campaign to speak out against the dam project. They visited 17 countries during the campaign and met important people, including King Juan Carlos (1938–) of Spain, President François Mitterrand (1916–1996) of France, and religious leader Pope John Paul II (1920–2005).

The most important part of Raoni's campaign against the dam was a rally held at Altamira. Raoni and the Kayapo gathered with people from 40 other indigenous groups at the five-day rally to protest the dam project. The protesters called on the Brazilian government to respect their rights and stop plans for building a dam that would destroy their homes. Raoni and other leaders also met directly with government officials to persuade them to change their minds about the dam. The rally and the meeting captured the world's attention and convinced many people that something should be done to help the Kayapo.

British singer Sting (center) poses with Chief Raoni Metuktire (left) during a press conference in Madrid, Spain, on May 6, 1989, to promote funds for a natural reserve in the rain forests of Brazil. © AP IMAGES/DESMOND BOYLAN.

Results

Raoni's campaign put a great deal of pressure on the Brazilian government and the World Bank. This eventually led the World Bank to pull its support of the project. Unable to pay for the dam on its own, the Brazilian government was forced to cancel its plans. Raoni and the Kayapo successfully stopped the Belo Monte Dam from being built at that time.

Although the Belo Monte Dam project was stopped in 1989, the idea of building a dam on the Xingu did not go away forever. The Brazilian government announced its decision to build the dam once again in 2010. This time, however, the government was able to use tax money to fund the project. As a result, the Kayapo and other indigenous peoples could not stop the project from moving forward. Work on the dam was completed in 2016 and it was expected to be in operation in 2019. Raoni and other indigenous leaders again opposed the dam. They expressed frustration that the dam builders were not listening to their concerns. Raoni worried about the environmental impact of the dam on his people's way of life.

Dakota Access Pipeline Protest

LOCATION: North Dakota

DATE: 2016–2017

In the late 20th century, experts in the oil industry discovered a new way to drill for oil. This technology made it easier to find oil in layers of rock. In 2014 Energy Transfer Partners, a company headquartered in Texas, announced plans to build a pipeline from the oil fields in North Dakota to a transportation center in Illinois. The Dakota Access Pipeline was planned to stretch for more than 1,000 miles (1,609 kilometers) through four states.

One section of the pipeline was to run through an area in North Dakota near the Standing Rock Reservation. Members of the Sioux (pronounced SOO) tribe who live on the reservation were angry at the planned route of the pipeline. They were worried that a leak from the pipeline could pollute the reservation's water supply. They were also concerned that construction on the project could damage sacred land.

In 2016 the Standing Rock Sioux set up a protest camp with tents, trailers, and tepees near the site of the planned pipeline construction.

Other Native Americans and environmental activists joined them at the site. The government eventually approved the pipeline, but the Sioux asked a judge to stop the project. When construction began, the demonstrations grew larger. The protests began to interfere with work on the pipeline and at times turned violent.

In late 2016, the US government under President Barack Obama (1961–) ordered construction on the pipeline to stop until it could review the project. It wanted to see if the pipeline would have any harmful effects on the environment. The review was completed quickly in early 2017 and new President Donald Trump allowed the project to move forward. The protesters were removed from the camp in February, and oil began flowing through the pipeline in June. As of November 2017, the Standing Rock Sioux continued to battle the pipeline in court.

The proposed pipeline

There are many ways to get oil and natural gas from the ground. One of those ways is called hydraulic fracturing, or fracking. Fracking involves blasting a type of underground rock called shale with powerful jets of water and chemicals. The process forces the oil and gas out of the rock where it can be collected and transported. Fracking had been used to find oil since the early 20th century, but it was not considered very efficient.

In the 1990s, oil companies found a better way to access the oil trapped in shale. Instead of drilling a hole straight down, they drilled down and then sideways before shooting water and chemicals into the rock. This method made it possible to get more oil from areas with large amounts of shale. Shale rock is common in the United States, especially in the states of North Dakota and Montana.

In 2014 a company called Energy Transfer Partners wanted to build a pipeline to carry the oil from drilling sites in North Dakota to a place where it could be stored and shipped across the country. They suggested a 1,172-mile (1,886-kilometer) pipeline that began in North Dakota, traveled through South Dakota and Iowa, and ended in Illinois. The project was called the Dakota Access Pipeline (DAPL).

Before the pipeline could be built, its route had to be approved by the US Army Corps of Engineers. The corps is a government agency responsible for making sure projects like the DAPL are safe and will not harm the environment. In December 2015, the corps finished its review of the pipeline plan. It said the route did not endanger the environment and that it would not damage any important historic sites.

When construction began, the demonstrations grew larger. The protests began to interfere with work on the pipeline and at times turned violent.

Indigenous Peoples' Rights

Protest against the Trail of Tears

Although land rights protests by native people are more common today, indigenous people had few options in the past when treaties were broken or they were forced off their land and on to reservations. Often their only choices were to fight or to submit. On occasion, others spoke out in protest on their behalf.

Such was the case in the 1830s when the American population was growing so quickly that people were beginning to run out of space to live and work. At this time, a number of states began passing laws that took away or limited Native American land rights. The US government also began relocating Native Americans by force in some places. In other areas, the government tried to pay Native Americans to move off their traditional lands.

The US government made a deal with representatives of the Cherokee people in 1835. According to the Treaty of New Echota, the Cherokee agreed to give all of their land east of the Mississippi River to the United States for $5 million. After the treaty was signed, many Cherokee did not think they had been fairly represented in this agreement. Some believed that those who agreed to the treaty did not have the Cherokee's best interests in mind. A large number of Cherokee refused to leave the land.

As a result, the US government began making plans to remove the Cherokee from their land by force. By 1838 many Americans were against that idea. They protested the US government's plans using a common form of protest—signing petitions and writing letters. One such letter of

Native American concerns

The pipeline's route crossed hundreds of waterways, including 22 larger bodies of water such as lakes and rivers. The pipeline was to be drilled deep underground at such points to better protect the water from possible oil leaks. One of these crossings was under the Missouri River at the Lake Oahe (pronounced oh-WAH-hee) reservoir in North Dakota. A reservoir is a human-made lake created to store water for use by a community.

Lake Oahe provides water for the Standing Rock Reservation. The reservation is located on the border of North Dakota and South Dakota. According to the 2010 US census, Standing Rock was home to about 8,217 people. Members of the Standing Rock Sioux were worried that if the pipeline leaked, oil would pollute their drinking water. They were also concerned that nearby religious and cultural sites such as burial grounds could be damaged during construction.

Energy Transfer Partners, the company building the pipeline, argued that it followed all proper safety measures to prevent oil leaks. It noted the

Indigenous Peoples' Rights

protest was written by author and poet Ralph Waldo Emerson (1803–1882). To make his feelings known, Emerson wrote a letter to President Martin Van Buren (1782–1862) encouraging him not to take violent action against the Cherokee. Emerson argued that it would be wrong to remove the Cherokee by force.

Van Buren did not listen to Emerson or to the other protesters, however. Some 15,000 Cherokee were eventually forced from their lands in the Southeast. Many were made to march more than 1,200 miles (1,931 kilometers) to what was then called "Indian Territory," now Oklahoma. Known as the Trail of Tears, this march caused undue hardship. Starvation, disease, and exhaustion as well as the harsh environment along the way caused as many as 4,000 deaths. The plight of the Native Americans is commemorated at the Trail of Tears National Historic Trail, which runs through parts of nine states.

Ralph Waldo Emerson protested the treatment of the Cherokee. © EVERETT HISTORICAL/SHUTTERSTOCK.COM.

pipeline was being built on government-owned land and not reservation territory. The Standing Rock Sioux said the project was dangerous because all pipelines can leak oil. They also said that the pipeline's path crossed land originally given to them in an 1851 treaty with the US government. The government later took that portion of land away from the Sioux.

The protests begin

In April 2016, about 200 members of the Standing Rock Sioux set up a protest area called Sacred Stone Camp near the planned construction site. Reservation leaders also asked the Army Corps of Engineers to perform a more complete study to make sure the pipeline was safe for the environment. In late July 2016, the corps gave its final approval to the pipeline route. It included the crossing below Lake Oahe.

The Standing Rock Sioux were very upset by the ruling. They claimed the corps did not properly communicate with reservation leaders before making its decision. They also said the corps did not do enough to

Indigenous Peoples' Rights

Members of the Standing Rock Sioux and their supporters opposed to the Dakota Access Pipeline confront bulldozers working on the new oil pipeline in an effort to make them stop on September 3, 2016, near Cannon Ball, North Dakota. Private security guards used pepper spray and attack dogs to attempt to repel the protesters, but eventually the bulldozers and the security guards retreated. © ROBYN BECK/AFP/GETTY IMAGES.

make sure Sioux burial grounds and other cultural sites would be safe. The Sioux took their concerns to court and asked a judge to stop construction on the project.

The protests at Sacred Stone Camp grew larger after the court action. By early August, about 600 people were demonstrating at the camp. Members of other Native American groups joined the Standing Rock Sioux. Environmental activists, including several celebrities and politicians, also took part in the protests.

A violent turn

Construction was scheduled to begin on August 10, 2016. When workers from the pipeline company showed up at the site that morning, about 15 to 30 people met them there. The group blocked the workers from reaching the construction area. The crowd grew to about 100 by afternoon. Some demonstrators chained themselves to fences while others tore down blockades that were meant to keep them away from the work site. Several of the protesters were arrested.

During the next few weeks, the crowd of protesters at Sacred Stone Camp and the construction site grew to several thousand. On September 3, members of the Standing Rock Sioux said the pipeline construction had destroyed a tribal burial ground and an important religious site. That same day, several hundred protesters broke down a wire fence around the construction site and clashed with private security officers. Security officers used pepper spray on the crowd, and guard dogs bit some protesters. Pepper spray is made from cayenne peppers and can cause a burning feeling in a person's eyes and throat when applied.

On September 9, a judge denied the Standing Rock Sioux's request to stop construction on the pipeline. The judge said the Army Corps of Engineers had followed the rules and had "likely" done enough to discuss the project with tribal leaders. The US government, however, ordered the pipeline company to stop work at the Standing Rock site. The government wanted to examine the Army Corps of Engineers' environmental study on the project. It also wanted to discuss the situation with the Standing Rock Sioux.

As both sides battled the issue in court, the governor of North Dakota brought in the National Guard to help local police keep order at the protest site. On November 20, about 400 protesters tried to remove a burned-out vehicle that was blocking a bridge connecting their camp to the construction site. As they pushed forward on the bridge, police fired rubber incident and water cannons at them. Many people were injured in the incident and at least one person was arrested. Some protesters complained that the use of water cannons was dangerous on a night when temperatures fell below freezing. In mid-December a group of about 2,000 US military veterans called Veterans for Standing Rock arrived in North Dakota to join the protests.

Pipeline completed

In early January 2017, the Army Corps of Engineers began a new environmental study of the Lake Oahe construction site. The study was expected to take up to two years to complete. On January 24,

Indigenous Peoples' Rights

"Why We Take a Stand at Standing Rock"

This primary source excerpt was written by Dennis Banks, who was a leader of the American Indian Movement for many years. Appearing in the San Francisco Chronicle *on November 6, 2016, this article explains why Native Americans, as protectors of the water, soil, and air, oppose the Dakota Access Pipeline.*

I realized that it is we Native Americans who were entrusted by the Great Spirit to speak for the protection of the many species of life, the protection of the sacred sites of our ancestors, sites where our people are buried, sites where we gather herbs, roots and other leaves we use to heal our people. These are our duties and responsibilities that the Creator gave to us in the beginning. We accepted these instructions for eternity.

Now comes the Standing Rock Sioux Nation in North Dakota and South Dakota, who saw the impending doom that lay in the path of the Dakota Access Pipeline. The nation moved quickly to defend the sacredness of the lands that would be destroyed by the huge earthmoving machines.

The nation called out to other nations to send their medicine bundles, their sacred pipes, their sacred drums and to come and pray with the Standing Rock Nation. Today, 460 of the 567 Native American nations in the U.S. have come to Standing Rock, in addition to Canadian First Nations sending delegations.

On April 1, the Standing Rock Sioux Nation, with a permit in hand issued by the U.S. Army Corp[s]

President Donald Trump, who took office on January 20, signed an order directing the corps to speed up its review process. On February 8, the corps announced it would stop its review and granted permission for the project to continue.

The Standing Rock Sioux and a neighboring tribe again took the issue to court, but a judge denied their request to stop the pipeline. The protesters were ordered to leave their camp by February 22. Although most people did leave the camp, about 46 people refused and were arrested. Smaller groups continued their protests at other sites near the Standing Rock Reservation. Other protesters moved to different spots on the pipeline route. Some Native Americans staged a rally in Washington, DC.

Work on the project was completed and oil began flowing through the pipeline on June 1, 2017. In July a judge ruled that the Army Corps of Engineers should have conducted a more complete study of the environmental impact of the pipeline on the Standing Rock reservation. The judge ordered the corps to prepare a new report but allowed the pipeline to remain in operation.

of Engineers, opened its large main spiritual camp across the Cannonball River in North Dakota.

Each day begins with a ceremony welcoming the sun, giving thanks for another day. Then follows prayers to protect the soil, the water and the air. Every day there are pipe ceremonies, sweat lodge ceremonies, talking circles and the making of tobacco ties. We have built a small school to teach our young people the meaning of life.

Each day we walk to the site carrying our prayer ties to place them on the land near the digging and bulldozing sites. It is there that we meet the many police, sheriffs and their deputies, and the dogs that are trained to attack us. It is there we meet the young men in uniform, military forces of the same government that massacred our people at Sand Creek in 1864 and Wounded Knee in 1890, that also sent our sons and daughters to carry the same flag we fly today alongside our tribal nation flags, in World War I, World War II, and the wars in Korea, Vietnam, Iraq, Iran and Afghanistan.

We only want to carry out our spiritual duties and go home. We must, however, stay until Standing Rock releases us and tells us the sacred sites are protected now and the water is safe. We shall never abandon Standing Rock. Never. Standing Rock is who we are.

SOURCE: Banks, Dennis. "Why We Take a Stand at Standing Rock." *San Francisco Chronicle* (November 6, 2016). Available online at http://www.sfchronicle.com/opinion/openforum/article/Why-we-take-a-stand-at-Standing-Rock-10597021.php (accessed October 15, 2017). Courtesy of *San Francisco Chronicle*.

For More Information

BOOKS

Gitlin, Marty. *Wounded Knee Massacre.* Santa Barbara, CA: Greenwood, 2011.

Lennox, Corinne, and Damien Short, eds. *Handbook of Indigenous Peoples' Rights.* New York: Routledge, 2016.

Morris, Barry. *Protests, Land Rights, and Riots: Postcolonial Struggles in Australia in the 1980s.* New York: Berghahn Books, 2014.

Oberg, Michael Leroy. *Native America: A History.* 2nd ed. Hoboken, NJ: Wiley-Blackwell, 2017.

Zanotti, Laura. *Radical Territories in the Brazilian Amazon: The Kayapó's Fight for Just Livelihoods.* Tucson: University of Arizona Press, 2016.

PERIODICALS

Aisch, Gregor, and K. K. Rebecca Lai. "The Conflicts along 1,172 Miles of the Dakota Access Pipeline." *New York Times* (March 23, 2017). Available online at https://www.nytimes.com/interactive/2016/11/23/us/dakota-access-pipeline-protest-map.html (accessed August 21, 2017).

Chertoff, Emily. "Occupy Wounded Knee: A 71-Day Siege and a Forgotten Civil Rights Movement." *Atlantic* (October 23, 2012). Available online at https://www.theatlantic.com/national/archive/2012/10/occupy-wounded-knee-a-71-day-siege-and-a-forgotten-civil-rights-movement/263998/ (accessed August 21, 2017).

Johnston, Barbara Rose, ed. "Water, Cultural Diversity, and Global Environmental Change." UNESCO (2012). Available online at http://unesdoc.unesco.org/images/0021/002151/215119E.pdf (accessed August 21, 2017).

Meyer, Robinson. "The Standing Rock Sioux Claim 'Victory and Vindication' in Court." *Atlantic* (June 14, 2017). Available online at https://www.theatlantic.com/science/archive/2017/06/dakota-access-standing-rock-sioux-victory-court/530427/ (accessed August 21, 2017).

"A Timeline of the Dakota Access Oil Pipeline." *U.S. News & World Report* (February 22, 2017). Available online at https://www.usnews.com/news/north-dakota/articles/2017-02-22/a-timeline-of-the-dakota-access-oil-pipeline (accessed August 21, 2017).

WEBSITES

"Aboriginal People." Survival International. http://www.survivalinternational.org/tribes/aboriginals (accessed August 21, 2017).

"Australia Day Beginnings." Department of Premier and Cabinet. http://www.australiaday.vic.gov.au/about/timeline-2 (accessed August 21, 2017).

"Cree (First Nations) Stop Second Phase of James Bay Hydroelectric Project, 1989–1994." Global Nonviolent Action Database. http://nvdatabase.swarthmore.edu/content/cree-first-nations-stop-second-phase-james-bay-hydroelectric-project-1989-1994 (accessed August 21, 2017).

Hersher, Rebecca. "Key Moments in the Dakota Access Pipeline Fight." National Public Radio, February 22, 2017. http://www.npr.org/sections/thetwo-way/2017/02/22/514988040/key-moments-in-the-dakota-access-pipeline-fight (accessed August 21, 2017).

"History—Incident at Wounded Knee." U.S. Marshals Service. https://www.usmarshals.gov/history/wounded-knee/ (accessed August 21, 2017).

"Indigenous Peoples." Amnesty International. https://www.amnesty.org/en/what-we-do/indigenous-peoples (accessed August 21, 2017).

Johnson, Troy. "We Hold the Rock." National Park Service, February 27, 2015. https://www.nps.gov/alca/learn/historyculture/we-hold-the-rock.htm (accessed August 21, 2017).

"Māori Land Rights." Museum of New Zealand. http://sites.tepapa.govt.nz/sliceofheaven/web/html/landrights.html (accessed August 21, 2017).

"Who Are the Indigenous Peoples?" International Work Group for Indigenous Affairs. http://www.iwgia.org/culture-and-identity/identification-of-indigenous-peoples (accessed August 21, 2017).

13

Labor Rights

Mother Jones's
"Children's Crusade" **399**

Flint Sit-Down Strike against General Motors **407**

Delano Grape Strike and Boycott **414**

Fast-Food Workers' Strike **422**

Labor rights have existed as an idea since at least the mid- to late 18th century. Labor rights, also called workers' rights, are privileges that some people believe all employees should have. These rights cover issues such as wages, working conditions, and the ability of workers to organize into labor unions. Labor unions are organizations that protect workers in certain fields from unfair labor practices.

Labor rights developed in the late 18th century and early 19th century as a response to the Industrial Revolution (c. 1760–1840). This was a period when certain Western European countries and the United States transitioned from mostly farming societies to industrialized ones. Industry refers to the production of goods from raw materials in factories. The Industrial Revolution grew these countries' economies, but the factory workers who produced the goods often suffered on the job. Many of them worked in dangerous conditions for long hours and low pay.

In 1802 the United Kingdom passed one of the first labor laws, limiting the number of working hours in a day. Later in the 19th and 20th centuries, labor rights generally improved for workers in Europe and the United States. Workers did not always obtain these rights easily though. Many workers had to unite and protest their employers or governments for legal protection of their rights.

Most developed nations in the 21st century have labor laws that protect the rights of employees. Labor laws differ by country. Laws in some countries guarantee workers paid time off from their jobs. Laws in other countries set the maximum amount of hours employees may work in a shift. Different sets of laws guarantee certain working conditions for employees younger than 18 years of age. However, many undeveloped countries around the world still used child labor in the 21st century. Child labor is the use of children in industry. It is often difficult, hard

Labor Rights

> ## WORDS TO KNOW
>
> **American dream:** An ideal that stresses that US citizens can be successful through hard work.
>
> **Apprentice:** A student who learns skills from an experienced worker.
>
> **Boycott:** A refusal to buy or use certain items, products, or services as a form of protest.
>
> **Crusade:** An important mission, usually involving moral beliefs and often requiring a long journey.
>
> **Industry:** The production of goods from raw materials in factories.
>
> **Migrant worker:** A person who travels in search of work.
>
> **Minimum wage:** The lowest hourly rate that an employer can pay a worker.
>
> **Reformer:** A person who tries to bring changes to society.
>
> **Sit-down strike:** A protest in which a group of workers sit down on the job and refuse to work.
>
> **Strike:** An organized work stoppage to force employers to meet certain demands.
>
> **Sweatshop:** A small factory where people work long hours for low pay.
>
> **Union:** An organized group that protects workers' rights.

work for someone so young. The practice is illegal in many developed nations. Most countries with poor working conditions for adults and children are located in South America, Africa, the Middle East, and Asia.

Workers in the modern United States enjoy a variety of labor rights. They have the right to form unions, work in safe conditions, and be free from discrimination and harassment on the job. Discrimination is unfair treatment based race, gender, religion, or other factors. Harassment is the use of aggressive actions or words to offend or frighten people.

Rise of industry

Labor rights had not truly become a concept before the mid-18th century. People in Europe and elsewhere had mostly worked as farmers for hundreds of years. Farming was the center of people's lives. Many farmers made all their money from growing and selling their crops. Others worked for landowners, sowing crops or tending livestock. But the work was difficult, and most farmers did not make much money from what they sold. Many farmers simply made whatever goods they needed in their own homes or in shops. These goods included clothing, tools, and furniture.

Labor Rights

This kind of lifestyle began to change for many people during the Industrial Revolution. The revolution began in the United Kingdom around the mid- to late 18th century. The British were able to industrialize because their country had a great deal of natural coal and iron. These resources were useful in the building and powering of factories. Over the years, the United Kingdom became a major global producer of cloth and fabric, ships, and a variety of metal products.

People produced most of these goods in factories. Many factory owners became rich from the sale of their goods. However, working in the factories was very difficult. Employees worked near machinery that could seriously injure or kill them. They worked in shifts of about 10 hours, often 6 days a week. Workers who were not skilled in any particular trade could lose their jobs at any time. Managers could easily replace unskilled workers. Children also worked long shifts in the factories. Payment for factory work was low. Many employees were poor and lived in dirty, crowded housing.

The Industrial Revolution eventually spread to other Western European nations and the United States. Factory conditions in these countries were similar to those in the United Kingdom. These poor working conditions led people to protest for labor rights.

During the Industrial Revolution some people fought against having their jobs be replaced by machines. A group of weavers and textile workers called the Luddites took action and began destroying such machines in protest. Here, a factory owner tries to defend his workshop. © EVERETT HISTORICAL/SHUTTERSTOCK.COM.

Calls for labor rights

The Health and Morals of Apprentices Act of 1802 in the United Kingdom was one of the earliest examples of a labor law. Apprentices are students who learn skills from experienced workers. The act tried to improve life for apprentices by preventing them from working at night and allowing them to go to school while holding jobs. The main problem with the act was that no one could enforce it. As a result, not all young British workers enjoyed the labor rights described in the act.

Labor Rights

CRITICAL THINKING QUESTIONS

1. Do you believe that fast-food workers should earn $15 an hour? Why or why not?

2. Can a person afford to live on $7.25 an hour? Why or why not?

3. Do you think it is important for workers to be able to organize and join unions? Explain.

4. Do you think GM and other car companies treated their employees so poorly?

5. What are some of the reasons why joining a union was important to GM and other auto plant workers?

6. Do you think César Chávez's focus on non-violent methods of protest helped the Delano strike and boycott? Explain your reasoning.

7. How did the farmwork that children performed differ from the work they performed in factories and other industrial settings?

8. Why do you think reformers like Mother Jones became so concerned about children working in industrial settings?

9. Why do you think it took the United States such a long time to pass child labor laws?

By the late 18th and early 19th centuries in Western Europe and the United States, effective labor laws were still decades away. It would also be many years before truly influential labor unions started to organize. Even so, some groups of American workers had united as early as the 1760s to demand better working conditions. This began a long American tradition of fighting for fair and equal treatment in workplaces.

In 1768 a group of tailors in New York banded together to protest a decrease in their pay from their employers. Tailors make fitted clothing. In 1794 in Philadelphia, Pennsylvania, shoemakers came together to create the Federal Society of Journeymen Cordwainers (pronounced KORD-way-ners). A cordwainer is a shoemaker. The shoemakers had formed the society to oppose decreases their employers wanted to make to their pay.

These protests marked the unofficial start of the US labor movement. Over the next several decades, people in numerous American cities established labor societies that tried to make life better for local workers. The societies attempted to secure better pay and shorter shifts for workers. The societies charged fees for their efforts. Many labor groups in these early years formed to accomplish certain goals and then broke up.

American labor societies organized more formally later in the 19th century. In 1827 the Mechanics' Union of Trade Associations formed in Philadelphia. The union was one of the first of its kind to organize the multiple smaller unions of a particular industry in one city. The International Typographical Union formed in 1852. This was a union of publishers. It was among the first labor unions to represent a trade across the United States and Canada. Other national unions followed later. The National Labor Union, formed in 1866, worked to secure an eight-hour workday for employees of the US government.

Employer resistance

The American labor movement often did not proceed smoothly. Many business owners strongly opposed labor unions. The owners did not want to pay their workers more money or have them work fewer hours. Business owners sometimes threatened their workers with violence if the workers tried to form unions. In some cases, owners and managers had the US military physically stop union activity. Sometimes employers and employees went to court to settle their disagreements over unions. Most judges sided with the business owners.

Unions were not the only method that American workers used to try to secure labor rights. Striking was another option. Strikes occur when the employees of a certain company or industry all stop working at the same time. The purpose of a strike is to make an employer understand how much money he or she will lose if the employees all stop work at once. The goal is to force the employer to give in to the employees' demands.

The Knights of Labor, an American labor union, led a number of strikes in the 1880s. The Knights of Labor had formed in 1869 as a society of tailors. Over the years, the group welcomed workers from a variety of industries, including railroad employees. In 1886 about 200,000 Knights of Labor employees of the Union Pacific Railroad and the Missouri Pacific Railroad participated in a strike against their employers. The workers wanted safer working conditions, shorter hours, and higher pay. The railroad owners defeated the strike by simply hiring new employees who were not union members. The Knights of Labor broke up soon after this. American workers continued to use strikes to demand better conditions into the 20th century.

Sometimes the government helped American and European workers seeking better conditions. Effective labor laws were enacted in the United States beginning in the 1930s. The National Labor Relations Act of 1935 allowed the US government to enforce the power of labor unions. The Fair Labor Standards Act of 1938 described working conditions that employers throughout the United States had to meet. Children could no longer work, and employees had to be at least 16 years old. The law also forced employers to pay their employees extra for working more than 40 hours per week. Finally, the law created a minimum wage. This is the lowest amount employers are allowed to pay their employees.

Over the next several decades, American labor laws were put in place, creating standards used by labor unions to demand fair treatment of workers. The laws also banned discrimination in the hiring of employees. Labor laws in Australia and the countries of Western Europe caught up with American laws around the same period.

Modern labor rights around the world

In the 21st century, the International Trade Union Confederation (ITUC) annually ranks the best and worst countries in which to work. In the mid-2010s, the ITUC ranked even developed countries such as the United States somewhat low on its list. However, the United States simply had different labor standards than certain European countries that ranked higher. In the United States, employers do not have to give employees breaks during workdays. They also do not have to give employees paid time off. Breaks and vacation time are considered optional benefits in the American workplace. Countries that scored high on the ITUC's ranking included Austria, Finland, the Netherlands, and Norway.

At the same time, the ITUC ranked other countries around the world poorly in terms of labor rights. China was one of these. Many Chinese laborers work in dangerous conditions. China also does not allow its citizens to complain about unfair or unsafe working conditions. Strikes are illegal, and employers and the Chinese government can threaten employees who go on strike.

Egypt also placed low on the ITUC list. Employers can suspend workers who strike against unfair conditions. The Egyptian government also opposes striking and can prevent employees from ever working again if they strike. Foreign workers in the Middle Eastern country of Qatar (pronounced kah-TAR or KAH-ter) face a similar situation. Labor laws in Qatar do not apply to foreign workers. Workers may go to Qatar to perform a job believing they will receive a certain wage for their work. Once the workers are in the country, employers can set entirely new wages. These wages may be much lower than those promised. In addition,

Many Chinese laborers work in dangerous conditions. China also does not allow its citizens to complain about unfair or unsafe working conditions. Strikes are illegal, and employers and the Chinese government can threaten employees who go on strike.

working conditions in Qatar are often unsafe. Foreign workers who complain about any mistreatment can be arrested and held in prison for a long time.

Many countries around the world continued to use child labor in the 21st century. In the mid-2010s the global consulting firm Maplecroft ranked countries that use child labor. The African country of Eritrea (pronounced air-uh-TREE-uh) ranked first. It was followed by the African countries of Somalia, the Democratic Republic of the Congo, and Sudan. The countries of Afghanistan, Pakistan, and Yemen were also included on the list. Maplecroft claimed high poverty in those countries forced children to work to help their families. Many child laborers in these nations were between ages 5 and 17. The work they did could be dangerous. It included farming, working in the streets as food vendors and shoe shiners, and assisting in factories and workshops.

Mother Jones's "Children's Crusade"

LOCATION: Philadelphia, Pennsylvania, to Oyster Bay, New York
DATE: July 1903

The Children's Crusade of 1903, also known as the March of the Mill Children, was a march that helped bring attention to the problem of child labor. At that time, many thousands of children in the United States worked long hours, often in dangerous jobs. They received little pay and few, if any, protections. Many children were hurt or killed. Child workers often missed school and did not have much time to play.

A reformer named Mary Harris Jones (1837–1930), nicknamed "Mother Jones," decided to help these children. In 1903 she organized a march in which at least 100 child laborers walked from Philadelphia, Pennsylvania, to New York City. Along the way, the children raised awareness of the problem of child labor. They even attempted to meet with President Theodore Roosevelt (1858–1919), but he would not speak with them.

Although the Children's Crusade did not end child labor, it did help teach people about the practice. The march made people realize the horrible effect that child labor had on much of the nation's youth.

Labor Rights

Child labor

Throughout history children often worked to help support their families. Children of farming families traditionally helped pick crops, feed farm animals, and perform chores around the household. Sometimes a parent took a child as an assistant or an apprentice to teach him or her the skills needed for a certain profession.

In the 1800s many social factors were changing the way Americans lived and worked. One factor was industrialization, or the widespread use of machines and factories. Millions of Americans took jobs in factories to produce the goods that the growing and spreading population demanded. Another important factor was urbanization, or the growth of cities. Many families moved away from traditional countryside homes and occupations. They went to big cities in search of new opportunities.

Child labor remained a feature of American life, but it changed to fit the modern nation. Especially in slums, or poor areas of a city, child labor was everywhere. Children delivered goods, sold fruit or newspapers, and shined shoes on city streets. Many city children had to work in mills or sweatshops where they helped make numerous products. Sweatshops are small factories where people work long hours for low pay. Children outside cities often worked in mines, which were dangerous and required hard labor.

This little girl worked as a spinner in a mill in Macon, Georgia. She was so small she had to climb up on to the spinning frame to mend broken threads. Photo taken in 1909.
LEWIS WICKES HINE/LIBRARY OF CONGRESS.

A growing social problem

For many years few people questioned the use of child laborers. Until the late 1800s, most people considered children to be the property of their parents. Children had few, if any, protections from the government or other outside forces. Many families supported child labor simply because they needed the money that working children could provide. At the same time, many business leaders supported the practice because child labor was a cheap way to increase business profits.

Child labor was widespread in the United States, and it grew quickly. In 1870 about 750,000 children between the ages of 10 and 15 were working in cities. That figure did not count the many thousands more who worked on farms. The number of working children rose greatly in the following decades. By 1900 more than 1,750,000 children under the age of 16 worked. These children had little time for fun or education. Many were hurt or even killed while doing dangerous work.

The spirit of reform

Many reformers, people who try to bring changes to society, noticed the difficult situations child laborers faced. These reformers believed that child labor was unjust.

The reformers' messages began to spread throughout the country and gain support. The path to reform was slow and difficult, however. By 1881 only seven states had passed laws to protect child laborers. Many people ignored these laws.

Some laborers, including children, took the quest for reform into their own hands. Occasional strikes and other protests highlighted the workers' complaints. One of the largest early strikes took place in Kensington, a textile mill near Philadelphia, Pennsylvania. Textiles are different types of cloth. In 1903 between 75,000 and 100,000 workers in Kensington went on strike. At least 16,000 of them were children. The workers asked their bosses to reduce the workweek from 60 hours to 55 hours and to stop requiring women and children to work at night. The working environment is less safe when employees work longer hours. When people are tired they are more likely to make mistakes that cause accidents.

Mother Jones arrives

The Kensington strike continued for weeks. Business leaders paid little notice to the strikers or their demands. However, the demonstrations attracted the attention of Mary Harris Jones, an outspoken labor

Labor Rights

Child Labor Protest, 1909

By the late 1800s, many American workers led very difficult lives. It was common for workers, especially in cities, to labor for 12 hours a day. Workers had few, if any, days off. Their jobs were often grim and dangerous. They received very low pay and little respect or recognition, even though their hard work was making the United States a stronger nation with a bright future.

Workers began to protest for more rights, better pay, and more respect. On September 5, 1882, about 10,000 workers in New York City marched through the streets. They wanted to spread the idea that workers deserved respect. This was the first demonstration on what would eventually become the Labor Day holiday.

After many protests and other demonstrations, some of which ended in violence, the country began slowly recognizing its workers. Throughout the 1880s, cities and then states began making plans for a special day to celebrate working people. By 1894 more than half of the states had adopted such measures. That year the federal government ruled that the first Monday of each September would be Labor Day.

Labor Day was meant as a holiday to thank workers for their efforts. Some workers got the day off. They spent their free time enjoying parades and picnics. The day also became important for highlighting the continuing problems American workers faced.

On occasion, labor was celebrated or protested at other times of the year. In 1909 a labor parade in New York City became the center of a protest against child labor. In the early 19th century, hundreds of thousands of children worked in difficult and dangerous jobs. Many of these children were immigrants or the children of immigrants. These jobs stole their youth and deprived them of the education they needed to better themselves.

During the 1909 parade, many children wearing banners and carrying flags marched with other workers. Some of the banners had slogans such as "Abolish Child Slavery!" To abolish something means to stop or end it. The words made a strong connection between the unfair practices of child

reformer. Jones, who came to the United States from Ireland, had dedicated her life to helping poor workers some years after tragedy struck her family. Her husband and four children had died of yellow fever in 1867. Jones's kindness and compassion in helping workers earned her the nickname "Mother Jones."

In June 1903 Jones was helping coal miners in West Virginia when she heard about the Kensington strike. She rushed to Philadelphia to support the workers, especially the thousands of children. She was upset to learn that the owners of the textile mill were not cooperating. Local people did not support the workers either, largely because newspapers refused to report on the strike.

labor and slavery, which the United States abolished in 1865. Children of immigrant families displayed banners in other languages that expressed similar ideas. All were hoping to spread the message that children laborers needed to be treated fairly.

Reforming child labor laws received attention from various groups and people around the dawn of the 20th century. Here, two girls wear sashes with the slogan "Abolish Child Slavery!," one written in English and the other in Yiddish. This photograph was likely taken during the May 1, 1909, labor parade in New York City. COURTESY OF THE BAIN COLLECTION/LIBRARY OF CONGRESS.

Jones planned a demonstration march of child laborers from Philadelphia to New York to protest the workers' treatment and raise awareness of labor concerns. She announced her plans during a rally in Kensington. The march came to be known as the "Children's Crusade," or the "March of the Mill Children." A crusade is an important mission, usually involving moral beliefs and often requiring a long journey.

The crusade

On July 7, 1903, Jones assembled her "industrial army" of children in Kensington. Reports about the number of children who participated vary widely from about 100 to 300. Regardless of the number, the marching

March of the Mill Children

In this primary source excerpt from The Autobiography of Mother Jones, *Mary Harris Jones describes how she decided to undertake the Children's Crusade, also known as the March of the Mill Children, in 1903.*

In the spring of 1903 I went to Kensington, Pennsylvania, where seventy-five thousand textile workers were on strike. Of this number at least ten thousand were little children. The workers were striking for more pay and shorter hours. Every day little children came into Union Headquarters, some with their hands off, some with the thumb missing, some with their fingers off at the knuckle. They were stooped little things, round shouldered and skinny. Many of them were not over ten years of age, although the state law prohibited their working before they were twelve years of age.

The law was poorly enforced and the mothers of these children often swore falsely as to their children's age. In a single block in Kensington, fourteen women, mothers of twenty-two children all under twelve, explained it was a question of starvation or perjury. That the fathers had been killed or maimed at the mines.

I asked the newspaper men why they didn't publish the facts about child labor in Pennsylvania. They said they couldn't because the mill owners had stock in the papers.

"Well, I've got stock in these little children," said I, "and I'll arrange a little publicity."

We assembled a number of boys and girls one morning in Independence Park and from there we arranged to parade with banners to the court house where we would hold a meeting.

A great crowd gathered in the public square in front of the city hall. I put the little boys with their fingers off and hands crushed and maimed on a platform. I held up their mutilated hands and showed them to the crowd and made the statement that Philadelphia's mansions were built on the broken bones, the quivering hearts and drooping heads of these children. That their little lives went out to make wealth for others. That neither state or city officials paid any attention to these wrongs. That they did not care that these children were to be the future citizens of the nation.

The officials of the city hall were standing in the open windows. I held the little ones of the mills

children had an immediate effect. They drew attention from the people in the towns and cities they passed through.

The children played music and carried banners that called for shorter workweeks and access to education. People noticed the demonstration and came out to support Jones and the children. Thousands of onlookers attended speeches and rallies along the route of the march.

Jones gave many spirited talks in support of labor laws for children. Several children who had been seriously hurt by long hours of overwork joined Jones and aided in her lectures. One of these children was a 10-year-old boy who had developed a permanently crooked back from high up above the heads of the crowd and pointed to their puny arms and legs and hollow chests. They were light to lift.

I called upon the millionaire manufacturers to cease their moral murders, and I cried to the officials in the open windows opposite, "Some day the workers will take possession of your city hall, and when we do, no child will be sacrificed on the altar of profit."

The officials quickly closed the windows, just as they had closed their eyes and hearts. . . .

I concluded the people needed stirring up again. The Liberty Bell that a century ago rang out for freedom against tyranny was touring the country and crowds were coming to see it everywhere. That gave me an idea. These little children were striking for some of the freedom that childhood ought to have, and I decided that the children and I would go on a tour.

I asked some of the parents if they would let me have their little boys and girls for a week or ten days, promising to bring them back safe and sound. They consented. A man named Sweeny was marshal for our "army." A few men and women went with me to help with the children.

They were on strike and I thought they might well have a little recreation.

The children carried knapsacks on their backs in which was a knife and fork, a tin cup and plate. We took along a wash boiler in which to cook the food on the road. One little fellow had a drum and another had a fife. That was our band. We carried banners that said, "We want more schools and less hospitals." "We want time to play." "Prosperity is here. Where is ours?"

We started from Philadelphia where we held a great mass meeting. I decided to go with the children to see President Roosevelt to ask him to have Congress pass a law prohibiting the exploitation of childhood. I thought that President Roosevelt might see these mill children and compare them with his own little ones who were spending the summer on the seashore at Oyster Bay. I thought too, out of politeness, we might call on [J. P.] Morgan in Wall Street who owned the mines where many of these children's fathers worked.

SOURCE: Jones, Mother. "Chapter X: The March of the Mill Children." *The Autobiography of Mother Jones.* Chicago: Charles H. Kerr, 1925. Courtesy of Charles H. Kerr & Company.

---

constantly carrying heavy spools of yarn. Jones also organized stunts to get press attention. In one such display, she had children pose in empty cages in a zoo to demonstrate how their bosses treated them like animals.

The marchers left Pennsylvania and entered New Jersey. They passed through Trenton, Princeton, Newark, and other cities. From there the marchers proceeded into New York City. On the night of July 23, they marched on Second Avenue in Manhattan and then demonstrated in the entertainment area of Coney Island. Jones decided to highlight the group's efforts by marching directly to the summer home of President Theodore Roosevelt on Long Island.

Labor Rights

Mary Harris "Mother" Jones (center) poses with children and adults as they set off on their Children's Crusade. They intended to tell the people along their route about the conditions that children face working in the textile mills. COURTESY OF THE LIBRARY OF CONGRESS.

The march ends

The approximately 100-mile (160-kilometer) trip from Philadelphia to New York City took three weeks. During this time, the group made many stops and met thousands of sympathetic citizens. Many children greatly enjoyed the rare vacation. It was one of the few instances when they had time off from work. The trip was not easy, however. The marchers faced hot and challenging weather. Some children were unable to complete the trek and returned home.

By the time the group reached New York, it had greatly dwindled in number. Only Jones and a few children remained when they reached President Roosevelt's summer home. These faithful few were disappointed when the country's leader refused to meet them.

Jones and the children returned to Philadelphia in August. They returned to the same troubled situation they had briefly left. The strike ended, children returned to work, and Jones had little success at that time to show for her efforts.

Results

Mother Jones refused to stop her campaign. She wrote three letters to President Roosevelt, which he did not answer. A White House secretary responded to Jones saying that the president was powerless to change child labor laws. Rather, as stated in the US Constitution, only the states had the right and responsibility to choose their industries and industrial practices.

Although the Children's Crusade failed to influence the Kensington bosses, it had an effect on the nation. It helped make child labor an issue of debate and outrage. By 1904 an association called the National Child Labor Committee formed to continue Jones's advocacy. Advocacy is support for a cause. Shortly afterward, Pennsylvania passed laws that gave children some degree of protection. New Jersey and New York soon followed. Nationwide support grew slowly in the coming decades. In 1938 President Franklin D. Roosevelt (1882–1945), a distant cousin of Theodore, signed the Fair Labor Standards Act into law. The federal law created guidelines for all states that required strict regulation of child labor.

Thanks to this act, and the work of many brave reformers such as Mother Jones, child labor is almost gone in the modern United States. In most areas, children under 14 cannot work. Older children are not allowed to participate in dangerous jobs.

Child labor remains a serious concern in many other countries, however. In 2012 the International Labour Organization (ILO) reported that about 168 million children between 5 and 17 years old were workers. Although this figure is very high, it is lower than in previous years.

Flint Sit-Down Strike against General Motors

LOCATION: Flint, Michigan

DATE: 1936–1937

The Flint sit-down strike was held from December 1936 to February 1937 at several General Motors (GM) plants in Flint, Michigan. GM is an international automobile company located in the United States. The work stoppage was part of several held at numerous GM plants across the United States during this time. The demonstration was one of the first sit-down strikes and largest labor disputes in US history. During a sit-down strike, workers remain at their work areas and refuse to perform their jobs or leave.

GM automobile workers went on strike for better pay and working conditions. GM was and still is one of the largest automakers in the world. Michigan has been home to major automobile companies, including GM, Ford, and Chrysler, since the early 20th century. In the 1930s car manufacturers paid employees very little and expected them to work long hours under difficult working conditions. Many workers suffered from exhaustion, and some even died on the job.

GM did not want its employees to join unions. However, the United Automobile Workers (UAW) convinced workers that they needed a union to fight for their rights and protection. The UAW helped workers organize the sit-down strikes. The Flint sit-down strikes lasted 44 days. Afterward, GM allowed its employees to join the UAW and promised them increased wages and safer working conditions.

Working conditions at General Motors

During the early 20th century, many small automobile companies existed in the United States. William C. Durant (1861–1947) and Charles Stewart Mott (1875–1973), who both formerly produced horse-drawn carriages, formed GM in 1908. The company bought several of the smaller car companies and sold and manufactured different brands and types of automobiles.

GM became one of the largest auto manufacturers in the United States and one of the largest companies in the world during the early 20th century. It employed thousands of people. Many of these employees worked at the Flint plants during the 1930s. However, these jobs could be dangerous, and working conditions were sometimes unsafe.

The machinery was so loud in the plants that it caused some employees to lose their hearing. The plants also became very hot, especially during the summer months. The noise and heat sickened many workers. Some people vomited, and others fainted while working. Many workers developed a condition that made their skin appear yellow. Some employees died due to the poor conditions.

The pay for these jobs was very low for the difficulty of the work involved. In the 1930s, the average pay for an autoworker was $900 a

In the 1930s car manufacturers paid employees very little and expected them to work long hours under difficult working conditions. Many workers suffered from exhaustion, and some even died on the job.

year. The US average yearly income level for a family of four to live on was $1,600. In 1936 GM made an annual profit of about $225 million. It paid its executives thousands of dollars in salaries and bonuses each year. This was much more than it paid its plant workers.

GM workers could not afford to lose their jobs at the time because the nation was in the middle of the Great Depression (1929–1941). The Great Depression was a time of economic troubles that left many people without money and jobs. Some of the plant managers took advantage of this to make employees work as hard and as fast as they could. They threatened to fire employees who could not keep up with the demands. Some managers worked the employees so hard that they became exhausted and sick. The managers then replaced the sick workers. The company also let employees go without work for months at time and offered no guarantee of when work would begin again.

The poor working conditions and low pay angered many employees. Union officials tried to persuade employees to join them. GM, however, threatened to fire employees who tried to join the unions. It even hired detectives to make sure the unions did not try to organize employees. In 1930 and 1934, the workers unsuccessfully tried to organize strikes, which were against the law at the time. In 1935 the passage of the National Labor Relations Act, which was also known as the Wagner Act, made strikes legal.

The UAW union formed during the 1930s. It broke from the American Federation of Labor, which was a group of labor unions. UAW officials secretly visited the homes of GM workers in Flint in 1936. They persuaded many of them to join the union. That same year, conditions at the Flint plants worsened. The heat and difficult work claimed lives. According to the Library of Congress, hundreds of people died in Michigan car plants that year due to a heat wave in July. The UAW convinced workers that they could take a stand against GM. Union officials told the employees they could stop working to show the company how serious they were about their demands of increased pay and safer working conditions.

Strike begins

The UAW helped the workers organize a legal strike over the next few months. The work stoppage began in November 1936 at a GM plant in Atlanta, Georgia. Another strike followed at the Kansas City, Missouri,

Labor Rights

Battle of Blair Mountain, 1921

Another major labor protest was the Battle of Blair Mountain. It was the largest labor uprising in the United States as of 2017. It took place in West Virginia for several days in late August and early September 1921. It began with a group of coal miners who were unhappy with their employers, including the Stone Mountain Coal Company. The coal companies paid miners low wages or in credit that they could use to buy items at stores owned by their employers. The companies made them rent their tools and showed little concern about safe working conditions.

Unions tried to get the miners to organize, but the companies hired men from the Baldwin-Felts detective agency to make sure workers did not join the unions. The detectives made the miners leave their homes, which were owned by the coal companies, if they were caught trying to join a union. This angered many people, including Mayor Cabell Testerman (d. 1920) and Sheriff Sid Hatfield (d. 1921), who called a meeting with the Baldwin-Felts detectives in 1920. The meeting turned violent and resulted in the deaths of several people, including Testerman. This event was called the Matewan Massacre or the Battle of Matewan.

In response, the unions organized a strike at the mines and many miners joined the protest. The companies hired nonunion miners to replace the striking workers. Baldwin-Felts detectives killed Hatfield as he was heading to court for a trial. Hatfield and one of his deputies were gunned down in front of their wives as they tried to enter the courthouse on August 1, 1921. The deaths and other events resulted in the Mine Wars, in which both sides fought and several people died. During the fights, the coal companies jailed several union miners for going against their orders and other minor offenses.

The death of the sheriff angered the striking workers, so they planned an armed march to rescue the jailed miners and confront the coal company. About 10,000 miners took part in the march. Governor Ephraim Morgan (1869–1950) formed an armed group to stop the miners. The two groups met at Blair Mountain and engaged in battle for the next few days. Many people were

---

plant in mid-December. Next was the work stoppage at another GM plant in Cleveland, Ohio, at the end of the month.

At 8 p.m. on December 30, 1936, workers at Fisher Body Plant No. 1 in Flint joined the strike. A shout of "She's ours!" signaled workers to lock themselves inside the building. The Flint plant was much larger than other GM plants. It was also very valuable to the company since it contained one of the two necessary machines to make the bodies of the 1937 line of cars. The work stoppage at this plant greatly affected the company's production. On January 1, 1937, workers at the Fisher Body Plant No. 2 in Flint joined the sit-down strike.

Labor Rights

killed on both sides. The governor called on President Warren G. Harding (1865–1923) to send federal troops to the site. The conflict ended on September 4, 1921. The number of people killed was not known and could not be confirmed.

The Jefferson County Courthouse in Charles Town, West Virginia, was the site of the trial of some of the union coal miners who took part in the armed march in 1921 against an armed group organized by the governor. More than 60 years earlier, it was also where abolitionist John Brown was tried and sentenced to death for treason after his raid on Harpers Ferry. © GEORGE RINHART/CORBIS VIA GETTY IMAGES.

The GM workers decided to use sit-down measures to block their workstations to ensure that the company could not replace them with workers who were not in the union. They locked the doors of the buildings to prevent anyone from getting inside to stop the strike. GM managers became very angry. They could not enter the buildings. They asked the workers to open the doors, but the workers refused. GM then asked the courts to charge the striking workers with trespassing, which is the crime of being on someone else's property without permission. This did not change the strikers' minds, and they stayed put.

The decision to stay inside the buildings instead of picketing outside protected the workers from the cold weather conditions and violence

Labor Rights

During the sit-down strike at the General Motors Chevrolet plant in Flint, Michigan, striking workers are shown crossing off the number of days they have been off work during their protest. © TOM WATSON/NY DAILY NEWS ARCHIVE VIA GETTY IMAGES.

from those who did not support them. The workers relaxed inside the plants. They played games and listened to music. They also worked on their list of demands for the company. GM then came up with a plan to make the strikers leave the plant. They turned off the heat. They assumed the cold would force the workers to end the strike. The workers wrapped themselves in coats and stayed close to one another to stay warm. They had many supporters, who got them food, blankets, and other items. The strike continued.

On January 11, 1937, a riot began outside the second Fisher Body Plant when police officers attempted to stop a shipment of food from reaching the strikers inside the building. At what became known as the Battle of the Running Bulls, several strikers and about a dozen police officers were injured. Afterward, Governor Frank Murphy (1890–1949) of Michigan placed the National Guard outside the plants. Murphy was a union supporter so he did not order troops to enter the buildings. He did not want to break the strike with force and cause any injuries or deaths. He wanted to keep individuals on both sides safe.

By this time, many workers at the GM plants throughout the country joined the strike. It continued to grow. Workers at GM's largest plant,

Strike Heard 'Round the World

In this primary source excerpt from the July 11, 2008, edition of the Flint Journal, *reporter Kristin Longley interviews people who participated in the General Motors sit-down strike some 70 years earlier.*

More than 70 years later, Arthur Lowell still can feel the sting of tear gas in his eyes and the weight of the fire hose in his arms.

Barricaded inside a General Motors plant in the middle of winter, Lowell and other union workers struggled to keep police and management at bay during the Sit-Down Strike of 1936–37.

"They kept trying to get in the back, but I was waiting there for them," he said, chuckling. "You can't fight a fire hose. They didn't like to get drowned."

Lowell, 90, is one of only a handful of strikers in the area who still can share tales of the "strike heard 'round the world," as some historians called it. . . .

In Lowell's Thetford Township home, news clippings from the strike are kept within easy reach of his worn armchair, as are photos of him at recent UAW events. Wearing a white UAW ball cap and T-shirt with "Solidarity Forever" across the chest, Lowell proudly declares that he's still a union man and regularly pays his union dues.

"It means a lot to me, talking about the strike," said Lowell. "I'm proud of what we did. People come up to me and shake my hand and say, 'Thank you for the good life I have today.'"

"It really builds me up. . . . "

Geraldine (Green) Blankinship, 88, remembers how, before the strike, her father would come home from the plants so tired that he couldn't even eat—he would fall right into bed, greasy and sweaty from a long day's work. She was 17 when her father called home to tell his family about the strike and that he would be home when it was over.

Jay J. Green, vice chairman of the strikers in Fisher 1, made good on his word—he stayed in the plant for the entire 44 days.

"When he went into the strike, he had black sideburns and beard," said Blankinship, who picketed outside the plants. "When he came out, they were almost all white, just from the strain and the stress. . . . "

"I remember the terror that struck our hearts when the National Guard came in," she said. "We never knew if he was going to be brought home in a box or what."

SOURCE: Longley, Kristin. "UAW Sit-Down Striker Arthur Lowell: 'I'm Proud of What We Did.'" *Flint Journal* (July 11, 2008). Available online at http://www.mlive.com/flintjournal/business/index.ssf/2008/07/uaw_sitdown_striker_arthur_low.html (accessed October 15, 2017). Courtesy of MLive Media Group.

Chevrolet Engine Plant No. 4 in Flint, decided to join the fight and stopped work on February 1, 1937. This led to a large decrease in the company's production and further angered many company officials.

Labor Rights

At this time, President Franklin D. Roosevelt (1882–1945) asked GM to consider giving in to the strikers' demands.

The GM workers wanted safer working conditions and better wages. They wanted the company to set rules that would protect them from injury. They demanded job security. They asked that managers not threaten to fire them and for a slower-paced workday that would not make them exhausted or sick. The UAW wanted GM to stop using workers who were not in the union. It wanted to be the only union for GM's workers so it could protect their rights and interests. GM officials began to work on an agreement with the UAW and strikers. After 44 days, the strike ended on February 11, 1937.

Aftermath

After the strike, GM agreed to several new terms, including improved working conditions and higher pay. The following year, wages for the workers increased and union membership grew. GM made the UAW the official union for its employees. Other major American car companies, such as Chrysler and Ford, allowed its workers to join the UAW in the years that followed. The UAW eventually began to represent workers in other fields and changed its name to the International Union, United Automobile, Aerospace and Agricultural Implement Workers of America.

Delano Grape Strike and Boycott

LOCATION: Delano, California
DATE: 1965–1970

The Delano grape strike and boycott were protests organized by migrant workers in California. The strike began in 1965 when groups of Filipino and Mexican American workers refused to continue picking grapes until they received better wages and working conditions. Up to that time, many farm owners had paid workers poorly and refused to respect their rights.

The laborers, organized as the United Farm Workers (UFW) and led by César Chávez (pronounced SHA-vez; 1927–1993) and Dolores Huerta (pronounced WER-tuh; 1930–), won attention and sympathy in many ways. They held strikes in the grape fields. They marched in the streets. They also asked American consumers to boycott grapes. A boycott occurs when people refuse to buy a product to show their concern about a certain issue. The protesters refused to use force or violence during their struggle. By 1970 the protesters finally reached their goal. The farm owners agreed to meet the workers' demands. The Delano grape strike and boycott showed the power of determination, nonviolence, and boycotts in winning labor rights.

Migrant labor in the United States

Migrant workers are people who travel in search of work. Usually these people move temporarily to a new location for a seasonal job, such as picking crops on a farm. Migrant workers often perform difficult tasks for long hours and accept lower pay than native-born workers do. They also face problems such as bigotry (unkindness toward people who are different) and lack legal protections. Many migrant workers have hard lives.

In the 1800s, migrant labor became important to the economy in certain parts of the United States. During that time, the country was rapidly expanding westward. Railroads allowed people to cross the nation. Discoveries of valuable natural resources brought investors rushing into new territories. People claimed and attempted to settle large amounts of land in a short time. Businesspeople searched for ways to make their new lands useful and profitable. These factors all increased the need for migrant workers.

Migrant workers became very common in California and along other parts of the Pacific Coast. This occurred for several reasons. One reason was that the land in this region was thinly settled in the 1800s, and people had to be brought in to prepare the land for use. Another reason was that these areas had a good climate and soil for farming. Fruits and vegetables such as grapes, strawberries, and lettuce grew particularly well and in large amounts. In addition, the region was close to Mexico and directly across the ocean from Asia, two major sources of migrant workers.

The protesters refused to use force or violence during their struggle. By 1970 the protesters finally reached their goal.... The Delano grape strike and boycott showed the power of determination, nonviolence, and boycotts in winning labor rights.

Labor in California

Many immigrants moved to California in search of work and a better life in America. Some of the first immigrants to the region were Chinese. Many Chinese immigrants originally worked in the mines and on the railroads. Once the railroads were constructed, Chinese workers looked for jobs on farms. Later, many Japanese people migrated to the area as well. These workers faced backbreaking labor and poor treatment from locals, many of whom held racist ideas about Asian people.

By the early 1900s, the Chinese Exclusion Act (1882) and immigration quotas blocked most Asians from moving to the United States. Many Asian laborers already living in the United States had found better-paying, safer, and more secure jobs. California and other Pacific states again faced a lack of agricultural workers. To meet this demand for labor, leaders encouraged immigration from nearby Mexico and from the Philippines, which was a US colony at the time. A colony is a land controlled by another country. From around 1917 to 1930, tens of thousands of Mexicans and Filipinos immigrated to California.

Mexican and Filipino laborers worked hard on Californian farms. Entire families, including young children, labored for long days in the field. Many of their jobs involved stooping all day to pick crops or pull weeds. This led to crooked backs and damaged hands. Many workers were hurt by tools or by carrying heavy loads. Many others suffered illness due to the pesticides (pronounced PES-teh-sides) used on the crops. Pesticides are chemicals sprayed onto plants to kill insects and weeds. The workers had very poor housing. In addition, they had little time to rest, as they were paid by how much they produced.

Although these workers' were paid very little, most earned more than they would have in their home countries. However, they also faced racism and poor treatment by locals in the United States. They often lost their jobs in times of economic trouble when native-born Americans needed work. Some workers began to realize that they were missing out on the "American Dream," which seemed to promise so much more. A few of these workers started to wonder if they could work together to fight for better wages and working conditions.

Protests begin

Farmers did not want to pay workers more money. As a result, many farm owners in California tried to hire mixed groups of Mexican and Filipino workers. The owners believed that these groups' different cultures and languages would prevent them from uniting and calling for better wages. The groups also had to compete for work. If one group was too slow or complained about mistreatment, farm owners could easily give the work to the other group.

From Fields to Picket Lines

This primary source excerpt comes from the August 15, 1970, edition of El Malcriado: The Voice of the Farm Worker *newspaper of Delano, California. The newspaper includes an article highlighting the role of women in organizing the grape boycott.*

With 300 boycott centers stretching across the United States and reaching as far as Canada, Europe and Hong Kong, the grape boycott has been the major factor in the success of United Farm Workers Organizing Committee's grape strike. Activities such as organizing, picketing stores carrying scab grapes, handing out union literature, convincing and influencing people (and consumer power) in favor of the boycott, preventing trucks from unloading hot grapes at various markets have definitely curbed the economic power of nonunion farmers.

Approximately 200 persons are on the grape boycott; of this total about half are women. Past labor movements have disregarded the woman's role in union organizing. But UFWOC's realization that women are excellent organizers has been instrumental in the union's successful grape strike and economic boycott....

Heading the Montreal and Quebec boycott, for example, is 23-year-old Jessica Govea. Citing several reasons why she joined the union four years ago, Jessica said, "I did farm work, and I went to schools where children's futures were determined not by their intelligence but by the color of their skin and the size of their parents' pocketbooks. I hated the way we were made to exist by the present power without knowing what to do about it."

When she first arrived on the Montreal boycott two years ago, Jessica's two biggest obstacles were (1) not speaking French in a 75% French-speaking city, and (2) being the sole boycotter in the fourth largest grape eating city in the world.

"It has been difficult to come from the 'farm' to the big city (never having been in the big city before), but we are making tremendous headway in the boycott in Montreal now. Also, I was in Toronto nine months when I first went on the boycott, and under the 'directorship' of Marshall Ganz, we cut grape shipments about 50 percent," she states....

Jessica's boycott experiences haven't changed her general outlook on life. However, she feels she's grown and become a better person because "our movement has grown and become a stronger and more determined movement."

"I no longer belong to myself but to the thousands of people who are struggling to be free … farm workers, native Indians, blacks, Vietnamese. They are proud and they are brave, and I am happy that I am a part of them," she explained.

SOURCE: "Huelga Women and the Boycott: From the Fields to the Picket Line." *El Malcriado: The Voice of the Farm Worker* V, no. 5 (August 15, 1970): 12–13. Available online at https://libraries.ucsd.edu/farmworkermovement/ufwarchives/elmalcriado/1970/August%2015,%201970%20%20No%205_PDF.pdf (accessed October 15, 2017). Courtesy of United Farm Workers of America.

Labor Rights

Haymarket Square Riot, 1886

César Chávez was famous for his determination to avoid violence. However, not all protests in support of labor rights remain peaceful. The anger and tension of workers' rights disputes have led people on both sides to engage in violence. One of the most violent incidents in American history was the Haymarket Square Riot of 1886.

In early May 1886 workers held a strike at McCormick Reaper Works in Chicago, Illinois. The factory produced machines called reapers, which were used to harvest grain. During the strike, the Chicago police arrived and killed and injured several workers.

On May 4, 1886, labor radicals organized a rally at nearby Haymarket Square. A radical is someone who uses extreme measures to make a point or bring about change. The rally was meant not only to demonstrate for workers' rights but also to protest the recent police violence.

A group of Chicago police officers arrived to try to break up the Haymarket rally. Someone in the crowd threw a bomb at the police. In the confusion, the police began firing their guns. Other people may have fired weapons, too. The rally quickly became a riot. By the time the riot ended, eight people, mostly police officers, had died. Many more were badly hurt.

Chicago police and many other citizens called for justice. They believed the labor leaders were dangerous radicals and murderers. Many of these leaders were targeted because they were immigrants from Germany and other countries.

Several labor leaders were arrested and tried in August 1886. In a trial that many considered unfair, the laborers were found guilty. Several were hanged for their supposed roles in the crimes. This result further divided people's opinions on the matter. Some people believed that the labor leaders were criminals

---

For a while, this system worked well for the farm owners and created enormous profits. Yet, over time, the Mexicans and Filipinos began to find common ground. Both groups realized they were outsiders facing the constant threat of losing their jobs to native-born Americans, who also received higher wages. Many migrant workers, especially Filipinos, became increasingly bold in their attempts to improve their situations through labor unions and strikes. Labor unions are groups that help protect workers' rights.

In 1965 Filipino farmworkers established the Agricultural Workers Organizing Committee (AWOC). The main goal of the AWOC was to demand better wages and working conditions from grape growers in Delano, California, through strikes and demonstrations. The AWOC needed more help if it intended to have any influence against the powerful farm bosses.

Labor Rights

who were rightfully punished. Others believed that workers had important concerns and that the real issue was giving laborers the rights they deserved.

The Haymarket Square Riot in Chicago began as a strike rally. Things turned explosive when an unknown person threw a bomb, which resulted in the deaths of at least eight people, mostly policemen. © EVERETT HISTORICAL/SHUTTERSTOCK.COM.

Filipino union leaders offered a partnership with a mainly Mexican American labor organization, the National Farm Workers Association (NFWA).

Chávez and partnership

César Chávez and Dolores Huerta founded the NFWA. The two ran the organization together, with Chávez in a leadership position. Chávez, a Mexican American, was born in Arizona. The Chávez family owned a farm and some small businesses but lost it all during the Great Depression (1929–1941). The Great Depression was a time of major economic problems in the United States and other countries. The Chávez family could no longer keep their land. They were forced to join thousands of other poor families who moved to California in search of jobs.

César Chávez quickly learned the suffering of migrant workers. He worked long hours for low wages while facing widespread racism. As a young man, he became interested in activism, or ways of working to bring about change. The teachings of Indian activist Mohandas Gandhi (pronounced gahn-DEE; 1869–1948) and American civil rights leader the Rev. Dr. Martin Luther King Jr. (1929–1968) were of particular interest to Chávez. These leaders used nonviolent methods to overcome hate and unfair laws. Chávez became convinced that agricultural workers could peacefully win fair wages and better treatment. Though his activism, Chávez met Huerta, who also fought for the rights of workers. The two continued their partnership for many years and worked tirelessly to help migrant workers.

In 1965 Chávez agreed to join the Filipino workers in the Delano grape strike. The Mexican and Filipino labor organizations became one group, the United Farm Workers (UFW). Chávez ensured that the UFW would foster cooperation between the workers and use nonviolent methods in all their demonstrations. At last, the unified farmworkers had a chance to win their rights. Progress would be difficult to achieve and would take many years of effort.

A unique approach

The UFW fully supported the workers striking in the Delano grape fields. However, the organization also took other steps to help workers gain more rights. One approach involved organizing a march to rally support for the workers. Organizers called the march the *peregrinación* (pronounced pair-eh-GREE-noss-e-on), or pilgrimage. A pilgrimage is a long journey of great importance. Chávez led this 300-mile (483-kilometer) march from Delano to Sacramento, the capital city of California. It succeeded in raising public awareness of the workers' problems. People from many backgrounds wanted to help the workers.

Even more important, the UFW encouraged a boycott of grapes. The UFW sent representatives around the nation to ask consumers to stop buying California grapes or drinks made from them. Millions of Americans agreed to participate in the boycott. The strike plus the boycott hurt farm operators. Striking workers refused to pick the crops, and consumers refused to buy products made from them. Suddenly, farm owners saw their profits falling sharply.

Under Chávez's and Huerta's leadership, the Delano grape strike and boycott gained strength. Chávez insisted that all the protesters remain peaceful, and he put down any attempts to use violence during the protests. He held tight to the teachings of Gandhi and King, who said that determined but peaceful resistance was braver and more powerful than fighting. Chávez also tried different methods of protest, including some that put him at risk. For example, he stopped eating for 25 days to show his dedication and pure intentions.

Results

The grape strike and boycott lasted for five years. The workers suffered, and many lost all their money. Still, they kept working toward their goal. During this time, Chávez became an internationally famous leader and hero. King and US Senator Robert F. Kennedy (1925–1968) praised him and his work. Huerta also became well known for her efforts and received several awards for her work. Millions of Americans showed their support for the UFW by making small changes to their daily lives, mainly by not buying grapes or grape products. That helped the workers gain strength and showed Americans the power of small sacrifices to help people in need.

In 1970 the owners of the grape farms finally gave in. They could no longer afford to keep denying the workers' demands. The owners agreed to sign union contracts. These were agreements to provide better wages to workers and give them better benefits.

César Chávez (left, seated) claps after John Giumarra Sr. (right), one of California's largest table grape growers, waves his arms after signing a contract. © BETTMANN/GETTY IMAGES.

Labor Rights

After five difficult years, the UFW had won. People around the United States celebrated with them. Now the workers would be able to earn livable wages and provide for their families. The work of Chávez, Huerta, and the UFW did not end there though. In the coming years, these reformers moved to other places to continue helping workers in need. They held true to their nonviolent principles and their methods of boycotting unfairly produced goods to win many successes for agricultural workers.

Fast-Food Workers' Strike

LOCATION: United States
DATE: Beginning in 2012

Workers at various McDonald's and other fast-food restaurants throughout the United States organized several strikes beginning in 2012 to protest low wages. A strike is a work stoppage to force employers to meet certain demands. The employees also wanted the right to form unions. Unions are organizations that protect workers' rights. The first strike took place for one day in New York City on November 29, 2012. About 200 people participated.

The largest percentage of employees who walked off their jobs were from McDonald's. Workers from fast-food restaurants including Burger King, Taco Bell, KFC, Wendy's, and Pizza Hut also joined them. The organization New York Communities for Change (NYCC) helped to plan the strike and get people involved. The workers, whose pay in New York City ranged from $7.25 to about $9 an hour, fought for what they considered a livable wage of $15 an hour. The US government has set $7.25 an hour as the minimum amount that workers can be paid. The employees also wanted to organize unions without the fear of losing their jobs or being mistreated.

In the years that followed, fast-food workers staged several national and international strikes and formed Fight for $15. This movement, which aimed to raise the federal minimum wage to $15 an hour for all employees, gained much notice. During his term, US President Barack Obama (1961–) introduced bills, asking Congress to vote on raising the federal minimum wage. None of these passed, and as of 2017, the federal minimum wage remained at $7.25. Many states and cities have higher minimum wage rates. The Fight for $15 movement continued to plan and organize fast-food strikes throughout the 2010s.

Background

Prior to the 2012 strike, members from NYCC met with fast-food workers for months. They helped them realize that they needed to fight for better wages and the right to form and join unions so they had protections. Many fast-food workers did not work full time or enough hours to qualify for benefits such as health or dental insurance. Many also relied on second jobs or government assistance to help pay for food, housing, and health care.

NYCC members told the workers that they could help fight for change. It took the members a long time to convince people that they could make a difference. Workers were afraid to speak out because they needed their jobs. They also did not want to risk poor treatment by management or having their hours cut. In addition, it was hard to persuade fast-food workers to organize unions because many of these employees worked only part time and did not plan to stay at these jobs for a long time. However, due to the weakness of the economy and the decrease in available well-paying jobs, many people rely on fast-food restaurants for full-time work to support their families.

Eventually, workers began to trust the NYCC. The NYCC set several strikes at different locations throughout New York City on November 29, 2012. Some workers took the day off from work while others joined the protests after or before their work shifts. They held mostly peaceful protests outside of the different fast-food chains around the city. Some carried signs and chanted, "Hey, hey, what do you say? We demand fair pay." They returned to work the following day.

At fast-food chains, workers keep the companies operating from day to day. The workers outnumber managers and corporate executives. Workers felt that because of this they should at least be making enough money to support themselves. They noted how much the company spends on advertising campaigns in relation to their wages. For example, singer Justin Timberlake (1981–) was paid $6 million for a commercial featuring him singing the McDonald's jingle, "I'm Lovin' It," yet employees barely made more than minimum wage in many places.

They held mostly peaceful protests outside of the different fast-food chains around the city. Some carried signs and chanted, "Hey, hey, what do you say? We demand fair pay." They returned to work the following day.

Many people did not agree with the workers. While some restaurant owners wanted to pay their employees higher wages, they did not know where they would get the money. They said that the higher wages would have to come from the customers in the form of higher food prices. They also said they would have to cut hours and hire fewer employees to do the same amount of work. They also suggested they could replace employees with self-serve stations to make up the difference. All of this would limit jobs and force existing workers to perform more tasks.

Strikes

The NYCC along with another group called Fast Food Forward led by the Service Employees International Union continued to plan similar strikes throughout the United States. On December 5, 2013, workers in 100 cities held one-day walkouts. About 100 workers in New York City marched to the beat of a drum into a McDonald's restaurant while chanting "We can't survive on $7.25." Groups of workers in Detroit, Michigan, sang "Hey hey, ho ho, $7.40 has got to go!" outside of two McDonald's restaurants.

Some restaurants punished employees who participated in these events. Some warned employees that they would lose their jobs if they did not show up for their scheduled shifts. Others threatened to cut the workers' hours or give them additional duties.

Fast-food workers, along with health-care and other low-wage earners, rally together to demand a higher minimum wage. They are seeking $15 an hour and better working conditions. © MARIE KANGER BORN/SHUTTERSTOCK.OM.

Global recognition On May 15, 2014, Fast Food Forward helped to organize a one-day protest that stretched beyond the United States. More than 30 countries joined workers throughout the United States to demand $15 an hour at fast-food chains. Protesters in the United States continued marches and walkouts. While these protests were smaller than previous demonstrations, workers in cities around the globe joined them. For example, New Zealand workers marched holding banners while those in the Philippines organized a flash mob inside a McDonald's location. A flash mob is an organized group of people who gather at a specified spot at a specified time to perform.

Protests lead to arrests Protests in more than 150 cities were held on September 4, 2014. These gatherings were not as peaceful as previous ones. Hundreds of people arranged sit-ins and large demonstrations to get their voices heard. During a sit-in, groups of people sit in areas, usually blocking streets or entrances to buildings, as a form of protest. Home health-care workers and janitors also joined the fast-food protests. Many people hoped that the increase in numbers and the addition of people from other professions would strengthen the fight. Police responded to many of these protests around the nation. They arrested nearly 500 people, including US Representative Gwen Moore (1951–), a Democrat from Wisconsin, who took part in a Milwaukee sit-in.

Many restaurants and organizations spoke out against the protests. They criticized the use of sit-ins and called them dangerous to both workers in the streets and customers trying to enter the buildings. Some restaurants called the protests nothing more than a cry for attention from the news media. Many people accused Fast Food Forward and the other organizations of staging the demonstrations with protesters who were not even fast-food workers. None of the restaurants in the cities where the protests were held had to close because of a lack of employees. Many said the strikes did not affect business.

Gain in numbers and continued support On April 15, 2015, tens of thousands of people joined protests in more than 200 cities across the United States. This time the rallies forced some fast-food restaurants to close for the day. By this time, the movement, which began in 2012, had grown to include low-paid workers in other fields. The movement gained support from officials such as former US labor secretary Robert Reich (1946–), who led a strike in Oakland, California, that day.

The largest strike since the movement began was held in April 2016. Protesters in more than 300 cities in about 40 countries took part in the strikes. Workers from fast-food restaurants, home health-care agencies, airports, and retail stores along with many other low-paid individuals joined the marches. The demonstrations were held from New York City to Tokyo, Japan, and Toronto, Canada. The protests and work stoppages continued nationally and around the globe throughout the 2010s, with thousands of people joining the efforts.

Successes

The fight for $15 an hour made its way into politics and found support from various lawmakers. President Obama supported raising the federal minimum wage and urged Congress to pass legislation. US Senator Bernie Sanders (1941–), a politician from Vermont who ran for president in 2016, voiced his support. The 2016 Democratic presidential candidate Hillary Rodham Clinton (1947–) addressed wages during her campaign.

While the federal minimum wage remained unchanged at $7.25 an hour as of 2017, the movement for $15 an hour had some success. In response, several states passed laws to increase the state minimum wage for either all employees or workers in certain jobs. As of 2017, 29 states and Washington, DC, had a minimum wage higher than the national rate. Some states signed laws that would eventually raise the state minimum to $15 an hour over the next few years. Many cities also increased their minimum wage rates.

For More Information

BOOKS

Davis, Barbara J. *The National Grape Boycott: A Victory for Farmworkers.* Mankato, MN: Compass Point Books, 2008.

Kallen, Stuart A. *We Are Not Beasts of Burden: Cesar Chavez and the Delano Grape Strike, California, 1965–1970.* Minneapolis, MN: Twenty-First Century Books, 2011.

Kraft, Betsy Harvey. *Mother Jones: One Woman's Fight for Labor.* New York: Clarion, 1995.

Robinson, J. Dennis. *Striking Back: The Fight to End Child Labor Exploitation.* Mankato, MN: Compass Point Books, 2010.

Skurzynski, Gloria. *Sweat and Blood: A History of U.S. Labor Unions.* Minneapolis, MN: Twenty-First Century Books, 2009.

PERIODICALS

Greenhouse, Steven. "Hundreds of Fast-Food Workers Striking for Higher Wages Are Arrested." *New York Times* (September 5, 2014). Available online at https://www.nytimes.com/2014/09/05/business/economy/fast-food-workers-seeking-higher-wages-are-arrested-during-sit-ins.html?mcubz=3 (accessed August 25, 2017).

Greenhouse, Steven. "With Day of Protests, Fast-Food Workers Seek More Pay." *New York Times* (November 30, 2012). Available online at http://www.nytimes.com/2012/11/30/nyregion/fast-food-workers-in-new-york-city-rally-for-higher-wages.html?mcubz=3 (accessed August 25, 2017).

McDonnell, Steve. "Foreign vs. U.S. Labor Laws." *Houston Chronicle.* Available online at http://smallbusiness.chron.com/foreign-vs-us-labor-laws-77421.html (accessed August 25, 2017).

WEBSITES

Abbott, Franky. "The United Farm Workers and the Delano Grape Strike." Digital Public Library of America. https://dp.la/primary-source-sets/sets/the-united-farm-workers-and-the-delano-grape-strike (accessed August 25, 2017).

Cesar Chavez Foundation. http://www.chavezfoundation.org/ (accessed August 25, 2017).

"Child Labor Index 2014." Verisk Maplecroft. https://maplecroft.com/portfolio/new-analysis/2013/10/15/child-labour-risks-increase-china-and-russia-most-progress-shown-south-america-maplecroft-index/ (accessed October 16, 2017).

"Dolores Huerta." Dolores Huerta Foundation. http://doloreshuerta.org/dolores-huerta/ (accessed October 7, 2017).

"Early Factory Legislation." UK Parliament. http://www.parliament.uk/about/living-heritage/transformingsociety/livinglearning/19thcentury/overview/earlyfactorylegislation/ (accessed August 25, 2017).

Friedman, Gail. "March of the Mill Children." Encyclopedia of Greater Philadelphia. http://philadelphiaencyclopedia.org/archive/march-of-the-mill-children/ (accessed August 25, 2017).

"History of Labor Day." US Department of Labor. https://www.dol.gov/general/laborday/history (accessed August 25, 2017).

Hunt, Katie. "The 10 Worst Countries for Child Labor." CNN, October 15, 2013. http://www.cnn.com/2013/10/15/world/child-labor-index-2014/index.html (accessed August 25, 2017).

Kim, Inga. "The 1965–1970 Delano Grape Strike and Boycott." United Farm Workers, March 7, 2017. http://ufw.org/1965-1970-delano-grape-strike-boycott (accessed August 25, 2017).

"Labor Laws and Issues." USA.gov. https://www.usa.gov/labor-laws (accessed August 25, 2017).

"Mother Jones." AFL-CIO. https://aflcio.org/about/history/labor-history-people/mother-jones (accessed October 7, 2017).

Taylor, Beth. "A Right You Don't Want: The Right to Work." PayScale. https://www.payscale.com/career-news/2013/07/a-right-you-dont-want-the-right-to-work (accessed October 16, 2017).

"'They Bear All the Pain': Hazardous Child Labor in Afghanistan." Human Rights Watch. https://www.hrw.org/report/2016/07/14/they-bear-all-pain/hazardous-child-labor-afghanistan (accessed October 16, 2017).

"Topics in Chronicling America—The Haymarket Affair." Library of Congress. https://www.loc.gov/rr/news/topics/haymarket.html (accessed August 25, 2017).

Tuncer, Ertan. "The Flint, Michigan, Sit-Down Strike (1936–37)." Library of Congress, July 2012. https://www.loc.gov/rr/business/businesshistory/February/flint.html (accessed October 7, 2017).

"The 2016 ITUC Global Rights Index: The World's Worst Countries for Workers." International Trade Union Confederation (ITUC). https://www.ituc-csi.org/IMG/pdf/ituc-violationmap-2016-en_final.pdf (accessed August 25, 2017).

Yu, Titi. "A New Documentary Celebrates the Life and Work of Dolores Huerta." Moyers & Company, October 6, 2017. http://billmoyers.com/story/dolores-huerta-documentary (accessed October 16, 2017).

14

LGBTQ Rights

Stonewall Riots **435**

White Night Riots **441**

Westboro Protests of Matthew Shepard **445**

Shanghai Pride Festival **452**

Protests of North Carolina House Bill 2 **458**

The LGBTQ community includes a wide range of people from various backgrounds. The letters *LGBTQ* stand for lesbian, gay, bisexual, transgender, and queer. The terms represented by these letters have to do with sexual orientation, which refers to people's sexual identity and the people to whom they are attracted. For instance, lesbians are women who are attracted to other women. Gay men are attracted to other men. Bisexuals can be attracted to people of the same gender or a different gender. In contrast, straight people are attracted only to people of the opposite gender. Homosexuals are people who are attracted to the same sex; heterosexuals are people who are attracted to the opposite sex.

Transgender men and women are people whose gender identity and gender expression differ from the sex they were assigned at birth. Gender identity is a person's internal experience of gender. Gender expression refers to how people present themselves to the outside world. It is visible in the clothes individuals wear, the pronouns they use to refer to themselves, and the way they style or cut their hair. As transgender individuals transition from living life as one gender to another gender, they often alter their gender expression.

Queer is a term used by some individuals in the community who feel that the terms *gay, lesbian,* or *bisexual* are too limiting to accurately describe their sexual orientation. *Genderqueer* is a similar term that is sometimes used to describe a person who expresses a gender identity that is not entirely feminine or masculine. People sometimes refer to this as being nonbinary.

In the past, *queer* was once offensive to many people in the LGBTQ community. However, many people now use the term in a more positive manner to describe individuals who do not conform to traditional definitions of sexual orientation or gender identity. Some people recognize the Q at the end of LGBTQ to mean "questioning." This refers to

429

LGBTQ Rights

WORDS TO KNOW

Conservative: A person who holds traditional beliefs concerning social issues and favors limited government spending.

Gender expression: Individuals' external presentation of gender, including how they dress, style their hair, and refer to themselves.

Gender identity: Individuals' personal inner experience of their gender, which may not match the sex they were assigned at birth.

Hate crime: A crime committed against a person because of his or her race, religion, national origin, gender, sexual orientation, or disability.

Hate group: A group that supports hatred, anger, and/or violence toward members of a certain race, religion, national origin, gender, or sexual orientation.

Liberal: A person who believes that government should actively support social and political change.

Picket: To stand or march in a public place to protest something.

Repeal: To cancel or withdraw something, especially a law.

Sexual orientation: A person's sexual identity, which relates to the people to whom a person is attracted. Sexual orientation includes gay, lesbian, bisexual, straight, and asexual.

Voluntary manslaughter: A sentence for a crime in which a person has no previous intent or plans to kill another person, which usually happens in the moment.

individuals who are uncertain of their sexual orientation or gender identity or interpret their identity as not conforming to rigid choices from a set of limited options.

LGBTQ individuals are part of every society around the world. Some countries are more welcoming to LGBTQ people than others. Countries with strict governments or strong religious traditions often do not recognize LGBTQ rights. Often, leaders of these governments or religions will argue that homosexuality goes against traditional values or religious beliefs. Since the early 20th century, LGBTQ communities in many countries have made great strides in gaining civil rights and marriage equality. Marriage equality means that same-sex couples are afforded the same right to marry as opposite-sex couples. Nevertheless, the fight for certain rights and recognition continues.

History of LGBTQ rights

LGBTQ individuals have existed throughout history. In ancient Egypt a queen named Hatshepsut (1538–1458 BCE) declared herself pharaoh

CRITICAL THINKING QUESTIONS

1. What more could be done to help the LGBTQ community gain social acceptance and equal rights? Explain your reasoning.

2. Do you think the Shanghai Pride festival will help Chinese society become more accepting of LGBTQ people? Why or why not?

3. Do you think the modern LGBTQ movement would exist if the Stonewall Riots had not occurred? Why or why not?

4. How did Matthew Shepard's death advance the LGBTQ rights movement? How did it harm the movement? Explain your reasoning.

5. What do you think made Harvey Milk so popular with his supporters?

6. What do you think most contributed to the repeal of HB2? Explain your reasoning.

---

after her husband's death and wore male clothing while she ruled. Men had relationships with other men in ancient Greece. The Greek poet Sappho (c. 675–c. 570 BCE) was a lesbian. She lived on the island of Lesbos, which is where the term *lesbian* comes from. Some historians also believe that the Macedonian emperor Alexander the Great (356–323 BCE) was bisexual.

Despite this, LGBTQ individuals in many societies had to hide their sexual orientation or gender identity from the rest of the world for much of history. As civilizations developed, many governments created laws against homosexuality. In some places, gays and lesbians faced imprisonment or even death when others discovered their sexual orientation. For example, the famous British playwright Oscar Wilde (1854–1900) was gay and was arrested in 1895 for "gross indecency between males." Wilde was imprisoned for two years.

Being openly LGBTQ was often dangerous. Still, many gay and lesbian communities began forming in major cities around the world in the beginning of the 20th century. These areas typically had spaces, especially bars, where LGBTQ people could socialize with one another. Members of these communities had to keep their identities secret but now had places where they could be themselves.

The beginning of the modern LGBTQ rights movement Many historians contend that the Stonewall Riots in New York City in 1969 were the start of the modern LGBTQ movement. However, people were fighting for equal treatment for LGBTQ citizens for decades before Stonewall. In the

United States, one of the first LGBTQ rights organizations was the Society for Human Rights. Activist and postal worker Henry Gerber (1892–1972) founded the organization in Chicago, Illinois, in 1924. An activist is someone who fights for a certain cause or issue. The society lasted less than a year, and officials at the postal service fired Gerber when they learned he was gay.

During the 1940s and 1950s, the US government banned LGBTQ individuals from openly serving in the armed forces and working for the federal government. Such laws spurred some LGBTQ activists into action. Actor and activist Harry Hay formed the Mattachine (pronounced MATT-a-sheen) Society in Los Angeles, California, in 1950 to fight for the acceptance of gay people. Supporters eventually established other branches of the society in cities such as Chicago, New York City, and Philadelphia, Pennsylvania. Other similar organizations started forming around the country during the 1950s and 1960s.

LGBTQ people were not only fighting laws that discriminated against them. They also had to deal with the stigma created by medical organizations that insisted that being gay or transgender was a disorder. Stigma refers to a set of negative beliefs about a person or group. For example, in 1952 the American Psychiatric Association (APA) referred to homosexuality as a personality disorder in its manual, the *Diagnostic and Statistical Manual of Mental Disorders*. This description contributed to the idea that LGBTQ people had something wrong with them or could be "cured" of being gay or transgender. The APA did not remove this listing until 1973.

Challenging times The LGBTQ community fought for victories and faced challenges in the 1960s. In 1961 Illinois became the first state to repeal, or cancel, its laws against homosexuality. Activists were also able to repeal some laws that made it illegal for bars to serve alcohol to LGBTQ customers. These successes were rare, though. In 1967 the US Supreme Court upheld a ruling that allowed authorities to deport noncitizens who were LGBTQ in *Boutilier v. Immigration and Naturalization Service*.

In addition, police still targeted LGBTQ citizens and the places where they socialized. In late June 1969, police raided a gay bar in New York City called the Stonewall Inn. However, instead of following police orders or quickly leaving the scene of the raid, the LGBTQ customers stayed and fought back. Riots and protests lasted for several days. Known as the Stonewall Riots, this event helped launch the modern LGBTQ rights movement. The riots made the fight for equal treatment under the law more visible. They also led to the establishment of annual gay pride marches across the country and, eventually, around the world.

The 1970s continued to be a time of great change for LGBTQ citizens in the United States. In 1973 Lambda Legal became the first civil rights organization dedicated to fighting for legal protections for the LGBTQ community. Gay men and lesbians were also becoming more openly involved in politics. In 1974 Kathy Kozachenko (1954–) became the first openly gay candidate to win an election in the United States when she ran for a seat on the city council of Ann Arbor, Michigan. Harvey Milk (1930–1978) became the first openly gay man to hold a public office in California when he was sworn in as city supervisor of San Francisco in 1978. He and the city's mayor were murdered by a former employee a few months later. The following year, the San Francisco LGBTQ community rioted when Milk's killer was given a light sentence.

The LGBTQ community faced a new set of challenges in the 1980s. In 1981 several gay men in Los Angeles were diagnosed with what doctors thought was pneumonia, a disease that can trigger breathing complications and lead to death. These patients also seemed to have a compromised immune system, which is what protects the body from diseases. Eventually, scientists discovered that this disease was actually acquired immunodeficiency syndrome (AIDS). AIDS is caused by human immunodeficiency virus (HIV). People contract HIV through unprotected sex and through contact with HIV-positive blood or other body fluids.

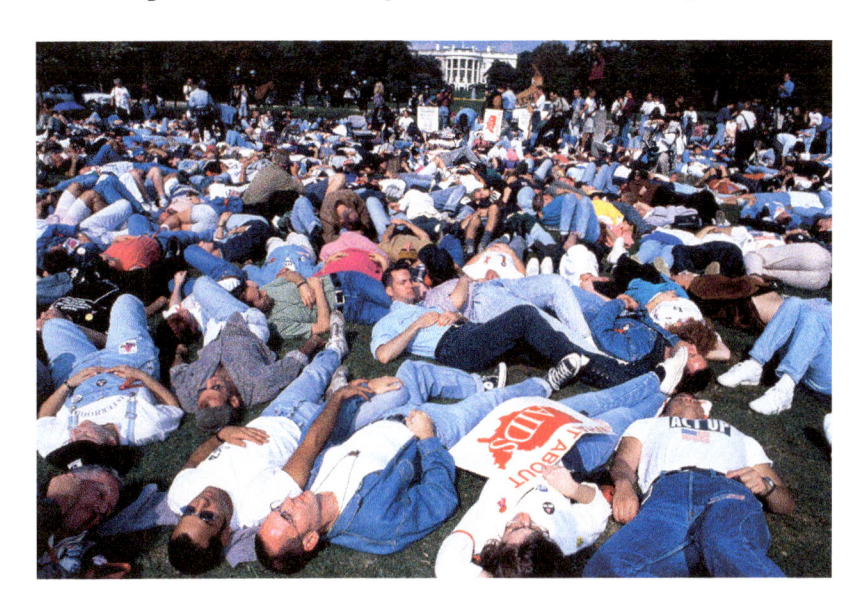

Many protests have been held to demand the government take more action to stop HIV/AIDS. Here, in 1992, activists from ACT UP held a die-in on the lawn in front of the US Capitol building. © JEFFREY MARKOWITZ/SYGMA VIA GETTY IMAGES.

HIV/AIDS particularly affected gay and bisexual men. However, HIV/AIDS can be contracted by people of all sexual orientations, not just LGBTQ people. Many LGBTQ rights activists turned their attention to fighting for the care of HIV/AIDS patients. Others created education programs to inform members of the LGBTQ community about how to protect themselves against the disease.

Continued fight for rights The 1990s brought more attention to LGBTQ rights. In 1993 President Bill Clinton (1946–) signed a military policy that prevented openly LGBTQ people from serving in the military. However, the bill also prevented discrimination against LGBTQ military members who were not out. The policy was known as "Don't Ask, Don't Tell." Popular culture was also starting to represent the LGBTQ community more frequently. Mainstream media introduced the first LGBTQ leading TV characters during this decade. Comedian Ellen DeGeneres (1958–) came out as gay in 1997. The character she played on her TV sitcom also came out. DeGeneres's character became the first lesbian leading character on a network TV show. The following year the show *Will and Grace* featured the first gay male leading character on TV.

In 1998 the murder of college student Matthew Shepard (1976–1998) in Laramie, Wyoming, shocked the country. His death and the trial of his killers led to protests and calls for changes to hate-crime laws so that they included LGBTQ individuals. A hate crime occurs when an individual targets another person based on his or her race, religion, gender, or sexual orientation. It took 11 years for the federal government to pass a hate-crime prevention law in Shepard's name.

In 1993 President Bill Clinton signed a military policy that prevented openly LGBTQ people from serving in the military. However, the bill also prevented discrimination against LGBTQ military members who were not out. The policy was known as "Don't Ask, Don't Tell."

LGBTQ rights in the 21st century For the first 15 years of the 21st century, LGBTQ activists focused on the fight for marriage equality. Several other countries had already legalized same-sex marriage by this time. However, many countries, like China and Russia, continued to ban same-sex marriage. Some US states, such as California in 1999 and Vermont in 2000, had legalized civil unions or domestic partnerships. However, such unions did not extend these partners the same rights as married couples. Some states also legalized same-sex marriage, but the fight for marriage equality across the nation continued. Finally, in 2015, the US Supreme Court ruled in *Obergefell v. Hodges* that denying gay couples the right to marry was illegal under the 14th Amendment to the US Constitution. This legalized same-sex marriage in all 50 states.

Also in the early 21st century, the fight for transgender rights and recognition gained national attention. In 2016 the North Carolina General Assembly passed a state law that prevented transgender men and women from using restrooms and locker rooms in public schools and government buildings that corresponded to their gender identity. Instead, the law said they had to use the facilities that matched the sex that doctors and caretakers had assigned them at birth. This led to protests from citizens. The law also resulted in a loss of jobs and money in the state because many companies and entertainers refused to do business there. Other states debated the passage of such laws and their potential consequences in the late 2010s.

Transgender men and women also fought for the right to serve openly in the military. President Barack Obama (1961–) signed the Don't Ask, Don't Tell Repeal Act in 2010, allowing gay men and lesbians to serve openly beginning in 2011. However, transgender officers were still not granted the same rights. On June 30, 2016, the military announced that it was lifting the ban on transgender people serving. But this did not last long. On July 26, 2017, President Donald Trump (1946–) announced on Twitter that transgender individuals would not be allowed to serve in the military in any capacity. Many LGBTQ organizations and veterans organizations criticized the president's decision. The ban was challenged in court and blocked. In late November 2017 a federal judge ruled that the military had to allow qualified transgender people to enlist as of January 1, 2018.

While LGBTQ individuals have gained many rights over the years, many battles remain. Progress is often overshadowed by incidents of persecution and discrimination toward LGBTQ people, especially in countries with strict expectations for traditional societal behaviors. As in the past, social acceptance and equal treatment under the law continue to be major goals of the worldwide LGBTQ rights movement in the late 2010s.

Stonewall Riots

LOCATION: Greenwich Village, New York

DATE: June 28 to July 3, 1969

The Stonewall Riots were not the first protest against discrimination by the American LGBTQ community. Lesbian, gay, bisexual, transgender, and queer US citizens have been fighting for their rights for years.

However, historians often recognize the events that occurred in the early morning hours of June 28, 1969, in the Greenwich Village section of New York City as the start of the modern LGBTQ rights movement. Following the riots, LGBTQ rights groups formed in most major cities across the country. Organizers held marches to mark the one-year anniversary of the Stonewall Riots in several large cities. These marches eventually became the inspiration for the gay pride parades held throughout the nation, and ultimately around the world, every year to celebrate the LGBTQ community.

Climate for LGBTQ New Yorkers in 1969

The 1960s were a difficult time for LGBTQ Americans. In many places, it was not legal or safe for gay, lesbian, bisexual, or transgender people to be open about their sexual orientation or gender identity. Many states still had laws against LGBTQ citizens expressing affection toward one another in public. In addition, some cities and states even had laws requiring people to dress in clothing that was "appropriate" to their assigned sex at birth. New York City was one of the places with laws like this.

Another problem was that many bars would not openly serve LGBTQ individuals because the New York State Liquor Authority would shut them down if they did so. The organization claimed that any location where LGBTQ people organized was "disorderly." The New York State Liquor Authority is the organization that gives bars licenses to serve alcohol. In 1966 LGBTQ activists fought against this policy, and it was reversed. Even though LGBTQ people could now be served in bars, they were still not allowed to display affection toward their partners or even dance together in public.

Because of this, many LGBTQ people would go only to gay bars. Members of organized crime families, sometimes referred to as the Mafia, often owned these bars. Most of the time, these bars did not have licenses from the New York State Liquor Authority to serve alcohol, but the Mafia paid police officers to ignore this. In some cases, organized crime families opened "bottle bars," bars where people brought their own alcohol. Bottle bars charged customers an entrance fee. Often, gay bars charged high admission fees. Bar owners knew that LGBTQ customers often had nowhere else to go, so they would pay the high fees.

The Stonewall Inn on Christopher Street in Greenwich Village was one of these gay bars. Greenwich Village is a section of New York City where many LGBTQ people lived or worked in the 1960s. The Stonewall Inn was once a restaurant. The Mafia purchased the inn in 1966 and made it a gay bar. The Stonewall was a bottle bar, so it did not need a liquor license. The owners also paid off local police to overlook activities at the bar. The police were then supposed to alert the bar owners about possible raids, so customers could leave and workers could remove any illegal alcohol. This allowed LGBTQ customers to feel somewhat comfortable at the Stonewall Inn although police still occasionally raided the bar.

The night of the riot

The Stonewall Inn had already been raided on June 24, 1969. During that raid, police officers led by Deputy Inspector Seymour Pine (1919–2010) searched the bar and removed any alcohol they found that had been served without a license. This gave Pine the evidence he needed to support the call for another raid. At the time, law enforcement officials believed the Mafia was involved in the theft of international bonds. Bonds are issued by banks and governments to raise money for projects and services and can be redeemed after a certain period for a profit. The police suspected that some of the Mafia's illegal activities regarding these bonds took place at the Stonewall Inn. They prepared for a larger raid on the bar later that week.

On Friday, June 27, 1969, about 200 people were gathered at the bar. Many of them danced, while others drank and talked. Undercover officers were in the bar as well. In the early morning hours of June 28, police in uniform entered the bar. Some LGBTQ customers were able to leave before the police blocked the doors. The officers then started separating men, women, and gender-nonconforming customers into groups. People who are gender-nonconforming do not automatically follow traditional expectations for male and female appearance and presentation. Police began inspecting customers to see if they were wearing at least three gender-appropriate items of clothing, according to the New York City law. They also checked customers' IDs to see if they were underage. Those who had appropriate clothing and IDs were let out of the bar.

Often, LGBTQ customers would leave the area immediately after a raid. They did not protest for fear that police would arrest them. If they were arrested, their names would appear in newspapers. At the time,

In the early morning hours of June 28, police in uniform entered the bar. Some LGBTQ customers were able to leave before the police blocked the doors. The officers then started separating men, women, and gender-nonconforming customers into groups.

LGBTQ Rights

Marriage Equality

Gay and lesbian citizens in the United States fought for many years for the right to marry their partners. Many states had laws banning marriage between same-sex couples. On the federal level, President Bill Clinton even signed the Defense of Marriage Act in 1996. This law denied federal benefits to married same-sex partners.

Although some states strongly opposed same-sex marriage, others wanted to extend marriage rights to LGBTQ people. In the late 1990s, some states granted same-sex couples the right to domestic partnerships or civil unions. Critics argued that this was not the same as obtaining marriage equality. Partners in civil unions did not have the same rights as spouses. Their relationships were also not always recognized in other states.

Because of this, the fight for marriage equality continued. In the early 21st century, several states legalized same-sex marriage. However, it was still not legal on a federal level. This eventually led to the US Supreme Court case *Obergefell v. Hodges*. Jim Obergefell was the partner of John Arthur. The two spent 18 years together before marrying in Maryland in 2013. They lived in Ohio, where same-sex marriage was still illegal.

Their marriage, however, lasted only a few months. Arthur had been very ill when they married and died shortly after. Obergefell wanted his name on Arthur's death certificate as the surviving spouse. The state of Ohio opposed this and won a court case against Obergefell.

Obergefell appealed the decision to the Supreme Court. His case and the cases of several other same-sex couples were grouped together in *Obergefell v. Hodges*. The case asked if states were required to recognize and license same-sex marriages based on the 14th Amendment. This amendment says that states cannot create or enforce laws that limit

people identified in the media as LGBTQ risked losing their homes, jobs, and friends. Yet, that morning many of the Stonewall customers stayed outside, waiting for their friends and partners. A crowd soon gathered there.

What happened to start the riots is a matter of some debate. Most accounts claim that an officer pushed a woman in handcuffs as he was loading her into a police vehicle. She resisted the officer and yelled at the crowd to do something. This encouraged people to act. Soon, they were throwing spare change at the police. They also threw bottles, cans, and stones. Pine and his officers had to lock themselves in the bar to avoid the violence outside. However, the rioting continued. Protesters shouted "Gay power!" Some even tried to light the bar on fire with the police officers still inside. Fighting continued until firefighters and additional

LGBTQ Rights

citizens' rights. In a 5–4 decision on June 26, 2015, the Supreme Court found in favor of Obergefell and the other couples. This made same-sex marriage legal throughout the United States.

According to the *New Republic*, Supreme Court Justice Anthony Kennedy (1936–) wrote in the majority decision, "No union is more profound than marriage, for it embodies the highest ideals of love, fidelity, devotion, sacrifice, and family. In forming a marital union, two people become something greater than once they were."

Justice Kennedy added: "It would misunderstand these men and women to say they disrespect the idea of marriage. Their plea is that they do respect it, respect it so deeply that they seek to find its fulfillment for themselves. Their hope is not to be condemned to live in loneliness, excluded from one of civilization's oldest institutions. They ask for equal dignity in the eyes of the law. The Constitution grants them that right."

A supporter of same-sex marriage protests in front of the US Supreme Court while counterprotesters conduct the March for Marriage in Washington, DC, on June 25, 2016. The March for Marriage event is held by people who believe in traditional marriage, which is marriage between a man and a woman. © RENA SCHILD/SHUTTERSTOCK.COM.

police officers showed up to rescue those inside the Stonewall Inn and break up the crowd.

Aftermath

Later that morning, newspapers and radio stations reported news of the riot. People from the Greenwich Village community decided to continue the protests against the unfair treatment of LGBTQ citizens. By Saturday afternoon, the Stonewall Inn had reopened, despite the damage to the building. The owners were serving only soda pop to customers that evening and did not charge them. Many people gathered at the bar. Some historians believe about 2,000 people attended what eventually became a kind of party.

LGBTQ Rights

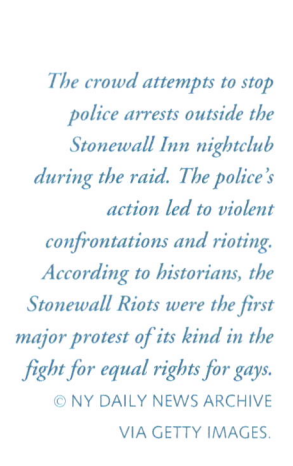

The crowd attempts to stop police arrests outside the Stonewall Inn nightclub during the raid. The police's action led to violent confrontations and rioting. According to historians, the Stonewall Riots were the first major protest of its kind in the fight for equal rights for gays.
© NY DAILY NEWS ARCHIVE VIA GETTY IMAGES.

LGBTQ community members and supporters spilled out of the Stonewall Inn into Christopher Street and even across the street to a park. They chanted, calling for equal rights. LGBTQ partners held hands and kissed in defiance of the laws against public displays of affection. Eventually, protesters turned violent. They attacked police cars. They started fires in trash cans. The police were not able to clear Christopher Street until the early morning hours of June 29. For the next several days, people continued to protest. Police and LGBTQ citizens clashed in the streets around Stonewall until July 3.

Influence of the Stonewall Riots

The Stonewall Riots had an immediate effect on the LGBTQ community and the fight for equality. Just one month later, organizers held a march in New York City to support LGBTQ rights. About 200 people attended the event. Activists then made plans to hold a march on the one-year anniversary of the riots. This is regarded by many as the start of the modern LGBTQ movement.

In 1970 the LGBTQ community in Chicago held a weeklong celebration at the end of June to mark the anniversary of the Stonewall Riots.

The celebration included speeches and marches. The march in New York City took place on June 28 and covered 51 blocks. Marchers then rallied in Central Park to show that the LGBTQ community would not stay silent anymore. On the same day as the New York City march, LGBTQ citizens in Los Angeles, California, also took to the streets to demonstrate the pride they felt for their community. Protesters also came out in San Francisco, California, to mark the Stonewall anniversary.

Over the years, these marches became known as gay pride parades. Major cities like New York, Chicago, and San Francisco continued to hold gay pride parades on the last weekend in June in honor of the events at Stonewall. In 1999 US President Bill Clinton declared June to be Gay and Lesbian Pride Month. In the early 21st century, the month became known as LGBT Pride Month. In June 2016 President Barack Obama (1961–) declared the Stonewall Inn, Christopher Street, and the surrounding area a national landmark. Stonewall was recognized for the important role it played in the fight for LGBTQ rights.

White Night Riots

LOCATION: San Francisco, California

DATE: May 21, 1979

The White Night Riots took place on May 21, 1979, in San Francisco, California. The protests were in response to the sentencing of Dan White (1946–1985), who shot and killed both San Francisco Mayor George Richard Moscone (1929–1978) and city supervisor Harvey Milk (1930–1978) in 1978.

White had served as a city supervisor with Milk, who was an openly gay activist in the community. Moscone regularly sided with Milk on many issues. Moscone's and Milk's views differed from those of White, who had quit his job because he said it did not pay well enough. He later asked for it back, but the mayor refused. White then killed both Moscone and Milk.

At his trial, White blamed the murders on a mental health condition brought on by the loss of his job and eating too much junk food. The jury found him guilty and sentenced him to voluntary manslaughter. People who commit this crime do not intend or make plans to kill. The killing usually happens in the moment. It is a lesser crime than murder and carries a less severe punishment. This outraged many people, including Milk's supporters in the LGBTQ community, who thought the jury should have sentenced White for double murder. The sentencing led to the protests known as the White Night Riots.

Harvey Milk

Harvey Milk was born on May 22, 1930, in New York. After college, he served in the navy but resigned. He then held various jobs. He taught school, worked on the stock exchange, and was a producer for Broadway. He also was an activist who protested the Vietnam War (1954–1975). He moved to San Francisco in 1972 and opened a camera store in the Castro neighborhood, which was home to many LGBTQ individuals and business owners. Milk quickly became involved in the community.

Milk decided to enter politics in 1973 and ran for a seat on the San Francisco Board of Supervisors. He lost but became very involved in politics. He wanted to fight for the rights of the city's LGBTQ community. Milk then helped to found the Castro Village Association, an organization of LGBTQ businesses, and served as its president.

In 1975 Milk again ran for the board of supervisors but lost. He continued his work with the LGBTQ community and became friends with Mayor George Moscone, who appointed him to the Board of Permit Appeals. Milk then decided to run for a seat on the California State Assembly but lost this election. He finally secured a position on the board of supervisors in 1977. Milk was one of the first openly gay individuals to be elected to a political position in the United States.

As supervisor, Milk worked to protect LGBTQ rights. He also fought for equal rights for women, the poor, the disabled, and minorities. He spoke out about many of the problems these groups faced and worked to ensure they received protections. On November 27, 1978, a former city supervisor assassinated both Milk and the mayor. Members of the Castro community gathered that evening to remember Milk's work as a champion for equal rights.

George Richard Moscone

George Richard Moscone was born in San Francisco on November 24, 1929. He earned a law degree and worked as a private lawyer after college. He decided to run for the California State Assembly in 1960 but lost. He was elected to the San Francisco Board of Supervisors three years later. During this time, he fought for rights for the poor, minorities, and small business owners. He wanted to make a difference in the changing city.

Moscone's reputation helped him earn a state Senate seat in 1966. He continued to fight for the rights of disadvantaged groups, including the LGBTQ community. He was reelected in 1970 and 1974. He then decided to run for mayor of San Francisco in 1975. He won the election, but his opponent requested a recall vote in which people recast their votes. Moscone again defeated John Barbagelata (1919–1994) in the race.

While mayor he appointed many minorities who were previously excluded from political office to serve in city government posts, including LGBTQ activist Milk. Milk later won a spot on the board of supervisors with Dan White. White later resigned, and on November 27, 1978, he killed both Moscone and Milk. After his death, Moscone was remembered for his liberal thinking, support for minorities, and his mission to make San Francisco a more accepting city for all individuals.

Dan White

Dan White was born in San Francisco. He served in the army and then worked as a police officer and firefighter. The police force in San Francisco urged him to run for a seat on the city's board of supervisors. The police wanted White to fight against the liberal policies of the mayor and others in local government.

White was elected to the board of supervisors in 1977. He supported causes in opposition to those supported by Milk and Moscone. White served for only one year before he resigned because he said his salary was too low to support his family. Also leading to his resignation were his frequent arguments with the mayor and Milk over their differences.

White then reconsidered his resignation and asked Moscone to give him back his position. Moscone refused. Then White discovered that, at Milk's urging, the mayor was going to appoint another liberal representative to fill White's empty seat. A few days later, White shot and killed both Moscone and Milk.

After his death, Moscone was remembered for his liberal thinking, support for minorities, and his mission to make San Francisco a more accepting city for all individuals.

LGBTQ Rights

When Dan White received a light sentence for killing San Francisco City Supervisor Harvey Milk and Mayor George Moscone, many people were outraged. Here, demonstrators are shown smashing the front doors of City Hall after learning the verdict in 1979. © AP PHOTO/ PAUL SAKUMA.

Trial

White turned himself in after the murders. His trial began on May 1, 1979. Douglas Schmidt acted as White's defense lawyer. Schmidt said the job loss led White to eat an unhealthy diet filled with junk food. This new diet decreased his mental abilities and made him occasionally violent. The media dubbed it the "Twinkie defense." Schmidt said that one of these violent episodes was to blame for the murders and that White did not plan in advance for the killings to occur.

After a three-week trial, the jury found White guilty of voluntary manslaughter, which was not nearly as severe as double murder. A judge sentenced White to seven years and eight months in jail. This sentence was mild compared to what White would have served had he been found guilty of deliberately planning the murders.

White Night Riots

When news of the sentencing broke on May 21, 1979, a crowd of about 500 people from the Castro neighborhood gathered to plan a peaceful march. Many of them belonged to the LGBTQ community. They wanted to protest what they thought was weak punishment for the murder of two people.

Thousands joined the march, which became a riot by the time it reached city hall. Rioters were angry with the police because they thought White got a lesser sentence because he was once a cop. Rioters damaged property and set police cars on fire. The police responded with force, beating and arresting people.

The violence lasted a few hours. Police officers used tear gas to control the crowds and end the riot. In the aftermath, more than 100 people, including protesters and police officers, suffered injuries. Police arrested several individuals. The city lost several police cars and suffered more than $1 million in damages.

LGBTQ Rights

The violence continued a few hours later when several police officers raided mostly LGBTQ businesses in the Castro neighborhood. They entered these establishments and assaulted people. The police chief stopped the violence but did not punish the police officers for their actions. The following day, which would have marked Milk's 49th birthday, more than 20,000 people organized a peaceful demonstration to remember him.

Aftermath

White served only part of his sentence. He was released early on January 6, 1984. He returned home to San Francisco, where he killed himself on October 21, 1985. He never apologized for murdering Moscone and Milk.

The White Night Riots led to changes in San Francisco. The community elected more LGBTQ politicians who continued to fight for equal rights. Community members remembered Milk as an outspoken supporter of equality and Moscone as a champion for minorities. Milk was the subject of several projects including the 2008 film *Milk*, for which actor Sean Penn (1960–) won a best actor Oscar for playing the city official. In his old Castro neighborhood, a school, multiple buildings, and streets are named in honor of Milk.

Westboro Baptist Church Protests of Matthew Shepard

LOCATION: Casper, Wyoming, and Laramie, Wyoming

DATE: October 16, 1998 and April 1999

On October 12, 1998, a 21-year-old college student named Matthew Shepard (1976–1998) died in a hospital bed in Fort Collins, Colorado. Five days earlier, two men robbed and beat Shepard. They tied him to a fence outside the town of Laramie, Wyoming, and left him to die in the cold. A bicyclist found Shepard 18 hours later and called for help. Barely alive, Shepard was unconscious when he arrived at the hospital. He never woke up.

LGBTQ Rights

Shepard's murder shocked people across the United States. News coverage of the murder led many to believe that the young man was the victim of a hate crime, a crime committed against a person because of his or her race, religion, national origin, gender, sexual orientation, or disability. Police investigating the crime believed Shepard's attackers chose to target the young man because he was gay.

The murder made people reconsider the definition of a hate crime. At the time, hate-crime laws covered crimes committed against others on the basis of race, religion, or national origin. Crimes committed against people on the basis of gender, sexual orientation, or disability were not included. Shepard's murder began a national conversation about expanding hate-crime laws to protect these other groups.

Shepard's murder also captured the attention of the Westboro Baptist Church (WBC). The Reverend Fred Phelps (1926–2014) founded the WBC in Topeka, Kansas, in 1955. Phelps and the WBC have openly opposed homosexuality and have stood firmly against LGBTQ rights. They have regularly staged antigay protests in Kansas and around the nation. The group is also known for its anti-Semitism (pronounced an-tee-SEH-muh-ti-zum), which is hatred toward or bias against Jews. Westboro is also anti-Catholic. Organizations such as the Southern Poverty Law Center (SPLC) and the Anti-Defamation League (ADL) consider the WBC to be a hate group. Hate groups support hatred, anger, and/or violence toward members of a certain race, religion, national origin, gender, or sexual orientation.

On October 16, 1998, Phelps and the WBC staged a protest at Shepard's funeral. They held signs with words and phrases disrespecting gay people. They yelled antigay slogans. The WBC returned to Wyoming in the spring of 1999 during the trial for Shepard's accused murderers. They again held antigay signs and shouted antigay phrases during their protest. In both cases, other groups gathered to counter the WBC's protest.

Background on Matthew Shepard

Matthew Shepard was born to Judy (1952–) and Dennis Shepard on December 1, 1976, in Casper, Wyoming, where he spent most of his childhood. In his junior year of high school, Shepard and his family moved to Saudi Arabia for his father's job. Because Saudi Arabia had no American schools, Shepard finished high school in Switzerland.

Living outside the United States, Shepard made many friends from different cultures. He enjoyed traveling and learned to speak several languages. These interests likely inspired his studies in college. When he enrolled at the University of Wyoming, he studied political science, foreign relations, and languages. He also participated in a group for LGBTQ students.

According to the website for the Matthew Shepard Foundation, which was established after his death, Shepard wanted "to foster a more caring and just world." However, the events of October 7, 1998, took away his opportunity to pursue that dream.

A robbery, a murder, and an arrest

On the night of October 6, 1998, Shepard went to a bar in Laramie, Wyoming, where he met two men, Aaron McKinney and Russell Henderson. Sometime after midnight on October 7, Shepard accepted a ride from McKinney and Henderson. The three rode in McKinney's truck to a deserted area outside town. There, McKinney and Henderson attacked Shepard. Shepard, who stood 5 feet, 2 inches tall and weighed between 105 and 110 pounds, could not fight off his attackers.

The men robbed Shepard and took his wallet and shoes. They beat and kicked him. They struck him in the head with the butt of a gun many times, which cracked his skull. McKinney and Henderson then tied Shepard to a fence post. They left him there to die, cold and alone.

A bicyclist passed the fence about 18 hours later. At first the bicyclist thought Shepard's body was a scarecrow, but then the passerby realized he was looking at a real person. Shepard was unconscious. His face was bloody except for two streaks on his cheeks where tears had washed away the blood.

The cyclist called for help, and the police arrived. Shepard was rushed to the hospital. Shepard's family returned to the United States from Saudi Arabia to be by his side. Shepard died in the hospital five days later.

Police found the bloody gun used to strike Shepard in McKinney's truck. They also found Shepard's shoes and wallet. They arrested and charged McKinney and Henderson with murder.

At first the bicyclist thought Shepard's body was a scarecrow, but then the passerby realized he was looking at a real person. Shepard was unconscious. His face was bloody except for two streaks on his cheeks where tears had washed away the blood.

Redefining hate crimes

News that two men had been accused of murdering a gay college student because of his sexual orientation quickly spread throughout the country.

LGBTQ Rights

Shepard's murder turned the nation's attention toward the need for a broader definition of hate crimes under the law. Many argued that the definition should include crimes committed against others not only because of their race, religion, and national origin but also because of their gender, sexual orientation, or disability.

Not all who paid attention to the case believed in redefining hate crimes. One group in particular wanted to use Shepard's death to advance a message of hate. The Westboro Baptist Church, or WBC, openly opposes homosexuality. The WBC is well known for its harsh antigay slogans. The WBC, led by Phelps, decided to travel to Casper, Wyoming, to picket Shepard's funeral. To picket is to stand or march in a public place to protest something.

A funeral and a protest

Casper's city council members heard rumors that antigay protesters planned to picket Shepard's funeral. The council quickly passed a ban on protests near the church immediately before and after the funeral.

Shepard's funeral was scheduled to take place on October 16, 1998, at St. Mark's Episcopal Church in Casper, Wyoming. Several hours before the funeral, about 12 members of the WBC, including Phelps, picketed in a park across the street from the church. They held brightly colored signs with words and phrases that were disrespectful toward gays. They shouted antigay phrases. Some shouted hurtful phrases specifically about Matthew Shepard.

Other demonstrators gathered to form a counterprotest against the WBC. Police separated the two groups with fences to avoid conflicts. They watched the protesters carefully. Still, the protests made people nervous. As a precaution, police sent bomb-sniffing dogs into the church before the funeral to make sure mourners were safe.

The WBC's protest did little to stop people from coming to the funeral. More than 700 people arrived at the church to mourn Shepard. President Bill Clinton sent two people to attend the funeral on his behalf. Many of the mourners did not know Shepard personally. Some were members of the LGBTQ community who felt a connection to Shepard. They believed that what happened to him could happen to them, too. Most of the mourners had to stand outside in the cold, snowy weather during the 90-minute funeral service.

LGBTQ Rights

WBC returns for a second protest

A few months later, in April 1999, Phelps and about a dozen of his WBC followers traveled to Laramie. This time they planned to picket during the court trial for Shepard's accused killers. Again the protesters brought disrespectful signs and shouted hurtful phrases about Matthew Shepard and members of the LGBTQ community.

Members of the counterprotest were better prepared to face the WBC this time. Romaine Patterson (1978–), one of Shepard's close friends, saw the WBC's protest before her friend's funeral. She saw the hateful signs they held. She listened to the harsh words they shouted about her friend and about members of the LGBTQ community like herself. When she heard that Phelps and the WBC planned to return for the murder trial in 1999, she formed a group called Angel Action. The group planned to protest peacefully against the WBC.

Members of the Westboro Baptist Church held signs of disrespect toward gay people outside the courthouse where Matthew Shepard's accused killers were standing trial in Laramie, Wyoming, in April 1999. In a counterprotest that blocked the antigay demonstrators, people dressed as angels and raised their arms, which looked like wings. © AP IMAGES/CASPER STAR-TRIBUNE, DAN CEPEDA.

Hate Crimes Prevention Act

This primary source excerpt is from an interview between Jacki Lyden, a host on Tell Me More *from NPR News, and Judy Shepard, who cofounded the Matthew Shepard Foundation. During the interview that took place on October 12, 2010, Shepard talks about her son, Matthew, and antigay hate crimes.*

Ms. JUDY SHEPARD (Co-founder, Matthew Shepard Foundation): Well, [Matt] was a 21-year-old college student who, like most college students I remember in my past, drank too much and didn't study enough. He was gay and out and proud of who he was and who he was becoming. He had a smile, like all mothers say, that would light up a room, great sense of humor, very empathetic and kind, really cared about humanity.

[JACKI] LYDEN [host]: And how do you feel about the progress that this country's made in acceptance and diversity awareness and education in the years since his death? Because his murder was absolutely a galvanizing force.

Ms. SHEPARD: I started speaking at colleges soon after the trials were over of the two men who murdered Matt. And I found on the students' faces then, and their loved ones, this great fear and trepidation about their future.

Now when I meet with them, I see a sense of entitlement, that they understand they're being denied basic civil rights. They have every right to everything that every American has access to, equality across the board, and they know how to get it. And that's what they're going to do....

But I still in my heart of hearts think that, overall, things have gotten much, much better.

LYDEN: About a year ago, Congress passed the Matthew Shepard and James Byrd, Jr., Hate Crimes Prevention Act, which President Obama signed into law. Now, James Byrd, we'll remember, was the African-American man who was brutally killed by white men in rural Texas. Would you explain what this law covers, please?

Ms. SHEPARD: There was a federal hate crime law already on the books that covered race, religion and ethnicity. The Matthew Shepard–James Byrd, Jr., Hate Crimes Prevention Act added to the existing law sexual orientation, gender identity, women and disability. And it expands the parameters of the law so that the federal government can step in, in cases where the community cannot afford or is unwilling to prosecute a hate crime.

And we know it's not going to prevent crimes. If laws prevented crimes, we wouldn't need prisons. But what the law did do was send a message of respect to the law enforcement agencies and to the public at large that we recognize the gay community as an oppressed group.

SOURCE: "Matthew Shepard's Mom Weighs In on Anti-Gay Hate Crimes." *Tell Me More.* National Public Radio, October 12, 2010. Available online at http://www.npr.org/templates/story/story.php?storyId=130513712 (accessed October 15, 2017). Courtesy of National Public Radio Inc.

Members of Angel Action arrived at the WBC's protest outside the courthouse in Laramie. They wore white angel costumes with huge wings that stretched 7 feet (2 meters) high and 10 feet (3 meters) wide. The angels did not say a word. They simply took their position in front of the WBC protesters. With their backs turned toward Phelps and members of the WBC, the angels stood quietly and smiled at those who walked past. Their huge wings completely blocked the antigay protesters from view.

Aftermath

Shepard's brutal murder started a national conversation about hate crimes. During their trial, Henderson and McKinney claimed that Shepard made sexual advances toward them, which is why they attacked and killed him. Since then they have changed their story several times. At one point, they claimed the murder was a robbery gone wrong. At another time they said the crime was drug-related. At the trial, Henderson pleaded guilty to the crime and was sentenced to life in prison. A jury found McKinney guilty. He, too, was sentenced to life in prison.

Following Shepard's death, lawmakers expanded the definition of hate crimes to include sexual orientation. Additionally, lawmakers passed the Matthew Shepard and James Byrd, Jr., Hate Crimes Prevention Act. Byrd was an African American man who was brutally murdered by three white men in 1998. The act allows the federal government to help local and state law enforcement agencies investigate and prosecute hate crimes. To prosecute is to take legal action against someone who has committed a crime. President Barack Obama signed the act into law in 2009.

The protests that took place at Shepard's funeral and at the court trial for his murderers had several effects. A negative effect is that media coverage of the protests gave Phelps and the WBC a national audience. Before 1998 the WBC was not well-known outside of Kansas. Since 1998 the WBC has continued to spread its message of hate. Members of the church argue that events such as the September 11, 2001, terrorist attacks on the United States and Hurricane Katrina in 2005 are God's punishments for the wicked. The WBC pickets at various events but often protests at military funerals. The group opposes LGBTQ people in the military and often protests the funerals of fallen soldiers to spread this message.

However, the WBC's protests against Shepard led to the formation of counterprotest groups. Angel Action's successful protest against the WBC in 1999 inspired other groups within the United States. Such groups have made their own angel costumes to protest hate groups at other events. Not all of these counterprotest groups dress in angel costumes, however.

The Patriot Guard Riders, for example, is a motorcycle group with deep respect for all who serve in the military. Members of the group do not care about a soldier's race, religion, or sexual orientation. They consider all soldiers killed while serving in the armed forces to be national heroes. Families of fallen soldiers invite the group to attend funerals to shield mourners from hate-group protesters. These counterprotest groups work to prevent hate groups such as the WBC from spreading their anti-LGBTQ message.

Shanghai Pride Festival

LOCATION: Shanghai, China
DATE: June 2009

China's record on LGBTQ rights is complicated, but some progress has been made over the years. Chinese LGBTQ people have some more freedoms than they did before. Nevertheless, these few advances have not resulted in changing most people's opinions of LGBTQ citizens in China. Chinese LGBTQ people still face great social discrimination. However, events like Shanghai Pride allowed members of the LGBTQ community to come together to celebrate their identities in a country that is often hostile toward them.

Background

Same-sex relationships have a long history in Chinese culture. Chinese social scientist Li Yinhe (1952–) says there are records of gay and lesbian relationships dating back to at least 650 BCE. Emperors would sometimes engage in sexual relationships with young male attendants at court. According to *Newsweek*, Li also notes that most Chinese religions have no objection to LGBTQ people. China made homosexuality legal in 1997. Four years later, homosexuality was removed from the *Chinese Classification of Mental Disorders*.

The Chinese government permits transgender men and women to change their gender on ID cards to match their gender identity, but only if they have had sex reassignment surgery. This is surgery to remove or change sex organs to help individuals transition to their inner gender identity. Not all transgender men and women wish to undergo such surgery, though. Those who do not cannot change the gender on their IDs. In 2014 a Chinese court also ruled that so-called conversion therapies were illegal. These treatments use a variety of methods to supposedly "cure" gay and lesbian people and make them straight. Some treatments may involve physical pain through electric shock. Despite the court's ruling, many clinics throughout China still offered conversion therapy in the late 2010s.

As of August 2017, members of the LGBTQ community in China still lacked many basic legal protections. For example, same-sex couples cannot get married or adopt a child. They also have no protection against discrimination when they apply for a job or look for a home. Modern Chinese society does not support LGBTQ individuals for the most part. A Pew Research Center poll in 2013 found that 57 percent of Chinese citizens did not believe that society should accept LGBTQ people. This is likely due to the focus on traditional family structures in Chinese culture. In addition, the Chinese government, which is ruled by a Communist party, has control over the media. In Communist societies, the government typically controls many businesses, newspapers, and TV stations. Governments such as the one in China also do not allow citizens to protest laws or call for additional rights. Often, the Chinese government bans films featuring LGBTQ themes and characters. Books and other forms of art that focus on expressing LGBTQ ideas are also censored, or blocked.

Despite many obstacles, the Chinese LGBTQ movement has made progress over the years. In 2009 Shanghai, the country's largest city, hosted the first LGBTQ pride festival on the Chinese mainland. Events celebrating LGBTQ pride had previously been held in Hong Kong. Still, organizers of this first celebration of the mainland LGBTQ community faced many challenges in making Shanghai Pride happen.

Members of the LGBTQ community in China still lacked many basic legal protections. For example, same-sex couples cannot get married or adopt a child. They also have no protection against discrimination when they apply for a job or look for a home.

Planning the event

In 2005 organizers attempted to hold an LGBTQ festival in Beijing, China. Police shut down the festival before it could begin, though. Authorities also shut down queer film festivals in Beijing on their opening days several times over the years. Holding an LGBTQ celebration in mainland China seemed to be almost impossible. In 2009 two Americans living in China decided to try to organize a gay and lesbian pride event

LGBTQ Rights

Russia and LGBTQ Rights

Although Russia is not a Communist nation like China, the government still has great control over citizens' lives. During the 20th century, Russia was part of the Communist Soviet Union, which did not permit same-sex relationships. At the time, LGBTQ citizens in Russia could face prison or worse if someone learned about their sexual orientation. The Soviet Union fell in the early 1990s. Russia became its own country, and homosexuality was no longer deemed a crime in the country.

Regardless, many organizations considered Russia to have one of the worst records on LGBTQ rights in the 2010s. One of the reasons for this was a bill passed in 2013 by the Russian parliament and signed into law by President Vladimir Putin (1952–). The bill discriminated against LGBTQ people. Russian lawmakers claimed this law was created to protect traditional family values. Critics argued that the law was so broad that it made it nearly impossible for Russian LGBTQ citizens to call for equal rights or even display affection with their partners in public.

This law led to international outcry because Russia was set to host the Winter Olympics in 2014. Many people around the globe protested against the law. Right before the games, people in Australia, France, the United Kingdom, and even Russia called on Olympic sponsors to speak out against the Russian government's policy. Three Russian activists later sued the government after police arrested and fined them for protesting against the law. The case went all the way to the European Court of Human Rights in France. The court sided with the activists in June 2017, finding that the law served no public benefit and discriminated against LGBTQ people. Russia intended to appeal the ruling.

More public uproar occurred in 2017 when Russian LGBTQ activists claimed that authorities in Chechnya were kidnapping and torturing gay men. Chechnya is a territory of Russia. Some reports even said that authorities had killed gay

anyway. Because of the government's strict rules about protests and marches, Hannah Miller and Tiffany Lemay had to be careful about how they presented the event. In 2006 Miller, a teacher, had helped create the city's first online gay and lesbian mailing list. Miller had also lived in China for several years, so she knew they had to be cautious about how they handled this event. For this reason, Miller and other organizers discussed their plans with a lawyer.

In the end, the organizers decided that the event should seem like a big party. They promoted the festival mostly in English instead of Chinese. If the police believed that the event was mainly a celebration held by foreigners, they would be less likely to shut it down. The organizers also decided to hold events in private spaces rather than in public places. They did not have a parade, either. Instead, the organizers

LGBTQ Rights

men or told their families to kill them. Chechen officials denied that such events had taken place because they declared that there were no gay people in the region.

Some activists have protested against Russia's antigay laws. Here, pro-gay activists hold signs asking companies who are sponsoring the Sochi Winter Olympic Games in Russia in 2014 to speak out against such laws. © PAUL CROCK/AFP/GETTY IMAGES.

planned film screenings, plays, and parties to be held from June 7 to June 14, 2009.

Shanghai Pride 2009

Shanghai Pride began on Sunday, June 7, with an art show and a film screening at private venues, or sites. Other activities were planned to take place throughout the week. The government's response to the event was difficult to determine. *China Daily*, the country's official English-language newspaper, praised the celebration. There was even a front-page story about Shanghai Pride. An editorial, or an opinion article, said that Shanghai Pride was a sign of positive social change in the country. Yet, none of the Chinese-language newspapers mentioned the festival.

LGBTQ Rights

Entertainers perform at the gay pride day festival during the Shanghai Pride Week in China in 2009. Nearly 3,000 people, including hundreds of LGBTQ individuals, participated in the first festival of its kind in Shanghai. © AP IMAGES/JUN YING.

Because of this, organizers were not sure how Chinese authorities would respond to the various events held during the weeklong celebration.

Some of the activities went on without a problem. However, police officers dressed as civilians attended many of the events and even videotaped them. Some of the officers told owners of private venues that they would get into trouble if they allowed scheduled LGBTQ events to continue. Organizers had to cancel several activities during the week. One of these events was a staging of the play *The Laramie Project*. The play focuses on the reaction to the death of Matthew Shepard. Shepard was a gay college student at the University of Wyoming in Laramie. He was beaten and left to die in a field because of his sexual orientation. Shepard eventually died in a hospital from his injuries. His death was a major event in the fight for LGBTQ rights in the United States.

During Shanghai Pride 2009, authorities learned about plans to stage *The Laramie Project*. Police officers came to a play practice and wrote down the names of the actors. Some of the actors said they would not perform for fear of what would happen to them. The owners of the venue where the play was supposed to take place also told the organizers they would have to find another space. Finally, the scheduled performance of *The Laramie Project* was canceled. Police also shut down a film screening during the week. Authorities claimed the venue did not have the proper license to show the movie.

One of the last events of the festival was a daylong party held at a restaurant in Shanghai. Scheduled events included a barbecue, a fashion show, and a drag show. A drag show often features male performers dressed in feminine clothing as they sing or dance. At one point during the party, organizers were afraid that the police would shut it down. Miller spoke with a police officer and promised to keep the noise down and limit the crowd size. The authorities then allowed the party to continue. The event ended with several same-sex weddings. Although the Chinese government would not recognize the marriages, the couples believed the weddings showed their commitment to their partners. At the end of the festival, organizers estimated that about 3,000 people had taken part in Shanghai Pride during the week.

Influence of Shanghai Pride

In 2009 *China Daily* featured the first Shanghai Pride festival in a year-end story called "Year of Gay China." The article said that 2009 had been a historic year for the Chinese LGBTQ community. The paper recognized Shanghai Pride for being the first LGBTQ pride event held in mainland China. In the article, *China Daily* made note of the festival along with several other LGBTQ-focused celebrations that took place in China that year.

Organizers have continued to hold Shanghai Pride events each year since 2009. As of 2017, the event was the longest-running pride festival in mainland China. That pride festival was shorter than those held in previous years. This was in anticipation of the 10th Shanghai Pride celebration in 2018. In 2017 organizers put together several events before and after the pride festival. These included a talent show in April and a queer bike ride in May. Throughout June, organizers held

LGBTQ Rights

various events, including film festivals, to continue the celebration of the Chinese LGBTQ community.

Although many people feel that Shanghai Pride and similar events show how China is changing, others argue that there is still much to be done in terms of LGBTQ acceptance. A report by the Human Rights Campaign in 2015 found that LGBTQ people still face much discrimination in China. In addition to facing pressure to marry a person of the opposite sex and raise a family, many young Chinese LGBTQ people do not have the opportunity to see themselves represented in their culture. The government continues to censor LGBTQ plays, movies, and TV shows. When LGBTQ individuals are discussed in the media, it is usually in a negative manner.

Nevertheless, LGBTQ citizens in China continue to find ways to connect and celebrate their community. Social networking sites help individuals communicate and organize events. There are also several LGBTQ groups in China's larger cities. Many citizens are hopeful that events like Shanghai Pride will lead to more acceptance of the LGBTQ community in China. With social acceptance, the possibility of gaining additional rights for LGBTQ citizens becomes more likely.

Protests of North Carolina House Bill 2

LOCATION: Raleigh, North Carolina

DATE: April 25, 2016

In early 2016 the North Carolina General Assembly made international news when it passed House Bill 2 (HB2), also known as the Public Facilities Privacy and Security Act. The bill required people in public schools or government buildings to use only restrooms that corresponded with the sex they were assigned at birth. The media often referred to HB2 as the "bathroom bill." However, the Gay and Lesbian Alliance against Defamation (GLAAD) deemed this term offensive.

The bill was a direct response to a local law set to go into effect in Charlotte, North Carolina, on April 1, 2016. This law would have prevented discrimination against LGBTQ people based on sexual orientation or gender identity in public places. It would have allowed them to use the bathroom of the gender with which they identified. But HB2 had the power to override all local laws regarding LGBTQ citizens' rights in housing, wages, and public accommodations, which included restrooms. The law led to protests on both sides and created problems for the state. Many companies and organizations refused to do business or hold events in North Carolina following the passage of the bill.

Background

In 2016 North Carolina's General Assembly was controlled by Republican lawmakers. The General Assembly is the lawmaking branch of North Carolina's government. It is made up of the House and the Senate and located in Raleigh, North Carolina. Many Republican politicians have conservative views concerning social issues. Conservatives uphold traditional beliefs regarding life and society. Some conservative politicians are against same-sex marriage and other LGBTQ rights. At the time, North Carolina also had a Republican governor, Pat McCrory (1956–).

The General Assembly was not in session in late March 2016. Yet, the Republican leaders wanted to hold a special meeting to push through a bill that would block a local law that was about to go into effect in Charlotte. This was an anti-discrimination law. It would prevent people in Charlotte from discriminating against LGBTQ people in several areas, including housing and employment. It also allowed transgender individuals to use public restrooms that matched their gender identity rather than the sex they were assigned at birth.

The Republican lawmakers in the General Assembly disliked this law. They claimed that allowing transgender individuals to use restrooms or locker rooms that matched their gender identity put other citizens in danger. In particular, many politicians claimed that male sexual predators might use the law to gain access to women's restrooms and locker rooms. A sexual predator is someone who commits a sexually violent act against another person. These lawmakers said that sexual predators might claim they were transgender to get into women's facilities. Republican politicians believed this put women and young girls at risk of sexual assault, which is illegal sexual contact that is forced on one person by another.

Many Democrats in the General Assembly and many LGBTQ rights activists did not agree with these lawmakers. According to ABC News, the

The law led to protests on both sides and created problems for the state. Many companies and organizations refused to do business or hold events in North Carolina following the passage of the bill.

LGBTQ Rights

NCAA Protest of HB2

The National Collegiate Athletic Association (NCAA) was one of the most vocal opponents of North Carolina's House Bill 2 (HB2). The NCAA oversees many college athletics programs across the country. In September 2016 the organization announced that it was moving seven events that had been scheduled to take place in North Carolina during the 2016–2017 season out of the state. A statement posted on the NCAA's website at the time said, "The Board of Governors emphasized that NCAA championships and events must promote an inclusive atmosphere. . . . Current North Carolina state laws make it challenging to guarantee that host communities can help deliver on that commitment if NCAA events remained in the state."

In December 2016 players from the University of Maine basketball team traveled to North Carolina to play against Duke University. Both teams are Division 1 teams in the NCAA. The Maine players wore shirts with rainbow-colored logos during their warm-up to show support for the LGBTQ community and their opposition to HB2. The rainbow is a symbol of gay pride.

The NCAA continued to pressure North Carolina to change its laws in early 2017. On March 23 the organization announced that the state needed to repeal HB2 or risk losing NCAA championship events through 2022. Such events add a great deal of money to local economies. Shortly after the NCAA's statement, the General Assembly repealed HB2 and replaced it with HB142. In early April officials at the NCAA said that the new bill met the organization's basic standards. However, the NCAA expressed concerns over the new bill, which many LGBTQ rights organizations argued was still discriminatory against transgender people. Despite this, NCAA officials said they would consider holding championship events in North Carolina for 2018 through 2022.

North Carolina branch of the American Civil Liberties Union (ACLU) claimed that transgender people were more likely to be assaulted in a public restroom than to assault someone. Nevertheless, the General Assembly held a special session on March 23 to vote on a bill that would block the Charlotte law. This bill was called House Bill 2 (HB2).

Passage of HB2

There were two main parts of HB2. First, the bill declared that state law would overrule local laws concerning wages, employment, and public services. This would make the Charlotte law and the protections it extended to the LGBTQ community meaningless. Second, the bill also required that multi-stall restrooms in public schools and government buildings be set aside only for use by people based on the sex they were assigned at birth. This meant that transgender women and men could not use restrooms or locker rooms that matched their gender identity.

LGBTQ Rights

The University of Maine's men's basketball team protested North Carolina's HB2 during a nationally televised game with the Duke University team in December 2016 by wearing special warm-up T-shirts featuring a rainbow, a symbol associated with gay pride. © AP IMAGES/BEN MCKEOWN.

The bill was introduced on Wednesday, March 23, 2016. Just 12 hours later, McCrory signed it into law. The House in North Carolina voted 83–25 in favor of the bill. The bill then passed in the state Senate with a 32–0 vote. The Democrats in the state Senate refused to vote on the bill and walked out in protest.

Republicans and the governor claimed that the bill was simply about protecting the safety and privacy of North Carolina citizens. Many critics claimed that HB2 was nothing more than discrimination against LGBTQ people. Those against the bill argued that there are no known cases in which a sexual predator posed as a transgender woman to assault anyone.

Swift fallout

The passage of HB2 created problems for North Carolina almost immediately. The North Carolina branch of the ACLU brought a lawsuit against the state on March 28. The organization claimed HB2 went against the 14th Amendment, which provides equal protection to all citizens under the law. Roy Cooper (1957–) was North Carolina's attorney general at the time. He was also running as a Democrat against McCrory for governor in the 2016 election. Cooper said he would not defend the state against the lawsuit.

On April 5, the online money-transfer company PayPal announced that it would cancel its plans to open a center in Charlotte due to HB2. The center would have brought 400 jobs to the area and would have added about $2.66 billion to the state's economy, according to the Associated Press.

The state also lost money when entertainers started canceling shows in North Carolina to protest HB2. American rock musician Bruce Springsteen (1949–) was one of the first acts to cancel a performance in the state on April 8. According to *Charlotte Magazine*, Springsteen wrote on his website, "Some things are more important than a rock show, and this fight against prejudice and bigotry, which is happening as I write, is one of them."

Protest

The North Carolina General Assembly did not open for its regular session until late April 2016. When lawmakers came back to work, protesters greeted them. Hundreds of people on both sides of HB2 came out to protest in the state capital on April 25, 2016.

Many of the protesters were calling for the governor and the General Assembly to repeal, or cancel, the bill. These people believed that the bill was hateful and targeted transgender people. They did not feel that it would do anything to ensure public safety. Many groups also brought petitions signed by citizens asking for the government to repeal the bill. Still, some protesters were there to defend the bill. These citizens believed that transgender individuals should use only public facilities that correspond to the sex they were assigned at birth.

All afternoon, protesters from both sides demonstrated outside the legislative building. Late in the day, authorities allowed protesters inside in groups of 100 as the assembly was set to come to order. Some of the protesters gathered in and around the office of state house Speaker Tim Moore (1970–). They chanted, calling for the repeal of HB2. Police arrested 18 protesters who refused to leave the area.

More people continued protesting in other parts of the building. Some shouted as the lawmakers tried to start their session. Another group of protesters sat on the floor outside Moore's office and refused to move. Police then arrested an additional 36 protesters, bringing the number of arrests that day to 54.

Aftermath

Shortly after the protests in April, the US Justice Department told McCrory that HB2 violated federal civil rights laws. The governor then sued the Justice Department, which then sued the state of North Carolina. The US attorney general at the time, Loretta Lynch (1959–), said the law "provides no benefit to society," according to *Charlotte Magazine*. Legal battles continued even after McCrory dropped his lawsuit in September 2016.

While this was happening, more organizations were pulling events out of North Carolina in protest of HB2. In July the National Basketball Association (NBA) announced that it would not hold its 2017 All-Star Game in Charlotte as planned. The Atlantic Coast Conference, a college athletic association, also announced that it would cancel events in North Carolina. This did not bode well for McCrory, who was running against Cooper for reelection. The bill was costing the state jobs and money.

In the November election, Cooper defeated McCrory by about only 10,000 votes. However, McCrory challenged the election. He finally gave up his challenge on December 5, and Cooper became governor on January 1, 2017. Many suspected that HB2 was partly to blame for McCrory's loss. Although a Democrat was now governor, the Republicans kept control of the General Assembly.

Armed with creative signs and symbolic flags, people protest North Carolina's HB2 law in Asheville in 2016. For many, the bill discriminates against transgender people. © J. BICKING /SHUTTERSTOCK.COM.

Repeal

In early 2017, the General Assembly and new governor Cooper faced mounting pressure from businesses and other organizations to repeal HB2.

In an article published on March 27, 2017, the Associated Press estimated that the bill would cost the state about $3.76 billion over 12 years if it was not repealed.

Three days later, on March 30, the General Assembly voted to repeal HB2 and replace it with HB142. However, this bill still maintained some of the most objectionable parts of HB2. Only the state legislature could regulate access to public restrooms and locker rooms. In addition, HB142 prevented local governments from passing any antidiscrimination laws regarding employment or public accommodations until 2020.

Although Cooper claimed the bill was not what he wanted, he still signed it into law. He also said he wanted to pass laws protecting LGBTQ citizens, but the Republicans in the General Assembly would be unlikely to support such legislation. LGBTQ organizations immediately came out against the bill, claiming it was no better than HB2. In July 2017 the ACLU and Lambda Legal, an LGBTQ rights organization, filed a revised lawsuit that now focused on HB142. The fight over HB2's replacement continued through the summer of 2017.

For More Information

BOOKS

Johnson, Michael, Jr. "Shepard, Matthew (1976–1998)." In *Culture Wars in America: An Encyclopedia of Issues, Viewpoints, and Voices.* 2nd ed. Edited by Roger Chapman and James Ciment, 856–858. New York: M. E. Sharpe, 2014.

Leonard, Bill J. "Westboro Baptist Church." In *Encyclopedia of Religious Controversies in the United States.* 2nd ed. Vol. 2. Edited by Bill J. Leonard and Jill Y. Crainshaw, 835–836. Santa Barbara, CA: ABC-CLIO, 2013.

Poehlmann, Tristan. *The Stonewall Riots: The Fight for LGBT Rights.* Minneapolis, MN: Abdo, 2017.

Pohlen, Jerome. *Gay & Lesbian History for Kids: The Century-Long Struggle for LGBT Rights, with 21 Activities.* Chicago: Chicago Review Press, 2016.

PERIODICALS

Blythe, Anne. "54 HB2 Opponents Arrested Inside NC Legislative Building." *Charlotte Observer* (April 25, 2016). Available online at http://www.charlotteobserver.com/news/politics-government/article73805467.html (accessed August 22, 2017).

Davis, Julie Hirschfeld, and Helene Cooper. "Trump Says Transgender People Will Not Be Allowed in the Military." *New York Times* (July 26, 2017).

Available online at https://www.nytimes.com/2017/07/26/us/politics/trump-transgender-military.html (accessed August 23, 2017).

Jacobs, Andrew. "Gay Festival in China Pushes Official Boundaries." *New York Times* (June 15, 2009). Available online at http://www.nytimes.com/2009/06/15/world/asia/15shanghai.html (accessed August 16, 2017).

Lacour, Greg. "HB2: How North Carolina Got Here (Updated)." *Charlotte Magazine* (March 30, 2017). Available online at http://www.charlottemagazine.com/Charlotte-Magazine/April-2016/HB2-How-North-Carolina-Got-Here/ (accessed August 22, 2017).

Laskowski, Christine. "Year of Gay China." *China Daily* (December 28, 2009). Available online at http://www.chinadaily.com.cn/cndy/2009-12/28/content_9235395.htm (accessed August 16, 2017).

Leber, Rebecca. "The Most Powerful Paragraph in the Supreme Court's Gay Marriage Decision." *New Republic* (June 24, 2015). Available online at https://newrepublic.com/article/122168/most-powerful-paragraph-supreme-courts-gay-marriage-decision (accessed August 18, 2017).

Liu, Melinda. "China Gay-Pride Event Meets Obstacles." *Newsweek* (June 12, 2009). Available online at http://www.newsweek.com/china-gay-pride-event-meets-obstacles-80291 (accessed August 16, 2017).

Patterson, Romaine. "Let Westboro Baptist Have Their Hate Speech. We'll Smother It with Peace." *Washington Post* (March 6, 2011). Available online at http://www.washingtonpost.com/wp-dyn/content/article/2011/03/04/AR2011030406330.html (accessed August 14, 2017).

Rosenwald, Michael S. "How Jim Obergefell Became the Face of the Supreme Court Gay Marriage Case." *Washington Post* (April 6, 2015). Available online at https://www.washingtonpost.com/local/how-jim-obergefell-became-the-face-of-the-supreme-court-gay-marriage-case/2015/04/06/3740433c-d958-11e4-b3f2-607bd612aeac_story.html?utm_term=.2a0ea1440ba5 (accessed August 18, 2017).

WEBSITES

"About Us." Matthew Shepard Foundation. http://www.matthewshepard.org/about-us/ (accessed August 14, 2017).

Dalesio, Emery P., and Jonathan Drew. "AP Exclusive: Price Tag of North Carolina's LGBT Law: $3.76B." Associated Press, March 27, 2017. https://apnews.com/fa4528580f3e4a01bb68bcb272f1f0f8/ap-exclusive-bathroom-bill-cost-north-carolina-376b (accessed August 22, 2017).

"The Global Divide on Homosexuality." Pew Research Center, June 4, 2013. http://www.pewglobal.org/2013/06/04/the-global-divide-on-homosexuality/ (accessed August 16, 2017).

"Hate Crimes Law." Human Rights Campaign. http://www.hrc.org/resources/hate-crimes-law (accessed August 15, 2017).

Lim, Louisa. "China's Gay Pride Week Mixes Celebration, Caution." National Public Radio, June 15, 2009. http://www.npr.org/templates/story/story.php?storyId=105405434 (accessed August 16, 2017).

"The Matthew Shepard and James Byrd, Jr., Hate Crimes Prevention Act of 2009." US Department of Justice. https://www.justice.gov/crt/matthew-shepard-and-james-byrd-jr-hate-crimes-prevention-act-2009-0 (accessed August 15, 2017).

"NCAA to Relocate Championships from North Carolina for 2016–17." NCAA, September 12, 2016. http://www.ncaa.org/about/resources/media-center/news/ncaa-relocate-championships-north-carolina-2016-17 (accessed August 22, 2017).

"Our History." Patriot Guard Riders. https://www.patriotguard.org/content.php?162-PGR-History (accessed August 15, 2017).

"Shanghai to Show Pride with Gay Festival." BBC, June 6, 2009. http://news.bbc.co.uk/1/hi/world/asia-pacific/8083672.stm (accessed August 16, 2017).

Tan, Avianne. "North Carolina's Controversial Anti-LGBT Bill Explained." ABC News, March 24, 2016. http://abcnews.go.com/US/north-carolinas-controversial-anti-lgbt-bill-explained/story?id=37898153 (accessed August 22, 2017).

"With HB2 Repeal, NCAA Satisfied with North Carolina." ABC 11 Eyewitness News, April 4, 2017. http://abc11.com/sports/with-hb2-repeal-ncaa-satisfied-with-north-carolina/1835204/ (accessed August 22, 2017).

Research and Activity Ideas

Animal Rights

Some of the animals discussed in this chapter include whales, elephants, and monkeys. Choose one animal mentioned in the chapter, or select an animal you would like to learn more about. Research that animal on the Internet or in the school library. Create a poster that includes a picture of the animal and facts about it. Be sure to include information about where the animal lives, what makes it unique, and how it interacts with humans. Present your poster to the rest of the class, and explain why you chose the animal you did.

Civil Rights, African American

The Freedom Riders protested segregation in the southern United States. The Freedom Riders' protests helped bring about the desegregation of public transportation. Many Freedom Riders were threatened and some were beaten for their protests. Write an editorial to a newspaper about why you think the Freedom Riders' protests were important and should be remembered today. Include specific details about the Freedom Riders and explain specific outcomes of their protests.

Civil Rights, Hispanic and Latino

Dolores Huerta was the cofounder of the National Farm Workers Association, which later became United Farm Workers (UFW). Huerta advocated for workers' rights throughout her life. Use the Internet or school library resources to research Huerta's life. Write a paragraph describing one event in which Huerta participated or one part of her life story that most interests you. Share your writing with the group.

Economic Discontent

The citizens of the United Kingdom launched campaigns for and against Britain's break from the European Union, which became known as "Brexit." Demonstrate the opposing sides by organizing into two groups: one to research economic arguments in support of leaving the European Union and the other to research economic arguments in support of staying in the European Union. With your group, prepare a speech explaining why the UK should leave or stay in the European Union. Then choose one representative from each group to present the speech to the whole class.

Environment

The Pacific Climate Warriors tried to prevent coal ships from leaving an Australian port in 2014. Use the Internet or school library resources to search for images of the Pacific Climate Warriors' protest. Have the class vote on one image to print. Post the image at the front of the class. Then, break into small groups to discuss what the image shows and how the people in the picture most likely felt. With your group, write a journal entry from the point of view of one of the protesters in the picture. Explain how that person felt during the protest and why that person wanted to protest. Also describe what the person hoped to change by protesting.

Free Speech

In 2001 a church group burned Harry Potter books. People have burned and banned books for many reasons throughout history. Use the Internet or your school library to learn about one of these banned books: *The Absolutely True Diary of a Part-Time Indian, The Adventures of Huckleberry Finn, The Call of the Wild, The Catcher in the Rye, Go Ask Alice, The Handmaid's Tale, I Know Why the Caged Bird Sings, The Outsiders,* or *Twilight.* Read about the history of the book and why it is considered controversial. Pretend leaders in your community are planning to ban the book you chose from the community library. Write and present a speech about why they should or should not ban the book from the library's shelves.

Globalization

Banksy is an artist whose works have shared messages about many topics, including globalization. Do you agree or disagree with Banksy's opinions about consumerism and globalization? Use the Internet or the school library to find images of anti-globalization artwork. Imagine that you are an artist. Create a piece of art in response to Bansky's art shown in this chapter. You may create a drawing, a painting, or a collage with pictures from magazines or the Internet. Present your artwork to the class.

Gun Control/Gun Rights

The Black Panther protest of 1967 and the "I Will Not Comply" rally in 2014 both supported gun rights. However, these protests had different goals and different methods pertaining to gun rights. Create a compare-contrast chart on a poster. Fill in details about each protest to show how they were similar and how they were different. Present your poster to the class.

Human Rights

In 1971 prisoners at the Attica prison rioted in response to overcrowding, lack of food, and a lack of medical care. The riot ended in a great deal of violence. In 2016 prisoners from at least a dozen prisons in the United States commemorated the Attica Prison Riot by refusing to work. Use the Internet or your school library to research this protest from 2016. Which conditions were the prisoners protesting in 2016? How did those conditions compare to the conditions at Attica in 1971? How did the 2016 protest differ from the 1971 protest? How was it similar? Write a two-paragraph essay comparing and contrasting the conditions both groups were protesting.

Immigrant Rights

The 1844 riots in Philadelphia focused on Irish immigrants, most of whom were Catholic. The 2017 travel ban protests focused mostly on Middle Eastern and African immigrants, most of whom were Muslim. Use the Internet or the school library to research immigration in the United States from the early 1800s to the present. How have immigration rates from various parts of the world changed over time? How did this change most likely affect protests for immigrants' rights? What role has religion or race played in who was allowed into the country? Write a short essay

RESEARCH AND ACTIVITY IDEAS

(a couple of paragraphs) about how changes in immigration over time have affected protests for immigrants' rights in the United States.

Independence Movements

Imagine that you are a citizen of India in 1930. You want India to have independence from the United Kingdom. One day you see Mohandas Gandhi and a few hundred followers marching toward the sea. Some of them tell you about their plans to collect salt. You decide to join the march. Write a letter to a friend about your experience on the Salt March with Gandhi. Tell your friend why you joined the march and how you felt after collecting salt. Describe to your friend your hope for the future of India.

Indigenous Peoples' Rights

Imagine that you have a friend from another part of the world who learned about the Dakota Access Pipeline and the protests by the Standing Rock Sioux in the news. Your friend wants to learn more about the protests. He or she wants to know about the protesters' goals. Gather information about the protest from the chapter. Use the Internet or your school library to do research if you need more information. Then, write a two-paragraph email to your friend explaining the reasons for the protests, the protesters' goals, and the outcome of the protests.

Labor Rights

In 1936 and 1937 workers at a General Motors plant went on strike. Imagine that you are a newspaper journalist living in Flint, Michigan, in the 1930s. You just learned that the workers at General Motors have gone on strike. Write a newspaper article about the strike. Include at least one made-up quotation from a striking worker in your article. If you need more information about the strike, use the Internet or school library resources to research the topic.

LGBTQ Rights

The Stonewall Riots are one of the earliest protests for LGBTQ rights. Since then, many important events have helped shape the LGBTQ rights movement. Use the Internet or school library resources to research important events that happened around the world and shaped this movement. Then create a timeline poster starting in the 1960s and ending in

RESEARCH AND ACTIVITY IDEAS

the present. Mark at least 10 important events that happened in the LGBTQ rights movement during that time.

Political/Government Uprisings

The Arab Spring started in December 2010 in Tunisia. Many protests followed the one in Tunisia. The effects of the Arab Spring are still being felt in the Middle East today. Use the Internet or the school library to research the events of the Arab Spring. Make a poster with a timeline listing the most important events from the Arab Spring. Start the timeline in 2010 and end it in the present. Present your timeline to the class and compare it to the timelines your classmates made. Discuss with classmates how the timelines are similar or different.

Racial Conflict

In 1976 thousands of black students in Soweto, South Africa, protested unfair government laws. Imagine that you are a news reporter covering the Soweto uprising. You have an opportunity to interview a number of protesters after the uprising ends. Write a list of questions you would ask them about their protest. Then make up answers that you think the protesters might give based on what you have read. Share your questions and answers with a small group.

Reproductive Rights

Reproductive rights differ from one country to another. Track the reproductive rights of different countries around the world. Organize into five groups and have each group choose a different continent (Africa, Asia, Europe, North America, and South America). Try to determine which country on your chosen continent offers the most reproductive rights and which country offers the fewest reproductive rights. Use the Internet or your school library to research the reproductive rights in different countries. With your group, prepare a two-minute presentation about the reproductive rights in the countries you studied. Share your presentation with the class.

Resistance to Nazis

The White Rose movement published informational pamphlets as a way to resist Nazis. Consider the information the White Rose movement most likely included in its pamphlets. Organize into small groups. Imagine you are members of the White Rose movement, and you are

RESEARCH AND ACTIVITY IDEAS

designing another pamphlet to hand out in Germany. Use the Internet or school library resources to research the White Rose movement's pamphlets. Make a similar pamphlet with your group. Include information in the pamphlet that you want other Germans to know about the Nazis. Present your finished pamphlets to the class.

Slavery

Enslaved Africans were unable to protest to gain their freedom. People who escaped enslavement, however, often wanted to share their stories. They wanted people to understand the horrors of slavery and the terrible conditions enslaved people faced. Many enslaved people who were freed or who escaped wrote stories about their lives. Using the Internet or the school library, find one of these stories written by Frederick Douglass, Olaudah Equiano, Harriet Ann Jacobs, Solomon Northup, William Wells Brown, Briton Hammon, or Mary Prince. Read part of the story. Write a paragraph explaining how anti-slavery protesters could have benefited from reading the story.

War

In 1965 a group of students in Des Moines, Iowa, decided to wear black arm bands to protest the Vietnam War. Their school tried to stop them. In response, the students' families sued the school. The court case, *Tinker v. Des Moines*, eventually reached the US Supreme Court. Imagine that you are a lawyer defending one of the students in *Tinker v. Des Moines*. Write a one- or two-paragraph statement that you want to present in the courtroom to support your client's protest. Be sure to include information about why the students protested and why you think they should be allowed to take part in such a protest.

Women's Rights

Both the women from Saudi Arabia who were involved in the Baladi campaign in 2015 and the American women who were involved in the women's suffrage protest in 1918 were protesting to gain the right to vote. Talk about the two protests with a partner. Discuss what one of the Saudi protesters and one of the American protesters might say to each other about their protests if they could meet each other. Write down notes about this imaginary conversation. Then, perform a short skit in front of the class to show what the two protesters might say when talking about their protests.

Where to Learn More

Books

Amison Lüsted. *Tiananmen Square Protests.* Edina, MN: ABDO, 2011.

Arsenault, Raymond. *Freedom Riders: 1961 and the Struggle for Racial Justice.* New York: Oxford University Press, 2006.

Bledsoe, Karen E. *Consumption and Waste.* New York: Bloomsbury, 2014.

Çinar, Özgür Heval. *Conscientious Objection to Military Service in International Human Rights Law.* New York: Palgrave Macmillan, 2013.

Cunningham, Anne. *Critical Perspectives on Gun Control.* Berkeley Heights, NJ: Enslow, 2017.

David, Laurie, and Cambria Gordon. *The Down-to-Earth Guide to Global Warming.* New York: Scholastic, 2007.

Fredrickson, George M. *Racism: A Short History.* Princeton, NJ: Princeton University Press, 2002.

Gitlin, Todd. *Occupy Nation: The Roots, the Spirit, and the Promise of Occupy Wall Street.* New York: HarperCollins Publishers, 2012.

Henderson, Timothy J. *The Mexican Wars for Independence.* New York: Hill and Wang, 2009.

Jenkins, Henry. *Convergence Culture: Where Old and New Media Collide.* New York: New York University Press, 2006.

Kelly, Nigel. *The Fall of the Berlin Wall: The Cold War Ends.* Rev. ed. Chicago: Heinemann, 2006.

Kinsbruner, Jay. *Independence in Spanish America: Civil Wars, Revolutions, and Underdevelopment.* Albuquerque: University of New Mexico Press, 2000.

Laine, Carolee. *Book Banning and Other Forms of Censorship.* Minneapolis, MN: ABDO, 2017.

Lennox, Corinne, and Damien Short, eds. *Handbook of Indigenous Peoples' Rights.* New York: Routledge, 2016.

WHERE TO LEARN MORE

Mize, Ronald L., and Grace Peña Delgado. *Latino Immigrants in the United States.* Cambridge, UK: Polity Press, 2012.

Oberg, Michael Leroy. *Native America: A History.* 2nd ed. Hoboken, New Jersey: Wiley-Blackwell, 2017.

Parks, Rosa. *Rosa Parks: My Story.* New York: Penguin, 1992.

Poehlmann, Tristan. *The Stonewall Riots: The Fight for LGBT Rights.* Minneapolis, MN: ABDO, 2017.

Reagan, Leslie J. *When Abortion Was a Crime: Women, Medicine, and Law in the United States, 1867–1973.* Berkeley: University of California Press, 1998.

Regan, Tom. *The Case for Animal Rights.* 2nd ed. Berkeley: University of California Press, 2004.

Robinson, J. Dennis. *Striking Back: The Fight to End Child Labor Exploitation.* Mankato, MN: Compass Point Books, 2010.

Rosinsky, Natalie M. *The Kent State Shootings.* Minneapolis: Compass Point Books, 2009.

Singer, Peter. *Animal Liberation: The Definitive Classic of the Animal Movement.* 40th anniversary ed. New York: Open Road Media, 2015.

Shuter, Jane. *Resistance to the Nazis.* Chicago: Heinemann, 2003.

Skocpol, Theda, and Vanessa Williamson. *The Tea Party and the Remaking of Republican Conservatism.* Oxford, UK: Oxford University Press, 2012.

Skurzynski, Gloria. *Sweat and Blood: A History of U.S. Labor Unions.* Minneapolis, MN: Twenty-First Century Books, 2009.

Stienstra, Deborah. *Women's Movements and International Organizations.* New York: St. Martin's Press, 1994.

Townsend, Riley M. *The European Migrant Crisis.* Morrisville, NC: Lulu, 2015.

Periodicals

Abend, Lisa. "In Spain, Human Rights for Apes." *Time* (July 18, 2008). Available online at http://content.time.com/time/world/article/0,8599,1824206,00.html (accessed July 10, 2017).

Abouzeid, Rania. "Bouazizi: The Man Who Set Himself and Tunisia on Fire." *Time* (January 21, 2011). Available online at http://content.time.com/time/magazine/article/0,9171,2044723,00.html (accessed August 18, 2017).

Aisch, Gregor, and K. K. Rebecca Lai. "The Conflicts along 1,172 Miles of the Dakota Access Pipeline." *New York Times* (March 23, 2017). Available online at https://www.nytimes.com/interactive/2016/11/23/us/dakota-access-pipeline-protest-map.html (accessed August 21, 2017).

Alexander, Harriet. "Who Is Chelsea Manning and Why Is She Being Released from Prison?" *Telegraph* (May 17, 2017). Available online at http://www.telegraph.co.uk/news/2017/05/17/chelsea-manning-released-prison/ (accessed September 20, 2017).

Anderson, John Ward. "Cartoons of Prophet Met with Outrage." *Washington Post* (January 31, 2006). Available online at http://www.washingtonpost.com/wp-dyn/content/article/2006/01/30/AR2006013001316.html (accessed July 25, 2017).

Archibold, Randal C. "Immigrants Take to U.S. Streets in Show of Strength." *New York Times* (May 2, 2006). Available online at http://www.nytimes.com/2006/05/02/us/02immig.html (accessed July 17, 2017).

"A Background Guide to 'Brexit' from the European Union." *Economist* (February 24, 2016). Available online at https://www.economist.com/blogs/graphicdetail/2016/02/graphics-britain-s-referendum-eu-membership (accessed July 24, 2017).

Bacon, John, and Alan Gomez. "Protests against Trump's Immigration Plan Rolling in More than 30 Cities." *USA Today* (January 29, 2017). Available online at https://www.usatoday.com/story/news/nation/2017/01/29/homeland-security-judges-stay-has-little-impact-travel-ban/97211720/ (accessed August 3, 2017).

Blair, David. "The World Has Over 45 Million Slaves—Including 1.2 Million in Europe—Finds New Study." *Telegraph* (May 31, 2016). Available online at http://www.telegraph.co.uk/news/2016/05/31/the-world-has-over-45-million-slaves---including-12-million-in-e/ (accessed August 28, 2017).

Blythe, Anne. "NC Law Replacing HB2 Is Still a Bathroom Bill That Discriminates, Challengers Claim." *News & Observer* (July 21, 2017). Available online at http://www.newsobserver.com/news/politics-government/state-politics/article162850673.html (accessed August 22, 2017).

Burton, Lynsi. "WTO Riots in Seattle: 15 Years Ago." *Seattle Post Intelligencer* (November 29, 2014). Available online at http://www.seattlepi.com/local/article/WTO-riots-in-Seattle-15-years-ago-5915088.php (accessed July 25, 2017).

"Casting Ballots, Saudi Women Proudly 'Make History.'" *Times of Israel* (December 13, 2015). Available online at http://www.timesofisrael.com/casting-ballots-saudi-women-proudly-make-history (accessed August 21, 2017).

Chertoff, Emily. "Occupy Wounded Knee: A 71-Day Siege and a Forgotten Civil Rights Movement." *Atlantic* (October 23, 2012). Available online at https://www.theatlantic.com/national/archive/2012/10/occupy-wounded-knee-a-71-day-siege-and-a-forgotten-civil-rights-movement/263998/ (accessed August 21, 2017).

Cobb, James C. "The Voting Rights Act at 50: How It Changed the World." *Time* (August 6, 2015). Available online at http://time.com/3985479/voting-rights-act-1965-results/ (accessed July 18, 2017).

Cohen, Sascha. "The Day Women Went on Strike." *Time* (August 26, 2015). Available online at http://time.com/4008060/women-strike-equality-1970 (accessed August 21, 2017).

Collins, Mike. "The Pros and Cons of Globalization." *Forbes* (May 6, 2015). Available online at https://www.forbes.com/sites/mikecollins/2015/05/06/the-pros-and-cons-of-globalization/#60ffb291ccce (accessed July 27, 2017).

"Dalit Anger Singes West India." *Times of India* (December 1, 2006). Available online at https://www.pressreader.com/india/the-times-of-india-new-delhi-edition/20061201/281552286366605 (accessed September 21, 2017).

Davis, Julie Hirschfeld, and Helene Cooper. "Trump Says Transgender People Will Not Be Allowed in the Military." *New York Times* (July 26, 2017). Available online at https://www.nytimes.com/2017/07/26/us/politics/trump-transgender-military.html (accessed August 23, 2017).

Davis, Kenneth C. "America's True History of Religious Tolerance." *Smithsonian* (October 2010). Available online at http://www.smithsonianmag.com/history/americas-true-history-of-religious-tolerance-61312684/ (accessed August 1, 2017).

Day, Elizabeth. "#BlackLivesMatter: The Birth of a New Civil Rights Movement." *Guardian* (July 19, 2015). Available online at https://www.theguardian.com/world/2015/jul/19/blacklivesmatter-birth-civil-rights-movement (accessed September 15, 2017).

Drezner, Daniel W. "A Clash between Administrators and Students at Yale Went Viral. Why That Is Unfortunate for All Concerned." *Washington Post* (November 9, 2015). Available online at https://www.washingtonpost.com/posteverything/wp/2015/11/09/a-clash-between-administrators-and-students-at-yale-went-viral-why-that-is-unfortunate-for-all-concerned/?utm_term=.bdfae3d5f34b (accessed July 25, 2017).

Eddy, Melissa. "Big Anti-Immigration Rally in Germany Prompts Counterdemonstrations." *New York Times* (January 12, 2015). Available online at https://www.nytimes.com/2015/01/13/world/europe/big-anti-immigration-rally-in-germany-prompts-counterdemonstrations.html (accessed July 27, 2017).

"800 Arrested at Berkeley; Students Paralyze Campus." *Harvard Crimson* (December 4, 1964). Available online at http://www.thecrimson.com/article/1964/12/4/800-arrested-at-berkeley-students-paralyze/ (accessed July 25, 2017).

Eilperin, Juliet. "The Keystone XL Pipeline and Its Politics, Explained." *Washington Post* (February 4, 2014). Available online at https://www.washingtonpost.com/news/the-fix/wp/2013/04/03/the-keystone-xl-pipeline-and-its-politics-explained/?utm_term=.2b02fc9a65c7 (accessed July 22, 2017).

Ellingwood, Ken. "In Mexico City, Crowds Protest Drug Violence." *Los Angeles Times* (May 8, 2011). Available online at http://articles.latimes.com/2011/may/08/world/la-fg-mexican-violence-protest-20110509 (accessed July 18, 2017).

Engler, Mark, and Paul Engler. "How Did Gandhi Win? Lessons from the Salt March." *Dissent* (October 10, 2014). Available online at https://www.dissentmagazine.org/blog/gandhi-win-lessons-salt-march-social-movements (accessed August 2, 2017).

Erb, Kelly Phillips. "Considering the Death Penalty: Your Tax Dollars at Work." *Forbes* (May 1, 2014). Available online at https://www.forbes.com/

sites/kellyphillipserb/2014/05/01/considering-the-death-penalty-your- tax-dollars-at-work/#3dbe69c7664b (accessed September 7, 2017).

Federoff, Nina. "Can We Trust Monsanto with Our Food?" *Scientific American* (July 25, 2013). Available online at https://www.scientificamerican.com/article/can-we-trust-monsanto-with-our-food/ (accessed July 25, 2017).

Fitz, Nicholas. "Economic Inequality: It's Far Worse than You Think." *Scientific American* (March 31, 2015). Available online at https://www.scientificamerican.com/article/economic-inequality-it-s-far-worse-than-you-think/ (accessed July 28, 2017).

Ford, Matt. "Can Europe End the Death Penalty in America?" *Atlantic* (February 18, 2014). Available online at https://www.theatlantic.com/international/archive/2014/02/can-europe-end-the-death-penalty-in-america/283790/ (accessed September 7, 2017).

Gaffey, Conor. "South Africa: What You Need to Know about the Soweto Uprising 40 Years Later." *Newsweek* (June 16, 2016). Available online at http://www.newsweek.com/soweto-uprising-hector-pieterson-memorial-471090 (accessed September 15, 2017).

Gopalakrishnan, Amulya, and Vaibhav Ganjapure. "10 Years Later, Khairlanji Shows How Caste Crimes Fester." *Times of India* (September 28, 2016). Available online at http://timesofindia.indiatimes.com/city/nagpur/10-years-later-Khairlanji-shows-how-caste-crimes-fester/articleshow/54568908.cms (accessed September 19, 2017).

Gordon, Noah. "The Little Rock Nine: How Far Has the Country Come?" *Atlantic* (September 25, 2014). Available online at https://www.theatlantic.com/politics/archive/2014/09/the-little-rock-nine/380676/ (accessed July 18, 2017).

Greenhouse, Steven. "With Day of Protests, Fast-Food Workers Seek More Pay." *New York Times* (November 30, 2012). Available online at http://www.nytimes.com/2012/11/30/nyregion/fast-food-workers-in-new-york-city-rally-for-higher-wages.html?mcubz=3 (accessed August 25, 2017).

Gregory, Alice. "A Brief History of the Zoot Suit: Unraveling the Jazzy Life of a Snazzy Style." *Smithsonian* (April 2016). Available online at http://www.smithsonianmag.com/arts-culture/brief-history-zoot-suit-180958507 (accessed September 15, 2017).

Grossman, David. "The Dakota Pipeline Controversy Explained." *Popular Mechanics* (January 24, 2017). Available online at http://www.popularmechanics.com/technology/infrastructure/a23658/dakota-pipeline-protests (accessed August 21, 2017).

Grossman, Ron. "Flashback: 'Swastika War': When the Neo-Nazis Fought in Court to March in Skokie." *Chicago Tribune* (January 1, 2002). Available online at http://www.chicagotribune.com/news/opinion/commentary/ct-neo-nazi-skokie-march-flashback-perspec-0312-20170310-story.html (accessed July 25, 2017).

WHERE TO LEARN MORE

Hall, Sarah. "Harry Potter and the Sermon of Fire." *Guardian* (January 1, 2002). Available online at https://www.theguardian.com/world/2002/jan/01/books.harrypotter (accessed July 25, 2017).

Havard, Kate, and Lori Aratani. "Nearly 1,000 March in D.C. for Gun Control." *Washington Post* (January 26, 2013). Available online at https://www.washingtonpost.com/local/trafficandcommuting/newtown-residents-among-those-at-dc-march-for-gun-control/2013/01/26/1813a3f6-67cb-11e2-85f5-a8a9228e55e7_story.html?utm_term=.c1c727450d42 (accessed August 8, 2017).

Hendel, John. "The Freedom Riders for Civil Rights, Half a Century Later." *Atlantic* (May 4, 2011). Available online at https://www.theatlantic.com/national/archive/2011/05/the-freedom-riders-for-civil-rights-half-a-century-later-life-photos/238342/ (accessed July 18, 2017).

Herszenhorn, David M. "Armenia, on Day of Rain and Sorrow, Observes 100th Anniversary of Genocide." *New York Times* (April 24, 2015). Available online at https://www.nytimes.com/2015/04/25/world/europe/armenian-genocide-100th-anniversary.html?mcubz=1&module=ArrowsNav&contentCollection=Europe&action=keypress&region=FixedLeft&pgtype=article (accessed September 8, 2017).

Herszenhorn, David M., and Emmarie Huetteman. "House Democrats' Gun-Control Sit-In Turns into Chaotic Showdown with Republicans." *New York Times* (June 23, 2016). Available online at https://www.nytimes.com/2016/06/23/us/politics/house-democrats-stage-sit-in-to-push-for-action-on-gun-control.html (accessed August 8, 2017).

Hingston, Sandy. "Bullets and Bigots: Remembering Philadelphia's 1844 Anti-Catholic Riots." *Philadelphia Magazine* (December 17, 2015). Available online at http://www.phillymag.com/news/2015/12/17/philadelphia-anti-catholic-riots-1844/ (accessed August 1, 2017).

Holmes, Steven A. "Disabled Protest and Are Arrested." *New York Times* (March 14, 1990). Available online at http://www.nytimes.com/1990/03/14/us/disabled-protest-and-are-arrested.html (accessed September 21, 2017).

Iracheta, Michelle. "Houston Group Protests Texas' Death Penalty." *Houston Chronicle* (October 26, 2014). Available online at http://www.chron.com/news/houston-texas/houston/article/Houston-group-protests-Texas-death-penalty-5848226.php (accessed September 7, 2017).

Iyengar, Rishi. "6 Questions You Might Have about Hong Kong's Umbrella Revolution." *Time* (October 5, 2014). Available online at http://time.com/3471366/hong-kong-umbrella-revolution-occupy-central-democracy-explainer-6-questions/ (accessed August 21, 2017).

Jacobs, Andrew. "Gay Festival in China Pushes Official Boundaries." *New York Times* (June 15, 2009). Available online at http://www.nytimes.com/2009/06/15/world/asia/15shanghai.html (accessed August 16, 2017).

Jaschik, Scott. "Racial Tensions Escalate." *Inside Higher Ed* (November 9, 2015). Available online at https://www.insidehighered.com/news/2015/

11/09/racial-tensions-escalate-u-missouri-and-yale (accessed July 25, 2017).

Kafanov, Lucy. "Turkey, Armenians Battle over Genocide 100 Years Later." *USA Today* (April 23, 2015). Available online at https://www.usatoday.com/story/news/world/2015/04/23/turkey-armenia-genocide-massacre-anniversary/26261059/ (accessed September 8, 2017).

Kaleem, Jaweed. "The Death Penalty Has Long Divided Americans. Here's Why Those Who Oppose It Are Winning." *Los Angeles Times* (April 27, 2017). Available online at http://www.latimes.com/nation/la-na-death-penalty-arkansas-20170427-htmlstory.html (accessed September 7, 2017).

Kifner, John. "Armenian Genocide of 1915: An Overview." *New York Times*, n.d. Available online at http://www.nytimes.com/ref/timestopics/topics_armeniangenocide.html?mcubz=0 (accessed September 8, 2017).

Koch, Wendy. "Tens of Thousands Demand Action on Climate Change." *USA Today* (February 17, 2013). Available online at https://www.usatoday.com/story/news/nation/2013/02/17/climate-change-rally-human-pipeline/1925719/ (accessed July 22, 2017).

Kopel, David. "The Warsaw Ghetto Uprising: Armed Jews vs. Nazis." *Washington Post* (October 10, 2015). Available online at https://www.washingtonpost.com/news/volokh-conspiracy/wp/2015/10/10/the-warsaw-ghetto-uprising-armed-jews-vs-nazis/?utm_term=.914e605236fd (accessed August 8, 2017).

Levitin, Michael. "The Triumph of Occupy Wall Street." *Atlantic* (June 10, 2015). Available online at https://www.theatlantic.com/politics/archive/2015/06/the-triumph-of-occupy-wall-street/395408/ (accessed July 27, 2017).

Liu, Melinda. "China Gay-Pride Event Meets Obstacles." *Newsweek* (June 12, 2009). Available online at http://www.newsweek.com/china-gay-pride-event-meets-obstacles-80291 (accessed August 16, 2017).

Lueck, Thomas J. "Threats and Responses: Protests; Candlelight Vigils Are Held around the World to Oppose Military Action against Iraq." *New York Times* (March 17, 2003). Available online at http://www.nytimes.com/2003/03/17/world/threats-responses-protests-candlelight-vigils-are-held-around-world-oppose.html?mcubz=1 (accessed September 22, 2017).

"Marchers in over 400 Cities Protest Monsanto." *Washington Post* (May 25, 2013). Available online at https://www.washingtonpost.com/politics/marchers-in-over-400-cities-protest-monsanto/2013/05/25/938dd988-c59b-11e2-914f-a7aba60512a7_story.html?utm_term=.cd0efcd95a22 (accessed July 25, 2017).

McCarthy, Tom. "Under the Umbrellas: What Do Hong Kong's Protesters Want from China?" *Guardian* (September 29, 2014). Available online at https://www.theguardian.com/world/2014/sep/29/hong-kong-democracy-protests-china-umbrellas-police (accessed August 21, 2017).

McFadden, Robert D. "The Republicans: The Convention in New York—The March; Vast Anti-Bush Rally Greets Republicans in New York." *New York Times* (August 30, 2004). Available online at http://www.nytimes.com/

2004/08/30/us/republicans-convention-new-york-march-vast-anti-bush-rally-greets-republicans.html?mcubz=1 (accessed September 22, 2017).

Mejia, Brittny, et al. "Armenian Genocide: Massive March Ends at Turkish Consulate in L.A." *Los Angeles Times* (April 24, 2015). Available online at http://www.latimes.com/local/lanow/la-me-ln-armenian-genocide-march-los-angeles-20150424-story.html (accessed September 8, 2017).

Meyer, Robinson. "The Standing Rock Sioux Claim 'Victory and Vindication' in Court." *Atlantic* (June 14, 2017). Available online at https://www.theatlantic.com/science/archive/2017/06/dakota-access-standing-rock-sioux-victory-court/530427/ (accessed August 21, 2017).

"Millions March against GM Crops." *Guardian* (May 25, 2013). Available online at https://www.theguardian.com/environment/2013/may/26/millions-march-against-monsanto (accessed July 25, 2017).

Minder, Raphael. "Animal Welfare Activists to Protest Bullfighting in Spain." *New York Times* (August 20, 2010). Available online at http://www.nytimes.com/2010/08/21/world/europe/21iht-spain.html (accessed July 12, 2017).

Patterson, Romaine. "Let Westboro Baptist Have Their Hate Speech. We'll Smother It with Peace." *Washington Post* (March 6, 2011). Available online at http://www.washingtonpost.com/wp-dyn/content/article/2011/03/04/AR2011030406330.html (accessed August 14, 2017).

Peters, Jeremy W., et al. "Pence Tells Anti-Abortion Marchers That 'Life Is Winning.'" *New York Times* (January 27, 2017). Available online at https://www.nytimes.com/2017/01/27/us/politics/march-for-life.html (accessed August 30, 2017).

"Prophet Mohammed Cartoon Controversy: Timeline." *Telegraph* (May 4, 2015). Available online at http://www.telegraph.co.uk/news/worldnews/europe/france/11341599/Prophet-Muhammad-cartoons-controversy-timeline.html (accessed July 25, 2017).

Rayman, Noah. "6 Things You Should Know about the Tiananmen Square Massacre." *Time* (June 4, 2014). Available online at http://time.com/2822290/tiananmen-square-massacre-facts-time/ (accessed August 23, 2017).

Remnick, Noah. "Yale Grapples with Ties to Slavery in Debate over a College's Name." *New York Times* (September 12, 2015). Available online at https://www.nytimes.com/2015/09/12/nyregion/yale-in-debate-over-calhoun-college-grapples-with-ties-to-slavery.html (accessed July 25, 2017).

Richmond, Emily. "Civics Lessons from the House Democrats' Sit-in." *Atlantic* (June 28, 2016). Available online at https://www.theatlantic.com/education/archive/2016/06/civics-lessons-from-the-house-democrats-sit-in/489167/ (accessed August 8, 2017).

Ross, Winston. "Protests Hit Netherlands in Wake of Paris Attack." *Newsweek* (January 7, 2015). Available online at http://www.newsweek.com/protests-hit-netherlands-wake-paris-attack-297459 (accessed July 25, 2017).

Rothman, Lily. "What We Still Get Wrong about What Happened in Detroit in 1967." *Time* (August 3, 2017). Available online at http://time.com/4879062/detroit-1967-real-history/ (accessed September 15, 2017).

Sanchez, Raf. "WikiLeaks Q & A: Who Is Bradley Manning and What Did He Do?" *Telegraph* (July 30, 2013). Available online at http://www.telegraph.co.uk/news/worldnews/wikileaks/10210160/WikiLeaks-Q-and-A-who-is-Bradley-Manning-and-what-did-he-do.html (accessed September 20, 2017).

Santora, Marc. "Yale Report Clears Police Officer in Encounter with Student." *New York Times* (March 5, 2015). Available online at https://www.nytimes.com/2015/03/05/nyregion/yale-report-clears-police-officer-in-encounter-with-student.html (accessed July 25, 2017).

Smith, Mitch. "Standing Rock Protest Camp, Once Home to Thousands, Is Razed." *New York Times* (February 23, 2017). Available online at https://www.nytimes.com/2017/02/23/us/standing-rock-protest-dakota-access-pipeline.html (accessed July 22, 2017).

Smith, Noah. "The Dark Side of Globalization: Why Seattle's 1999 Protesters Were Right." *Atlantic* (January 6, 2014). Available online at https://www.theatlantic.com/business/archive/2014/01/the-dark-side-of-globalization-why-seattles-1999-protesters-were-right/282831/ (accessed July 27, 2017).

Stack, Liam. "A Brief History of Deadly Attacks on Abortion Providers." *New York Times* (November 29, 2015). Available online at https://www.nytimes.com/interactive/2015/11/29/us/30abortion-clinic-violence.html (accessed August 31, 2017).

Steinfels, Peter. "Paris, May 1968: The Revolution That Never Was." *New York Times* (May 11, 2008). Available online at http://www.nytimes.com/2008/05/11/world/europe/11iht-paris.4.12777919.html (accessed July 24, 2017).

Steyn, Paul. "African Elephant Numbers Plummet 30 Percent, Landmark Survey Finds." *National Geographic* (August 31, 2016). Available online at http://news.nationalgeographic.com/2016/08/wildlife-african-elephants-population-decrease-great-elephant-census/ (accessed July 11, 2017).

Swarns, Rachel L. "Yale College Dean Torn by Racial Protests." *New York Times* (November 15, 2015). Available online at https://www.nytimes.com/2015/11/16/nyregion/yale-college-dean-torn-by-racial-protests.html (accessed July 25, 2017).

"Tiananmen Square 25 Years On: 'Every Person in the Crowd Was a Victim of the Massacre.'" *Guardian* (June 1, 2014). Available online at https://www.theguardian.com/world/2014/jun/01/tiananmen-square-25-years-every-person-victim-massacre (accessed August 23, 2017).

"A Timeline of the Dakota Access Oil Pipeline." *U.S. News & World Report* (February 22, 2017). Available online at https://www.usnews.com/news/north-dakota/articles/2017-02-22/a-timeline-of-the-dakota-access-oil-pipeline (accessed August 21, 2017).

Tremlett, Giles. "Spain Protesters Vote to Dismantle Puerta del Sol Tent City." *Guardian* (June 8, 2011). Available online at https://www.theguardian.com/

world/2011/jun/08/spain-protesters-dismantle-puerta-sol (accessed August 1, 2017).

"Why Islam Prohibits Images of Muhammad." *Economist* (January 19, 2015). Available online at https://www.economist.com/blogs/economist-explains/2015/01/economist-explains-12 (accessed July 25, 2017).

Wilkinson, Tracy. "New Report Raises Chilling Possibility That Mystery of 43 Mexican Students' Disappearance Will Never Be Solved." *Los Angeles Times* (April 25, 2016). Available online at http://www.latimes.com/world/mexico-americas/la-fg-mexico-students-20160425-story.html (accessed July 18, 2017).

Winkler, Adam. "The Secret History of Guns." *Atlantic* (September 2011). Available online at https://www.theatlantic.com/magazine/archive/2011/09/the-secret-history-of-guns/308608/ (accessed August 8, 2017).

Woo, Elaine. "'60s 'Blowouts': Leaders of Latino School Protest See Little Change." *Los Angeles Times* (March 7, 1988). Available online at http://articles.latimes.com/1988-03-07/local/me-488_1_lincoln-high-school-graduate (accessed July 13, 2017).

Worthington, Danika. "Meet the Disabled Activists from Denver Who Changed a Nation." *Denver Post* (July 5, 2017). Available online at http://www.denverpost.com/2017/07/05/adapt-disabled-activists-denver/ (accessed September 21, 2017).

Yee, Vivian, Kenan Davis, and Jugal K. Patel. "Here's the Reality about Illegal Immigrants in the United States." *New York Times* (March 2, 2017). Available online at https://www.nytimes.com/interactive/2017/03/06/us/politics/undocumented-illegal-immigrants.html (accessed July 19, 2017).

Yong, Ed. "How the March for Science Finally Found Its Voice." *Atlantic* (April 23, 2017). Available online at https://www.theatlantic.com/science/archive/2017/04/how-the-march-for-science-finally-found-its-voice/524022/ (accessed July 22, 2017).

Websites

"About." 18th Annual March to Abolish the Death Penalty – Oct 28, 2017. http://marchforabolition.org/about-2/ (accessed September 7, 2017).

Badcock, James. "Will Spain Ever Ban Bullfighting?" BBC News, December 3, 2016. http://www.bbc.com/news/world-europe-38063778 (accessed July 12, 2017).

Batha, Emma. "Europe's Refugee and Migrant Crisis in 2016. In Numbers." World Economic Forum, December 5, 2016. https://www.weforum.org/agenda/2016/12/europes-refugee-and-migrant-crisis-in-2016-in-numbers (accessed July 27, 2017).

Black, Richard. "Copenhagen Climate Accord: Key Issues" BBC News, December 19, 2009. http://news.bbc.co.uk/2/hi/science/nature/8422186.stm (accessed July 22, 2017).

WHERE TO LEARN MORE

Botelho, Greg. "Arab Spring Aftermath: Revolutions Give Way to Violence, More Unrest." CNN, March 2015. http://www.cnn.com/2015/03/27/middleeast/arab-spring-aftermath/index.html (accessed August 18, 2017).

"Chicano Movement." Brown University. http://www.brown.edu/Research/Coachella/chicano.html (accessed July 13, 2017).

"Civil Rights at Stonewall National Monument." National Park Service, October 17, 2016. https://www.nps.gov/places/stonewall.htm (accessed August 17, 2017).

Connolly, Katie. "What Exactly Is the Tea Party?" BBC News, September 16, 2010. http://www.bbc.com/news/world-us-canada-11317202 (accessed July 14, 2017).

Convention on International Trade in Endangered Species of Wild Fauna and Flora (CITES). https://www.cites.org/ (accessed July 10, 2017).

"Czech Republic Slovakia: Velvet Revolution at 25." BBC News, November 17, 2014. http://www.bbc.com/news/world-europe-30059011 (accessed August 4, 2017).

"The Death Penalty in United States of America." Cornell Center on the Death Penalty Worldwide, March 10, 2014. http://www.deathpenaltyworldwide.org/country-search-post.cfm?country=united+states+of+america (accessed September 7, 2017).

Dwyer, Colin. "Protests against Planned Parenthood Rouse Dueling Rallies Nationwide." National Public Radio, February 11, 2017. http://www.npr.org/sections/thetwo-way/2017/02/11/514717975/protests-against-planned-parenthood-rouse-dueling-rallies-nationwide (accessed August 31, 2017).

"Episode 337: The Secret Document That Transformed China." *Planet Money*, National Public Radio, May 14, 2014. http://www.npr.org/sections/money/2014/05/14/312488659/episode-337-the-secret-document-that-transformed-china (accessed July 19, 2017).

Fessenden, Marissa. "How a Nearly Successful Slave Revolt Was Intentionally Lost to History." *Smithsonian*. http://www.smithsonianmag.com/smart-news/its-anniversary-1811-louisiana-slave-revolt-180957760 (accessed August 25, 2017).

"45.8 Million People Are Enslaved across the World." Global Slavery Index, May 30, 2016. https://www.globalslaveryindex.org/media/45-8-million-people-enslaved-across-world/ (accessed August 28, 2017).

"The Freedom Rides: CORE Volunteers Put Their Lives on the Road." Congress of Racial Equality (CORE). http://www.core-online.org/History/freedom%20rides.htm (accessed July 18, 2017).

Friedman, Gail. "March of the Mill Children." Encyclopedia of Greater Philadelphia. http://philadelphiaencyclopedia.org/archive/march-of-the-mill-children/ (accessed August 25, 2017).

Gamboa, Suzanne. "For Latinos, 1965 Voting Rights Act Impact Came a Decade Later." NBC News, August 6, 2015. http://www.nbcnews.com/

WHERE TO LEARN MORE

news/latino/latinos-1965-voting-rights-act-impact-came-decade-later-n404936 (accessed July 20, 2017).

"The Global Divide on Homosexuality." Pew Research Center, June 4, 2013. http://www.pewglobal.org/2013/06/04/the-global-divide-on-homosexuality/ (accessed August 16, 2017).

"Globalization." *National Geographic*, March 28, 2011. https://www.nationalgeographic.org/encyclopedia/globalization/ (accessed July 27, 2017).

Goodman, Al. "Thousands of Spaniards Call for Economic Reform in New Protest." CNN, June 19, 2011. http://www.cnn.com/2011/WORLD/europe/06/19/spain.protests/ (accessed August 1, 2017).

"The Grito de Lares: The Rebellion of 1868." Library of Congress. https://www.loc.gov/collections/puerto-rico-books-and-pamphlets/articles-and-essays/nineteenth-century-puerto-rico/rebellion-of-1868 (accessed July 31, 2017).

"Gun Violence." Brady Campaign to Prevent Gun Violence. http://www.bradycampaign.org/gun-violence (accessed August 8, 2017).

"Hate Crimes Law." Human Rights Campaign. http://www.hrc.org/resources/hate-crimes-law (accessed August 15, 2017).

Hersher, Rebecca. "Key Moments in the Dakota Access Pipeline Fight." National Public Radio, February 22, 2017. http://www.npr.org/sections/thetwo-way/2017/02/22/514988040/key-moments-in-the-dakota-access-pipeline-fight (accessed August 21, 2017).

"Hispanics in the US Fast Facts." CNN, March 31, 2017. http://www.cnn.com/2013/09/20/us/hispanics-in-the-u-s-/index.html (accessed July 27, 2017).

"History—Incident at Wounded Knee." US Marshals Service. https://www.usmarshals.gov/history/wounded-knee/ (accessed August 21, 2017).

"Hong Kong Protests: Timeline of the Occupation." BBC News, December 11, 2014. http://www.bbc.com/news/world-asia-china-30390820 (accessed August 21, 2017).

"How the United States Immigration System Works." American Immigration Council, August 12, 2016. https://www.americanimmigrationcouncil.org/research/how-united-states-immigration-system-works (accessed July 19, 2017).

"India's Dalits: Between Atrocity and Protest." Human Rights Watch, January 12, 2007. https://www.hrw.org/news/2007/01/12/indias-dalits-between-atrocity-and-protest (accessed September 21, 2017).

"Indigenous Peoples." The World Bank. http://www.worldbank.org/en/topic/indigenouspeoples (accessed August 21, 2017).

International Congress of Women. "Final Programme." Gothenburg University Library. http://www.ub.gu.se/kvinndata/portaler/fred/samarbete/pdf/program_1915.pdf (accessed September 8, 2017).

Johnson, Troy. "We Hold the Rock." National Park Service, February 27, 2015. https://www.nps.gov/alca/learn/historyculture/we-hold-the-rock.htm (accessed August 21, 2017).

Jones, Owen. "The People Are Revolting—the History of Protest." BBC. http://www.bbc.co.uk/timelines/ztvxtfr (accessed August 15, 2017).

Kauffman, Stephen. "They Abandoned Their Wheelchairs and Crawled Up the Capitol Steps." ShareAmerica, March 12, 2015. https://share.america.gov/crawling-up-steps-demand-their-rights/ (accessed September 21, 2017).

Kennedy, Merrit. "A Look at Egypt's Uprising, 5 Years Later." National Public Radio, January 25, 2016. http://www.npr.org/sections/thetwo-way/2016/01/25/464290769/a-look-at-egypts-uprising-5-years-later (accessed August 15, 2017).

Kim, Inga. "The 1965–1970 Delano Grape Strike and Boycott." United Farm Workers, March 7, 2017. http://ufw.org/1965-1970-delano-grape-strike-boycott (accessed August 25, 2017).

Kurtzleben, Danielle. "100 Days In, Women's March Still Inspires. But Can the Enthusiasm Hold?" National Public Radio, April 28, 2017. http://www.npr.org/2017/04/28/525764938/100-days-in-womens-march-still-inspires-but-can-the-enthusiasm-hold (accessed August 21, 2017).

Lee, Brianna, and Danielle Renwick. "Mexico's Drug War." Council on Foreign Relations, May 25, 2017. https://www.cfr.org/backgrounder/mexicos-drug-war (accessed July 18, 2017).

Lee, Trymaine. "Justice for All: Thousands March against Police Violence." MSNBC, July 21, 2015. http://www.msnbc.com/msnbc/justice-all-thousands-expected-march-washington-against-police-violence (accessed September 15, 2017).

Lewis, Jerry M., and Thomas R. Hensley. "The May 4 Shootings at Kent State University: The Search for Historical Accuracy." Kent State University. http://www.kent.edu/may-4-historical-accuracy (accessed September 7, 2017).

"LGBT Rights Milestones Fast Facts." CNN, July 4, 2017. http://www.cnn.com/2015/06/19/us/lgbt-rights-milestones-fast-facts/index.html (accessed August 23, 2017).

"Little Rock Central High School: Crisis Timeline." National Park Service. https://www.nps.gov/chsc/learn/historyculture/timeline.htm (accessed July 18, 2017).

López, Gustavo, and Kristen Bialik. "Key Findings about U.S. Immigrants." Pew Research Center, May 3, 2017. http://www.pewresearch.org/fact-tank/2017/05/03/key-findings-about-u-s-immigrants/ (accessed July 17, 2017).

"Malala's Story." Malala Fund. https://www.malala.org/malalas-story (accessed August 21, 2017).

Malik, Asad. "Charles Deslondes and the American Uprising of 1811." Pan-African Alliance. https://www.panafricanalliance.com/charles-deslondes (accessed August 25, 2017).

"Māori Land Rights." Museum of New Zealand. http://sites.tepapa.govt.nz/sliceofheaven/web/html/landrights.html (accessed August 21, 2017).

"March for Science." EarthDay.org, April 22, 2017. http://www.earthday.org/marchforscience/ (accessed July 22, 2017).

"March on Washington for Jobs and Freedom." National Park Service. https://www.nps.gov/articles/march-on-washington.htm (accessed July 18, 2017).

"The Matthew Shepard and James Byrd, Jr., Hate Crimes Prevention Act of 2009." US Department of Justice. https://www.justice.gov/crt/matthew-shepard-and-james-byrd-jr-hate-crimes-prevention-act-2009-0 (accessed August 15, 2017).

Meincke, Paul. "Protests Mark 100th Anniversary of Armenian Massacres." ABC News 7, April 24, 2015. http://abc7chicago.com/news/protests-mark-100th-anniversary-of-armenian-massacres-/679914/ (accessed September 8, 2017).

Michals, Debra. "Ruby Bridges (1954–)." National Women's History Museum, 2015. https://www.nwhm.org/education-resources/biography/biographies/ruby-bridges (accessed July 18, 2017).

"The Modern Environmental Movement." Public Broadcasting Service. http://www.pbs.org/wgbh/americanexperience/features/earth-days-modern-environmental-movement/ (accessed July 22, 2017).

"Murder in Mississippi." Public Broadcasting Service. http://www.pbs.org/wgbh/americanexperience/features/freedomsummer-murder/ (accessed July 18, 2017).

"Muslims Protest Danish Muhammad Cartoons." NBC News, February 15, 2008. http://www.nbcnews.com/id/23186467/ns/world_news-europe/t/muslims-protest-danish-muhammad-cartoons/#.WW9wZITyuUl (accessed July 25, 2017).

National Rifle Association (NRA). https://home.nra.org/ (accessed August 8, 2017).

"1943: Zoot Suit Riots." *National Geographic.* https://www.nationalgeographic.org/thisday/jun3/zoot-suit-riots (accessed September 15, 2017).

"Obergefell v. Hodges." Oyez. https://www.oyez.org/cases/2014/14-556 (accessed August 18, 2017).

"The Official Harvey Milk Biography." Milk Foundation. http://milkfoundation.org/about/harvey-milk-biography (accessed August 22, 2017).

"Our History." Royal Society for the Prevention of Cruelty to Animals (RSPCA). https://www.rspca.org.uk/whatwedo/whoweare/history (accessed July 11, 2017).

Pao, Maureen. "Cesar Chavez: The Life behind a Legacy of Farm Labor Rights." National Public Radio, August 12, 2016. http://www.npr.org/2016/08/02/488428577/cesar-chavez-the-life-behind-a-legacy-of-farm-labor-rights (accessed July 14, 2017).

WHERE TO LEARN MORE

Pilgrim, David. "What Was Jim Crow." Ferris State University, September 2000. https://ferris.edu/HTMLS/news/jimcrow/what/ (accessed August 23, 2017).

"Polish Resistance and Conclusions." United States Holocaust Memorial Museum. https://www.ushmm.org/learn/students/learning-materials-and-resources/poles-victims-of-the-nazi-era/polish-resistance-and-conclusions (accessed August 2, 2017).

"The Raid on Harpers Ferry." Public Broadcasting Service. http://www.pbs.org/wgbh/aia/part4/4p2940.html (accessed August 21, 2017).

Ravitz, Jessica. "The Surprising History of Abortion in the United States." CNN, June 27, 2016. http://www.cnn.com/2016/06/23/health/abortion-history-in-united-states/index.html (accessed August 31, 2017).

"Rescue in Denmark." United States Holocaust Memorial Museum. https://www.ushmm.org/outreach/en/article.php?ModuleId=10007740 (accessed August 2, 2017).

"Rock Hill, South Carolina, Students Sit-In for US Civil Rights, 1960." Global Nonviolent Action Database at Swarthmore College. http://nvdatabase.swarthmore.edu/content/rock-hill-south-carolina-students-sit-us-civil-rights-1960 (accessed July 18, 2017).

"'Satanic' Harry Potter Books Burnt." BBC News, December 31, 2001. http://news.bbc.co.uk/2/hi/entertainment/1735623.stm (accessed July 25, 2017).

Schwartz, Daniel. "What Happened after the Arab Spring?" CBC News, August 4, 2014. http://www.cbc.ca/news/world/what-happened-after-the-arab-spring-1.2723934 (accessed August 18, 2017).

"September 11th Terror Attacks Fast Facts." CNN, August 24, 2017. http://www.cnn.com/2013/07/27/us/september-11-anniversary-fast-facts/index.html (accessed September 22, 2017).

"Shanghai to Show Pride with Gay Festival." BBC News, June 6, 2009. http://news.bbc.co.uk/1/hi/world/asia-pacific/8083672.stm (accessed August 16, 2017).

Smith, Natalie. "What Is Occupy Wall Street?" Scholastic. http://www.scholastic.com/browse/article.jsp?id=3756681 (accessed July 27, 2017).

"Spain's Indignados Protest Here to Stay." BBC News, May 15, 2012. http://www.bbc.com/news/world-europe-18070246 (accessed July 18, 2017).

"Syrian War Monitor Says 465,000 Killed in Six Years of Fighting." Reuters, March 13, 2017. http://www.reuters.com/article/us-mideast-crisis-syria-casualties-idUSKBN16K1Q1 (accessed August 18, 2017).

"Timeline: Iraq War." BBC News, July 5, 2016. http://www.bbc.com/news/magazine-36702957 (accessed September 22, 2017).

"Timeline: Tiananmen Protests." BBC News, June 2, 2014. http://www.bbc.com/news/world-asia-china-27404764 (accessed August 23, 2017).

WHERE TO LEARN MORE

"Tinker v. Des Moines Independent Community School Dist." Cornell Law School. https://www.law.cornell.edu/supremecourt/text/393/503 (accessed August 31, 2017).

"Topics in Chronicling America—The Haymarket Affair." Library of Congress. https://www.loc.gov/rr/news/topics/haymarket.html (accessed August 25, 2017).

"Trafficking in Persons Report." US Department of State, June 2017. https://www.state.gov/documents/organization/271339.pdf (accessed August 23, 2017).

"Treblinka Death Camp Revolt." United States Holocaust Memorial Museum. https://www.ushmm.org/research/the-center-for-advanced-holocaust-studies/miles-lerman-center-for-the-study-of-jewish-resistance/medals-of-resistance-award/treblinka-death-camp-revolt (accessed July 31, 2017).

"The Triangular Slave Trade: Overview." BBC. http://www.bbc.co.uk/bitesize/ks3/history/industrial_era/the_slave_trade/revision/2/ (accessed August 28, 2017).

Tuysuz, Gul. "What Is Sharia Law?" CNN, August 16, 2016. http://www.cnn.com/2016/08/16/world/sharia-law-definition/index.html (accessed August 21, 2017).

"2015 Charlie Hebdo Attacks Fast Facts." CNN, December 22, 2016. http://www.cnn.com/2015/01/21/europe/2015-paris-terror-attacks-fast-facts/index.html (accessed July 25, 2017).

"The 2016 ITUC Global Rights Index: The World's Worst Countries for Workers." International Trade Union Confederation (ITUC). https://www.ituc-csi.org/IMG/pdf/ituc-violationmap-2016-en_final.pdf (accessed August 25, 2017).

"The Velvet Revolution, November 1989." Association for Diplomatic Studies and Training. http://adst.org/2015/10/the-velvet-revolution-november-1989 (accessed August 4, 2017).

"Warsaw." United States Holocaust Memorial Museum. https://www.ushmm.org/wlc/en/article.php?ModuleId=10005069 (accessed August 8, 2017).

Weeks, Linton. "Whatever Happened to the Anti-War Movement?" National Public Radio, April 15 2011. www.npr.org/2011/04/15/135391188/whatever-happened-to-the-anti-war-movement (accessed September 22, 2017).

"What Are Human Rights?" United Nations Human Rights Office of the High Commissioner. http://www.ohchr.org/EN/Issues/Pages/WhatareHumanRights.aspx (accessed September 19, 2017).

"What Does Free Speech Mean?" US Courts. http://www.uscourts.gov/about-federal-courts/educational-resources/about-educational-outreach/activity-resources/what-does (accessed July 25, 2017).

"What Is Fracking and Why Is It Controversial?" BBC News, December 16, 2015. http://www.bbc.com/news/uk-14432401 (accessed July 22, 2017).

"What Is the Americans with Disabilities Act (ADA)?" ADA National Network. https://adata.org/learn-about-ada (accessed September 21, 2017).

"White Rose." United States Holocaust Memorial Museum. https://www.ushmm.org/wlc/en/article.php?ModuleId=10007188 (accessed August 4, 2017).

"WikiLeaks Fast Facts." CNN. http://www.cnn.com/2013/06/03/world/wikileaks-fast-facts/index.html (accessed September 20, 2017).

"Woman Suffrage Timeline (1840–1920)." National Women's History Museum. https://www.nwhm.org/education-resources/history/woman-suffrage-timeline (accessed August 21, 2017).

"World Trade Organization Protests in Seattle." Seattle.gov. https://www.seattle.gov/cityarchives/exhibits-and-education/digital-document-libraries/world-trade-organization-protests-in-seattle (accessed July 25, 2017).

"Yale Students March over Concerns of Racism." CBS News, November 9, 2015. http://www.cbsnews.com/news/yale-students-march-over-concerns-of-racism/ (accessed July 25, 2017).

Zhou, David. "Operation Rescue Activists Resist Abortion Clinic in Wichita, Kansas (Summer of Mercy), 1991." Global Nonviolent Action Database, April 30, 2012. http://nvdatabase.swarthmore.edu/content/operation-rescue-activists-resist-abortion-clinic-wichita-kansas-summer-mercy-1991 (accessed August 28, 2017).

Other

Blackfish. Documentary. Directed by Gabriela Cowperthwaite. New York: Magnolia Pictures, 2013.

Britches. Documentary. Directed by Lori Gruen, Norfolk, VA: PETA, 1986.

A Day without a Mexican. DVD. Directed by Sergio Arau. Los Angeles: Altavista Films, 2004.

Gasland. Documentary. Directed by Josh Fox. Brooklyn, NY: International WOW Company, 2010.

An Inconvenient Truth. Documentary. Directed by Davis Guggenheim. Los Angeles: Paramount Pictures, 2006.

The Ivory Game. Documentary. Directed by Richard Ladkani and Kief Davidson. Vienna, Austria: Terra Mater Factual Studios, 2016.

General Index

Italic type indicates volume numbers; **boldface** indicates main entries. Illustrations are marked by (ill.).

A

A21 Campaign, *3:* 647
Abdullah bin Abdulaziz al Saud, King of Saudi Arabia, *3:* 715–716
Abernathy, Ralph, *1:* 36 (ill.)
Ableism, *2:* 276
Abolition of slavery, *2:* 267–268; *3:* 511–512. *See also* **Slavery**
   Harpers Ferry Raid (1859), *3:* 638–643, 642 (ill.)
   Mauritania, *3:* 643
   United Kingdom, *3:* 637
   United States, *3:* 633
   Washington, D.C., *3:* 633
Abolitionist movement, *3:* 622, 638, 639
Aboriginal Land Rights Protest (1988), *2:* 375–379, 378 (ill.). *See also* **Indigenous peoples' rights**
Aboriginals, *2:* 365–366, 375–379
Abortion, *3:* 549. *See also* **Reproductive rights**
   anti-abortion laws, *3:* 552–553
   blocking access to clinics, *3:* 557–558, 562–568, 566–567
   history, *3:* 551–553
   late-term, *3:* 566
   legalization of, *3:* 575–576
Abzug, Bella, *3:* 560
ACCD (American Coalition of Citizens with Disabilities), *2:* 279
ACLU (American Civil Liberties Union), *2:* 460, 461–462, 464

ACT UP, HIV/AIDS demonstration, *2:* 433 (ill.)
Activists
   animal rights, *1:* 4, 7–11, 10 (ill.), 12–13, 25–26
   labor, *1:* 75–76
   scientists, *1:* 168
ADA (United States. Americans with Disabilities Act), *2:* 277, 280–283
ADAPT (American Disabled for Accessible Public Transit), *2:* 279–280, 283
Addams, Jane, *3:* 660, 660 (ill.)
ADL (Anti-Defamation League), *2:* 446
Afghanistan War, *3:* 681–682
   civilian casualties, *3:* 684
   refugees, *2:* 319
AFL (American Federation of Labor), *2:* 409
Africa
   child labor, *2:* 399
   slavery, *3:* 620–621
African American civil rights, *1:* **35–70**, 36 (ill.), 39 (ill.), 45 (ill.), 52 (ill.), 53 (ill.), 56 (ill.), 58 (ill.), 61 (ill.), 65 (ill.). *See also* Civil rights; **Racial conflict**
   Bridges, Ruby, *1:* 53, 53 (ill.)
   desegregation in Birmingham, Alabama, *1:* 62
   Freedom Rides (1961), *1:* 54–59, 56 (ill.)
   Little Rock Nine Crisis (1957), *1:* 47–52, 52 (ill.)
   Lunch Counter Protest, McCrory's (1961), *1:* 59–63, 61 (ill.)
   March on Washington for Jobs and Freedom (1963), *1:* 39 (ill.), 63–69, 65 (ill.)

GENERAL INDEX

Mississippi Summer Project/Freedom Summer Voter Registration, *1:* 58, 58 (ill.)
Montgomery Bus Boycott (1955–1956), *1:* 36 (ill.), 42–47
African Americans
　racial discrimination, *1:* 36–37; *3:* 512, 513–515
　violence against, *1:* 38, 40, 56–57, 56 (ill.), 58, 62; *3:* 526–527
　voting rights, *1:* 40
African slave trade, *3:* 620–621, 621 (ill.)
　end of, *3:* 622
　triangular trade, *3:* 621
Afrikaans, *3:* 534–535
Afrikaners, *3:* 533
Agent Orange, *1:* 223
Agha-Soltan, Neda, *3:* 490–491, 491 (ill.)
Agricultural Workers Organizing Committee (AWOC), *2:* 418
Ahmadinejad, Mahmoud, *3:* 490
AIM (American Indian Movement), *2:* 364–365, 371–372
AIM (American Indian Movement) Occupation of Wounded Knee (1973), *2:* 364–365, 367–375, 374 (ill.). *See also* **Indigenous peoples' rights**
Airports, anti-Trump travel ban protests, *2:* 330–331, 330 (ill.)
Alabama
　desegregation, *1:* 62
　Freedom Rides, *1:* 56, 56 (ill.), 57
　Montgomery Bus Boycott (1955–1956), *1:* 36 (ill.), 42–47
Alamagordo, NM, book burning, *1:* 181 (ill.)
Alamagordo Public Library, *1:* 182
Alcatraz, occupation by Native Americans, *2:* 370–371, 371 (ill.)
Alexander the Great, *2:* 430
Alexis, Aaron, *2:* 253
ALF (Animal Liberation Front), *1:* 7–11
　activists, *1:* 10 (ill.)
　debate over methods, *1:* 11
　founding, *1:* 8
　use of arson, *1:* 10–11
Allende, Salvador, *1:* 106–107, 107 (ill.)
Alliance of Small Island States (AOSIS), *1:* 146, 147
Allred, Gloria, *3:* 577 (ill.)

Alt Right, *3:* 542, 543
Amazon rain forest, *2:* 366, 379–384
Amazonian indigenous peoples, *2:* 366, 379–384. *See also* Indigenous peoples
Ambedkar, Bhimrao Ramji, *2:* 291–293, 295
American Airlines Flight 11, *3:* 677, 678
American Airlines Flight 77, *3:* 677
American Civil Liberties Union (ACLU), *2:* 460, 461–462, 464
American Coalition of Citizens with Disabilities (ACCD), *2:* 279
American Federation of Labor (AFL), *2:* 409
American Horse, *2:* 373
American Indian Movement (AIM), *2:* 364–365, 371–372
American Indian Movement (AIM) Occupation of Wounded Knee (1973), *2:* 364–365, 367–375, 374 (ill.)
American Library Association, *1:* 180
American Protestant Association, *2:* 315, 316
American Psychiatric Association (APA), *2:* 432
American Recovery and Reinvestment Act (ARRA), *1:* 113
American Republican Association, *2:* 315
American Revolutionary War (1775–1783), *2:* 233, 335–337; *3:* 471. *See also* United States
American Society for the Prevention of Cruelty to Animals (ASPCA), *1:* 3
　circus animals, *1:* 29
　position on ALF methods, *1:* 11
American War of Independence (1775–1783), *2:* 233, 335–337; *3:* 471. *See also* United States
American westward expansion, *3:* 638, 639–640. *See also* United States
Americans for Responsible Solutions, *2:* 248
Americans with Disabilities Act (ADA), *2:* 277, 280–283
Amherst, NY, Operation Rescue protests, *3:* 562–568
Amnesty International, *3:* 474
Anarchists, *1:* 213–214
Ancient Greece
　free speech, *1:* 172
　slavery, *3:* 617–619
Anderson, John Ward, *1:* 185

Andry, Manuel, *3:* 625–627
Angel Action, *2:* 449–451, 449 (ill.), 451
Anielewicz, Mordechai, *3:* 605
Animal cruelty, *1:* 4
Animal experimentation, *1:* 7–11. *See also* **Animal rights**
Animal Liberation: A New Ethics for Our Treatment of Animals (1975), *1:* 3–4
Animal Liberation Front (ALF), *1:* 7–11
  activists, *1:* 10 (ill.)
  debate over methods, *1:* 11
  founding, *1:* 8
  use of arson, *1:* 10–11
Animal rights, *1:* **1–33**, 6 (ill.), 10 (ill.), 13 (ill.), 17 (ill.), 23 (ill.), 24 (ill.)
  Bilbao Anti-bullfighting Protest (2010), *1:* 12–18, 17 (ill.)
  Blackfish Documentary and SeaWorld Protests (2013-2014), *1:* 25–31
  Circus animals, *1:* 5, 29, 29 (ill.)
  Global March for Elephants and Rhinos, *1:* 18–25, 24 (ill.)
  Greenpeace and whaling, *1:* 22–23, 23 (ill.)
  ongoing fight for, *1:* 4–5
  PETA antifur campaign, *1:* 12–13, 13 (ill.)
  protests, *1:* 5–7
  UCR Lab Raid (1985), *1:* 7–11
Animal rights activists, *1:* 4
  ALF, *1:* 10 (ill.)
  anti-fur campaign, *1:* 12–13
  SeaWorld protests, *1:* 25–26
  UCR lab raid, *1:* 7–11
Animal rights movement
  history, *1:* 1–7
  modern, *1:* 3–4
Animal rights organizations, *1:* 2–3
Animal Welfare Act of 1966, *1:* 3
Anima-Naturalis, *1:* 17, 17 (ill.)
Anniston, Alabama, *1:* 56
Anthony, Susan B., *3:* 697 (ill.), 713
Anti-abortion laws, *3:* 552–553, 561, 580
Anti-abortion protesters, *3:* 558, 564 (ill.), 567 (ill.)
Anti-Catholicism, *2:* 313
Anti-Defamation League (ADL), *2:* 446
Antifa, *3:* 542

Anti-fur campaign, *1:* 12–13, 13 (ill.)
Anti-gay laws. *See also* **LGBTQ rights**
  protests against in Russia, *2:* 455 (ill.)
  Russia, *2:* 454–455
  United States, *2:* 432
Anti-gay protests
  counterprotests, *2:* 448, 449–451
  Westboro Baptist Church, *2:* 448, 449–451, 451
Anti-immigrant riots, *2:* 328–329, 329 (ill.)
Anti-Islam movement, *2:* 322–323
Anti-migrant protests
  Dresden, Germany, *2:* 321, 323 (ill.)
  Warsaw, Poland, *2:* 323
Anti-slavery Day, *3:* 647
Anti-slavery petitions, *3:* 628–634
Anti-war protests, *3:* **651–692**, 656 (ill.), 660 (ill.), 667 (ill.), 668 (ill.), 679 (ill.), 674 (ill.), 679 (ill.), 682 (ill.), 686 (ill.). *See also* Pacifists
  burning draft cards, *3:* 666–667, 667 (ill.)
  Candlelight Vigils against Invasion of Iraq (2003), *3:* 676–683, 682 (ill.)
  Democratic National Convention (DNC) (1968), *3:* 656 (ill.)
  International Congress of Women, *3:* 657–663, 660 (ill.)
  Iraq War (2003–2011), *3:* 657, 682 (ill.)
  Manning, Chelsea, and WikiLeaks, *3:* 684–690, 686 (ill.)
  One Thousand Coffins Protest (2004), *3:* 678–679, 679 (ill.)
  Student Armband Protest of Vietnam War (1965–1969), *3:* 663–668, 668 (ill.)
  United States, *3:* 653–657
  Vietnam War (1954–1975), *3:* 655–656, 663–668, 669–676
AOSIS (Alliance of Small Island States), *1:* 146, 147
APA (American Psychiatric Association), *2:* 432
Apartheid, *3:* 531, 534, 539. *See also* Desegregation/Segregation; Racial discrimination
Apprentices, *2:* 395
Arab Spring, *1:* 90, 120, 219; *3:* 486–493. *See also* **Political/Government uprisings**
  Bahrain, *3:* 489
  Egypt, *3:* 495
  Libya, *3:* 489–490

origins, *3:* 487–488
spread of, *3:* 489–490
Syria, *3:* 491–493, 492 (ill.)
Tunisia, *2:* 318–319
Yemen, *3:* 488–489
Argentina, March against Monsanto, *1:* 228
Aristophanes, *3:* 651–652
Arizona, mass shooting, *2:* 248
Arkansas, school integration, *1:* 47–52
Armenia
genocide survivors, *2:* 298–300, 299
history, *2:* 297–298
Armenian Genocide Protests (2015), *2:* 297–302, 301 (ill.). *See also* Genocide; **Human rights**
Army of God, *3:* 558
ARRA (United States. American Recovery and Reinvestment Act), *1:* 113
Arson, *1:* 10–11
Aryan race, *3:* 598–599
Asia. *See also* Specific Asian countries
independence movements, *2:* 339–340
use of rhino horn, *1:* 19
Asia for Educators, *3:* 569
Asner, Ed, *3:* 560
ASPCA (American Society for the Prevention of Cruelty to Animals), *1:* 3
circus animals, *1:* 29
position on ALF methods, *1:* 11
Assad, Bashar al-, *2:* 319; *3:* 487, 491–492
Assange, Julian, *3:* 685, 687
Assassination attempts, Hitler, Adolf, *3:* 590–591
Assault weapons, *2:* 234–235
Athens (city state), *1:* 172
Athletes, protests by, *3:* 516–517
Atkins v. Virginia, *2:* 285
Atlantic, *1:* 198
ATSIC (Aboriginal and Torres Strait Islander Commission), *2:* 379
Attica Prison Riot (1971), *2:* 270–276, 274 (ill.). *See also* **Human rights**
investigation and outcome, *2:* 275–276
manifesto of demands, *2:* 273
prisoner conditions, *2:* 271–272
Austerity measures, Spain, *1:* 116–122, 117–118, 121

Austin, TX, March to Abolish the Death Penalty, *2:* 287
Australia
aboriginals, *2:* 365–366, 375–379
land rights protests, *2:* 375–379
pro-migrant rallies, *2:* 318–325
Australia Day, *2:* 365–366, 375, 376–377
Australian aboriginals, *2:* 365–366, 375–379
Automobile industry, working conditions, *2:* 408–409
AWOC (Agricultural Workers Organizing Committee), *2:* 418
Axis Powers, *3:* 585

B

Background checks, *2:* 236, 252. *See also* **Gun control/Gun rights**
federal law, *2:* 253
gun shows, *2:* 257
private sales, *2:* 256
Washington (state), *2:* 253–254
Baez, Joan, *1:* 68, 198, 199 (ill.); *3:* 670
Bahrain, Arab Spring, *3:* 489
Baladi campaign, *3:* 699, 714–718, 716 (ill.). *See also* **Women's rights**
goals of, *3:* 716–717
leaders, *3:* 716 (ill.)
Balch, Emily G., *3:* 660
Bald and Golden Eagle Protection Act, *1:* 135
Baldwin, James, *1:* 68
Baldwin-Felts, *2:* 410
Banks, Dennis, *2:* 372, 374, 390–391
Banksy, *1:* 212, 212 (ill.)
Banned books, *1:* 180. *See also* Censorship
Baptist War (1831–1832), *3:* 634–638. *See also* **Slavery**
Barbagelata, John, *2:* 443
Bassey, Nnimmo, *1:* 148
Bates, Berke, M.M., *3:* 543
Bates, Daisy, *1:* 50–51
Battle in Seattle, World Trade Organization Protests (1999), *1:* 209–216, 214 (ill.). *See also* **Globalization**

Battle of Blair Mountain (1921), *2:* 410–411
Battle of Matewan, *2:* 410
Battle of Stalingrad (1943), *3:* 594–595, 609. *See also* World War II (1939–1945)
Bavaud, Maurice, *3:* 590–591
Bear Runner, Oscar, *2:* 374 (ill.)
Bearbaiting, *1:* 2
Beijing, China, Tiananmen Square protests, *3:* 473–478, 476 (ill.)
Belarus, human rights protests, *2:* 270
Belo Monte Dam, *2:* 381, 384
Belvis, Segundo Ruiz, *2:* 344–345
Ben Ali, Zine El-Abidine, *3:* 488, 495
Bergh, Henry, *1:* 3
Berlin, Germany
  division of, *3:* 480
  fall of the Berlin Wall (1989), *3:* 478–486
Berlin Wall, *3:* 483 (ill.)
  building of, *3:* 482–483
  fall of, *3:* 485–486
  history, *3:* 478–479
  Reagan, Ronald speech, *3:* 484–485
Bernard, Sheila C., *3:* 530–531
Betances, Ramón Emeterio, *2:* 344–345, 345 (ill.)
Bhopal, India
  torch rally, *1:* 136 (ill.)
  toxic chemical spills, *1:* 136
Bhotmange family, *2:* 293–294, 296
Bialystok Ghetto, Poland, *3:* 607
Bias, danger of, *1:* 167
Bible, *2:* 314–316
Biden, Joe, *2:* 250
Big Pharma, *1:* 226–227, 227 (ill.)
Biko, Steve, *3:* 532–533
Bilbao (Spain) Anti-bullfighting Protest (2010), *1:* 12–18, 17 (ill.). *See also* **Animal rights**
bin Laden, Osama, *3:* 681
Binghamton, NY, Operation Rescue protests, *3:* 563
Birmingham, AL
  desegregation, *1:* 62
  Freedom Rides, *1:* 56, 57
Birth control, *3:* 550. *See also* One child policy; **Reproductive rights**
  access to information, *3:* 553, 575
  China, *3:* 568–574
  health insurance plans and, *3:* 556
  laws limiting, *3:* 555
  oral contraceptives, *3:* 558–559
Birth rate, China, *3:* 569, 573
Bisexuals. *See* LGBTQ people
Black armbands, *3:* 664, 665
Black consciousness movement, *3:* 532–533
Black Lives Matter, *2:* 244; *3:* 515, 539
  demonstrators, *3:* 540 (ill.)
  origins, *3:* 540–544
Black Panthers, *2:* 239–245, 240–241, 243 (ill.)
Blackfish (2013), *1:* 4–5, 25–31, 28, 30
Blair Mountain, Battle of (1921), *2:* 410–411
Blake, James F., *1:* 44–45
Blankenship, Geraldine Green, *2:* 413
Blasphemy, *1:* 183
Blow, Charles M., *1:* 196
Blow, Tahj, *1:* 196
Blowouts, Mexican American students, *1:* 77–82
Blue Star Boy, Suzanne, *2:* 247–249
Bly, Nellie, *2:* 278, 278 (ill.)
Boehner, John, *1:* 115
Boko Haram, *3:* 700, 722–723
Bolívar, Simón, *2:* 338, 338 (ill.)
Book burning. *See also* Censorship; **Free speech**
  Alamagordo, New Mexico, *1:* 181 (ill.)
  Harry Potter (book series), *1:* 175, 177–183, 181 (ill.)
  history, *1:* 178–179
  Mayan texts, *1:* 178
  Nazi Germany, *1:* 179
  protests against in Alamagordo, *1:* 182
Boston Harbor, *2:* 337 (ill.)
Boston Tea Party (1773), *1:* 99, 111–112; *2:* 336–337, 337 (ill.); *3:* 471
Bouazizi, Mohamed, *3:* 487–488
Boutilier v. Immigration and Naturalization Service, *2:* 432
Boycotts. *See also* Protests
  defined, *1:* 35
  Delano Grape Strike and Boycott, *2:* 414–422, 421 (ill.)
  farm produce, *1:* 78–79
  Great American, *1:* 88
  Japan, *1:* 126–127

GENERAL INDEX

Montgomery Bus Boycott (1955–1956), *1:* 35, 36 (ill.)
NCAA, of North Carolina, *2:* 460–461
North Carolina, *2:* 461–462
South African products, *3:* 538
Boynton v. Virginia, 1: 55
Brady, James, *2:* 236
Brady Campaign to Prevent Gun Violence, *2:* 236–237, 250
Brady Handgun Violence Prevention Act, *2:* 236–237, 253
Brancheau, Dawn, *1:* 26, 27 (ill.)
Brando, Marlon, *1:* 68; *2:* 375
Brazil
    Malê Revolt of 1835, *3:* 626–627
    Preservation of Amazon Rain Forest Awareness Campaign, *2:* 379–384
Bressler, Isak, *1:* 215
Brexit, *1:* 103–104, 103 (ill.), 122–129, 124 (ill.). *See also* **Economic discontent**
    demonstrations, *1:* 103 (ill.), 124 (ill.), 125–128
    EU anniversary demonstration, *1:* 127–128
    May, Theresa, speech, *1:* 128–129
    referendum, *1:* 124–125
Bridges, Ruby, *1:* 53, 53 (ill.)
Bring Back Our Girls, *3:* 722–723
    demonstrators, *3:* 723 (ill.)
    Obama, Michelle, speech, *3:* 700–701
Britches, *1:* 8, 9
Britches (1986), *1:* 9
British colonies, *2:* 336–337. *See also* Colonization; United Kingdom
    Australia, *2:* 376
    Hong Kong, *3:* 499
    India, *2:* 347–349
    women's rights, *3:* 693–695
British East India Company (EIC), *2:* 347–348
British Raj, *2:* 348–349
Brock, Jack, *1:* 178, 181–182
Brotherhood of Sleeping Car Porters, *1:* 64
Brown, John, *3:* 640–643, 640 (ill.), 642 (ill.)
    anti-slavery activity in Kansas, *3:* 640
    Douglass, Frederick speech, *3:* 641
    Harpers Ferry Raid, *3:* 641–643, 642 (ill.)
Brown, Minnijean, *1:* 50, 51

Brown v. Board of Education, 1: 38–39, 49
BUC (Buffalo United for Choice), *3:* 565
Buchanan, James, *3:* 642
Buenos Aires, Argentina, March against Monsanto, *1:* 228
Buffalo, NY, Operation Rescue protests, *3:* 562–568
Buffalo United for Choice (BUC), *3:* 565
Bull Moose Party, *3:* 710
Bullbaiting, *1:* 1–2
Bullfighting, *1:* 6, 12–13, 14–15 (ill.)
    arguments against, *1:* 15
    Bilbao, Spain, protest, *1:* 16–18, 17 (ill.)
    interview with former bullfighter, *1:* 16
Burgdorf, Robert L., Jr., *2:* 282
Burma. *See* Myanmar
Burns, Lucy, *3:* 710
Burwell v. Hobby Lobby, 3: 555
Bush, George H.W., *2:* 281; *3:* 478
Bush, George W., *1:* 112
    position on reproductive rights, *3:* 561
    protests at RNC, *3:* 678–679
    speech on Iraq invasion, *3:* 680–681

C

Cacerolaza protests, *1:* 106–107. *See also* **Economic discontent**
Caesar, Julius, *3:* 469, 469 (ill.)
Cairo, Egypt, Tahrir Square Protests (2011), *3:* 495–498, 496 (ill.)
Calderón, Felipe, *1:* 91, 94–95
Calhoun, John C., *1:* 195
California. *See also* East Los Angeles, CA; Los Angeles, CA
    Black Panthers protest Mulford Act, *2:* 239–245, 243 (ill.)
    Delano Grape Strike and Boycott (1965–1970), *2:* 414–422, 421 (ill.)
    occupation of Alcatraz (1969–1970), *2:* 370–371, 371 (ill.)
    protest against Trump travel bans, *2:* 327, 330 (ill.)
    San Bernardino terrorist attack, *2:* 328
    San Diego SeaWorld protest, *1:* 30

California. Mulford Act, *2:* 242–243, 244
California. Senate. Resolution No. 16 (2017), *2:* 327
California redwoods, *1:* 152
California State Capitol, Sacramento, CA, *2:* 239–245, 243 (ill.)
Cameron, David, *1:* 124–125; *2:* 321
Camus, Albert, *1:* 93
Canada
    indigenous peoples, *2:* 365 (ill.), 382
    land rights protests, *2:* 365 (ill.), 382
Candlelight Vigils against Invasion of Iraq (2003), *3:* 676–683, 682 (ill.). *See also* **War protests**
Capital punishment, *2:* 284–285. *See also* **Human rights**
    declining use, 289
    history, *2:* 285
    legal challenges to, *2:* 285–286
    support and opposition, *2:* 286–287
Capitalism, *1:* 212
Capitol Crawl (1990), *2:* 276–284, 282 (ill.). *See also* **Human rights**
Carlos, John, *3:* 516, 517 (ill.)
Carpenter, Mary Chapin, *3:* 729
Carson, Rachel, *1:* 135
Carter, Jimmy, *1:* 143; *2:* 280–281
Cartoons, of Muhammad, *1:* 184–187
The Cartoons That Shook the World (2009), *1:* 184, 187
CAS International, *1:* 17, 17 (ill.)
The Case for Animal Rights (1983), *1:* 4
Casper, WY, anti-gay protests by WBC, *2:* 448
Caste systems, *2:* 290–291
    discrimination, *2:* 296
    India, *2:* 290–297
Castro, Fidel, *1:* 106
Castro, Sal, *1:* 80, 82
Castro Village Association, *2:* 442
Catalonia, Spain, *1:* 17–18
Catholic Church, *1:* 173
Cats, animal testing, *1:* 10 (ill.)
Catt, Carrie Chapman, *3:* 710, 711
La Causa, *1:* 78
Cavanagh, Jerome, *3:* 528
CCP (Chinese Communist Party), *1:* 105, 107

Censorship, *1:* 171. *See also* Banned books; Book burning
    Catholic Church, *1:* 173
    Nazi Germany, *1:* 179
CERCLA (United States. Comprehensive Environmental Response, Compensation, and Liability Act), *1:* 143
Chaillot Prize, *3:* 716 (ill.)
Chaney, James Earl, *1:* 58, 58 (ill.)
Charlie Hebdo, *1:* 176, 187, 190–191
    publication of Muhammad cartoons, *1:* 191
    terrorist attack on offices, *1:* 191
Charlotte Magazine, *2:* 462, 463
Charlottesville Protests (2017), *3:* 542–543, 543 (ill.). *See also* **Racial conflict**
Chávez, César
    Delano Grape Strike and Boycott (1965–1970), *2:* 414–415, 419–421, 421 (ill.)
    Hispanic and Latino civil rights, *1:* 75–76, 78–79, 79 (ill.), 86
    state holiday, *1:* 79
Chechnya, *2:* 454–455
Chemical weapons, use in Syria, *3:* 492
Chen Guangcheng, *3:* 571
Chernobyl nuclear accident, *1:* 136–137
Cherokees, *2:* 386–387
Chicago, IL
    DNC anti-war protests, *3:* 656 (ill.)
    Haymarket Square Riot, *2:* 418–419
Chicano movement, *1:* 76, 79
Child, Lydia Maria, *3:* 697 (ill.)
Child labor, *2:* 393–394, 400–401, 400 (ill.), 402–403, 403 (ill.). *See also* **Labor rights**
    Africa, *2:* 399
    labor laws, *2:* 407
    Mother Jones's "Children's Crusade," *2:* 399–407, 406 (ill.)
    NYC protest of 1909, *2:* 402–403, 403 (ill.)
    textile mills, *2:* 400 (ill.)
Children
    cruelty to animals, *1:* 4
    disabled, *2:* 277–278
    Love Canal protests, *1:* 143 (ill.)
    runaway, *3:* 645

GENERAL INDEX

Children's Crusade of 1903, *2:* 399–407, 406 (ill.).
See also **Labor rights**
Chile, *Cacerolaza* protests, *1:* 106–107
China, *1:* 103
    birth rate, *3:* 569, 573
    book burning, *1:* 178
    collective farms and communes, *1:* 108–110
    Cultural Revolution (1966), *1:* 108
    economic reforms, *1:* 110–111
    farmers' secret agreement, *1:* 105–111, 109 (ill.)
    fur production, *1:* 12, 13
    history, *1:* 105–108
    ivory trade, *1:* 25
    labor rights, *2:* 398
    LGBTQ rights, *2:* 452–453, 458
    one child policy, *3:* 568–574
    relationship with Hong Kong, *3:* 499–500
    rhino horn, *1:* 19
    sanctions by United States, *3:* 478
    Shanghai Pride Festival (2009), *2:* 452–458, 456 (ill.)
    Tiananmen Square protests, *3:* 473–478, 476 (ill.)
    transgender rights, *2:* 452–453
China Daily, 2: 455, 457
Chinese Classification of Mental Disorders, 2: 452
Chinese Communist Party (CCP), *1:* 105, 107
Chinese farmers
    one child policy, *3:* 570
    secret agreement, *1:* 105–111, 109 (ill.)
Chinese immigrants. See also Immigrants and immigration
    riots against, Denver, Colorado, *2:* 328–329, 329 (ill.)
    United States, *2:* 307, 415–416
Chinese traditional medicine, *1:* 19
Chinese workers, working conditions, *2:* 398
Christ Community Church, Alamagordo, New Mexico, *1:* 175, 177–183
Christakis, Erika, *1:* 195, 197–198, 200
Christakis, Nicholas, *1:* 197–198, 200
Christian X, King of Denmark, *3:* 600
Christmas Rebellion (1831–1832), *3:* 634–638.
    See also **Slavery**

Cigar workers, *1:* 85 (ill.)
    strikes, *1:* 84
    violence against, *1:* 84
Circus animals, *1:* 5, 29, 29 (ill.)
CITES (Convention on International Trade in Endangered Species of Wild Fauna and Flora), *1:* 21
Citizen journalism, *3:* 490–491
Citizens for a Sound Economy, *1:* 111
Citrin, Jack, *1:* 177
City of Hope National Medical Center, *1:* 9
Civic Forum, *2:* 355
Civil disobedience, *1:* 139. See also Nonviolent resistance
    "I Will Not Comply" Rally, *2:* 254
        Indian independence movement, *2:* 346–347, 349, 350
Civil rights. See also **African American civil rights**; **Free speech**; **Hispanic and Latino civil rights**; **Human rights**; **Indigenous peoples' rights**; **LGBTQ rights**
    defined, *1:* 71
    DOJ lawsuit against North Carolina, *2:* 463
    farm workers, *1:* 78–79
    summary of laws, *1:* 41
Civil rights, African American. See **African American civil rights**
Civil rights, Hispanic and Latino. See **Hispanic and Latino civil rights**
Civil Rights Act of 1957, *1:* 41
Civil Rights Act of 1960, *1:* 41
Civil Rights Act of 1964, *1:* 40, 41, 69
Civil Rights Act of 1968, *1:* 40, 41
Civil rights movement, *1:* 35–36, 38–42, 42
    Freedom Rides, *1:* 54–59, 56 (ill.)
    Hispanic and Latino, *1:* 75–76
    legislation, *1:* 40–41
    origins, *1:* 38–39
    resulting legislation, *1:* 40–41
    United States, *3:* 472
Civilian casualties, *3:* 684, 686
Cleary, John, *3:* 674 (ill.)
Cleveland, Ohio, *1:* 135–136
Climate change. See also **Environment**; Global warming
    COP 15, *1:* 144–145
    greenhouse gases, *1:* 137, 145, 157
    island nations, *1:* 157–158
    US attitudes about, *1:* 164, 164 (ill.)

Climate deniers, *1:* 165–166
Climate Justice Action (CJA), *1:* 145, 146
Climate Justice Now (CJN), *1:* 146
Climate refugees, *1:* 159
Clinton, Bill, *1:* 52
    Gay and Lesbian Pride Month, *2:* 441
    gays in military policy, *2:* 434
    gun control laws, *2:* 253
    position on reproductive rights, *3:* 561
    support of gun control sit-in, *2:* 259
    WTO meeting, *1:* 211
Clinton, Hillary Rodham, *2:* 426; *3:* 578, 699, 725–726
Clovis, Sam, *1:* 168
Coal miners and coal mining
    environmental impact, *1:* 159
    global warming, *1:* 159
    strikes, *2:* 410–411
    working conditions, *2:* 312
Cockfighting, *1:* 2
Code Noir, *3:* 624
Coffee, Linda, *3:* 576
Cold War (1945–1991), *1:* 178; *3:* 479, 483, 484, 486, 655
Collective farms, *1:* 108–110
Collin, Frank, *1:* 189 (ill.)
Collins, Susan, *2:* 260
Colonization, *1:* 204; *2:* 335. *See also* British colonies; French colonies; Portuguese colonies; Spanish colonies
    impact on indigenous peoples, *2:* 361, 375–376
    impact on Native Americans, *2:* 362–363, 386–387
    North America, *1:* 72
    prison colonies, *2:* 376
    South America, *1:* 72; *3:* 533
Colorado, A Day without Immigrants protests, *1:* 88
Columbus, Christopher, *2:* 343
Comfort Women (Korean), protests, *2:* 269 (ill.)
Communes, *1:* 108–110
Communism and communists, *2:* 352; *3:* 587, 663–664, 669
    Chile, *1:* 106
    China, *1:* 107–108
    resistance to Nazis, *3:* 587–588

Compensated Emancipation Act, *3:* 633, 633 (ill.)
Comprehensive Environmental Response, Compensation, and Liability Act (CERCLA), *1:* 143
Compton, Jim, *1:* 215
Comstock Act, *3:* 553, 575
Conception, *3:* 562
Confederate symbols, *3:* 515–517
Congress of Racial Equality (CORE), *1:* 54–57
    Berkeley free speech movement, *1:* 198
    sit-ins, *1:* 60–61, 62
Congressional Union for Woman Suffrage, *3:* 710
Connecticut, Sandy Hook mass shooting, *2:* 246–247
Conscientious objectors, *3:* 652–653
Constitution of India, *2:* 292
Consumerism, *1:* 212
Contraceptives, *3:* 549
Convention on International Trade in Endangered Species of Wild Fauna and Flora (CITES), *1:* 21
Cooper, Roy, *2:* 462, 463
COP 15 (Conference of the Parties 15), *1:* 144–145, 145–146, 146–148. *See also* **Environment**
Copenhagen, Denmark, protests (2009), *1:* 144–151, 150 (ill.). *See also* **Environment**
    clashes with police, *1:* 148–150
    protest groups plan, *1:* 146–148
    response of Danish government, *1:* 147–150
Copernicus, Nicolaus, *1:* 173
CORE (Congress of Racial Equality), *1:* 54–57
    Berkeley free speech movement, *1:* 198
    sit-ins, *1:* 60–61, 62
Cornell Center on the Death Penalty Worldwide, *2:* 284
Coulter, Ann, *1:* 176
Cowperthwaite, Gabriela, *1:* 26–27
Cree First Nations, *2:* 382. *See also* Indigenous peoples
Creedence Clearwater Revival, *3:* 670
Criminal justice system, human rights abuses, *2:* 270–271
Cruz, Sophie, *3:* 729
C-SPAN, *2:* 259
Cuba, independence movements, *2:* 338–339
Cuernavaca, Mexico, *1:* 91 (ill.), 93–94
Cullen, H. Jay, *3:* 542–543

GENERAL INDEX

Cullors, Patrice, *3:* 541
Cultural exchange, *1:* 206
Cultural Revolution (1966), *1:* 108; *3:* 473. See also China
Cultural studies, Los Angeles Unified School District, *1:* 82
Cuomo, Mario, *2:* 382
Cuyahoga River, *1:* 135–136
Cyrus the Great, King of Persia, *2:* 265
Czech Republic, *2:* 357–358
Czech resistance (World War II), *3:* 589
Czechoslovakia
    independence movements, *2:* 341–342, 352–358
    invasion of 1968, *2:* 354 (ill.)
    under Soviet Union, *2:* 353–354

D

Dakota Access Pipeline (DAPL), *1:* 140; *2:* 384, 385
    Native American opposition, *1:* 144; 366–367, 367 (ill.), 384–391, 388 (ill.)
    Trump, Donald, *2:* 367
Dakota Access Pipeline (DAPL) Protest (2016–2017), *2:* 366–367, 367 (ill.), 384–391, 388 (ill.). See also **Indigenous peoples' rights**
    Dennis Banks, *2:* 390–391
    Native Americans, *2:* 367 (ill.), 388 (ill.)
Dalit Protests in India (2006), *2:* 290–297, 295 (ill.). See also **Human rights**
Dalits, *2:* 290, 291–293, 295 (ill.)
    continuing discrimination, *2:* 296–297
    murder of family in Khairlanji, India, *2:* 293–294
    violence against, *2:* 293–294, 297
Dallas, TX, Huey P. Newton Gun Club demonstrations, *2:* 244
Dams
    land rights protests by Cree First Nations, *2:* 382
    land rights protests by Kayapo, *2:* 379–384
Dandi March, *2:* 346–352, 351 (ill.)
Danish Jews, *3:* 597, 601–602
Danish resistance (World War II), *3:* 589, 597–602
DAPL (Dakota Access Pipeline), *1:* 140; *2:* 384, 385
    Native American opposition, *1:* 144
    Trump, Donald, *2:* 367

DAPL (Dakota Access Pipeline) Protest (2016–2017), *2:* 366–367, 367 (ill.), 384–391, 388 (ill.). See also **Indigenous peoples' rights**
    Dennis Banks, *2:* 390–391
    Native Americans, *2:* 367 (ill.)
Dart, Justin, Jr., *2:* 282
Davis, Sammy, Jr., *1:* 68
Davison, Emily Wilding, *3:* 705, 705 (ill.)
A Day without a Mexican (2004), *1:* 86
A Day without a Woman (2017), *3:* 731
A Day without Immigrants, *1:* 83–89, 88 (ill.)
DDT, *1:* 135
De Klerk, F.W., *3:* 539
Death camps, *3:* 585–586, 587, 604–605, 608–609
Death penalty, *2:* 284–285. See also **Human rights**
    declining use, *2:* 289
    history, *2:* 285
    legal challenges to, *2:* 285–286
    support and opposition, *2:* 286–287
Declaration of Independence, *2:* 337
Declaration of Sentiments, *3:* 708, 709 (ill.)
Declaration of the Rights of Animals, *1:* 3
Declaration of the Rights of Man and of the Citizen, *2:* 267
Defense of Marriage Act, *2:* 438
Deforestation, *1:* 138
DeGeneres, Ellen, *2:* 434
Delano (CA) Grape Strike and Boycott (1965–1970), *2:* 414–422, 421 (ill.). See also **Labor rights**
Democracia Real Ya (DRY), *1:* 116, 120
Democracy, *3:* 467, 493, 669
Democratic Congressional Representatives Sit-in for Gun control (2016), *2:* 256–260, 259 (ill.). See also **Gun control/Gun rights**
Democratic National Convention (DNC), *3:* 564, 656 (ill.)
Deng, Xiaoping, *1:* 108, 110
Denmark
    Holocaust Resistance in Denmark (1943), *3:* 597–602, 601 (ill.)
    Nazi occupation, *3:* 598–600
    Nazi occupation ends, *3:* 602
    protests against *Jyllands-Posten* cartoons, *1:* 183–188
    response to Copenhagen protests, *1:* 147–148

Denver, CO, A Day without Immigrants protests, *1:* 88
Deportations
 to death camps, *3:* 604–605
 to Mexico by the United States, *1:* 74
Derby Day Protest (1913), *3:* 705
Des Moines, IA, Vietnam War protest (1965–1969), *3:* 663–668
Desegregation/Segregation, *1:* 38–39, 42. *See also* **Apartheid**
 Birmingham, Alabama, *1:* 62
 Little Rock, Arkansas, *1:* 47–52
 national defense jobs, *1:* 64
Desertification, *1:* 138
Deslondes, Charles, *3:* 625–627
Detroit Riots (MI) (1967), *3:* 524–530, 528 (ill.). *See also* **Racial conflict**
 aftermath, *3:* 529–530
 origins in "blind pig," *3:* 525
 Romney, George, interview, *3:* 530–531
Developing countries, advantages of globalization, *1:* 206
Development, Relief, and Education for Alien Minors Act (United States. DREAM Act), *1:* 89
Diagnostic and Statistical Manual of Mental Disorders, *2:* 432
Dickinson, Anna E., *3:* 697 (ill.)
Dictators, *3:* 467–468
Disability rights, *2:* 276–284. *See also* **Human rights**
 ADA passage, *2:* 280–283
 legislation, *2:* 278–279
 ongoing efforts, *2:* 283–284
 organizations, *2:* 279–280
Disabled children, education, *2:* 277–278
Discrimination. *See also* Racial discrimination
 against LGBTQ people, *2:* 431, 432, 436, 454–455
 Mexican American students, *1:* 79–80
District of Columbia. *See* Washington, D.C.
DNC (Democratic National Convention), *3:* 564, 656 (ill.)
"Don't Ask, Don't Tell," *2:* 434, 435
Douglass, Frederick, *3:* 638, 641
Dowell, Denzil, *2:* 241
Draft cards, burning, *3:* 666–667, 667 (ill.)

Draft (military)
 United States Civil War, *3:* 526, 654
 Vietnam War, *3:* 666
Drag shows, *2:* 457
DREAM Act, *1:* 89
Dresden, Germany, anti-migrant protests, *2:* 321, 323 (ill.)
Drug trade
 Mexico, *1:* 75, 90, 91
 violence, *1:* 91–92
DRY (Democracia Real Ya), *1:* 116, 120
Dubček, Alexander, *2:* 353
Dublin, Ireland, Easter Rebellion (1916), *3:* 480–481, 481 (ill.)
Duckwitz, Georg Ferdinand, *3:* 600–601
Duncan, Arne, *2:* 249
Dunlop, Marion Wallace, *3:* 704, 706
Durant, William C., *2:* 408
Dutilleux, Jean-Pierre, *2:* 381–382
Dylan, Bob, *1:* 68; *3:* 670

Earth Day, *1:* 136, 164; *3:* 730–731
Earth Liberation Front (ELF), *1:* 11
Earthquakes, *1:* 154
East Los Angeles, CA. *See also* California; Los Angeles, CA
 blowouts, *1:* 77–82
 commemoration of East LA blowouts, *1:* 81 (ill.)
 Mexican American students, *1:* 77
Easter Rebellion (1916), *3:* 480–481, 481 (ill.). *See also* **Political/Government uprisings**
Eckford, Elizabeth, *1:* 50–51, 52 (ill.)
Eckhardt, Christopher, *3:* 664, 665
Economic discontent, *1:* **99–131**, 103 (ill.), 109 (ill.), 114 (ill.), 119 (ill.), 121 (ill.), 124 (ill.). *See also* **Globalization**
 Brexit, *1:* 103, 103 (ill.), 122–129, 124 (ill.)
 Cacerolazo Protests in Chile (1971), *1:* 106–107
 15-M Movement (2011), *1:* 116–122, 121 (ill.)
 Porkulus Protests, Tea Party (2009–2010), *1:* 111–116, 114 (ill.)
 Rice Riots of 1918 (Japan), *1:* 126–127

Secret Document of the Farmers of Xiaogang (1978), *1:* 105–111, 109 (ill.)
student protests in France (May 1968), *1:* 118–119, 119 (ill.)
Economic inequality, *1:* 208
protest against, *1:* 216–217
Wall Street, *1:* 218
Ecoterrorism, *1:* 11. *See also* Terrorism
Education
for disabled children, *2:* 277–278
discrimination against Mexican American students, *1:* 79–80
for girls and women, *3:* 718–724
Education for All Handicapped Children Act, *2:* 278
Educational Issues Coordinating Committee (EICC), *1:* 82
EEC (European Economic Community), *1:* 123
Egypt
labor rights, *2:* 398
post-revolution, *3:* 497–498
Tahrir Square Protests (2011), *3:* 493–498, 495–498, 496 (ill.)
Egyptian Revolution (2011), *3:* 488, 493–498, 496 (ill.). *See also* **Political/Government uprisings**
EIA (United States. Energy Information Administration), *1:* 155
EIC (British East India Company), *2:* 347–348
EICC (Educational Issues Coordinating Committee), *1:* 82
8888 Uprising, Myanmar (1988), *3:* 502–503, 503 (ill.)
Eilperin, Juliet, *1:* 141
Eisenhower, Dwight D., *1:* 48, 52
El Rhazoui, Zineb, *1:* 194
Elections
disputed, Iran, *3:* 490
source of unrest in Hong Kong, *3:* 499–500
US presidential (2016), *3:* 725–726
Elephants
poaching, *1:* 18–19, 25
population decline, *1:* 20–22
postage stamp, *1:* 29 (ill.)
in Ringling Bros. circus, *1:* 29, 29 (ill.)
ELF (Earth Liberation Front), *1:* 11

Elizabeth I, Queen of England, *1:* 173; *2:* 347
Elser, Georg Johann, *3:* 591
Emancipation Proclamation, *3:* 633
Emergency Economic Stabilization Act of 2008, *1:* 112
Emerson, Ralph Waldo, *2:* 387, 387 (ill.)
Encyclopedia of Environmental Issues, *3:* 573
Endangered Species Act, *1:* 136
Energy Transfer Partners, *2:* 384, 385, 386–387
England. Bill of Rights, *1:* 173; *2:* 266–267
ENGOs (Environmental nongovernmental organizations), *1:* 146
Enlightenment, *2:* 265–267
Environment, *1:* **133–170**, 135 (ill.), 136 (ill.), 142 (ill.), 143 (ill.), 150 (ill.), 153 (ill.), 155 (ill.), 161 (ill.), 162 (ill.), 165 (ill.). *See also* Climate change; Global warming
Copenhagen Protests (2009), *1:* 144–151, 150 (ill.)
Forward on Climate Rally (2013), *1:* 139–144, 142 (ill.)
Fukushima nuclear power protests, *1:* 160–161, 161 (ill.)
Global Frackdown (2014), *1:* 151–156, 155 (ill.)
Gore, Al, *1:* 148–149
Hill, Julia "Butterfly," *1:* 152, 153 (ill.)
human impact, *1:* 137–138
Love Canal, NY, *1:* 136, 143, 143 (ill.)
March for Science (2017), *1:* 163–168, 165 (ill.)
Pacific Climate Warriors Blockade (2014), *1:* 157–163, 162 (ill.)
21st century challenges, *1:* 137–138
Environmental movement
history, *1:* 133–137
methods, *1:* 138–139
Environmental nongovernmental organizations (ENGOs), *1:* 146
Environmentalists, *1:* 133, 138–139
EPA (United States. Environmental Protection Agency), *1:* 136
Equal pay, *3:* 728–729
Equal Rights Amendment (ERA), *3:* 558–559
Equanimal, *1:* 17, 17 (ill.)
Espionage, *2:* 285
Estonia, independence movements, *2:* 348
Ethnicity, *3:* 509

EU (European Union)
    exit of United Kingdom, *1:* 103–104, 122–129
    immigrants and immigration, *2:* 309–310
    refugee crisis, *2:* 324–325
    refugees, *2:* 319–321
Europe, pro-migrant rallies, *2:* 318–325, 324 (ill.)
European Court of Human Rights, *2:* 454
European Economic Community (EEC), *1:* 123
European Union (EU)
    exit of United Kingdom, *1:* 103–104, 122–129
    immigrants and immigration, *2:* 309–310
    refugee crisis, *2:* 324–325
    refugees, *2:* 319–321
Euroscepticism, *1:* 125
Eviction protests, *1:* 120
Evidence-based policies, *1:* 163–164
Executions
    declining use, 2890
    lethal injection, 2890
    Texas, *2:* 284

F

FACE Act (United States. Freedom of Access to Clinic Entrances Act), *3:* 568
Fair Housing Act of 1968, *1:* 40, 41
Fair Labor Standards Act of 1938, *2:* 397–398, 407
Fairchild, Morgan, *3:* 560
Fall of the Berlin Wall (1989), *3:* 478–486, 483 (ill.). *See also* **Political/Government uprisings**
Fallata, Iman, *3:* 716 (ill.)
Famines, *3:* 569
Farage, Nigel, *1:* 125
Farm workers. *See also* Workers
    civil rights, *1:* 78–79
    labor unions, *1:* 75–76
    Mexican, *1:* 75 (ill.)
    working conditions, *2:* 416
Fast Food Forward, *2:* 424, 425
Fast-food Workers' Strike (2012), *2:* 422–426, 424 (ill.). *See also* **Labor rights**
    global recognition, *2:* 425
    sit-ins, *2:* 425
Faubus, Orbal, *1:* 48, 50–52

Fawcett, Millicent, *3:* 703
FBI (United States. Federal Bureau of Investigation), *3:* 686–687, 725
Federal Assault Weapons Ban, *2:* 234–235
Federal Society of Journeymen Cordwainers, *2:* 396
Federalists, *1:* 175
Feld Entertainment, *1:* 29
Feminists, *3:* 558. *See also* **Women's rights**
Ferdinand II, King of Spain, *2:* 343
Ferrera, America, *3:* 729
Feudal societies, *3:* 469–470, 619–620
Fields, James Alex, *3:* 542
15-M Movement, *1:* 90, 116–122, 121 (ill.). *See also* **Economic discontent**
Fight for $15, *2:* 422
Fight to Stop Human Trafficking, *3:* 643–647. *See also* **Slavery**
Filipino workers, *2:* 416, 418–419. *See also* Workers
Final Solution, *3:* 608
Finding Dory, 1: 28
Firearms Owners' Protection Act, *2:* 234
First Landing Day (Australia), *2:* 365–366, 375, 376–377
Fisher Body Plant No. 1, Flint, MI, *2:* 410
Fisher Body Plant No. 2, Flint, MI, *2:* 410
Fitz, Nicholas, *1:* 100
Flag burning, Palestinian students, *1:* 186 (ill.)
Flint (MI) Sit-Down Strike against General Motors (1936–1937), *2:* 407–414, 412 (ill.). *See also* **Labor rights**
Florida
    mass shootings at Pulse nightclub, *2:* 257
    Tea Party movement, *1:* 114 (ill.)
    Ybor City Cigar Strike (1931), *1:* 84
Floyd, John, *3:* 632
Fonda, Jane, *3:* 560
Food & Water Watch, *1:* 155
Food labeling, *1:* 229–230
Forced abortions, *3:* 571
Forced labor, *3:* 644–646
Forced sterilization, *3:* 571
Force-feeding, *3:* 702, 706, 713
Ford v. Wainwright, 2: 285
Fort Myers, FL, Tea Party movement, *1:* 114 (ill.)

Forward on Climate Rally (2013), *1:* 139–144, 142 (ill.). See also **Environment**
Fossey, Dian, *1:* 20
Foundation Day (Australia), *2:* 365–366, 375, 376–377
Fox, Helen, *3:* 703–704
Fox, Maggie, *3:* 556
Fracking, *1:* 151–154; *2:* 385. See also **Environment**
   bans on, *1:* 156
   environmental impact, *1:* 154–155
   origins, *1:* 153–154
   toxic wastes, *1:* 153–154
France
   attack on *Charlie Hebdo* offices, *1:* 191
   student protests of 1968, *1:* 118–119, 119 (ill.)
Frantz (William) Elementary School, *1:* 53
Free blacks, *3:* 630–632. See also African Americans
Free speech, *1:* **171–202**, 177 (ill.), 181 (ill.), 186 (ill.), 189 (ill.), 190 (ill.), 192 (ill.), 197 (ill.), 199 (ill.). See also Civil rights
   Banned book list, *1:* 180
   Harry Potter Book Burning (2001), *1:* 177–183, 181 (ill.)
   history of, *1:* 171–174
   "Je Suis Charlie" protests (2015), *1:* 189–194, 192 (ill.)
   limits of, *1:* 171, 175–177
   Muslim protests against *Charlie Hebdo*, *1:* 190 (ill.), 193
   Muslim protests of Danish cartoons (2005–2008), *1:* 183–188, 186 (ill.)
   Nazi Book Burning, *1:* 179
   proposed Skokie neo-Nazi march, *1:* 188–189, 189 (ill.)
   religion and, *1:* 176, 183
   Supreme Court decisions, *3:* 667–668
   United States, *1:* 173–174
   University of California, Berkeley, *1:* 176–177, 177 (ill.), 198–199, 199 (ill.)
   Yale Student Protests (2015), *1:* 194–201, 197 (ill.)
Free Syrian Army, *3:* 492
Free trade. See also **Globalization**
   defined, *1:* 203
   opponents of, *1:* 211

Free trade agreements, *1:* 205–206
Freedom of Access to Clinic Entrances Act (FACE Act), *3:* 568
Freedom of religion, *2:* 265
Freedom of speech. See **Free speech**
Freedom Riders, *1:* 39, 56 (ill.)
Freedom Rides (1961), *1:* 39, 54–59, 56 (ill.). See also **African American civil rights**
   first ride, *1:* 56–57
   origins, *1:* 54–55
Freedom Sunday, *3:* 647
French colonies. See also Colonization
   Haitian Revolution (1791–1804), *3:* 625
   independence movements, *2:* 338
   slavery in, *3:* 624–625
French resistance (World War II), *3:* 589
French Revolution (1789–1799), *2:* 267; *3:* 471
French Student Protests of 1968, *1:* 118–119, 119 (ill.)
Friedan, Betty, *3:* 558, 728, 729 (ill.)
Friendship Junior College, *1:* 59, 61
Friendship Nine, *1:* 59, 61, 63
Frost, Robert, *1:* 149
Fryberg, Jaylen, *2:* 253
Fugitive Slave Law, *3:* 631
Fukushima nuclear power protests, *1:* 160–161, 161 (ill.)
Fulton, Sybrina, *3:* 545–546
Fur farms, *1:* 11
Furman v. Georgia, *2:* 285
Furs, PETA protests against, *1:* 12–13, 13 (ill.)

G

G20 Summit, Hamburg, Germany (2017), *1:* 208–209, 208 (ill.)
Gandhi, Mahatma, *1:* 78; *2:* 340–341, 341, 351 (ill.)
   Indian independence movement, *2:* 348–352
   Salt March, *2:* 341–342, 346–352, 351 (ill.)
   speech before the Salt March, *2:* 349
Gandhi, Mohandas. See Gandhi, Mahatma
Gandhi's Salt March (1930), *2:* 340–341, 346–352, 351 (ill.). See also **Independence movements**
Garfield High School, East LA, *1:* 81

Garner, Eric, *3:* 541–542, 544–545
Garner, Esaw, *3:* 546
Garza, Alicia, *3:* 541
Gasland (2010), *1:* 154
Gaulle, Charles de, *1:* 118–119
Gay and Lesbian Alliance against Defamation (GLAAD), *2:* 458
Gay and Lesbian Pride Month, *2:* 441
Gay pride
    parades, *2:* 441
    Shanghai Pride Festival, *2:* 452–458, 456 (ill.)
Gaye, Marvin, *3:* 670
Gays. *See* LGBTQ people
Gdansk Shipyard Strike, Poland (1980), *2:* 356–357, 357 (ill.)
Gender identity, *2:* 429, 435
Genderqueer, *2:* 429–430
General Motors Co. (GM)
    Flint Sit-Down Strike, *2:* 407–414, 412 (ill.)
    working conditions, *2:* 408–409
Genetically modified organisms (GMOs), *1:* 224
    food, *1:* 223
    labeling, *1:* 229–230
    seeds, *1:* 223
Genocide, *2:* 297, 300. *See also* Holocaust
George III, King of Great Britain, *2:* 376
Gerber, Henry, *2:* 432
German immigrants, *2:* 307. *See also* Immigrants and immigration
Germany. *See also* Nazi Germany
    anti-migrant protests, *2:* 321, 323 (ill.)
    Fukushima nuclear energy protests, *1:* 161 (ill.)
    Nazi resistance, *3:* 592–597
    nuclear energy policy, *1:* 161
    post–World War II division, *3:* 479–481
    reunification, *3:* 486
Gestapo, *3:* 592, 593, 594. *See also* Nazi Germany
Ghettos, *3:* 602
    Bialystok, Poland, *3:* 607
    Warsaw, Poland, *3:* 602–605
Ghost dance, *2:* 369, 369 (ill.)
Giffords, Gabrielle, *2:* 248, 248 (ill.)
Giumarra, John, Sr., *2:* 421 (ill.)
GLAAD (Gay and Lesbian Alliance against Defamation), *2:* 458

Glacier Point, Yosemite Valley, *1:* 135 (ill.)
Global Frackdown (2014), *1:* 151–156, 155 (ill.). *See also* **Environment**
Global March for Elephants and Rhinos (GMFER), *1:* 18–25, 24 (ill.). *See also* **Animal rights**
Global Recession of 2008, *1:* 219
    Spain, *1:* 104–105, 116–117
    United States, *1:* 112–113
Global Slavery Index, *3:* 623
Global warming, *1:* 145, 159. *See also* Climate change; **Environment**
Globalization, *1:* **203–231**, 208 (ill.), 212 (ill.), 214 (ill.), 222 (ill.), 227 (ill.), 228 (ill.). *See also* **Economic discontent**
    Banksy street art protests, *1:* 212, 212 (ill.)
    Battle in Seattle, World Trade Organization protests (1999), *1:* 209–216, 214 (ill.)
    benefits and disadvantages, *1:* 206–207
    Big Pharma, *1:* 226–227, 227 (ill.)
    history, *1:* 204–205
    March against Monsanto (2013), *1:* 223–230, 228 (ill.)
    Occupy Wall Street (2011), *1:* 216–222, 222 (ill.)
    21st century, *1:* 205–206
Glover, Danny, *3:* 678
Glyphosate, *1:* 224
GM (General Motors Co.)
    Flint Sit-Down Strike, *2:* 407–414, 412 (ill.)
    working conditions, *2:* 408–409
GMFER (Global March for Elephants and Rhinos), *1:* 18–25, 24 (ill.). *See also* **Animal rights**
GMOs (Genetically modified organisms), *1:* 224
    foods, *1:* 223
    labeling, *1:* 229–230
    seeds, *1:* 223
Goddard, Colin, *2:* 249–250
Goebbels, Joseph, *1:* 179
Goldsmith, Judy, *3:* 559–560
Goodman, Andrew, *1:* 58, 58 (ill.)
Gorbachev, Mikhail, *3:* 476, 478, 484, 485
Gore, Al, *1:* 148–149
Gorillas, *1:* 20
Gorsuch, Neil, *3:* 579
Govea, Jessica, *2:* 417
Graffiti, *1:* 212

GENERAL INDEX

Graves, Goddard C., *3:* 667 (ill.)
Gray, Freddie, *3:* 544
Gray, Nellie, *3:* 559
Gray, Vincent, *2:* 250
Great American Boycott, *1:* 88. *See also* Boycotts
Great Britain. Tea Act, *2:* 336–337
Great Depression, *1:* 74, 218; *2:* 409, 419
Great Recession. *See* Global Recession of 2008
Green, Ernest, *1:* 50, 52
Green, Jay J., *2:* 413
Greenhouse gases. *See also* **Environment**
    from agriculture, *1:* 225–226
    climate change, *1:* 137, 145, 157
    Newcastle Harbor, New South Wales, *1:* 160–161
Greenpeace, *1:* 22–23, 23 (ill.)
Greensboro, NC, sit-ins, *1:* 59, 60
Greenwich Village, NY, *2:* 436–437, 441
Greenwood, Grace, *3:* 697 (ill.)
Grito de Lares (1868), *2:* 340, 342–346. *See also* **Independence movements**
Guangdong, China, *3:* 570–573
Guangxi, China, *3:* 570–573
Guardian, 1: 158, 181
Guggenheim Museum, Bilbao, Spain, *1:* 12, 16–18
Guiliani, Rudolph, *3:* 680
Gun Control Act, *2:* 234
Gun control laws
    background checks, *2:* 253
    California, *2:* 242–243
    history in the United States, *2:* 233–235
Gun control/Gun rights, *2:* **233–262**, 237 (ill.), 238 (ill.), 243 (ill.), 248 (ill.), 249 (ill.), 254 (ill.), 259 (ill.)
    Black Panthers Protest Mulford Act (1967), *2:* 239–245, 243 (ill.)
    Democratic Congressional Representatives Sit-in for Gun Control (2016), *2:* 256–260, 259 (ill.)
    demonstrators, *2:* 237 (ill.), 238 (ill.)
    gun control arguments, *2:* 235–237
    gun rights arguments, *2:* 237–238
    Huey P. Newton Gun Club demonstrations, *2:* 244
    "I Will Not Comply" Rally (2014), *2:* 252–256, 254 (ill.)
    March on Washington for Gun Control (2013), *2:* 246–252, 249 (ill.)
    Seale, Bobby, on Mulford Act, *2:* 240, 242
    Vocal Majority Tour (2016), *2:* 248, 248 (ill.)
Gun ownership
    history in United States, *2:* 233–235
    United States, *2:* 235, 235 (ill.)
Gun shows, *2:* 257
Gunn, David, *3:* 554
Gutenberg, Johannes, *1:* 172
Guttmacher Institute, *3:* 556

H

The Hague, Netherlands, International Congress of Women (1915), *3:* 657–663, 660 (ill.)
Haitian Revolution (1791–1804), *2:* 338; *3:* 625
Hamid bin Isa Al Khalifa, King of Bahrain, *3:* 489
Hamilton, Alice, *3:* 660
Handguns, *2:* 235
Harbor blockades, *1:* 157–163
Harding, Warren G., *2:* 411
Harpers Ferry Raid (1859), *3:* 638–643, 642 (ill.). *See also* **Slavery**
Harry Potter Book Burning (2001), *1:* 177–183, 181 (ill.). *See also* **Free speech**
Harry Potter (book series), *1:* 175
    book burning, *1:* 177–183, 181 (ill.)
    opposition to, *1:* 179–180
Hate crimes
    expanding definition, *2:* 447–448, 451
    laws, *2:* 434, 446, 450
    United States, *3:* 518 (ill.)
Hate groups, *3:* 518 (ill.), 542
Hatfield, Sid, *2:* 410
Hatshepsut, *2:* 430–431
Havel, Václav, *2:* 355, 356
Hawke, Bob, *2:* 378–379
Haymarket Square Riot (1886), *2:* 418–419, 419 (ill.)
HDI (Human Development Index), *1:* 102
Health insurance plans, birth control and, *3:* 555, 556
Heart (music group), *1:* 30
Heine, Heinrich, *1:* 179
Heller, Aron, *3:* 610

Henderson, Russell, *2:* 447, 451
Henry VII, King of England, *2:* 265
Henry VIII, King of England, *1:* 173; *2:* 285
Heston, Charlton, *1:* 68
Heydrich, Reinhard, *3:* 589
Heyer, Heather, *3:* 542
Heymann, Lida Gustava, *3:* 660
Hidalgo, Miguel, *2:* 338
Hill, Julia "Butterfly," *1:* 152, 153 (ill.)
Himmler, Heinrich, *3:* 604, 605
Hinckley, John, Jr., *2:* 236–237
Hinduism, *2:* 290–291
Hispanic and Latino civil rights, *1:* **71–98**, 76 (ill.), 81 (ill.), 88 (ill.), 91 (ill.), 95 (ill.). *See also* Civil rights
   Day without Immigrants protests (2006), *1:* 83–89, 88 (ill.)
   Day without Latinos (2006), *1:* 87
   early history, *1:* 73
   East LA blowouts (1968), *1:* 77–82, 81 (ill.)
   Mexican Indignados movement, *1:* 90–96, 91 (ill.), 95 (ill.)
   Sicilia, Javier, *1:* 90, 91 (ill.), 92–93, 94
   Tlatelolco Massacre (1968), *1:* 94, 95
   Ybor City Cigar Strike (1931), *1:* 84–85
Hispanics and Latinos. *See also* Mexican Americans
   definitions, *1:* 71
   United States population, *1:* 75–76
Hitler, Adolf, *1:* 179; *3:* 479–480, 585–586, 590–591, 592, 607
HIV/AIDS
   demonstrations, *2:* 433 (ill.)
   drugs protests, *1:* 226–227, 227 (ill.)
   epidemic, *2:* 433–434
Hobby Lobby, *3:* 555
Holloway, Jonathan, *1:* 200
Holocaust, *1:* 179; *2:* 297; *3:* 586, 613. *See also* Genocide
Holocaust Resistance in Denmark (1943), *3:* 597–602, 601 (ill.). *See also* **Resistance to Nazis**
Homosexuality. *See also* LGBTQ people
   as mental disorder, *2:* 432, 452
   opposition to by WBC, *2:* 448, 452
   as personality disorder, *2:* 432
Hong Kong
   relationship with China, *3:* 499–500
   Umbrella Revolution (2014), *3:* 498–505, 500 (ill.), 504 (ill.)
Hopper, Grace Murray, *1:* 200
Horn, Jerry, *3:* 560
Houston, TX
   anti-abortion demonstrators, *3:* 564 (ill.)
   March to Abolish the Death Penalty, *2:* 287
HPI (Human Poverty Index), *1:* 102
Hu Yaobang, *3:* 473–474
Huerta, Dolores, *1:* 75, 76 (ill.), 78, 86; *2:* 414–415, 419–420
Human development, *1:* 101–102
Human Development Index (HDI), *1:* 102
Human migrations, *2:* 305–306
Human Poverty Index (HPI), *1:* 102
Human rights, *2:* **263–304**, 269 (ill.), 274 (ill.), 278 (ill.), 282 (ill.), 287 (ill.), 295 (ill.), 301 (ill.). *See also* Civil rights; Disability rights; **Immigrant rights**
   Americans with Disabilities Act (ADA), *2:* 277, 280–283
   Armenian Genocide Protests, *2:* 297–302, 301 (ill.)
   Attica Prison Riot (1971), *2:* 270–276, 274 (ill.)
   Bly, Nellie, investigation of mental hospital, *2:* 278, 278 (ill.)
   Capitol Crawl (1990), *2:* 276–284, 282 (ill.)
   Dalit Protests in India (2006), *2:* 290–297, 295 (ill.)
   definition and nature of, *2:* 263
   history, *2:* 264–268
   March to Abolish the Death Penalty, *2:* 284–289, 287 (ill.)
   Strangeways Prison Riot (1990), *2:* 271
Human Rights Campaign, *2:* 458
Human trafficking, *3:* 623, 643–647. *See also* **Slavery**
Humane Society of the United States, *1:* 11
Hunger strikes, *3:* 476, 701–702
   Manning, Bradley/Chelsea, *3:* 689
   Pankhurst, Sylvia, *3:* 704 (ill.)
   by Suffragettes in Prison, *3:* 701–707
   Women's Suffrage Protest at the White House, *3:* 713
Hunt, Jane, *3:* 708
Hussein, Saddam, *3:* 682

Hutton, Bobby, *2:* 245
Hyde Amendment, *3:* 578
Hydro-Quebec, *2:* 382

I

"I Have a Dream" speech, *1:* 39, 63, 68
"I Will Not Comply" Rally (2014), *2:* 252–256
    See also **Gun control/Gun rights**
IAT (Indians of All Tribes), *2:* 370–371
Idle No More, *2:* 365 (ill.)
Iglesias, Pablo, *1:* 121–122
Iguala, Mexico, *1:* 95–96
IJM (International Justice Mission), *3:* 647
Illinois
    DNC anti-war protests, *3:* 656 (ill.)
    Haymarket Square Riot, *2:* 418–419
    proposed Skokie neo-Nazi march, *1:* 188–189
ILO (International Labour Organization), *3:* 644
Immigrant rights, *2:* **305–334**, 313 (ill.), 317 (ill.). 323 (ill.), 324 (ill.), 329 (ill.), 330 (ill.). *See also* **Human rights**
    anti-Chinese riots, Denver, CO (1980), *2:* 328–329, 329 (ill.)
    California. Senate. Resolution No. 16 (2017), *2:* 327
    Molly Maguires, *2:* 312–313, 313 (ill.)
    Nativist Riots (1844), *2:* 311–318, 317 (ill.)
    Patriotic Europeans against the Islamization of the West (PEGIDA), *2:* 322–323, 323 (ill.)
    Pro-migrant Rallies in Europe and Australia (2015-2016), *2:* 318–325, 324 (ill.)
    Protests against President Trump's Travel Ban (2017), *2:* 325–332, 330 (ill.)
Immigrants and immigration. *See also* Refugees
    Chinese, *2:* 307, 328–329, 329 (ill.), 415–416
    Day without Immigrants protests, *1:* 83–89
    EU (European Union), *2:* 309–310
    German, *2:* 307
    Irish, *2:* 307, 312, 314
    Latin American, *2:* 308–309
    Mexican, *2:* 308–309
    undocumented immigrants, *1:* 74, 83–84; *2:* 325
    United Kingdom, *1:* 123, 124
    United States, *1:* 74, 83–85; *2:* 306–309

INC (Indian National Congress), *2:* 348–349
Income inequality, *1:* 99–100
Indentured servants, *3:* 510–511, 694
Independence movements, *2:* **335–359**, 345 (ill.), 337 (ill.), 345 (ill.), 351 (ill.), 354 (ill.), 357 (ill.)
    Asia, *2:* 339–340
    Cuba, *2:* 338–339
    Czechoslovakia, *2:* 341–342, 352–358, 354 (ill.)
    Estonia, Singing Revolution, *2:* 348
    French colonies, *2:* 338; *3:* 625
    Gandhi leads Salt March (1930), *2:* 340–341, 346–352, 351 (ill.)
    Gdansk Shipyard Strike, Poland (1980), *2:* 356–357, 357 (ill.)
    Grito de Lares (1868), *2:* 342–346, 345 (ill.)
    history, *2:* 335–340
    India, *2:* 340–341, 346–352
    Jamaica, *2:* 339
    Mexico, *2:* 338
    Puerto Rico, *2:* 342–346
    Spanish colonies, *2:* 338–339
    Velvet Revolution (1989), *2:* 352–358
India
    caste systems, *2:* 290–297
    colonial history, *2:* 347–349
    Dalit protests, *2:* 290–297, 295 (ill.)
    8888 anniversary protest, *3:* 503 (ill.)
    independence movements, *2:* 340–341, 346–352
    reservation system, *2:* 292–293, 294–295
India. Constitution, *2:* 292
India. National Crime Record Bureau, *2:* 296–297
Indian Mutiny (1857–1858), *2:* 348
Indian National Congress (INC), *2:* 348–349
Indian reservations. *See also* Native Americans
    land rights, *2:* 362–363
    Pine Ridge Reservation, *2:* 370, 372, 374
    Standing Rock Reservation, *2:* 369, 370, 384
Indians of All Tribes (IAT), *2:* 370–371
Indigenous Australians. *See* Aboriginals
Indigenous peoples. *See also* Native Americans
    Amazonian, *2:* 366, 379–384
    Canada, *2:* 365 (ill.)
    Copenhagen protests, *1:* 146, 149
    Cree First Nations, *2:* 382
    impact of colonization, *2:* 361, 375–376

Kayapo, *2:* 366, 380–384
land rights, *2:* 361
New Zealand, *2:* 364
Pacific Climate Warriors Blockade, *1:* 162, 162 (ill.)
South Africa, *3:* 532–533, 534
Taino, *2:* 343
Indigenous peoples' rights, *2:* 361–392, 365 (ill.), 367 (ill.), 369 (ill.), 371 (ill.), 374 (ill.), 378 (ill.), 383 (ill.), 388 (ill.). *See also* Civil rights
 Aboriginal Land Rights Protest (1988), *2:* 365–366, 375–379, 378 (ill.)
 AIM Occupation of Wounded Knee (1973), *2:* 364–365, 367–375, 374 (ill.)
 Cree First Nations dam protest, *2:* 382
 Dakota Access Pipeline Protest (2016–2017), *2:* 366–367; 367 (ill.), 384–391, 388 (ill.)
 history, *2:* 362–364
 occupation of Alcatraz, *2:* 370–371, 371 (ill.)
 Preservation of Amazon Rain Forest Awareness Campaign (1989), *2:* 366, 379–384, 383 (ill.)
 Trail of Tears protest, *2:* 386–387, 387 (ill.)
Indignados movement, *1:* 90–96
Indigo Girls, *3:* 729
Individuals with Disabilities Education Act (IDEA), *2:* 278
Industrial Revolution, *1:* 133–134; *2:* 393, 395, 395 (ill.)
Industrialization, *2:* 400
International Congress of Women (1915), *3:* 657–663, 660 (ill.). *See also* Anti-war protests
 goals of, *3:* 661
 impact of, *3:* 661–663
 resolutions, *3:* 662
International Justice Mission (IJM), *3:* 647
International Labour Organization (ILO), *2:* 407; *3:* 644
International March for Elephants, *1:* 22–23. *See also* **Animal rights**
International Union, United Automobile, Aerospace and Agricultural Implement Workers of America, *2:* 414. *See also* UAW (United Auto Workers)
International Whaling Commission (IWC), *1:* 22
International Woman Suffrage Alliance, *3:* 658
International Workers Day, *1:* 86

Internet
 citizen journalism, *3:* 490–491
 role in organizing protests, *1:* 213
Interstate Commerce Commission, *1:* 54–55, 57, 59
Iowa, Student Armband Protest of Vietnam War (1965–1969), *3:* 663–668, 668 (ill.)
IPCC (United Nations. Intergovernmental Panel on Climate Change), *1:* 137, 148
Iranian demonstrators, violence against, *3:* 490–491, 491 (ill.)
Iranian Green Movement (2009), *3:* 490–491, 491 (ill.)
Iraq War (2003–2011), *3:* 682–683
 anti-war protests, *3:* 657, 682 (ill.)
 Bush, George W., speech, *3:* 680–681
 Candlelight Vigils against Invasion of Iraq (2003), *3:* 676–683
 civilian casualties, *3:* 684
Ireland
 Brexit demonstrations, *1:* 126
 Easter Rebellion (1916), *3:* 480–481, 481 (ill.)
Irish immigrants, *2:* 307, 312, 314. *See also* Immigrants and immigration
Irish Republican Brotherhood, *3:* 480
Irish War of Independence (1919–1921), *3:* 481
Irwin, Lord, *2:* 351
Islam, *1:* 184
Islamic extremists, *2:* 326–328
Islamic law, *3:* 715, 718, 719
Islamization, *2:* 322
Island nations, *1:* 146
 climate change, *1:* 157–158
 Pacific Climate Warriors Blockade, *1:* 162
Ivory trade, *1:* 18–19
IWC (International Whaling Commission), *1:* 22

J

Jackson, Jesse, *3:* 678
Jackson, Mahalia, *1:* 67, 68
Jackson, MS, Freedom Rides, *1:* 57
Jacobs, Aletta, *3:* 657, 658–659
"Jail, no bail," *1:* 61

GENERAL INDEX

Jamaica
    Christmas Rebellion/Baptist War (1831–1832), *3:* 634–638
    history, *3:* 634–635
    independence movements, *2:* 339
James II, King of England, *1:* 173; *2:* 266
Japan
    nuclear energy policy, *1:* 160
    rice riots of 1918, *1:* 126–127
    Tokyo Big March, *1:* 160
Jati, *2:* 291
"Je Suis Charlie" Protests (2015), *1:* 189–194, 192 (ill.). *See also* **Free speech**
    Muslim protests against *Charlie Hebdo*, *1:* 190 (ill.), 193
    pro free speech, *1:* 192–193
Jefferson County Courthouse, West Virginia, *2:* 411 (ill.)
Jewish Combat Organization (ZOB), *3:* 604–606, 605
Jewish Holocaust, *1:* 179; *2:* 297; *3:* 586, 613. *See also* Genocide
Jews
    assistance to, *3:* 588–589
    Danish, *3:* 597, 601–602
    under Nazis, *3:* 585–586, 607
Jim Crow laws, *1:* 37, 43–44. *See also* Racial discrimination
    changes to, *1:* 48
    school segregation, *1:* 48–49
    segregation, *1:* 55
John, King of England, *3:* 470
Johnson, Lyndon B., *1:* 69
    civil rights, *1:* 40
    Detroit Riots, *3:* 529
Jones, Mary Harris
    crusade against child labor, *2:* 399–407, 406 (ill.)
    excerpt from autobiography, *2:* 404–405
    Kensington textile mill strike, *2:* 401–403
Journey of Reconciliation (1947), *1:* 55
Judd, Ashley, *3:* 729
July 20 Plot (1944), *3:* 591
Juste, Carsten, *1:* 186
Justice for All March (2014), *3:* 515, 539–546, 545 (ill.). *See also* **Racial conflict**
Jyllands-Posten, *1:* 183–188, 191

K

Kadhem, Laila al-, *3:* 716 (ill.)
Kaepernick, Colin, *3:* 515, 516–517, 517 (ill.)
Kansas
    Brown, John, anti-slavery activity, *3:* 640
    debate over slavery, *3:* 640
    Summer of Mercy Protest, *3:* 566–567
Kayany Foundation, *3:* 724
Kayapo, *2:* 366, 380–384. *See also* Indigenous peoples
Keelan, Jennifer, *2:* 282 (ill.)
Keller, Helen, *1:* 179
Kelly, Mark, *2:* 248, 248 (ill.)
Kennedy, Anthony, *2:* 439
Kennedy, John F., *1:* 54
    assassination, *2:* 234
    Freedom Rides, *1:* 57, 59
    March on Washington, *1:* 66–67
Kennedy, Robert, *1:* 57, 69
Kennedy (John F.) International Airport, *2:* 330
Kenrick, Francis Patrick, *2:* 314–315, 316
Kensington Textile Mill Strike (1903), *2:* 401–403
Kent State University student protests, *3:* 669–676, 674 (ill.). *See also* Anti-war protests
Kenya, Global March for Elephants and Rhinos, *1:* 22–23, 24 (ill.)
Kerner Commission, *3:* 529–530
Kerr, Clark, *1:* 199
Kerr, Stanley, *2:* 299
Keys, Alicia, *3:* 729
Keystone XL project, *1:* 139, 140–141, 144
Khairlanji, India, Dalit family murder, *2:* 293–294
Kifner, John, *3:* 672–673
Killer whales, *1:* 4–5
    SeaWorld protests, *1:* 25–31
    treatment by SeaWorld, *1:* 26–27, 30–31
King, Martin Luther, Jr., *1:* 36, 78
    assassination, *1:* 41, 69
    Birmingham, AL, desegregation, *1:* 62
    civil rights movement, *1:* 75; *3:* 472
    "I Have a Dream" speech, *1:* 39
    March on Washington, *1:* 63, 67, 68
    Montgomery bus boycott, *1:* 36 (ill.), 45–46, 47

King, Rodney, *3:* 522
KKK (Ku Klux Klan), *1:* 47, 58; *3:* 542
Klausen, Jytte, *1:* 184, 185
KMT (Kuomintang), *1:* 107
Knights of Labor, *2:* 397
Koch, Charles, *1:* 111
Koch, David, *1:* 111
Kopp, James C., *3:* 563–564
Koran, *3:* 498, 715, 718
Kozachenko, Kathy, *2:* 433
Krause, Allison, *3:* 675
Ku Klux Klan (KKK), *1:* 47, 58; *3:* 542
Kulach, Adam, *3:* 716 (ill.)
Kuomintang (KMT), *1:* 107
Kyoto Protocol, *1:* 146

L

Labeling, genetically modified organisms, *1:* 229–230
Labor activists, *1:* 75–76
Labor Day, *2:* 402
Labor laws, *2:* 393
    child labor, *2:* 407
    United States, *2:* 397–398
Labor movement, *2:* 395–398, 401
Labor rights, *2:* **393–428,** 395 (ill.), 400 (ill.), 403 (ill.), 406 (ill.), 411 (ill.), 412 (ill.), 419 (ill.), 421 (ill.), 424 (ill.). *See also* Child labor; Workers
    Battle of Blair Mountain strike (1921), *2:* 410–411, 411 (ill.)
    Delano Grape Strike and Boycott (1965–1970), *2:* 414–422, 421 (ill.)
    Fast-Food Workers' Strike (2012), *2:* 422–426, 424 (ill.)
    Flint Sit-down Strike against General Motors (1936–1937), *2:* 407–414, 412 (ill.)
    Haymarket Square Riot (1886), *2:* 418–419, 419 (ill.)
    Mother Jones's "Children's Crusade" (1903), *2:* 399–407, 406 (ill.)
    Solidarity movement, *2:* 356–357, 357 (ill.)
    United States, *2:* 394
    worldwide, *2:* 398–399
Labor unions, *2:* 396–397
    employer resistance to, *2:* 397–398
    farmworkers, *1:* 75–76

Lafayette, LA, mass shooting, *2:* 251
Lake Oahe, *2:* 386
Lakota Sioux, *2:* 369, 369 (ill.), 370, 372. *See also* Native Americans
Lam, Carrie, *3:* 504–505
Lambda Legal, *2:* 433, 464
Land rights
    Indian reservations, *2:* 362–363
    indigenous peoples, *2:* 361
    Māori, *2:* 363–364
Land rights protests, *2:* 364–367. *See also* **Indigenous peoples' rights**
    Aboriginals, *2:* 365–366
    Amazonian indigenous peoples, *2:* 366, 379–384
    Australia, *2:* 375–379
    Canada, *2:* 365 (ill.)
    Cree First Nations, *2:* 382
    Native Americans, *2:* 364–365, 366–367, 384–391, 388 (ill.)
Lanza, Adam, *2:* 246–247, 253
Laramie, WY
    anti-gay protests by Westboro Baptist Church, *2:* 449–451
    murder of Matthew Shepard, *2:* 445–446
The Laramie Project, *2:* 456–457
Las Vegas, NV, mass shootings, *2:* 260
Lasn, Kalle, *1:* 219
Latin America, *1:* 71, 72
Latin American immigrants, *2:* 308–309. *See also* Immigrants and immigration; Mexican Americans
Latino civil rights. *See* **Hispanic and Latino civil rights**
Latinos. *See* Hispanics and Latinos
Law Center to Prevent Gun Violence, *2:* 256
Law Enforcement Officers Protection Act, *2:* 234
Lebanon, Yousafzai, Malala, All-Girls School, *3:* 718–724
Lectors, *1:* 84, 85 (ill.)
Lee, Robert E., *3:* 642
Lee, Ronnie, *1:* 8
Lemay, Tiffany, *2:* 454
Lennon, John, *3:* 670, 671 (ill.)
Lesbians, *2:* 430. *See also* LGBTQ people
Lethal injection, *2:* 289. *See also* Death penalty
Leung, Trini, *3:* 474–475
Leung Chun-ying, *3:* 500–501, 504–505

GENERAL INDEX

Levi-Strauss, Claude, *1:* 166
Lewis, John, *1:* 56, 66–67, 68; *2:* 258, 259 (ill.)
LGBTQ people. *See also* Homosexuality
    definition, *2:* 429–430
    discrimination against, *2:* 431, 432, 436, 454–455
    lesbians, *2:* 430
    transgender people, *2:* 429, 435
LGBTQ rights, *2:* **429–466,** 433 (ill.), 439 (ill.), 440 (ill.), 444 (ill.), 449 (ill.), 455 (ill.), 456 (ill.), 461 (ill.), 463 (ill.). *See also* Civil rights
    China, *2:* 452–453, 458
    history, *2:* 430–431
    Marriage equality, *2:* 438–439, 439 (ill.)
    modern movement, *2:* 431–435
    NCAA boycott of North Carolina, *2:* 460–461, 461 (ill.)
    organizations, *2:* 432, 436
    protests against, *2:* 445–452
    Protests of North Carolina House Bill 2 (2016), *2:* 458–464, 461 (ill.), 463 (ill.)
    Russia, *2:* 454–455, 455 (ill.)
    Shanghai Pride Festival (2009), *2:* 452–458, 456 (ill.)
    Stonewall Riots (1969), *2:* 435–441, 440 (ill.)
    Westboro Baptist Church Protests of Matthew Shepard (1998–1999), *2:* 445–452, 449 (ill.)
    White Night Riots (1979), *2:* 441–445, 444 (ill.)
Li Peng, *3:* 475
Li Yinhe, *2:* 452
Liberal Democratic Party (Japan), *1:* 160
Libya
    Arab Spring, *3:* 489–490
    civil war, *3:* 490
Lincoln, Abraham, *3:* 654, 654 (ill.)
Little Rock, AR, school integration, *1:* 47–52
Little Rock Central High School, *1:* 47–52
Little Rock Nine Crisis (1957), *1:* 47–52, 52 (ill.). *See also* **African American civil rights**
Livermore, Mary, *3:* 697 (ill.)
Lloyd George, David, *3:* 705
Lobbyists, *1:* 139
Locke, John, *2:* 266
Loeak, Milañ, *1:* 158
London, UK, anti-fracking protesters, *1:* 155 (ill.)

Longley, Kristin, *2:* 413
Los Angeles, CA. *See also* California; East Los Angeles, CA
    Armenian genocide protests, *2:* 301 (ill.), 302
    A Day without Immigrants protests, *1:* 88
    King, Rodney, riots, *3:* 522–523, 523 (ill.)
    March for Women's Lives (1986), *3:* 556–561
    Occupy Wall Street demonstration, *1:* 222 (ill.)
    race riots (1992), *3:* 522–523, 523 (ill.)
    Watts Riots, *3:* 514 (ill.)
    Zoot Suit Riots, *3:* 518–524, 521 (ill.)
Los Angeles Race Riots (1992), *3:* 522–523, 523 (ill.)
Los Angeles Unified School District
    cultural studies introduced, *1:* 82
    discrimination in education, *1:* 79–80
Loughner, Jared Lee, *2:* 248
Louisiana
    mass shooting, *2:* 251
    school desegregation, *1:* 53
    slavery, *3:* 624–625
Louisiana Rebellion (German Coast) (1811), *3:* 623–628. *See also* **Slavery**
Love, William T., *1:* 143
Love Canal, NY, *1:* 136, 143, 143 (ill.)
Lowell, Arthur, *2:* 413
Luddites, *2:* 395 (ill.)
Lunch Counter Protest, McCrory's (1961), *1:* 59–63, 61 (ill.). *See also* **African American civil rights**
Luther, Martin, *2:* 312
Lyden, Jack, *2:* 450
Lysistrata, *3:* 651–652

M

Macy's Thanksgiving Parade, *1:* 28, 30
Madonna, *3:* 729
Mafia, *2:* 436–437
Magazinet, *1:* 185
Magna Carta (1215), *2:* 265; *3:* 470
Maharashtra, India, *2:* 296
Malala Fund, *3:* 724
Malala Yousafzai All-Girls School, *3:* 718–724
El Malcriado: The Voice of the Farm Worker, *2:* 417

Malê Revolt of 1835, *3:* 626–627, 627 (ill.). *See also* **Slavery**
Mallory, Tamika, *3:* 728
Malloy, Annie E., *3:* 660 (ill.)
Manama, Bahrain, *3:* 489
Manchester, England, Strangeways Prison riot, *2:* 271
Mandela, Nelson, *3:* 539
Manning, Bradley/Chelsea, *3:* 684–690, 686 (ill.). *See also* Transgender people
  arrest and trial, *3:* 686–688
  communication with WikiLeaks, *3:* 685–686
Mao Zedong, *1:* 107, 108; *3:* 473, 569
Māori, land rights, *2:* 363–364
March against Monsanto (2013), *1:* 223–230, 228 (ill.). *See also* **Globalization**
March for Life (1986), *3:* 558, 559
March for Life Education and Defense Fund, *3:* 559
March for Marriage, *2:* 439 (ill.)
March for Science (2017), *1:* 163–168, 165 (ill.); *3:* 730–731. *See also* **Environment**
March for Women's Lives (1986), *3:* 556–561, 557 (ill.), 559. *See also* **Reproductive rights**
March of the Mill Children, *2:* 399–407, 406 (ill.). *See also* **Labor rights**
March on Washington for Gun Control (2013), *2:* 246–252, 249 (ill.). *See also* **Gun control/Gun rights**
March on Washington for Jobs and Freedom (1963), *1:* 39, 39 (ill.), 63–69, 65 (ill.); *3:* 472. *See also* **African American civil rights**
  King Jr., Martin Luther, *1:* 63, 67, 68
  leaders, *1:* 65–66, 65 (ill.)
  Lewis, John, *1:* 66–67
  origins, *1:* 64
March to Abolish the Death Penalty, *2:* 284–289, 287 (ill.). *See also* **Human rights**
Marine Mammal Protection Act, *1:* 136
Maroons, *3:* 636
Marriage equality, *2:* 434
  defined, *2:* 430
  legal battle, *2:* 438–439
  Washington, D.C., protest against, *2:* 439 (ill.)
Married women, rights of, *3:* 693–695
Marshall, Thurgood, *1:* 39

Marshall Islands, *1:* 158
Martin, Richard, *1:* 2
Martin, Trayvon, *3:* 540–541
Martin's Act, *1:* 2
Mary II, Queen of England, *1:* 173
Marysville Pilchuck High School shootings, *2:* 253
Mass shootings, *2:* 239, 253–254, 257
  Lafayette, Louisiana, *2:* 251
  Las Vegas, Nevada, *2:* 260
  Obama, Barack speech, *2:* 251
  Sandy Hook Elementary School, *2:* 246–247
  Tucson, Arizona, *2:* 248
  Umpqua Community College, *2:* 251
  Virginia Tech, *2:* 249
Mateen, Oscar, *2:* 257
Matewan Massacre (1921), *2:* 410
Mattachine Society, *2:* 432
Matters, Muriel, *3:* 703–704
Matthew Shepard and James Byrd, Jr., Hate Crimes Prevention Act, *2:* 450, 451
Mauritania, abolition of slavery, *3:* 643
Maximilian, Saint, *3:* 652
Maximilianus, *3:* 652
May, Theresa, *1:* 125, 128–129
May Day, *1:* 86
Mayan texts, book burning, *1:* 178
McAuliffe, Terry, *3:* 542
McCartney, Stella, *1:* 12–13
McCormick Reaper Works, *2:* 418
McCorvey, Norma, *3:* 576–577, 577 (ill.)
McCoy, Rose, *1:* 28, 30
McCrory, Pat, *2:* 459
McCrory's Lunch Counter Protest (1961), *1:* 59–63, 61 (ill.). *See also* **African American civil rights**
McDonald's, *2:* 422, 424, 425
McGuire, Barry, *3:* 670
McKinney, Aaron, *2:* 447, 451
M'Clintock, Mary Ann, *3:* 708
McSpadden, Lesley, *3:* 545–546
Means, Russell, *2:* 372, 374
Mechanics' Union of Trade Associations, *2:* 396–397
Medicaid, *2:* 283–284; *3:* 578
Medina, Francisco Ramírez, *2:* 345

Melchior, Bent, *3:* 598–599, 599 (ill.)
Meltdowns. *See* Nuclear accidents
Mental institutions, *2:* 278
Mercado, Mark, *2:* 255–256
Merkel, Angela, *1:* 161; *2:* 321, 322
Merkley, Jeff, *1:* 230
Methane gas, *1:* 159
Metropolitan Coalition against Nukes, *1:* 160
Mexican American students
    discrimination in education, *1:* 79–80
    East LA blowouts, *1:* 77–82
Mexican-American War (1846–1848), *1:* 73
Mexican Americans. *See also* Hispanics and Latinos
    racial conflict, *3:* 518–524
    racial discrimination, *3:* 519
    Zoot Suit Riots, *3:* 512 (ill.), 521 (ill.)
Mexican farm workers, *1:* 75 (ill.). *See also* Workers
Mexican immigrants, *2:* 308–309. *See also* Immigrants and immigration
Mexican Indignados movement, *1:* 90–96
Mexican students
    demonstrations, *1:* 95 (ill.)
    murder of in Iguala, *1:* 95–96
    Tlatelolco massacre, *1:* 94
    violence against, *1:* 90, 94
Mexican workers, *2:* 416, 418–419. *See also* Workers
Mexico
    drug trade, *1:* 75, 90, 91
    independence movements, *2:* 338
    Indignados movement, *1:* 90–96
    Tlatelolco Massacre (1968), *1:* 94, 95
    war on drugs, *1:* 91–95
Mexico City, Mexico, *1:* 93–94
MIA (Montgomery Improvement Association), *1:* 45–46
Michigan
    Detroit Riots (1967), *3:* 524–530
    strike against GM, *2:* 407–414, 412 (ill.)
Middle Ages
    political/government uprisings, *3:* 469–470
    slavery, *3:* 619–620
Middle East, Arab Spring, *1:* 90; *3:* 486–493
Middle Eastern refugees, *2:* 318–319
Migrant workers, *2:* 415, 416. *See also* Workers

Military draft
    United States Civil War, *3:* 526, 654
    Vietnam War, *3:* 666
Military servicemen, Zoot Suit Riots, *3:* 520–522
Milk (2008), *2:* 445
Milk, Harvey, *2:* 433, 441, 442, 445
Mill, John Stuart, *3:* 703
Miller, David, *3:* 666
Miller, Hannah, *2:* 454
Miller, Jeffrey, *3:* 675
Minimum wage, *2:* 422–423, 426. *See also* **Labor rights**
Minks, *1:* 11
Mississippi, Freedom Rides, *1:* 57
Mississippi Summer Project/Freedom Summer Voter Registration, *1:* 58, 58 (ill.). *See also* **African American civil rights**
Mitchell, George P., *1:* 154
Molly Maguires, *2:* 312–313, 313 (ill.)
Moms Demand Action, *2:* 238 (ill.)
Monáe, Janelle, *3:* 729
Monkeys, animal testing, *1:* 7–8, 10
Monopolies, *1:* 224–225, 228
Monsanto Co., *1:* 223–230
    concerns about products, *1:* 224–225
    product benefits, *1:* 225–226
Montgomery, AL
    bus boycott, *1:* 42–47
    Freedom Rides, *1:* 57
Montgomery Bus Boycott (1955–1956), *1:* 36 (ill.), 42–47. *See also* **African American civil rights**
Montgomery Improvement Association (MIA), *1:* 45–46
Moore, Gwen, *2:* 425
Moore, Michael, *3:* 678, 729
Moore, Tim, *2:* 462
Morgan, Ephraim, *2:* 410
Morgan, J.P., *1:* 217–218
Morgan v. Virginia, *1:* 55
Morsi, Mohamed, *3:* 498
Moscone, George Richard, *2:* 441, 442, 443, 445
Mother Jones
    crusade against child labor, *2:* 399–407, 406 (ill.)
    excerpt from autobiography, *2:* 404–405
    Kensington textile mill strike, *2:* 401–403

Mother Jones's "Children's Crusade" (1903), *2:* 399–407, 406 (ill.). *See also* **Labor rights**
Mothershed, Thelma, *1:* 50
Mott, Charles Stewart, *2:* 408
Mott, Lucretia, *3:* 697 (ill.), 708
Movement for Peace with Justice and Dignity, *1:* 93
Mubarak, Hosni, *3:* 488, 494, 496–497
Muhammad, images of, *1:* 176, 183, 184, 190
Muir, John, *1:* 135, 135 (ill.)
Mulford, Donald, *2:* 242–243
Mulford Act (California), *2:* 242–243, 244
Múnera, Álvaro, *1:* 16
Murder. *See also* Violence
    of Dalit family in Khairlanji, India, *2:* 293–294
    by pro-life advocates, *3:* 554–555, 563–564, 567
Murphy, Christopher, *2:* 258
Murphy, Frank, *2:* 412
Muslim Brotherhood, *3:* 498
Muslim protesters
    against *Charlie Hebdo* use of images of Muhammad, *1:* 190 (ill.), 193
    Muhammad cartoons, *1:* 186–187, 186 (ill.)
Muslim Protests of Danish Cartoons, *1:* 183–188, 186 (ill.). *See also* **Free speech**
Muslims, Trump travel bans, *2:* 325–326, 328–329, 330 (ill.)
Mutawa, *3:* 715
Myanmar
    8888 Uprising (1988), *3:* 502–503
    violence against the Rohingya, *3:* 503

N

NAACP (National Association for the Advancement of Colored People)
    founding, *1:* 35
    legal actions, *1:* 38–39
    March on Washington, *1:* 65
    Montgomery bus boycott, *1:* 44
NAFTA (North American Free Trade Agreement), *1:* 205
Naidu, Sarojina, *2:* 351 (ill.)
NAN (National Action Network), *3:* 539, 544

Nat Turner's Rebellion (1831–1832), *3:* 628–634, 629 (ill.). *See also* **Slavery**
National Action Network (NAN), *3:* 539, 544
National Advisory Commission on Civil Disorders, *3:* 529–530
National American Woman Suffrage Association (NAWSA), *3:* 710
National Association for the Advancement of Colored People (NAACP)
    founding, *1:* 35
    legal actions, *1:* 38–39
    March on Washington, *1:* 65
    Montgomery bus boycott, *1:* 44
National Center for Missing and Exploited Children, *3:* 645
National Child Labor Committee, *2:* 407
National Collegiate Athletic Association (NCAA), *2:* 460–461, 461 (ill.)
National Conference of Dalit Organizations, *2:* 295 (ill.), 296
National Council on the Handicapped (NCH), *2:* 282
National defense jobs, desegregation, *1:* 64
National Democratic Party (Egypt), *3:* 495
National Family Planning Program, *3:* 577–578
National Farm Workers Association (NFWA), *1:* 75, 78; *2:* 419
National Firearms Act, *2:* 234
National Football League (NFL), *3:* 515
National Geographic, *1:* 21–22
National Guard, *2:* 275, 389
    Arkansas, *1:* 48, 50–52, 52 (ill.)
    Michigan, *3:* 528, 528 (ill.), 531
    Ohio, *3:* 674–675
National Instant Criminal Background Check System, *2:* 253
National Labor Relations Act of 1935, *2:* 397
National Socialist German Workers' Party (Nazi Party), *3:* 585, 592, 607
National Socialist Party of America, *1:* 188
National Socialists German Students' Association, *1:* 179
National Urban League (NUL), *1:* 35
National Women's Party (United States), *3:* 698 (ill.), 710, 712 (ill.)

National Youth Peace Prize (Pakistan), *3:* 719
Nationwide Tea Party Coalition, *1:* 114
Native Americans. *See also* Indian reservations; Indigenous peoples
    Dakota Access Pipeline Protest, *2:* 366–367, 367 (ill.), 384–391, 388 (ill.)
    impact of colonization, *2:* 362–363, 386–387
    Lakota Sioux, *2:* 369, 369 (ill.), 370, 372
    land rights protests, *2:* 364–365, 366–367, 384–391, 388 (ill.)
    occupation of Alcatraz, *2:* 370–371, 371 (ill.)
    opposition to oil pipelines, *1:* 144
    slavery, *3:* 624
    Standing Rock Sioux, *2:* 384–385, 387–388, 388 (ill.)
    treaties with federal government, *2:* 368, 386
    treatment in the United States, *2:* 368–369
Nativism, *2:* 314
Nativist Riots (1844), *2:* 311–318, 317 (ill.). *See also* **Immigrant rights**
    eyewitness account, *2:* 314–315
    Protestant-Catholic conflict, *2:* 312–313
NATO (North Atlantic Treaty Organization), *3:* 490
NAWSA (National American Woman Suffrage Association), *3:* 710
Nazi Germany, *3:* 585–586, 592. *See also* Germany; Gestapo; **Resistance to Nazis**
    book burnings, *1:* 179
    deportations to death camps, *3:* 604–605
Nazi Party (National Socialist German Workers' Party), *3:* 585, 592, 607
Nazis, *1:* 188. *See also* Neo-Nazis
NCAA (National Collegiate Athletic Association), *2:* 460–461, 461 (ill.)
NCH (National Council on the Handicapped), *2:* 282
Ne Win, *3:* 502–503
Nelson, Willie, *1:* 30
Neo-Nazis, *1:* 188–189; *3:* 542, 543 (ill.). *See also* Nazis
Neumann-Ortiz, Christine, *1:* 87
Nevada, mass shootings, *2:* 260
New Delhi, India, 8888 anniversary protest, *3:* 503 (ill.)

New Mexico, Alamagordo book burning, *1:* 181 (ill.)
New Orleans, LA, school desegregation, *1:* 53
New York, NY
    child labor protest of 1909, *2:* 402–403, 403 (ill.)
    draft riots of 1863, *3:* 526–527, 527 (ill.)
    Occupy Wall Street, *1:* 216–222
    One Thousand Coffins Protest (2004), *3:* 678–679, 679 (ill.)
    racial conflict, *3:* 526–527
New York. State Police, *2:* 275
New York Act (1866), *1:* 3
New York City Draft Riots (1863), *3:* 526–527, 527 (ill.), 654. *See also* **Racial conflict**
New York Communities for Change (NYCC), *2:* 422, 423, 424
New York (state)
    Love Canal, *1:* 136, 143, 143 (ill.)
    Operation Rescue protests, *3:* 562–568, 563
New York State Liquor Authority, *2:* 436
New York Times, *3:* 555–556
New Zealand, indigenous peoples, *2:* 364
Newcastle Harbor, New South Wales, *1:* 160–161
Newman, Paul, *1:* 68
Newsweek, *2:* 452
Newton, Huey P., *2:* 240, 242
Newton (Huey P.) Gun Club, *2:* 244
Newtown, Connecticut, mass shooting, *2:* 246–247
NFL (National Football League), *3:* 515
NFWA (National Farm Workers Association), *1:* 75, 78; *2:* 419
Nigeria, Boko Haram kidnappings, *3:* 700, 722–723
Nixon, Richard M., *2:* 371
    decision to invade Cambodia, *3:* 671
    expansion of Vietnam War, *3:* 656
    moves to end Vietnam War, *3:* 676
    Women's Equality Day, *3:* 729
No Taxpayer Funding for Abortion and Abortion Insurance Full Disclosure Act, *3:* 580
NOAA (United States. National Oceanic and Atmospheric Administration), *1:* 136
Nobel Peace Prize
    Gore, Al, speech, *1:* 148–149
    Suu Kyi, Aung San, *3:* 503
    Yousafzai, Malala, *3:* 718, 720–721

Nonviolent resistance, *2:* 341, 420–421. *See also* Civil disobedience
Norman, Peter, *3:* 516, 517 (ill.)
North America
    British colonies, *2:* 336–337
    colonization, *1:* 72
North American Free Trade Agreement (NAFTA), *1:* 205
North Atlantic Treaty Organization (NATO), *3:* 490
North Carolina
    boycott, *2:* 461–462
    NCAA boycott, *2:* 460–461
    sit-ins, *1:* 59, 60
    transgender rights, *2:* 458–464
North Carolina. General Assembly. HB2, *2:* 458–459
    protests, *2:* 458–464, 461 (ill.), 463 (ill.)
    repeal, *2:* 463–464
North Carolina. General Assembly. HB142, *2:* 460, 464
North Dakota
    Dakota Access Pipeline protest, *2:* 366–367, 367 (ill.), 388 (ill.)
    land rights protests, *2:* 384–391, 388 (ill.)
North Vietnam, *2:* 340 (ill.). *See also* Vietnam
Northern Ireland, Brexit demonstrations, *1:* 126
Norway
    publication of cartoons of Muhammad, *1:* 185
    whaling, *1:* 22–23
No-till farming, *1:* 225–226
NOW (National Organization for Women), *3:* 554, 558–561, 560–561, 728
NPS (United States. National Park Service), *1:* 135
NRA (National Rifle Association), *2:* 238–239, 245, 250, 252, 257
Nuclear accidents
    Chernobyl, Ukraine, *1:* 136–137
    Fukushima, Japan, *1:* 160–161
Nuclear power plants, post-Fukushima protests, *1:* 160–161, 161 (ill.)
NUL (National Urban League), *1:* 35
Nunez, David, *2:* 255–256
NUWSS (National Union of Women's Suffrage Societies), *3:* 703
NYCC (New York Communities for Change), *2:* 422, 423, 424
Nye, Bill, *1:* 165 (ill.)

O

Oakes, Richard, *2:* 370
Oakland, CA, Global Frackdown, *1:* 156
Obama, Barack, *1:* 76 (ill.), 113
    Dakota Access Pipeline, *2:* 385
    declares Stonewall Inn a national landmark, *2:* 441
    hate crimes laws, *2:* 451
    Keystone XL project, *1:* 139, 141, 144
    Manning, Chelsea, sentence reduction, *3:* 685, 690
    on mass shootings, *2:* 251
    minimum wage, *2:* 422–423, 426
    repeal of "Don't Ask, Don't Tell," *2:* 435
    support of gun control sit-in, *2:* 259
Obama, Michelle, *3:* 700–701, 727
Obergefell, Jim, *2:* 438–439
Obergefell v. Hodges, *2:* 434, 438–439
Occupation of Alcatraz (1969–1970), *2:* 370–371, 371 (ill.)
Occupy Central with Love and Peace, *3:* 500–501
Occupy Wall Street (2011), *1:* 216–222, 222 (ill.). *See also* **Globalization**
    declaration of principles, *1:* 220–221
    expansion beyond NYC, *1:* 220–221, 222 (ill.)
    origins, *1:* 219
Ochs, Phil, *3:* 670
Ogallala Aquifer, *1:* 141
Ohio, Kent State University student protests, *3:* 669–676, 674 (ill.)
Oil leaks, *1:* 140
Oil pipelines, *1:* 140–141, 142. *See also* Dakota Access Pipeline (DAPL); Keystone XL project
Olympic Games, Mexico City (1968), *3:* 516, 517 (ill.)
One child policy, *3:* 568. *See also* Birth control; **Reproductive rights**
    enforcement of, *3:* 570–572
    introduction of, *3:* 569–570
    results of, *3:* 573
    revision of, *3:* 573–574

GENERAL INDEX

One Child Policy Riots (2007), *3:* 568–574, 572 (ill.)
One Million Moms for Gun Control, *2:* 248
One Thousand Coffins Protest (2004), *3:* 678–679, 679 (ill.). *See also* Anti-war protests
Open carry, *2:* 235. *See also* **Gun control/Gun rights**
    Black Panthers protest, *2:* 239–245, 243 (ill.)
    Huey P. Newton Gun Club demonstrations, *2:* 244
Operation Rescue (1992), *3:* 562–568. *See also* **Reproductive rights**
    demonstrators, *3:* 564 (ill.), 567 (ill.)
    history, *3:* 562–563
    methods, *3:* 563–564
Operation Save America, *3:* 563
Opletal, Jan, *2:* 355
Orcas, *1:* 4–5
    SeaWorld protests, *1:* 25–31
    treatment by SeaWorld, *1:* 26–27, 30–31
Orestiada, Greece, pro-migrant rally, *2:* 324 (ill.)
Origliasso, Jessica, *1:* 13 (ill.)
Origliasso, Lisa, *1:* 13 (ill.)
Orlando, FL, mass shootings at Pulse nightclub, *2:* 257
O'Sullivan, Michael, *1:* 28
Oswald, Lee Harvey, *2:* 234
Oswald, Russell, *2:* 273
Ottoman Empire, *2:* 297–300
Outsourcing, *1:* 207
Oxfam, *1:* 100
Oxford, Mississippi, *1:* 58

P

Pacific Climate Warriors Blockade (2014), *1:* 157–163, 162 (ill.). *See also* **Environment**
Pacific Lumber Company, *1:* 152
Pacifists, *3:* 652, 661. *See also* Anti-war protests
Paddock, Stephen, *2:* 260
PAH (Platform for People Affected by Mortgages), *1:* 120
Palestinian students, flag burning, *1:* 186 (ill.)
Paltrow, Gweneth, *1:* 229
Pankhurst, Emmeline, *3:* 703
Pankhurst, Sylvia, *3:* 704 (ill.)

Pantaleo, Daniel, *3:* 541–542, 544–545
Pantsuit Nation, *3:* 726
Parent, Elena, *2:* 238 (ill.)
Paris, France
    attack on *Charlie Hebdo* offices, *1:* 191
    student protests of 1968, *1:* 118–119, 119 (ill.)
Paris Agreement, *1:* 168
Paris Peace Accords, *3:* 676
Parks, Rosa, *1:* 36 (ill.), 42–43, 45 (ill.), 47
Partial-Birth Abortion Act, *3:* 561
Partisans, *3:* 589
Patents, genetically modified seeds, *1:* 224
Patriot Guard Riders, *2:* 452
Patriotic Europeans against the Islamization of the West (PEGIDA), *2:* 322–323, 323 (ill.)
Patterson, Romaine, *2:* 449
Pattillo, Melba, *1:* 50
Paul, Alice, *3:* 698 (ill.), 710, 713
Paul, Rand, *1:* 115–116
PayPal, *2:* 462
Pearse, Patrick, *3:* 480
Peasants' Revolt of 1381, *3:* 470
PEGIDA (Patriotic Europeans against the Islamization of the West), *2:* 322–323, 323 (ill.)
Pence, Mike, *3:* 559, 578–579
Penn, Sean, *2:* 445
Pennsylvania
    Kensington textile mill strike, *2:* 401–403
    Nativist Riots (1844), *2:* 311–318, 317 (ill.)
Peño Nieto, Enrique, *1:* 95, 96
Pentagon terror attack (2001), *2:* 326; *3:* 677–680. *See also* Terrorism
People for the Ethical Treatment of Animals (PETA)
    antifur campaign, *1:* 12–13, 13 (ill.)
    circus animals, *1:* 29
    founding, *1:* 4
    SeaWorld protests, *1:* 30
    support for ALF, *1:* 11
People's Climate March, *1:* 156
Perez, Carmen, *3:* 728
Periscope, *2:* 259
Perry, John B., *2:* 314–315
Perry, Rick, *2:* 288
Pesticides, *1:* 135, 224

PETA (People for the Ethical Treatment of Animals)
    antifur campaign, *1:* 12–13, 13 (ill.)
    circus animals, *1:* 29
    founding, *1:* 4
    SeaWorld protests, *1:* 30
    support for ALF, *1:* 11
Peter, Paul, and Mary, *3:* 670
Pethick-Lawrence, Emmeline, *3:* 660 (ill.), 661
Pew Research Center, *2:* 308, 453; *3:* 541 (ill.)
Pharmaceutical industry, *1:* 226–227, 227 (ill.)
Phelps, Fred, *2:* 446, 448
Philadelphia, PA, Nativist Riots (1844), *2:* 311–318, 317 (ill.)
Phipps, Benjamin, *3:* 629 (ill.)
Picketing, *3:* 563
Pieterson, Hector, *3:* 537
Pine Ridge Reservation, *2:* 370, 372, 374
Pixar Animation Studios, *1:* 28
Planned Parenthood, *3:* 558, 574, 575–576, 728. *See also* **Reproductive rights**
    anti-abortion demonstrators, *3:* 564 (ill.)
    debate over government funding for, *3:* 577–579
    pro-choice supporters, *3:* 579 (ill.)
    protests (2017), *3:* 574–580, 579 (ill.)
Planned Parenthood of Southeastern Pennsylvania v. Casey, 3: 561
Platform for People Affected by Mortgages (PAH), *1:* 120
Plessy v. Ferguson, 1: 48–49
Poaching
    elephants, *1:* 18–19, 25
    gorillas, *1:* 20
    rhinos, *1:* 18–19, 25
Podemos, *1:* 121–122
Poitier, Sidney, *1:* 68
Poland, Bialystok Ghetto, *3:* 607
Poland. Home Army, *3:* 589–590, 604
Polaris Project, *3:* 644, 646
Police
    impact of police shootings, *3:* 541 (ill.)
    racial discrimination, *3:* 513–514
    Watts Riots, *3:* 514 (ill.)
Police brutality, *3:* 525
Polish Home Army, *3:* 589–590, 604

Polish resistance (World War II), *3:* 589–590, 590 (ill.)
Political prisoners, *3:* 706
Political/Government uprisings, *3:* 467–507, 476 (ill.), 481 (ill.), 483 (ill.), 491 (ill.), 492 (ill.), 496 (ill.), 500 (ill.), 503 (ill.), 504 (ill.)
    Arab Spring and the Syrian Civil Uprising (2011), *3:* 486–493, 492 (ill.)
    causes of, *3:* 467–468
    Easter Rebellion (1916), *3:* 480–481, 481 (ill.)
    8888 Uprising, Myanmar (1988), *3:* 502–503, 503 (ill.)
    Fall of the Berlin Wall (1989), *3:* 478–486, 483 (ill.)
    history, *3:* 469–472
    Iranian Green Movement (2009), *3:* 490–491, 491 (ill.)
    Middle Ages, *3:* 469–470
    Tahrir Square Protests (Egyptian Revolution, 2011), *3:* 493–498, 496 (ill.)
    Tiananmen Square Protests (1989), *3:* 473–478, 476 (ill.)
    Umbrella Revolution (2014), *3:* 498–505, 500 (ill.), 504 (ill.)
PoliticsNation, 3: 544
Pollution, *1:* 134–135
Pompeo, Mike, *3:* 690
Popular Party (Spain), *1:* 121, 122
Populist movement, *1:* 218
Porkulus protests, Tea Party, *1:* 111–116, 114 (ill.). *See also* **Economic discontent**
Portuguese colonies. *See also* Colonization
    slave rebellions, *3:* 626–627
    slave trade, *3:* 621
    slavery, *3:* 511
Potter (Harry) Book Burning (2001), *1:* 177–183
Potter (Harry) (book series), *1:* 175
    book burning, *1:* 177–183
    opposition to, *1:* 179–180
Poverty, *1:* 101
Prague Spring, *2:* 353, 354 (ill.)
Preservation of Amazon Rain Forest Awareness Campaign (1989), *2:* 379–384
Presidential elections, *3:* 725–726
Presidential Medal of Freedom, *1:* 76 (ill.), 79

GENERAL INDEX

El Primer Congreso Mexicanista, *1:* 73
Prison colonies, *2:* 376. *See also* Colonization
Prisoners' rights, *2:* 270–276. *See also* **Human rights**
Prisons, human rights abuses, *2:* 270–271
Probst, Christoph, *3:* 593, 596
Pro-choice groups, *3:* 550–551, 554, 556, 574, 579 (ill.). *See also* **Reproductive rights**
Pro-democracy protests. *See* **Political/Government uprisings**
Progressive Party (United States), *3:* 710
Prohibition (1920–1933), *2:* 233–234
Project Confrontation, *1:* 62
Pro-life groups, *3:* 550, 554, 557, 574. *See also* **Reproductive rights**
   March for Life, *3:* 559
   murder by, *3:* 554–555
Pro-migrant rallies. *See also* **Immigrant rights**
   Europe and Australia, *2:* 318–325, 324 (ill.)
   Orestiada, Greece, *2:* 324 (ill.)
Protest literature, *3:* 631
Protest songs, *3:* 670–671
Protestant Reformation, *2:* 312–313
Protestants, *2:* 312
#ProtestPP, *3:* 574, 579–580
Protests. *See also* Boycotts; Riots; Sit-ins; Student protests
   African American civil rights, *1:* 35–70
   animal rights, *1:* 1–33
   athletes, *3:* 516–517
   economic discontent, *1:* 99–131
   environment, *1:* 133–170
   free speech, *1:* 171–202
   globalization, *1:* 203–231
   gun control/gun rights, *2:* 233–262, 237 (ill.), 238–239, 238 (ill.)
   Hispanic and Latino civil rights, *1:* 71–98
   HIV/AIDS drugs, *1:* 226–227
   human rights, *2:* 263–304
   immigrant rights, *2:* 305–334
   independence movements, *2:* 335–359
   indigenous peoples' rights, *2:* 361–392
   labor rights, *2:* 393–428
   LGBTQ rights, *2:* 429–466
   Mexican American students, *1:* 77–82
   political/government uprisings, *3:* 467–507
   racial conflict, *3:* 509–548
   reproductive rights, *3:* 549–583
   resistance to Nazis, *3:* 585–615
   slavery, *3:* 617–649
   in sports, *3:* 516–517
   tax, *1:* 111–116
   war, *3:* 651–692
   whaling, *1:* 22–23
   women's rights, *3:* 693–732
Protests against President Trump's travel ban (2017), *2:* 325–332, 330 (ill.). *See also* **Immigrant rights**
Protests of North Carolina House Bill 2 (2016), *2:* 458–464, 463 (ill.). *See also* **LGBTQ rights**
PSOE (Spanish Socialist Workers' Party), *1:* 120–121
Puerta del Sol, Madrid, Spain, *1:* 119, 121 (ill.)
Puerto Rico
   independence movements, *2:* 342–346
   as Spanish colony, *2:* 343–344
Pulse nightclub shootings, *2:* 257
Purple Teardrop Campaign, *3:* 646–647
Putin, Vladimir, *2:* 454

Q

Qaddafi, Mu'ammar al-, *3:* 488–489
al-Qaeda, *1:* 191
Qatar, labor rights, *2:* 398–399
Qin Shi Huang, *1:* 178
Qing Dynasty, *1:* 105–106
QR codes, *1:* 229
Quakers, *3:* 630, 652
Queer, *2:* 429. *See also* LGBTQ people
Quinn, William, *2:* 274

R

Race and racism, *3:* 509–510. *See also* White supremacists
   motivation for Zoot Suit riots, *3:* 523
   myth of racial superiority, *3:* 512–513

Racial conflict, *3:* **509–548**, 512 (ill.), 514 (ill.), 517 (ill.), 521 (ill.), 523 (ill.), 527 (ill.), 528 (ill.), 535 (ill.), 540 (ill.), 543 (ill.), 545 (ill.). *See also* **African American civil rights**; Black Lives Matter
  Black Consciousness Movement, *3:* 532–533
  Charlottesville Protests (2017), *3:* 542–543, 543 (ill.)
  Detroit Riots (1967), *3:* 524–530, 528 (ill.)
  Justice for All March (2014), *3:* 539–546, 545 (ill.)
  Los Angeles Race Riots (1992), *3:* 522–524, 523 (ill.)
  Mexican Americans, *3:* 518–524
  New York City Draft Riots (1863), *3:* 526–527, 527 (ill.)
  Soweto Uprising (1976), *3:* 530–539, 535 (ill.)
  Sports, protests in, *3:* 516–517, 517 (ill.)
  United States, *3:* 515–518
  Zoot Suit Riots (1943), *3:* 512, 512 (ill.), 518–524, 521 (ill.)
Racial discrimination, *1:* 35. *See also* Apartheid; Discrimination; Jim Crow laws
  African Americans, *1:* 36–37; *3:* 512, 513–515
  bus service, *1:* 54–59
  Mexican Americans, *3:* 519
  police, *3:* 513–514
  segregation and, *1:* 42
  South Africa, *3:* 513
Racial profiling, *3:* 539
Racial sensitivity, *1:* 194, 200
Racial superiority, *3:* 509–510, 512–513
Rain forests, *2:* 366, 379–380
Randolph, A. Philip, *1:* 64, 65–66, 68
Rankin, Jeannette, *3:* 711
Raoni (1977), *2:* 382
Raoni Metuktire, *2:* 366, 380–381, 383 (ill.)
Ray, Gloria, *1:* 50, 51
Reagan, Leslie J., *3:* 552
Reagan, Ronald, *2:* 245, 281
  Berlin Wall speech, *3:* 484–485
  position on reproductive rights, *3:* 559
  reproductive rights, *3:* 558
Redwoods, *1:* 152
Reed (Walter) Medical Center, *3:* 688–689, 689 (ill.)
Refugees. *See also* Immigrants and immigration
  Afghanistan, *2:* 319

  camps, *2:* 319–320, 320
  climate, *1:* 159
  crisis in Europe, *2:* 309–310, 324–325
  dangerous journeys, *2:* 323–324
  defined, *2:* 320
  EU (European Union), *2:* 319–321
  Middle Eastern, *2:* 318–319
  Syrian, *2:* 319, 321; *3:* 493, 720–724
Regan, Tom, *1:* 4
Reich, Robert, *2:* 425
Reid, Eric, *3:* 517 (ill.)
Religion, free speech and, *1:* 176, 183
Religious freedom, *2:* 311
Reproductive health services, *3:* 575
Reproductive rights, *3:* **549–583**, 557 (ill.), 564 (ill.), 567 (ill.), 572 (ill.), 577 (ill.), 579 (ill.). *See also* Abortion; Pro-choice groups; Pro-life groups; **Women's rights**
  debate over, *3:* 549–550
  history, *3:* 551–555
  laws limiting, *3:* 555
  March for Life (1986), *3:* 558, 559
  March for Women's Lives (1986), *3:* 556–561, 557 (ill.)
  McCorvey, Norma, *3:* 576–577, 577 (ill.)
  One Child Policy Riots (2007), *3:* 568–574, 572 (ill.)
  ongoing fight over, *3:* 555–556
  Operation Rescue (1992), *3:* 562–568, 564 (ill.)
  Planned Parenthood Protests (2017), *3:* 574–580, 579 (ill.)
  Summer of Mercy Protest (1991), *3:* 566–567
Republican National Convention (RNC), *3:* 564, 678
Reservation system
  India, *2:* 292–293
  private businesses, *2:* 294–295
Resistance to Nazis, *3:* **585–615**, 590 (ill.), 593 (ill.), 596 (ill.), 601 (ill.), 606 (ill.), 611 (ill.). *See also* Nazi Germany
  beginnings, *3:* 587–588
  Holocaust Resistance in Denmark (1943), *3:* 597–602, 601 (ill.)
  peaceful resistance, *3:* 588–589
  Treblinka Death Camp Revolt (1943), *3:* 607–614, 611 (ill.)

GENERAL INDEX

violent resistance, *3:* 590–591
Warsaw Ghetto Uprising (1943), *3:* 602–607, 606 (ill.)
White Rose Movement (1942–1943), *3:* 592–597, 593 (ill.), 596 (ill.)
Revolutionary Committee of Puerto Rico, *2:* 344–345
Rhino horn, *1:* 19
Rhinos
  poaching, *1:* 18–19, 25
  population decline, *1:* 21–22
Rhodes, James A., *3:* 674–675
Rice Riots of 1918 (Japan), *1:* 126–127
Richards, Cecile, *3:* 579, 728
Rig Veda, *2:* 290–291
Ringling Bros. and Barnum & Bailey Circus, *1:* 5, 29, 29 (ill.)
Riots. *See also* Protests; Violence
  anti-immigrant, *2:* 328–329
  Detroit Riots (MI) (1967), *3:* 524–530, 528 (ill.)
  Los Angeles Race Riots (1992), *3:* 522–523, 523 (ill.)
  Nativist riots, Philadelphia, Pennsylvania, *2:* 311–318, 317 (ill.)
  New York City Draft Riots (1863), *3:* 526–527, 527 (ill.), 654
  One Child Policy Riots (2007), *3:* 568–574, 572 (ill.)
  Rice Riots of 1918, *1:* 126–127
  Stonewall Riots (1969), *2:* 432–433, 435–441, 440 (ill.)
  White Night Riots (1979), *2:* 441–445, 444 (ill.)
  Zoot Suit Riots (1943), *3:* 512, 512 (ill.), 518–524, 521 (ill.)
RNC (Republican National Convention), *3:* 564, 678
Roberts, John, *1:* 87
Roberts, Terrence, *1:* 50
Robinson, Jackie, *1:* 68
Rock Hill, SC, Freedom Rides, *1:* 56
Rockefeller, Nelson, *2:* 273, 275
Roe v. Wade, 3: 554, 556, 575–576. *See also* McCorvey, Norma.
Roeder, Scott, *3:* 567
Rohingya, violence against, *3:* 503

Rolling Stone, 1: 177
Roman Empire (27 BCE–476 CE), *2:* 305–306; *3:* 617–619
Romney, George, *3:* 528, 529, 530–531
Roosevelt, Franklin D., *1:* 64; *2:* 277, 407, 414
Roosevelt, Theodore, *1:* 135 (ill.); *2:* 399, 405; *3:* 710
Roper v. Simmons, 2: 285
Rose Parade, SeaWorld protests, *1:* 30,
Rowling, J.K., *1:* 175, 177, 182–183
Royal Society for the Prevention of Cruelty to Animals (RSPCA), *1:* 2–3
RSPCA (Royal Society for the Prevention of Cruelty to Animals), *1:* 2–3
Rubio, Marco, *1:* 115
Rudd, Kevin, *2:* 379
Runaway children, *3:* 645
Russia, *2:* 454–455, 455 (ill.). *See also* Soviet Union
Rustin, Bayard, *1:* 65–66
Ryan, Paul, *1:* 115; *2:* 260

S

Sacramento, CA, Black Panthers protest Mulford Act, *2:* 239–245, 243 (ill.)
Sacred Stone Camp, *2:* 367, 387–388
Sadler, Barry, *3:* 671
Salazar, Sonia, *1:* 81 (ill.)
Saleh, Ali Abdullah, *3:* 488–489
Salman bin Abdulaziz al Saud, King of Saudi Arabia, *3:* 717
Salovey, Peter, *1:* 200
Salt Acts, *2:* 341
Same-sex marriage, *2:* 430, 434, 438–439, 439 (ill.)
San Bernardino, CA, terrorist attack, *2:* 328
San Diego, CA, SeaWorld protest, *1:* 30
San Francisco Chronicle, 2: 245
Sanctions, *3:* 538
Sanders, Bernie, *1:* 229, 230; *2:* 426
Sandy Hook Elementary School mass shooting, *2:* 246–247
Sanger, Margaret, *3:* 558, 575
Santelli, Rick, *1:* 113
Sappho, *2:* 430
Sarsour, Linda, *3:* 728

Satrom, LeRoy, *3:* 674
Saudi Arabia
　Baladi campaign, *3:* 699, 714–718, 716 (ill.)
　women's rights, *3:* 714–715
Saudi Arabia. Shura Council, *3:* 716
Savage, Adam, *1:* 166–167
Save the Rhino, *1:* 21
Savio, Mario, *1:* 198
Schell, Paul, *1:* 214–215
Scheuer, Sandra, *3:* 675
Schmidt, Douglas, *2:* 444
Schmorell, Alexander, *3:* 593, 596
Scholl, Hans, *3:* 588, 592, 593, 596
Scholl, Sophie, *3:* 588, 592, 593, 593 (ill.), 595–596, 596
School segregation. *See also* Desegregation/Segregation
　Little Rock, AR, *1:* 47–52
　New Orleans, LA, *1:* 53
Schroeder, William, *3:* 675
Schwerner, Michael Henry, *1:* 58, 58 (ill.)
Schwimmer, Rosika, *3:* 660
Science Champions, *1:* 168
Scientific American, 1: 100
Scientists, as activists, *1:* 168
Scott, Elizabeth, *2:* 254–255
Sea level rise, *1:* 137, 146, 157–158. *See also* **Environment**
Seale, Bobby, *2:* 240, 242
Seaman, Elizabeth Cochrane, *2:* 278
Seattle, Washington, WTO protests, *1:* 209–216, 214 (ill.)
SeaWorld
　protests against, *1:* 25–31, 28, 30
　treatment of orcas, *1:* 26–27, 30–31
Secret Document of the Farmers of Xiaogang (1978), *1:* 105–111, 109 (ill.). *See also* **Economic discontent**
Seeds, genetically modified, *1:* 223
Seeger, Pete, *3:* 670
Segregation. *See* Desegregation/Segregation
Seim, Gavin, *2:* 254
Selbekk, Vebjørn, *1:* 185
Self-censorship, *1:* 184, 187
Semiautomatic weapons, *2:* 247
Seneca Falls Convention (1848), *3:* 696, 708, 708 (ill.)

Seneca Falls Convention (1848). Declaration of Sentiments, *3:* 708, 709 (ill.)
Sensenbrenner, James, Jr., *1:* 84–86, 87
Serfdom, *3:* 619–620
Service Employees International Union, *2:* 424
Sex reassignment surgery, *2:* 452–453
Sexual orientation, *2:* 429
Sexual predators, *2:* 459
Shanghai Pride Festival (2009), *2:* 452–458, 456 (ill.). *See also* **LGBTQ rights**
Shapi Township, Guangdong, China, *3:* 572
Sharia, *3:* 715, 718, 719
Sharpe, Samuel, *3:* 634, 635–637, 635 (ill.)
Sharpeville Massacre (1960), *3:* 534
Sharpton, Al, *3:* 539, 544, 546
Shekau, Abubaka, *3:* 722
Sheldrick (David) Wildlife Trust, *1:* 22
Shepard, Judy, *2:* 446, 450
Shepard, Matthew, *2:* 434, 446–447
　The Laramie Project, 2: 456–457
　murder of, *2:* 445–446, 447
Shepard (Matthew) and James Byrd, Jr., Hate Crimes Prevention Act, *2:* 450, 451
Shepard (Matthew) Foundation, *2:* 447
Shook, Teresa, *3:* 726–727
Sicilia, Javier, *1:* 90, 91 (ill.), 92–93, 94
Sicilia, Juan Francisco, *1:* 92
Sidewalk counseling, *3:* 563
Sierra Club, *1:* 135, 213
Silent Spring (1962), *1:* 135
Singer, Peter, *1:* 3–4
Singh, Manmohar, *2:* 296
Singing Revolution (1988), *2:* 348
Single women, rights of, *3:* 693–695
Sisi, Abdel Fattah el-, *3:* 498
Sit-ins, *1:* 59–63; *2:* 256–257. *See also* Protests
　Democratic Congressional Representatives for Gun Control, *2:* 256–260, 259 (ill.)
　fast-food workers strikes, *2:* 425
　redwood trees, *1:* 152, 153 (ill.)
　University of California Berkeley, *1:* 198
Sitting Bull, *2:* 369
Skokie, Illinois, proposed neo-Nazi march, *1:* 188–189, 189 (ill.)
Slater, Amber, *2:* 242

GENERAL INDEX

Slave codes, *3:* 624
Slave rebellions, *3:* 623–624
    Christmas Rebellion/Baptist War (1831–1832), *3:* 634–638
    Louisiana Rebellion (German Coast), *3:* 623–628
    Malê Revolt of 1835, *3:* 626–627
    Turner's (Nat) rebellion (1831), *3:* 628–634, 629 (ill.)
Slave trade, *3:* 620–621, 621 (ill.)
    end of, *3:* 622
    triangular trade, *3:* 621
Slavery, *1:* 35, 36–37; *3:* 510–511, **617–649,** 619 (ill.), 621 (ill.), 629 (ill.), 633 (ill.), 635 (ill.), 639 (ill.), 640 (ill.), 642 (ill.), 644 (ill.), 647 (ill.). *See also* Abolition of slavery; Human trafficking
    Africa, *3:* 620–621
    American westward expansion, *3:* 638, 639–640
    ancient world, *3:* 617–619, 619 (ill.)
    Christmas Rebellion/Baptist War (1831–1832), *3:* 634–638, 635 (ill.)
    Fight to Stop Human Trafficking, *3:* 643–647, 644 (ill.)
    Harpers Ferry Raid (1859), *3:* 638–643, 642 (ill.)
    Louisiana Rebellion (German Coast) (1811), *3:* 623–628
    Malê Revolt of 1835, *3:* 626–627, 627 (ill.)
    Middle Ages, *3:* 619–620
    modern, *3:* 623
    Nat Turner's Rebellion/Anti-slavery petitions, *3:* 628–634, 629 (ill.). 633 (ill.)
    Native Americans, *3:* 624
    slave ships, *3:* 621, 621 (ill.)
    symbols of at Yale, *1:* 195, 196
Sleepy Lagoon murder, *3:* 520
Slovakia, *2:* 357–358
Smeal, Eleanor, *3:* 559–560
Smith, Molly, *2:* 247–249
Smith, Tommie, *3:* 516, 517 (ill.)
SNCC (Student Nonviolent Coordinating Committee), *1:* 57, 58
    Berkeley free speech movement, *1:* 198
    March on Washington, *1:* 65
    sit-ins, *1:* 60
Socialism, *3:* 587
Socialists, resistance to Nazis, *3:* 587–588

Society for Human Rights, *2:* 432
Solidarity movement, *2:* 356. *See also* **Labor rights**
Soroptimist International, *3:* 644 (ill.), 646–647
South Africa
    black consciousness movement, *3:* 532–533
    boycotts, *3:* 538
    brief history, *3:* 532–533
    HIV/AIDS drugs protests, *1:* 226–227, 227 (ill.)
    indigenous peoples, *3:* 532–533, 534
    racial discrimination, *3:* 513
    Soweto Uprising (1976), *3:* 530–539, 535 (ill.)
    student protests, *3:* 530–539, 535 (ill.)
    violence against blacks, *3:* 513
South America, *1:* 71, 72
South Carolina, Freedom Rides, *1:* 56
South Dakota
    AIM Occupation of Wounded Knee (1973), *2:* 367–375, 374 (ill.)
    Wounded Knee Massacre (1890), *2:* 369–370, 369 (ill.), 373
South Vietnam, *2:* 340 (ill.). *See also* Vietnam
Southern Christian Leadership Council, *1:* 65
Southern Poverty Law Center (SPLC), *2:* 446
Soviet Union. *See also* Russia
    book burning, *1:* 178
    break-up, *3:* 486
    control of Czechoslovakia, *2:* 353–354
    Estonian revolution, *2:* 348
    invasion of Czechoslovakia, *2:* 354 (ill.)
Soviet Union. Red Army, *2:* 354 (ill.)
Soweto Uprising (1976), *3:* 530–539, 535 (ill.). *See also* **Racial conflict**
    effects of, *3:* 538–539
    eyewitness account, *3:* 536–537
    spreading unrest, *3:* 537–538
Spain
    austerity measures, *1:* 117–118, 121
    Bilbao Anti-bullfighting Protest (2010), *1:* 12–18, 17 (ill.)
    15-M movement, *1:* 90, 116–122, 121 (ill.)
    Global Recession of 2008, *1:* 104–105, 116–117
Spanish colonies. *See also* Colonization
    independence movements, *2:* 338–339
    Puerto Rico, *2:* 343–344
    slave trade, *3:* 621
    slavery, *3:* 511

Spanish Socialist Workers' Party (PSOE), *1:* 120–121
Spanish-American War (1898), *2:* 338–339, 346
SPLC (Southern Poverty Law Center), *2:* 446
Sports, protests in, *3:* 516–517, 517 (ill.)
Spring of Life, *3:* 562, 564–565
    counterprotests, *3:* 565
    results of protest, *3:* 566–568
Springsteen, Bruce, *2:* 462
Stalingrad, Battle of (1943), *3:* 594–595, 609
Stand for Freedom, *3:* 647
Standing Rock Pipeline Protest (2016). *See* Dakota Access Pipeline (DAPL) Protest; **Indigenous peoples' rights**
    Dennis Banks, *2:* 390–391
    Native Americans, *2:* 367 (ill.)
Standing Rock Reservation, *2:* 369, 370, 384
Standing Rock Sioux, *2:* 384–385, 387–388, 388 (ill.). *See also* Native Americans
Stanton, Elizabeth Cady, *3:* 696, 697 (ill.), 708, 708 (ill.), 710
Starr, Edwin, *3:* 670
Stauffenberg, Claus von, *3:* 591
Steinem, Gloria, *3:* 560, 728
Sterilization, *3:* 549
Sting, *2:* 366, 383, 383 (ill.)
Stonewall Inn, *2:* 432, 436–437, 439, 441
Stonewall Riots (1969), *2:* 432–433, 435–441, 440 (ill.). *See also* **LGBTQ rights**
Stookey, N. Paul, *1:* 68
Stowe, Harriet Beecher, *3:* 631, 631 (ill.), 638
Strangeways Prison Riot (1990), *2:* 271
Street art, *1:* 212, 212 (ill.)
Strikes, *2:* 397. *See also* **Labor rights**; Protests
    cigar workers, *1:* 84
    coal miners, *2:* 410–411
    Delano Grape Strike and Boycott, *2:* 414–422
    equal pay for women, *3:* 728–729
    fast-food workers, *2:* 422–426, 424 (ill.)
    Flint strike against General Motors, *2:* 407–414, 412 (ill.)
    Gdansk Shipyard, Poland, *2:* 356–357, 357 (ill.)
    Kensington textile mill, *2:* 401–403
    legalization, *2:* 409
    McCormick Reaper Works, *2:* 418
    slaves, *3:* 634, 635–636
    University of California Berkeley, *1:* 199
Stroop, Jürgen, *3:* 605, 606
Student Armband Protest of Vietnam War (1965–1969), *3:* 663–668, 668 (ill.). *See also* Anti-war protests
Student Nonviolent Coordinating Committee (SNCC), *1:* 57, 58
    Berkeley free speech movement, *1:* 198
    March on Washington, *1:* 65
    sit-ins, *1:* 60
Student Protest at Kent State (1970), *3:* 669–676, 674 (ill.). *See also* Anti-war protests
    eyewitness account, *3:* 672–673
    wounded student, *3:* 674 (ill.)
Student protests. *See also* Protests
    counterprotests in Charlottesville, VA, *3:* 542
    Hong Kong, *3:* 500–501
    Kent State (1970), *3:* 669–676, 674 (ill.)
    Paris, France, *1:* 118–119, 119 (ill.)
    Soweto uprising, *3:* 530–539, 535 (ill.)
    Student Armband Protest of Vietnam War (1965–1969), *3:* 663–668, 668 (ill.)
    Vietnam War, *3:* 669–676
    White Rose movement, *3:* 588
The Suffragette, *3:* 705 (ill.)
Suffragettes. *See* Women's suffrage movement
Suffragists. *See* Women's suffrage movement
Summer of Mercy Protest (1991), *3:* 566–567
Sumner, Gordon, *2:* 366, 383, 383 (ill.)
Sun Yat-sen, *1:* 107
Supreme Court (United States). *See* United States. Supreme Court
Survivors, Armenian genocide, *2:* 299
Suu Kyi, Aung San, *3:* 502–503, 503 (ill.)
Sweden
    escape of Danish Jews to, *3:* 597, 601 (ill.)
    Melchior, Bent, escape to, *3:* 598–599
Sydney, Australia, aboriginal land rights protest, *2:* 375–379
Syria
    Arab Spring, *3:* 491–493, 492 (ill.)
    civil war, *2:* 319; *3:* 492–493, 720–721
Syrian refugees, *2:* 319, 321; *3:* 493, 720–724. *See also* Refugees

T

Tahrir Square protests (2011), *3:* 493–498, 494–495, 496 (ill.). *See also* **Political/Government uprisings**
Taigman, Kalman, *3:* 610
Taino (indigenous people), *2:* 343. *See also* Indigenous peoples
Taliban, *3:* 681, 719
Tariffs, *1:* 210
TARP (United States. Troubled Asset Relief Program), *1:* 112
Tax protests, *1:* 111–116
Tea Party movement, *1:* 103–104, 111–116, 114 (ill.)
    demonstration in Fort Myers, Florida, *1:* 114 (ill.)
    first events, *1:* 113–114
    membership statistics, *1:* 114–115
    mid-term elections of 2010, *1:* 115
Tema, Sophie Topsie, *3:* 536–537
Terauchi Masatake, *1:* 127, 127 (ill.)
Terra nullius, *2:* 376
Terrorism, *1:* 190; *2:* 285
    animal rights, *1:* 4
    ecoterrorism, *1:* 11
    fears of, *2:* 310
    San Bernardino, California, *2:* 328
    Syria, *3:* 489
    United States, *2:* 326
    World Trade Center/Pentagon terror attack (2001), *3:* 677–680
Terrorist watch list, *2:* 257, 260
Testerman, Cabell, *2:* 410
Texas
    executions, *2:* 284
    Huey P. Newton Gun Club demonstrations, *2:* 244
    March to Abolish the Death Penalty, *2:* 287, 287 (ill.)
Textile mills, child labor, *2:* 400 (ill.)
Thebes, *3:* 469
Thomas, Jefferson, *1:* 50
Thoreau, Henry David, *1:* 133
350.org, *1:* 157, 161

Tiananmen Square protests, *3:* 473–478, 476 (ill.). *See also* **Political/Government uprisings**
    eyewitness account, *3:* 474–475
    origins, *3:* 473–474
    use of military force, *3:* 477–478
Tilikum, *1:* 5, 26, 27 (ill.), 31
Tillard, Violet, *3:* 703–704
Tiller, George, *3:* 566–567
Timberlake, Justin, *2:* 423
Times of India, *2:* 296
Tinker, John, *3:* 664, 665, 668, 668 (ill.)
Tinker, Mary Beth, *3:* 664, 665, 668, 668 (ill.)
Tinker v. Des Moines Independent Community School District, *3:* 657, 667–668
Title X, *3:* 577–578
Tlatelolco Massacre (1968), *1:* 94, 95. *See also* **Hispanic and Latino civil rights**
Tokyo Big March, *1:* 160
Tometi, Opal, *3:* 541
Torture, *3:* 686
Toxic chemical spills, Bhopal, India, *1:* 136
Toxic wastes
    fracking, *1:* 153–154
    Love Canal, *1:* 136, 143
Trafficking Victims Protection Act (TVPA), *3:* 646
Trail of Tears protest, *2:* 386–387
TransCanada, *1:* 140
Transgender people, *2:* 429, 435. *See also* LGBTQ people; Manning, Bradley/Chelsea
Transgender rights, *2:* 435. *See also* **LGBTQ rights**
    China, *2:* 452–453
    North Carolina, *2:* 458–464
Travers, Mary, *1:* 68
Treason, *2:* 285
Treaty of New Echota, *2:* 386
Treblinka
    closing of, *3:* 613–614
    deportations to, *3:* 604, 606
Treblinka Death Camp Revolt (1943), *3:* 607–614. *See also* **Resistance to Nazis**
Tree sitting, *1:* 152
Tresckow, Henning von, *3:* 591
Trial by jury, *2:* 265
Triangular trade, *3:* 621
Trick (music group), *1:* 30

Troubled Asset Relief Program (TARP), *1:* 112
Trump, Donald, *1:* 89, 115
    ban on transgender people in military, *2:* 435
    birth control and health insurance plans, *3:* 556
    Charlottesville protests, *3:* 543
    climate change policies, *1:* 165–166
    criticism of NFL protesters, *3:* 515
    Dakota Access Pipeline, *2:* 367, 385, 391
    election of 2016, *3:* 725–726
    immigration policy, *2:* 310
    Keystone XL project, *1:* 139, 144
    reproductive rights, *3:* 578
    supporters, *1:* 177 (ill.)
    women's protest marches, *3:* 724–731
Trump travel bans (2017). *See also* **Immigrant rights**
    airport protests, *2:* 330–331, 330 (ill.)
    countries excluded in first travel ban, *2:* 326 (ill.)
    demonstrations against, *2:* 330 (ill.)
    lawsuit against, *2:* 331–332
    Muslims, *2:* 325–326
    protests against, *2:* 325–332, 330 (ill.)
    worldwide protests, *2:* 331
Tubman, Harriet, *3:* 639 (ill.)
Tucson, AZ, mass shooting, *2:* 248
Tunisia
    Arab Spring, *2:* 318–319; *3:* 487–488
    democracy in, *3:* 493
Tunisian Revolution, *3:* 488, 495
Turkey
    American protests against, *2:* 302
    Armenian genocide denial, *2:* 300–301
Turner, Nat, *3:* 628–629, 629 (ill.)
Turner's (Nat) Rebellion (1831–1832), *3:* 628–634, 629 (ill.). *See also* **Slavery**
Turning Hawk, *2:* 373
Tuvalu, *1:* 147
TVPA (United States. Trafficking Victims Protection Act), *3:* 646
12th Street Riots, Detroit, MI, *3:* 524–530, 528 (ill.)
    aftermath, *3:* 529–530
    origins in "blind pig," *3:* 525
    Romney, George, interview, *3:* 530–531
"Twinkie defense," *2:* 444

U

UAW (United Auto Workers), *2:* 408, 409, 414
UCR (University of California, Riverside)
    animal experimentation, *1:* 7–8
    lab raid to protest animal testing, *1:* 7–11
UFW (United Farm Workers), *2:* 414–415, 420
Umbrella Revolution (2014), *3:* 498–505, 500 (ill.), 504 (ill.). *See also* **Political/Government uprisings**
Umpqua Community College, mass shootings, *2:* 251
Unauthorized immigration. *See* Undocumented immigrants
Uncle Tom's Cabin, *3:* 631, 638
Underground Railroad, *3:* 639
Undocumented immigrants, *1:* 74, 83–84; *2:* 325. *See also* Immigrants and immigration
UNFCCC (United Nations. Framework Convention on Climate Change), *1:* 137, 145
Union of Concerned Scientists, *1:* 168
Unitarians, *3:* 652
United Airlines Flight 93, *3:* 677
United Airlines Flight 175, *3:* 677, 678
United Auto Workers (UAW), *2:* 408, 409, 414
United Farm Workers of America, *1:* 78
United Farm Workers (UFW), *2:* 414–415, 420
United for Peace and Justice, *3:* 678–679
United Kingdom. *See also* British colonies
    abolition of slavery, *2:* 268; *3:* 637
    anti-fracking protesters, *1:* 155 (ill.)
    Easter Rebellion, *3:* 480–481
    exit from EU, *1:* 103–104, 122–129
    immigrants and immigration, *1:* 123, 124
    Industrial Revolution, *2:* 395, 395 (ill.)
    women's suffrage movement, *3:* 471–472, 697–698, 701–707
United Kingdom. Act to Prevent the Cruel and Improper Treatment of Cattle in the United Kingdom (1822), *1:* 2
United Kingdom. Cat and Mouse Act, *3:* 706
United Kingdom. Equal Suffrage Act, *3:* 707
United Kingdom. Health and Morals of Apprentices Act of 1802, *2:* 395

GENERAL INDEX

United Kingdom. Pease's Act, *1:* 2
United Kingdom. Prisoners (Temporary Discharge for Ill-Health) Act, *3:* 706
United Kingdom. Representation of the People Act, *3:* 706–707
United Kingdom. Slavery Abolition Act of 1833, *2:* 268; *3:* 637
United Nations
    abolition of slavery, *3:* 643
    environmental protection, *1:* 137
    human rights, *2:* 264, 268–269
    measurement of human development, *1:* 101–102
United Nations. Climate Change Conference, *1:* 144–145
United Nations. Framework Convention on Climate Change (UNFCCC), *1:* 137, 145
United Nations. Intergovernmental Panel on Climate Change (IPCC), *1:* 137, 148
United States. *See also* American Revolutionary War (1775–1783); United States Civil War (1861–1865); Specific states and cities
    abolition of slavery, *2:* 268; *3:* 633
    anti-gay laws, *2:* 432
    anti-war protests, *3:* 653–657
    attitudes about climate change, *1:* 164, 164 (ill.)
    book burning, *1:* 178
    child labor, *2:* 401
    civil rights movement, *3:* 472
    Day without Immigrants protests, *1:* 83–89
    free speech, *1:* 173–174
    gun control, *2:* 233–235
    gun ownership, *2:* 233–235, 235 (ill.)
    gun protests, *2:* 238–239
    hate crimes, *3:* 518 (ill.)
    hate groups, *3:* 518 (ill.)
    Hispanic and Latino population, *1:* 75–76
    immigrants and immigration, *1:* 74, 83–85; *2:* 306–309
    immigration policy, *1:* 83–85, 89; *2:* 416
    income inequality, *1:* 99–100
    labor laws, *2:* 397–398
    labor rights, *2:* 394
    migrant workers, *2:* 415
    presidential election of 2016, *3:* 725–726
    racial conflict, *3:* 515–518
    recession of 2008, *1:* 112–113
    sanctions against China, *3:* 478
    slavery, *3:* 622
    Tea Party movement, *1:* 103–104
    terrorism, *2:* 326
    treatment of Native Americans, *2:* 368–369
    undocumented immigrants, *1:* 74; *2:* 325
    westward expansion, *1:* 72–73
    women in early United States, *3:* 696
    women's rights movement, *3:* 696–698
    women's suffrage movement, *3:* 707–713
United States. American Recovery and Reinvestment Act (ARRA), *1:* 113
United States. Americans with Disabilities Act (ADA), *2:* 277, 280–283
United States. Animal Welfare Act of 1966, *1:* 3
United States. Army Corp of Engineers, *2:* 385, 389–390
United States. Bald and Golden Eagle Protection Act, *1:* 135
United States. Bill of Rights, *1:* 174; *2:* 267
United States. Brady Handgun Violence Prevention Act, *2:* 236–237, 253
United States. Centers for Disease Control and Prevention, *3:* 556
United States. Chinese Exclusion Act, *2:* 329, 416
United States. Civil Rights Act of 1957, *1:* 41
United States. Civil Rights Act of 1960, *1:* 41
United States. Civil Rights Act of 1964, *1:* 40, 41, 69
United States. Civil Rights Act of 1968, *1:* 40, 41
United States. Comprehensive Environmental Response, Compensation, and Liability Act (CERCLA), *1:* 143
United States. Comstock Act, *3:* 553, 575
United States. Congress. House of Representatives, *2:* 256–260, 259 (ill.)
United States. Congress. HR 4437, *1:* 83–85, 89
United States. Constitution. 1st Amendment, *1:* 174–175
United States. Constitution. 2nd Amendment, *2:* 237, 252, 254–255
United States. Constitution. 13th Amendment, *2:* 268; *3:* 622, 633
United States. Constitution. 14th Amendment, *1:* 46, 49; *3:* 709

United States. Constitution. 15th Amendment, *3:* 709–710
United States. Constitution. 19th Amendment, *3:* 698 (ill.), 708, 713
United States. Defense of Marriage Act, *2:* 438
United States. Department of Justice (DOJ), *2:* 463
United States. DREAM Act (Development, Relief, and Education for Alien Minors Act), *1:* 89
United States. Education for All Handicapped Children Act, *2:* 278
United States. Emergency Economic Stabilization Act of 2008, *1:* 112
United States. Endangered Species Act, *1:* 136
United States. Energy Information Administration (EIA), *1:* 155
United States. Environmental Protection Agency (EPA), *1:* 136
United States. Fair Housing Act of 1968, *1:* 40, 41
United States. Fair Labor Standards Act of 1938, *2:* 397–398, 407
United States. Federal Assault Weapons Ban, *2:* 234–235
United States. Federal Bureau of Investigation (FBI), *3:* 686–687, 725
United States. Firearms Owners' Protection Act, *2:* 234
United States. Freedom of Access to Clinic Entrances Act (FACE Act), *3:* 568
United States. Gun Control Act, *2:* 234
United States. Individuals with Disabilities Education Act (IDEA), *2:* 278
United States. Interstate Commerce Commission, *1:* 54–55, 57, 59
United States. Law Enforcement Officers Protection Act, *2:* 234
United States. Marine Mammal Protection Act, *1:* 136
United States. Matthew Shepard and James Byrd, Jr., Hate Crimes Prevention Act, *2:* 450, 451
United States. National Firearms Act, *2:* 234
United States. National Guard, *2:* 275, 389
United States. National Guard (Arkansas), *1:* 48, 50–52, 52 (ill.)
United States. National Guard (Michigan), *3:* 528, 528 (ill.), 531
United States. National Guard (Ohio), *3:* 674–675
United States. National Instant Criminal Background Check System, *2:* 253
United States. National Institutes of Health, *1:* 9–10
United States. National Labor Relations Act (Wagner Act), *2:* 397, 409
United States. National Oceanic and Atmospheric Administration (NOAA), *1:* 136
United States. National Park Service (NPS), *1:* 135
United States. No Taxpayer Funding for Abortion and Abortion Insurance Full Disclosure Act, *3:* 580
United States. Partial-Birth Abortion Act, *3:* 561
United States. Supreme Court
    abortion rights, *3:* 554
    death penalty, *2:* 285
    defining free speech, *1:* 175
    LGBTQ rights, *2:* 432
    marriage equality, *2:* 434, 438–439
    neo-Nazi march, *1:* 188–189
    right to free speech, *3:* 667–668
United States. Trafficking Victims Protection Act (TVPA), *3:* 646
United States. Troubled Asset Relief Program (TARP), *1:* 112
United States. Voting Rights Act of 1965, *1:* 40, 41, 58, 69
United States Civil War (1861–1865), *2:* 268. *See also* United States
    anti-war protests, *3:* 653–654
    impact on women's rights movement, *3:* 709–710
    military draft, *3:* 526
Universal Declaration of Human Rights (UDHR), *2:* 268–269, 290; *3:* 646
University of California, Berkeley, *1:* 176–177, 177 (ill.), 198–199, 199 (ill.)
    free speech movement (1964), *1:* 198–199, 199 (ill.)
    free speech rally, *1:* 176–177, 177 (ill.)
University of California, Riverside
    animal experimentation, *1:* 7–8
    lab raid to protest animal testing, *1:* 7–11
University of Maine. Basketball team, *2:* 460, 461 (ill.)
University of Munich, *3:* 588, 593, 595, 597
University of Pennsylvania. Head Injury Lab, *1:* 9
Untouchability, *2:* 292. *See also* Dalits
Uprising of 1967 (Detroit, MI), *3:* 524–530, 528 (ill.)
    aftermath, *3:* 529–530
    origins in "blind pig," *3:* 525
    Romney, George, interview, *3:* 530–531
Urbanization, *2:* 400

GENERAL INDEX

V

Van Buren, Martin, *2:* 387 (ill.)
Varna, *2:* 291
Velvet Divorce, *2:* 357–358
Velvet Revolution (1989), *2:* 341–342, 352–358.
 See also **Independence movements**
Venezuela, human rights protests, *2:* 269
Vera, Raul, *1:* 91 (ill.)
Vietnam
 independence movements, *2:* 339–340
 partition, *2:* 340 (ill.)
Vietnam War (1954–1975), *2:* 339–340;
 3: 664–665, 669–671
 anti-war protests, *3:* 655–656, 663–668,
  669–676
 Nixon ends war, *3:* 676
 protest songs, *3:* 670–671
 student protests, *3:* 669–676
Villas Boas, Leonardo, *2:* 380–381
Villas Boas, Orlando, *2:* 380–381
Violence. *See also* Murder; Riots
 against African Americans, *1:* 38, 40, 56–57,
  56 (ill.), 58, 62; *3:* 526–527
 against black South Africans, *3:* 513
 against cigar workers, *1:* 84
 against Dalits, *2:* 293–294, 297
 drug trade, *1:* 91–92
 against Iranian demonstrators, *3:* 490–491
 against Mexican students, *1:* 90, 94
 against Myanmar protesters, *3:* 502
 racial conflict, *3:* 512
 against Rohingya, *3:* 503
 against Tiananmen Square protesters, *3:* 477–478
 against women's health clinics, *3:* 558
 against WTO protesters, *1:* 215
Virginia
 anti-slavery petitions, *3:* 628–634
 Charlottesville Protests (2017), *3:* 542–543, 543 (ill.)
 debate over slavery, *3:* 628, 632
 Harpers Ferry Raid (1859), *3:* 638–643, 642 (ill.)
 Turner's (Nat) Rebellion (1831), *3:* 628–634,
  629 (ill.)
Virginia Tech, mass shooting, *2:* 249

Virginia Yearly Meeting of the Society of Friends, *3:* 630
Vocal Majority Tour (2016), *2:* 248, 248 (ill.)
Votes for Women, *3:* 703
Voting rights, *1:* 40, 58. *See also* Civil rights;
 Women's suffrage movement
Voting Rights Act of 1965, *1:* 40, 41, 58, 69

W

Wade, Henry, *3:* 576
Wagner Act, *2:* 397, 409
Walentynowicz, Anna, *2:* 356
Walesa, Lech, *2:* 356, 357 (ill.)
Walk for Freedom, *3:* 647
Walk Free Foundation, *3:* 623
Walkouts, Mexican American students, *1:* 77–82
Wall Street
 economic inequality, *1:* 218
 history, *1:* 217–218
 Occupy Wall Street movement (2011), *1:* 216–222
 opposition movements, *1:* 218
Walls, Carlotta, *1:* 50
Walter Reed Medical Center, *3:* 688–689, 689 (ill.)
War on drugs, Mexico, *1:* 91–95
War on Terror, *3:* 681–682
War protests, *3:* **651–692**, 656 (ill.), 660 (ill.),
 667 (ill.), 668 (ill.), 671 (ill.), 674 (ill.), 679 (ill.),
 682 (ill.), 686 (ill.)
 burning draft cards, *3:* 666–667, 667 (ill.)
 Candlelight Vigils against Invasion of Iraq
  (2003), *3:* 676–683, 682 (ill.)
 International Congress of Women (1915),
  3: 657–663, 660 (ill.)
 Manning, Chelsea, and WikiLeaks, *3:* 684–690,
  686 (ill.)
 One Thousand Coffins Protest (2004),
  3: 678–679, 679 (ill.)
 protest songs, *3:* 670–671
 Student Armband Protest of Vietnam War
  (1965–1969), *3:* 663–668, 668 (ill.)
 Student Protest at Kent State (1970),
  3: 669–676, 674 (ill.)
Warren, Earl, *3:* 522–523
Warren, Elizabeth, *3:* 728

Warsaw, Poland
  anti-migrant protests, *2:* 323
  Polish resistance, *3:* 590 (ill.)
Warsaw Ghetto, *3:* 602–605
  creation of, *3:* 604
  deportations to death camps, *3:* 604–605
Warsaw Ghetto Uprising (1943), *3:* 590, 602–607, 606 (ill.). *See also* **Resistance to Nazis**
  end of the uprising, *3:* 606
  Willenberg, Samuel, *3:* 612
Washington, D.C.
  abolition of slavery, *3:* 633
  Capitol Crawl (1990), *2:* 276–284
  Forward on Climate rally (2013), *1:* 139–144, 142 (ill.)
  Justice for All March (2014), *3:* 515, 539–546, 545 (ill.)
  LGBTQ rights demonstrations, *2:* 433 (ill.)
  March for Gun Control (2013), *2:* 246–252
  March for Science (2017), *1:* 163–168, 165 (ill.)
  March for Women's Lives (1986), *3:* 556–561, 557 (ill.)
  Women's March on Washington (2017), *3:* 724–731, 730 (ill.)
  Women's Suffrage Protest at the White House (2017), *3:* 707–713, 712 (ill.)
Washington, D.C. Compensated Emancipation Act, *3:* 633, 633 (ill.)
Washington Post, 1: 141, 185; *3:* 688
Washington (state)
  background checks, *2:* 253–254
  WTO protests, *1:* 209–216, 214 (ill.)
Water pollution, *1:* 154
Watts Riots, *3:* 514 (ill.)
Weddington, Sarah, *3:* 576
Weiland, Hannah, *1:* 13
Weinberg, Jack, *1:* 198
West Virginia, Battle of Blair Mountain strike, *2:* 410–411
Westboro Baptist Church
  anti-gay protests, *2:* 449 (ill.), 451
  as hate group, *2:* 446
  protests of Matthew Shepard, *2:* 445–452
Westergaard, Kurt, *1:* 184–185, 187
Westwood, Vivienne, *1:* 13

WFL (Women's Freedom League), *3:* 703–704
Wheels of Justice March (1990), *2:* 282
When Abortion Was a Crime (1997), *3:* 552
Whistle-blowers, *3:* 684, 688
White, Dan, *2:* 441–442, 443–444
White, Micah, *1:* 219
White Night Riots (1979), *2:* 441–445, 444 (ill.). *See also* **LGBTQ rights**
White Rose Movement (1942–1943), *3:* 588, 592–597, 593 (ill.), 596 (ill.). *See also* **Resistance to Nazis**
  capture of leaders, *3:* 594–595
  methods, *3:* 594
  monument at University of Munich, *3:* 596 (ill.)
  origins, *3:* 593
White supremacists, *3:* 516–517, 542–543, 543. *See also* Race and racism
WHO (World Health Organization), *1:* 101; *3:* 550
Whole Women's Health v. Hellerstedt, 3: 555
Wichita, KS, Summer of Mercy Protest, *3:* 566–567
WikiLeaks and, Manning, Bradley/Chelsea, *3:* 684–690, 686 (ill.)
Wilde, Oscar, *2:* 430
Wildfire (ship), *3:* 621 (ill.)
Wilkins, N.B., *2:* 329
Wilkins, Roy, *1:* 51
Will and Grace, 2: 434
Willenberg, Samuel, *3:* 610, 611 (ill.), 612–613, 613 (ill.)
William Frantz Elementary School, *1:* 53
William III, King of England, *1:* 173
Willingham, Cameron Todd, *2:* 288
Wilson, Woodrow, *3:* 663, 710, 712
Wilson (Woodrow) High School, East LA, *1:* 81
Woman's Rights Convention (1848), *3:* 696, 708, 708 (ill.)
Woman's Rights Convention (1848). Declaration of Sentiments, *3:* 708, 709
Women's Equality Day, *3:* 713, 729
Women's Freedom League (WFL), *3:* 703–704
Women's health clinics, blocking access to, *3:* 557–558, 562–568, 566–567
Women's International League for Peace and Freedom, *3:* 661

GENERAL INDEX

Women's March on Washington (2017), *3:* 559, 724–731
 demonstrators, *3:* 730 (ill.)
 sister marches, *3:* 729–730
Women's Peace Congress (1915), *3:* 657–663, 660 (ill.)
 goals of, *3:* 661
 impact of, *3:* 661–663
 resolutions, *3:* 662
Women's rights, *3:* **693–732**, 697 (ill.), 698 (ill.), 704 (ill.), 705 (ill.), 708 (ill.), 709 (ill.), 712 (ill.), 716 (ill.), 719 (ill.), 723 (ill.), 729 (ill.), 730 (ill.). *See also* **Reproductive rights**
 Baladi campaign, *3:* 714–718, 716 (ill.)
 Bring Back Our Girls, *3:* 700–701, 722–723, 723 (ill.)
 British colonies, *3:* 693–695
 delayed by World War I, *3:* 658
 to education, *3:* 718–724
 Equal Rights Amendment, *3:* 558–559
 Hunger Strikes by Suffragettes in Prison, *3:* 701–707, 704 (ill.)
 Saudi Arabia, *3:* 714–715
 Seneca Falls Convention (1848), *3:* 696, 708, 708 (ill.)
 single v. married, *3:* 693–695
 21st century, *3:* 699–700
 Women's March on Washington (2017), *3:* 724–731, 730 (ill.)
 Women's Strike for Equality (1970), *3:* 728–729, 729 (ill.)
 Women's Suffrage Protest at the White House (1917), *3:* 707–713, 712 (ill.)
 Yousafzai, Malala, All-Girls School, *3:* 718–724
Women's Social and Political Union (WSPU), *3:* 703, 705
Women's Strike for Equality (1970), *3:* 728–729, 729 (ill.)
Women's suffrage movement, *3:* 696–698. *See also* Voting rights
 Derby Day Protest (1913), *3:* 705
 division over tactics, *3:* 703
 Hunger Strikes by Suffragettes in Prison, *3:* 701–707, 704 (ill.)
 impact of United States Civil War, *3:* 709–710
 impact of World War I (1914–1918), *3:* 710–711
 leaders, *3:* 697 (ill.)

Saudi Arabia, *3:* 714–718
United Kingdom, *3:* 471–472, 697–698, 701–707
United States, *3:* 696–698, 707–713
Women's Suffrage Protest at the White House (1917), *3:* 707–713, 712 (ill.)
Woodrow Wilson High School, East LA, *1:* 81
Woolworth's, Greensboro, NC, *1:* 60
Work hours, *2:* 393
Workers. *See also* **Labor rights**
 farm, *1:* 75–76, 75 (ill.), 78–79; *2:* 416
 Fast-food Workers' Strike, *2:* 422–426, 424 (ill.)
 Filipino, *2:* 416, 418–419
 Mexican, *2:* 416, 418–419
 migrant, *2:* 415, 416
Workers' rights. *See* **Labor rights**
Working conditions
 Chinese workers, *2:* 398
 coal mining, *2:* 312
 farm workers, *2:* 416
 General Motors Co., *2:* 408–409
 labor laws, *2:* 397–398
 migrant workers, *2:* 416
World Bank, *2:* 381, 384
World Conservation Congress, *1:* 21
World Day against Trafficking in Persons, *3:* 647
World Economic Forum, *2:* 323
World Health Organization (WHO), *1:* 101; *3:* 550
World Trade Center terror attack (2001), *2:* 326; *3:* 677–680. *See also* Terrorism
World Trade Organization (WTO). Accountability Review Committee of Seattle, Washington, *1:* 215
World War I (1914–1918), *2:* 298
 anti-war efforts, *3:* 655
 impact on women's suffrage movement, *3:* 658, 710–711
World War II (1939–1945), *1:* 74; *3:* 585, 607, 655
 Battle of Stalingrad, *3:* 594–595
 Germany, *3:* 479–481
Wounded Knee, SD
 AIM occupation (1973), *2:* 364–365, 367–375, 374 (ill.)
 massacre (1890), *2:* 369–370, 373
Wright, Martha, *3:* 708
WSPU (Women's Social and Political Union), *3:* 703, 705

GENERAL INDEX

WTO (World Trade Organization), *1:* 205–206
    goals, *1:* 210–211
    protests in Seattle, Washington, *1:* 209–216
WTO (World Trade Organization). Accountability Review Committee of Seattle, Washington, *1:* 215
Wuchang Revolt (1911), *1:* 106
Wyoming
    anti-gay protests by WBC, *2:* 448, 449–451
    murder of Matthew Shepard, *2:* 445–446

X

Xiaogang, China, *1:* 103
    collective farms and communes, *1:* 108–110
    farmers' secret agreement, *1:* 105–111, 109 (ill.)
Xingu River, *2:* 379–381

Y

Yale University
    history, *1:* 195–196
    racial tensions, *1:* 196–199
    student protests on free speech, *1:* 194–201, 197 (ill.)
Yale University. Calhoun College, *1:* 195, 200
Yale University. Intercultural Affairs Council, *1:* 195, 197
Yarrow, Peter, *1:* 68
Ybor City Cigar Strike (1931), *1:* 84–85
Yemen, Arab Spring, *3:* 488–489
Yiannopoulos, Milo, *1:* 176
York County Prison Farm, *1:* 62
Young, Neil, *3:* 670
Young Turks, *2:* 298
Yousafzai, Malala, *3:* 700–701, 718–720, 719 (ill.), 720–721
Yousafzai, Malala, All-Girls School, *3:* 718–724

Z

Zhou Enlai, *1:* 108
Zimmerman, George, *3:* 540–544
ZOB (Jewish Combat Organization), *3:* 604–606, 605
Zoot Suit Riots (1943), *3:* 512, 512 (ill.), 518–524, 521 (ill.). *See also* **Racial conflict**
Zoot suits, *3:* 519–520
Zuccotti Park, *1:* 219